POLITICAL ISLAM AND GLOBAL MEDIA

The development of new and social media, as well as the growth of transnational Arab television, has triggered a debate about the rise in transnational political and religious identification, as individuals and groups negotiate this new triad of media, religion and culture.

This book examines the implications of new media on the rise of political Islam and on Islamic religious identity in the Arab Middle East and North Africa (MENA), as well as among Muslim Arab diasporas. Undoubtedly, the process of globalization, especially in the field of media and information communication technologies, challenges the cultural and religious systems, particularly in terms of identity formation. Across the world, Arab Muslims have embraced new media not only as a source of information but also as a source of guidance and *fatwas*, thereby transforming Muslim practices and rituals. This volume brings together chapters from a range of specialists working in the field, presenting a variety of case studies on new media, identity formation and political Islam in Muslim communities both within and beyond the MENA region.

Offering new insight into the influence of media exposure on national, political and cultural boundaries of the Islamic identity, this book is a valuable resource for students and scholars of Middle Eastern politics, specifically political Islam and political communication.

Noha Mellor is Professor of Media at the University of Bedfordshire, United Kingdom. She has authored several books as well as journal articles about Arab media.

Khalil Rinnawi is a Lecturer at the College of Management in Tel Aviv, Israel.

POLITICAL ISLAM AND GLOBAL MEDIA

The boundaries of religious identity

Edited by Noha Mellor and Khalil Rinnawi

LONDON AND NEW YORK

First published 2016
by Routledge
2 Park Square, Milton Park, Abingdon, Oxon OX14 4RN

and by Routledge
711 Third Avenue, New York, NY 10017

Routledge is an imprint of the Taylor & Francis Group, an informa business

© 2016 selection and editorial material, Noha Mellor and Khalil Rinnawi; individual chapters, the contributors

The right of the editors to be identified as the authors of the editorial material, and of the authors for their individual chapters, has been asserted in accordance with sections 77 and 78 of the Copyright, Designs and Patents Act 1988.

All rights reserved. No part of this book may be reprinted or reproduced or utilised in any form or by any electronic, mechanical, or other means, now known or hereafter invented, including photocopying and recording, or in any information storage or retrieval system, without permission in writing from the publishers.

Trademark notice: Product or corporate names may be trademarks or registered trademarks, and are used only for identification and explanation without intent to infringe.

British Library Cataloguing in Publication Data
A catalogue record for this book is available from the British Library

Library of Congress Cataloging in Publication Data
Names: Mellor, Noha, 1969-, editor. | Rinnawi, Khalil, editor.
Title: Political Islam and global media : the boundaries of religious identity / Edited by Noha Mellor and Khalil Rinnawi.
Description: New York, NY : Routledge, 2016.
Identifiers: LCCN 2015047073| ISBN 9781138639539 | ISBN 9781138639577
Subjects: LCSH: Islam and politics. | Online social networks–Political aspects–Islamic countries. | Social media–Islamic countries. | Identification (Religion)–Political aspects–Islamic countries.
Classification: LCC BP173.7 .P637 2016 | DDC 302.23/1088297–dc23
LC record available at http://lccn.loc.gov/2015047073

ISBN: 978-1-138-63953-9 (hbk)
ISBN: 978-1-138-63957-7 (pbk)
ISBN: 978-1-315-63712-9 (ebk)

Typeset in Bembo
by Taylor & Francis Books

CONTENTS

List of illustrations vii
List of contributors viii

    Introduction 1
    Noha Mellor

PART I
The rise of political Islam **15**

1 Legitimate singularities: Ennahdha in search of plural identities? 17
   Ratiba Hadj-Moussa and Samar Ben Romdhane

2 Social media as a new identity battleground: The cultural comeback in Tunisia after the revolution of 14 January 2011 34
   Noureddine Miladi

3 Online aesthetics of martyrdom: A study of the Bahraini Arab Spring 48
   Magdalena Karolak

4 Rereading jihadi texts: Between subalternity and policy discourse 67
   Andrew Hammond

5 Friday *khutba* without borders: Constructing a Muslim audience 86
   Ehab Galal

PART II
Religious activism   103

6 The online response to the Quran-burning incidents   105
   Ahmed Al-Rawi

7 Working around the state: The micro-demise of
   authoritarianism in a digitally empowered Middle East   122
   Deborah L. Wheeler

8 Religious minorities in cyberspace: Identity and citizenship
   among European and British Muslims   138
   Dalia Yousef and Rasha Abdulla

9 British Arab youth: Reconstruction of virtual Islamic identities
   after the Arab Spring   158
   Khalil Alagha

10 Transnational media among the Muslim community in Europe   173
   Khalil Rinnawi

PART III
Mediated Islamic practices   185

11 The new Saudi nationalism of the new Saudi media   187
   Gilbert Ramsay and Sumayah Fatani

12 The dynamics of the Saudi Twitterverse   203
   Mohammed Ibahrine

13 The neo-liberal Islamic preachers: 'It is not enough to believe,
   but you must act on your faith'   219
   Nermeen Alazrak and Alamira Samah Saleh

14 *Fatwa* online: Novel patterns of production and consumption   231
   Roxanne D. Marcotte

15 How Islamic is Islam Online counselling?   246
   Mona Abdel-Fadil

16 Islam in the news: The case of Al Jazeera Arabic and the
   Muslim Brotherhood   265
   Mohammed-Ali Abunajela and Noha Mellor

Index   *280*

LIST OF ILLUSTRATIONS

Figures

1.1	Data sources	24
6.1	Comment tendencies	113
6.2	Tendencies noted in video clips	114
6.3	YouTube users' reactions to the videos	114
7.1	Committee for the Promotion of Virtue and Prevention of Vice Headquarters, Riyadh, Saudi Arabia	132
8.1	Muslim Community Helpline	150
8.2	BENI	151
9.1	Level of importance of religion amongst Arab youth in Britain	162
9.2	Level of importance of religion amongst heavy online media users	164

Tables

3.1	Comparison of the functions of the Internet for remembrance	54
3.2	Bahrain-wide anti-government websites	61
3.3	Facebook opposition district websites	62
3.4	Bahrain-wide pro-government websites	63
6.1	Top 15 self-proclaimed geographic locations of comment posters	115
6.2	Top 10 self-proclaimed geographic locations of video clip posters	115
9.1	Importance of religion among Arab Muslims and Christians	163
11.1	Popular Saudi channels on YouTube	189
12.1	Twitter in selected Arab countries	208
12.2	Network and Twitter activity	211
13.1	Reasons for following the new preachers	228

LIST OF CONTRIBUTORS

Mona Abdel-Fadil is an Egyptian-Norwegian ethnographer and holds a PhD from the University of Oslo. Abdel-Fadil's research interests and teaching experience include: media, religion and culture, media anthropology, anthropology of the Middle East, contemporary Islam, counselling psychology, migration and gender studies. Mona Abdel-Fadil is currently a postdoctoral researcher on the project Engaging with Conflicts in Mediatized Religious Environments: A Comparative Scandinavian Study, at the Department of Media and Communication, University of Oslo. Abdel-Fadil's publications include: *Counselling Muslim Selves on Islamic Websites: Walking a Tightrope Between Secular and Religious Counselling Ideals?* (2015), *Sowing the Seeds of The Message: Islamist Women Activists Before, During, and After the Egyptian Revolution* (2014), and *The Islam-Online Crisis: A Battle of Wasatiyya vs. Salafi Ideologies?* (2011). Abdel-Fadil is a regular contributor to the academic blogs 'The New Middle East Blog' and 'Religion: Going Public'.

Rasha Abdulla is Associate Professor of Journalism and Mass Communication at the American University in Cairo. She has a PhD in Communication from the University of Miami in Coral Gables, Florida. She is the recipient of several teaching and research awards, including, most recently, the AUC Excellence in Research and Creative Endeavors Award. Dr Abdulla's research interests include the uses and effects of new media, particularly the Internet, and the link between social media and political activism. She is the author of *The Internet in Egypt and the Arab World* (in Arabic, Afaq Publications, 2005), *The Internet in the Arab World: Egypt and Beyond* (Peter Lang, 2007), *Policing the Internet in the Arab World* (The Emirates Center for Strategic Study and Research, 2009), and numerous research articles and book chapters. She tweets avidly at @RashaAbdulla.

Mohammed-Ali Abunajela is Palestinian-born and grew up in the Gaza Strip. He completed his MSc in International Political Communications, Advocacy and Campaigning from Kingston University London, and was later awarded his PhD from the University of Bedfordshire, UK, for a thesis entitled *Al Jazeera (Arabic): A Platform for the Muslim Brotherhood in Egypt*. Abunajela is currently Internal and External Communications Adviser at the BBC World Service in London providing expert communications support to the BBC's Arabic service and other global language news services.

Khalil Alagha holds a PhD degree in Media Studies from the University of Northampton. He combined his 15 years' experience in online journalism with academic interest in online media and particularly Arab diaspora and online media. He has worked as a journalist and editor at many Arab online news sites, and he was a senior political editor specializing in covering Arab Spring countries in North Africa. He is now Online Editor at *Al Araby Al-Jadid*, London.

Nermeen Alazrak is Assistant Professor in Journalism at the Faculty of Mass Communication, Cairo University, Egypt. Her main interests are media laws and ethics, press freedom, and media regulation in the Arab world. She obtained her PhD degree from Cairo University for a thesis about press freedom in Egypt. She has lectured for more than 15 years at Cairo University in subjects related to media ethics. Her articles have appeared in several academic journals in Arabic or English.

Ahmed Al-Rawi is an Assistant Professor at the Department of Communication Studies of Concordia University in Canada and is a Research Fellow at Erasmus University in the Netherlands. He specializes in Middle East popular culture and media as well as global communication. He is the author of *Media Practice in Iraq* (Palgrave Macmillan, 2012), and his forthcoming book entitled *Islam on YouTube* will appear in 2016 (Palgrave Macmillan). His papers have appeared in a variety of journals such as *Information, Communication & Society*, *Public Relations Review*, *International Communication Gazette*, *Journal for the Scientific Study of Religion*, *Journal of International Communication* and *Global Media and Communication*.

Samar Ben Romdhane holds a PhD in Communications (Laval University, Quebec) which dealt with the public debate over religious pluralism in Quebec. Her research interests include polemical debates, political controversies, the challenges that the new religious pluralism presents to secular societies. She carries out this research in different communication and social interaction contexts, including interpersonal, intercultural, institutional and mass media by using qualitative, rhetorical and critical approaches. She has contributed to 'Constellations, Confrontations, and Aspirations: Reflections on Diaspora and Transnationalism Through the Lens of Youth Formations' (2011), and wrote 'Charte des valeurs québécoises: un mariage forcé entre laïcité et invisibilité des différences?' (2013).

Sumayah Fatani is completing her MA in International Relations at the University of St Andrews and is an Associate Fellow with the King Faisal Centre for Research and Islamic Studies. Her research interests include gender and security issues in the Middle East and North Africa (MENA). She is currently exploring the radicalization of Saudi women and an evolving female jihadi ideology by comparing women's involvement in al-Qaeda and the so-called Islamic State.

Ehab Galal is an Assistant Professor in Media and Society in the Middle East in the Department of Cross-Cultural and Regional Studies at the University of Copenhagen. His research focuses on Arab and Muslim media in the Middle East and transnationally. His recent publications include *Arab TV-Audiences: Negotiating Religion and Identity* (Peter Lang, 2014). He has also authored several chapters, including 'Conveying Islam: Arab Islamic satellite channels as new players', in *The New Media and Religious Transformations in Africa* (Indiana University Press, 2015), and 'Saleh Kamel: Investing in Islam', in *Arab Media Moguls* (I.B. Tauris, 2015).

Ratiba Hadj-Moussa is Professor of Sociology at York University (Toronto). Her work revolves around the issues of secularism in the French and Canadian societies, visual cultures, new and old media in North Africa, and the conceptualization of the political in non-Western contexts. She is the author of *La télévision par satellite au Maghreb et ses publics. Espaces de résistance, espaces critiques* (Presses Universitaires de Grenoble, 2015), and the co-editor of *Mondes Méditerranéens. L'Émeute au coeur du politique* (Revue l'Homme et la Société, l'Harmattan, 2013), and *Suffering, Art and Aesthetics* (Palgrave, 2014).

Andrew Hammond is a doctoral candidate in Arab and Turkish intellectual history at the University of Oxford. He previously worked for BBC Arabic radio, Reuters news agency in Egypt and Saudi Arabia, and as a political analyst with the European Council on Foreign Relations think tank. His publications include *The Islamic Utopia: The Illusion of Reform in Saudi Arabia, Popular Culture in the Arab World*, and articles on Arab media, sectarianism and judicial reform in Saudi Arabia.

Mohammed Ibahrine is an Associate Professor in the Department of Mass Communication at the American University of Sharjah (AUS), United Arab Emirates (UAE). Before coming to AUS, he served as an Assistant Professor at Al Akhawayn University in Ifrane (AUI), Morocco, and previously Lecturer at the Universities of Hamburg and Erfurt in Germany. He was also a visiting fellow at the London School of Economics, UK, and Scholar in Residence at the Johnson County Community College in Kansas City, USA. Ibahrine has worked for Deutsche Welle, International Telecommunication Union, UNESCO and the Open Society Foundation. He is the author of *New Media and Neo-Islamism*, and co-author of the report *Mapping Digital Media in Morocco*. Currently, he is working on a new book entitled *Communication Technologies and Socio-political Change in the Arab World*.

Magdalena Karolak (PhD in Linguistics, University of Silesia, Poland) is Assistant Professor of Interdisciplinary Studies at Zayed University, UAE. Her research interests include transformations of societies in the Arabian Gulf, and Slavic and comparative linguistics. For the past six years she has been conducting fieldwork in Bahrain. Dr Karolak has published more than 30 journal articles and book chapters on the shifting gender relations, social media, culture and identity and political system transformations. She is the author of a monograph, *The Past Tense in Polish and French: A Semantic Approach to Translation* (Peter Lang, 2013), and *Social Media Wars: Sunni and Shia Identity Conflicts in the Age of Web 2.0* (Academica, 2013).

Roxanne D. Marcotte is Associate Professor in Contemporary Islam at the Université du Québec à Montréal (Canada). For almost ten years, she was Assistant and Associate Professor in Islamic Studies at the University of Queensland (Australia), where she remains affiliated as an Honorary Research Senior Fellow. She has published 'Let's Talk about Sex: Australian Muslim Online Discussions' (2015), and 'Gender and Sexuality Online on Australian Muslim Forums' (2010) in *Contemporary Islam: Dynamics of Muslim Life* (both being reprinted). Currently, she is working on a five-year cross-Canada collaborative Social Sciences and Humanities Research Council of Canada (SSHRC)-funded research project (2013–18) on how English and French Canadian Muslims use the Internet and what role the Internet and digital technology play in their lives (canadianmuslimsonline.uqam.ca/en).

Noha Mellor is Professor of Media at the University of Bedfordshire, UK. She is the author of several books about Arab media including *The Making of Arab News* (Rowman & Littlefield, 2005), *Modern Arab Journalism* (Edinburgh University Press, 2007), *Arab Media* (Polity, 2011), and most recently *Reporting in the MENA Region* (Rowman & Littlefield, 2015).

Noureddine Miladi got an MA and PhD in Media and Communication from the University of Westminster, in London. Before joining Qatar University as Associate Professor in Mass Communication, then as Head of Department of Mass Communication, he had taught Journalism and Mass Communication since 2001 in various UK universities. His research interests are on diasporic media, Arab satellite TV, social media and social change, youth and the media, news and public opinion, Al Jazeera, and media and democracy. He is editor of the *Journal of Arab and Muslim Media Research*, an international academic refereed journal concerning Arab and Middle Eastern media and culture.

Gilbert Ramsay is a Lecturer in International Relations at the University of St Andrews, UK. His interests encompass the use of the Internet for political mobilization, online jihadi-Salafism, surveillance, theories of ideology and dehumanization, and citizen video-journalism as an activist tool, especially in the Middle East region.

Khalil Rinnawi is an Assistant Professor and researcher in the School of Social Behaviour in the College of Management in Rishon Letzion. He received his PhD in Political Sociology from the Free University of Berlin. He is the author of *Instant Nationalism: McArabism, Al Jazeera, and Transnational Media in the Arab World* (University Press of America, 2006), and *TV Consumption among the Arab Community in Israel* (Tel Aviv University, 2009), and co-author of *Arab Media and Globalization* (Polity, 2011).

Alamira Samah Saleh is an Assistant Professor in the Faculty of Mass Communication, Cairo University. She was previously a postdoctoral fellow at the University of Westminster, UK. Saleh completed her PhD in Media Studies from Cairo University. She is the holder of many scholarships and awards including the MENA Scholarship Programme (MSP), Radio Netherlands Training Centre (RNTC), and the Arab Council for the Social Sciences (ACSS) Fellowship. Saleh's main research interests are global and local crisis reporting and its impact on audience perception. Saleh has published a number of articles in both Arabic and English.

Deborah L. Wheeler is an Associate Professor of Political Science at the US Naval Academy. She received her PhD in Political Science from the University of Chicago. Her research focuses on two areas: digital citizen empowerment in the Middle East; and resource security and sustainability of Middle Eastern states. She has published a book, *Internet in the Middle East: Global Expectations and Local Imaginations in Kuwait* (State University of New York Press, 2006), and more than two dozen book chapters and articles. She has conducted fieldwork in Kuwait, Oman, UAE, Qatar, Saudi Arabia, Jordan, Syria, Turkey, Egypt, Tunisia and Morocco, and travelled extensively in Asia and Europe.

Dalia Yousef has a Master's degree in Journalism and Mass Communication from the American University in Cairo. She received a postgraduate diploma in Journalism from Cairo University. She worked for a decade at IslamOnline.net (2000–10), where she founded and managed a special page on European Muslims. She is the author of *Taglyat el adyan ala al internet* (or Manifestations of Religions on the Internet), published in the Digital Literacy Series (Egyptian Cultural Palaces Authority, 2012). She has contributed to research and publications addressing the issues of cyber-activism, religious minorities, women's issues, democratic transition and media diversity.

INTRODUCTION

Noha Mellor

The development of new and social media has sparked both media and academic interest in exploring the ways users share their views and religious beliefs online. This modern communication space has been particularly acclaimed as providing a new opportunity for interaction within Arab Muslim communities across the world, spurring a renewed sense of religious subjectivity; similarly, the growth of transnational Arab television has triggered a debate regarding the rise in transnational political and religious identification. Arab Muslims worldwide have embraced the new media, not only as a source of information, but also as a source of guidance and *fatwa*, and thereby transforming Muslim practices and rituals. While a number of Muslim clerics welcome the opportunity to use the new media to reach out to a global audience, others consider it a threat to native cultural identity, and a celebration of capitalist values. Scholars such as Peter Mandaville (2001a) argue that the Muslim *ummah* (nation) has emerged as a reimagined community where members engage in discussion through mediated communication across geographical boundaries. On the other hand, scholars such as Bunt (2003) argue that the new media have allowed a mix of voices and views including dissident voices, which may have weakened this sense of unified *ummah*.

The new media allowed for the proliferation of websites and forums where Muslim participants express their views, and Bunt (2003, 2) coins these sites as 'cyber Islamic environments'. It is within such environments that Muslims around the world can debate, whether amicably or not, issues germane to their faith and their practices, which has the power to transform Islamic understanding (Bunt, 2003, 4). Moreover, it has been argued that the lack of integration of some European Muslims may be due to the rigid Islamic practices taught by scholars who might be brought over from non-European countries and may lack insight into European societies (Mandaville, 2001a). Young generations use new media to explore Islam, find interpretations of the Quran online or share their experiences with peers

(Mandaville, 2001b). In this respect, new media supplement offline practices rather than substituting for them, while providing new methods to disseminate knowledge about Islam as a theology and way of life (ibid.). New media also provide new channels to communicate and interact with other Muslims rather than leaning on the traditional sphere of religious practices (Bunt, 2009).

This volume seeks to contribute to the ongoing debate about the role of new and global media in redefining Islamic practices and Muslims' sense of belonging and identity, focusing particularly on Arab Muslims in the Middle East and North Africa (MENA) region and in the diaspora. Such a debate is characterized by its inter-disciplinarity being situated at the intersection of religion and media studies. Media, religion and culture have become the focus of several commentaries, particularly with the rising radicalization amongst certain Muslim communities around the world, which, together with the rising political power of some European right extremist parties, has revived Samuel Huntington's theory of the 'Clash of Civilizations' (1993), pessimistically prophesying that cultural and religious differences would be the cause of international conflict. Indeed, the rising power of political Islam, particularly in the wake of the Arab uprisings, and the growing struggle these groups have had with military and liberal forces, coupled with the increasing tensions of failed multiculturalism in Western Europe, have all reinforced Huntington's argument. German Chancellor Angela Merkel declared in a speech to her party in 2010 that German multiculturalism had utterly failed, and that living happily side by side did not work (Weaver, 2010). Muslim communities in France have been at the centre of debate, particularly since the government's ban on the wearing of the *niqab* in public places, which triggered a wave of protests by the Muslim communities there: they saw this state ban as a way of curbing their religious freedom. Recent events exacerbated the debate about the possible conflict of Muslims and non-Muslims living together, such as the massacre of 130 people in Paris on 13 November 2015, or of 12 journalists and cartoonists at the Parisian satirical newspaper *Charlie Hebdo* on 7 January 2015. In addition, the rise of Islamic State in Iraq and Syria (ISIS, later Islamic State in Iraq and the Levant – ISIL), and the political debate surrounding European-based Muslim fighters, who voluntarily left Europe to join ISIS in Syria and Iraq, have stirred the heated debate. In the spirit of Huntington's theory, commentators such as Bawer (2006, 2009) argue that Muslim immigrants in Europe pose an inevitable threat to liberal Western values such as freedom of speech, while European leaders have failed to recognize the danger of multicultural policy by allowing Muslims to resist integration into their host societies. The aim of this volume is to advance current discussions regarding this intricate triad of media, religion and culture, and how individuals and groups may use new media to reconstruct religious meanings in their lives (White, 2007).

Media and religion – an emerging field

Although early works on media and religion, e.g. Arthur (1996, 1), suggest that every human religious expression is mediated, and although religious practices and beliefs continue to play a significant role in many societies including Western ones, Hoover and Venturelli (1996, 251) argue that religion has remained the 'blind-spot' of contemporary media theory.

In analysing new media and religion, Helland (2000) distinguishes between religion online and online religion, where the former refers to sharing prior knowledge and practices within the Internet interactive sphere, while the latter may refer to a new type of religion that adapts to the new media, thereby creating new practices. Moreover, Campbell (2005) distinguishes between sacramental and spiritual activities online, where the first type of activities may substitute for offline activity such as typing prayers, while the second type refers to experiences such as participating in a religious forum. Accordingly, new media can foster more individualist religious practices, with individuals, such as Muslims, seeking to explore their religion without necessarily seeking to join a particular group online or being alone together (Campbell, 2005, 46). Online communities then may not only replace offline ones but can also hinder the expansion of traditional communities online (Dawson & Hennebry, 2004). Campbell (2005, 12) argues that new media, particularly the Internet, provide new tools to promote religious practices. Other scholars (e.g. Wellman, 2011) divide the uses of the Internet into three stages: the first was dominated by experts and pundits, the second was driven by commercial interest, while the third and current stage is dominated by the analysis of how individuals really use the Internet and interact with peers online. Moreover, content provided online can be divided into author-focused and network-focused content (Hutchings, 2010, 14). The author-focused content (such as blogs) is controlled by the authors who also shape the message and its presentation according to their preference, while network-focused content aims to increase interaction with users (such as social media sites).

New media then facilitate a new form of agency or what some scholars (e.g. Helland, 2004) term interpretative agency. Such active agency challenges traditional authority vested in clerics, thereby allowing Muslims, for instance, to decide whether to follow traditional clerics (Mandaville, 2001b) or even subscribe to the so-called televangelists such as the Egyptian preachers Amr Khaled or Moez Massoud, whose talk shows mark a break from the old-style preacher in traditional robes preaching in eloquent classical Arabic (Mellor, 2014). The drawback, however, is that anyone can claim to be a religious authority (Bunt, 2009) addressing a vast audience of Muslim communities around the world while declaring that they are speaking the true essence of Islam (Roy, 1994, 95). Thus, the media have come to form a new resource and a communicative platform to disseminate the norms and rules. In so doing, the media serve as a bridge to other fields of power; they comprise a new form of interaction and discursive reflexivity. The media can be seen as a set of intersected resources, enabling and constraining at the same time: they connect people and accentuate their belonging to one unified, imagined community, while enabling their movement across diverse and unrelated fields, which threatens the foundation of this community.

Political Islam: an emerging force

The recent uprisings in the MENA region have attracted scholarly attention to the role of new and social media in reshaping participatory politics in the region with young people, in particular, using these media as new avenues for self-expression. Some Arab scholars and commentators have seen in new media, such as the Internet, a new resource for gaining global power by attracting more followers of Islam, thereby using such media as a vehicle of 'global *dawah*' or call to Islam. For instance, the veteran cleric Sheikh Qaradawi distinguishes between the use of the Internet for the good (*dawah*) versus using it for evil purposes: 'If we use the Internet to search for sex sites or to incite for hatred ... then it is haram, but if we use it for the good in life and spiritual matters ... because we can use this mysterious machine to teaching Islam to Muslims and in *dawah* amongst non-Muslims' (cited on Al Jazeera Arabic, 2004). In a special episode of *Al-Sharia wal Hayat* (Sharia and Life) programme on Al Jazeera Arabic, Qaradawi used the example of his site Islam Online as a model of modern *dawah*:

> We built our site on the Internet based in Qatar and called it Islam Online. The site is aimed at teaching the correct Islam and to call non-Muslims to Islam ... more than half of the world's population have not heard about Islam ... and the other half have a wrong image of Islam and that it was a religion in the Arabian Peninsula where people fought with swords and took beautiful women in their harem and used to worship statues ... what have we done to change this image?
>
> *(Al Jazeera Arabic, 2004)*

He added:

> When we set up Islam Online in October 1999, we called it Modern *Jihad*. What does Modern Jihad mean? To spread their *dawah*, Muslims in the past needed armies and troops to spread Islam to all nations because kings, emperors and Caesars would not allow Islam to spread in their nations [willingly] ... so it was necessary to fight them ... but now we do not need troops because this net can address all the peoples in all languages. I say that we do not need troops but people to teach [*da'eyah*] and teachers of all languages.
>
> *(Al Jazeera Arabic, 2004)*

Learning Internet skills, according to Qaradawi, is therefore a duty (*fard*) of all Muslims. Moreover, in his book *How to Serve Islam Using the Internet*, the Saudi Turki el-Ouseimi argues that the Internet is one of the *dawah* tools because the Prophet used all communication tools to reach his great goal, and thus, 'If the tool is not illegal like the computer and the aim is good [*dawah*], and the end goal is to attract others [to Islam] and not to spread evil, then we have to use that tool ... then it is a duty to use it' (El-Ouseimi, 2000, 19–20). This was perhaps why several sites were launched to propagate Islamic teachings amongst non-Muslim societies, such as eDialogue (or *Rokn elHewar*), which is an online site providing an opportunity to chat about Islamic matters. The site offers chat in several languages such as English, French, German, Spanish and Russian, but usually just English is available. The site's main page has this message to visitors:

> Dear valued visitor, Thank you for choosing eDialogue and taking the opportunity to find out about the meanings of life. We invite and encourage you to explore the depths of this unique experience, which will no doubt enrich your knowledge. Let's talk about your concerns regarding Islam. Our authorized specialists will help you to understand about Islam by sharing answers to the common misconceptions with foundational principle understanding. After that we provide you with 24/7 online support. Our online support will help you with a fresh start to tackle your life situation head on and feel the blessings of faith.
>
> *(edialogue.org/index/en)*

The site advertises its 'success' at attracting new followers of Islam from around the world. For instance, in an article in *Ar-Riyadh* newspaper on 17 March 2015 (Ash-Sheeban, 2015), it was reported that the site had attracted 5,000 new followers of Islam from 153 countries via their chat within four months (December 2014–March 2015) or about ten to twelve new followers daily. The site manager, Majid el-Ouseimi, told the newspaper that the site included more than 500 lectures in English followed by more than 10,000 new Muslims in just 1,000 days.

Moreover, Islamic rhetoric has informed the political sphere in many countries in the MENA region and South-East Asia, especially with the rise of Islamic movements, whether moderate or extremist (Esposito, 2000, 50). The resurgence of Islamic practices in public and private life, or what is known as political Islam, has been justified by the disappointment with secular and Western ideologies including nationalism and socialism (ibid.). Following the success of secular post-independence governments in the MENA region in monopolizing political and military powers within their respective countries, some Western scholars predicted prematurely the death of political Islamic movements (see e.g. Hamid, 2014, 16–17). Such authoritarian, and often repressive, regimes, however, had indirectly forced many Islamic movements such as the Muslim Brotherhood to moderate their politics. On the other hand, as Hamid (2014) argues, the success of such movements, following the recent uprisings since 2010, have forced the same movements back to their conservativism.

Islam and identity – a continuing debate

Social and national identities are constructs that depend on the presence of the *Other* for their significance: rather than seeing identity as signified and signifier, and hence with a meaning that is fixed in one spatial-temporal context, this identity should be seen as a construct with no fixed truth in the public domain, nor a centre from which it derives its meaning; instead, such a concept is dependent on, or subordinated to, other concepts, and thus its meaning oscillates from one sign to the next. Identity is also constituted through the processes of similarity and difference (Jenkins, 2004); accordingly, for the relationship to be identified by shared traits requires it to be defined against an Other identity in order to gain a foothold. The process of self-representation then is based on people's ability to see themselves and how others see them; in so doing, an infinite circle of meaning-making is entered, in which the definition of self keeps shifting and expanding as the meaning of self is constantly redefined and expanded in relation to others. Analysing national identity, for instance, can be unpacked through an exploration of how collective identity is formed. Group members are bound by similar norms and they are keen to abide by them (Power, 2004). Moreover, collective identity is expressed in cultural elements such as rituals and narratives: the 'cognitive, moral, and emotional connection with a broader community, category, practice, or institution' (Polletta & Jasper, 2001, 285). The sense of collective identity must rest on a shared historical memory and past tales with culturally identifiable values and morals. Diaspora can denote a process that binds several communities around the world who engage in building an imagined community based on their ethnic or religious identity (see e.g. Brubaker, 2005; Cohen, 1997). This process of building a certain diaspora identity is communicated through debates about the characteristics of this identity and what it means for these communities across the world. Diaspora is usually seen to rest on two coordinates: homeland orientation and boundary maintenance (Brubaker, 2005). Muslim communities provide an excellent case in point in analysing diaspora communities of Muslims scattered all over the world, and yet bound by one religious identity (as will be illustrated in Chapters 8, 9 and 10). The media here play a crucial role in articulating this diasporic identity through the subjective narratives of members of these communities. In these narratives, subjects engage in the process of (re)identifying their own cultural boundaries vis-à-vis other cultural groups in their host societies (see e.g. Hall, 1990). In so doing, they enforce a collective identity with their homeland by invoking memories of common history and geography in their cultural practices such as consumption of ethnic and transnational media. The media, then, are a valuable resource to enforce and appropriate identity in addition to serving as a fertile research ground providing evidence of identity contestation.

This volume aims to examine the implications of the new media and technology on Islamic religious identity in the Arab MENA, including Arab Muslims in the diaspora, while contributing to the argument regarding the influence of media exposure on national, political and cultural boundaries of this identity. Analysing identity necessitates the examination of the parts of this identity including religious, cultural and other identities (McPhee, 2005). It requires a re-examination of the communicative acts performed via global media platforms, the positioning of the producers of such acts, the aims and objectives of these acts, and the relationships that this communication aims to form, maintain or improve. The main focus of the following chapters is on three topical themes, namely the rise of political Islam, religious activism and mediated Islamic practices. What is notable in this collection is not only the variety of cases presented here but also the range of (at times opposing) opinions by the contributing authors, which gives a well-rounded discussion of these three themes.

The battle of political Islam

The political Islam phenomenon, or the intertwining of Islam as a religion into the political sphere, has been received with a considerable degree of fear and anxiety in Western societies. Here, the assumption is that Islam precludes the separation of religion and politics, and thus any political action may be driven not only by religious interests, but also by interpretations. A new political order was unleashed with the recent uprisings in the Arab region, characterized mainly by the rise of political Islam or Islamist movements such as the Muslim Brotherhood in Egypt, the Islah party in Yemen, and Ennahdha in Tunisia. Islamist movements were claimed to be the most dynamic political forces in the various regions and expected to stay in power for at least a decade (Wright, 2012). After many years of struggling for their political rights and freedom from the oppressive practices of the former regimes, more than 50 Islamist parties and movements managed to mobilize millions of supporters, subsequently winning landslide elections in several countries, including Egypt and Tunisia.

Following the terrorist attacks on the USA on 11 September 2001, Arab governments faced the pressure of political reforms, coupled with the need for many Islamist movements such as the Muslim Brotherhood to place emphasis on becoming moderate forces (*wasatiyya*), thereby distancing themselves from extremist and radicalized groups such as al-Qaeda; nonetheless, many such modernist Islamist movements faced the tension between the old goal of creating Islamic states based on Shari'a law, and the new goal of playing an active role in a modern, democratic system (Browne et al., 2006, 6). Although the 9/11 attacks roused Western fears of the rise of political Islam, Western policies towards Islamist parties have shifted since 2011, with the rise to power of these political parties in the Arab region; however, the schism between Islamist movements, the military sector and secular parties caused the fall of some of these parties, such as the Muslim Brotherhood in Egypt in 2013, when the newly formed government later declared it a terrorist group (Stein & Volpi, 2014, 2).

Chapter 1, by Ratiba Hadj-Moussa and Samar Ben Romdhane, focuses on the Tunisian Ennahdha party's use of social media to produce its own version of Tunisian identity, particularly by questioning the place of Islam in the political sphere by liberal movements and civil society in Tunisia. The discussion sheds new light on the role of religion, particularly Islam, in modern democracy and how supporters of political Islam attribute Islam to national identities and values. The discussion is continued in Noureddine Miladi's Chapter 2, which examines the religious debates in Tunisia facilitated by social media, and how religious activists appropriate and negotiate the cultural and religious identity of Tunisians. Miladi's chapter illustrates the use of social media as an ideological battleground between religious groups and secularists, but, unlike Hadj-Moussa and Ben Romdhane, he argues that the Ennahdha party has led a cautious media campaign taking a balanced response to recent chaotic media discourses in Tunisia.

The protests in Tunisia and Egypt had a domino effect, spreading to other states in the region. Protests in Bahrain, mostly by the Shi'a majority, erupted against King Hamad Al-Khalifa, who later blamed Iran for fomenting unrest. It is worth noting that the tiny Arabian state hosts the US Fifth Fleet, and is a close ally of the West and Saudi Arabia. The uprisings that occurred there in March 2011 left at least 30 civilians and five security officers dead, and 3,000 people were arrested. Magdalena Karolak's Chapter 3 discusses the practices related to the honouring of martyrs in Bahrain in 2011: social media sites were used to commemorate the deaths of both pro- and anti-government supporters.

The youth's sweeping protests across many parts of the Arab region in 2011 had sparked hopes for change and reform, but were soon stifled by the gradual end of uprisings and the fear of retaliation from the old regimes, not to mention the rise of radical groups such as ISIS. These groups ignited sectarian tensions in Syria and Iraq, while unleashing chaos in surrounding states. Chapter 4 by Andrew Hammond focuses on ISIS and its revival of the issue of an Islamic caliphate, reflecting on how it originally started with a strong rhetoric of nationalism and Sunni Islam religious sentiments. The chapter shows how the group reproduces themes in religious politics by focusing on ISIS' relationship with established movements such as Wahhabism in Saudi Arabia. The group has illustrated that it is adept at using new media to disseminate its propaganda across the world, and to ensure global media attention is fixed on the group's activities. The ISIS video of the execution of the US journalist James Foley was claimed to be stage-managed in order to spread fear and awe, although the exact moment of decapitation was not shown (Coughlin, 2014). The group's use of social media to propagate hatred and coordinate acts of violence has attracted much attention in scholarly and policymaking circles. It is argued that groups such as ISIS have a professional media machine at their disposal, aiming to produce and broadcast online material and videos to glorify the group and its mission (Hashem, 2014).

The so-called 'Arab Spring', by and large, suggests a central role for social media in disseminating information to the whole world about the Arab uprisings. The latest media in the MENA region have come to serve as new platforms for substantive virtual conversations that tend to become quite robust during crisis situations such as the Gaza conflict in July–August 2014, when numerous hashtags appeared on Twitter as part of either Israel's or Hamas' campaigns. It is such tension that triggers media and scholarly interest in questions regarding the triad of politics, social media and Islam. Ehab Galal's Chapter 5 offers a fresh analysis of a sample of Friday sermons or *khutba*, broadcast on satellite channels and reaching out to Muslim audiences around the globe. He illustrates the way *khutba* aims to influence public opinion, by focusing on selected sermons broadcast during the Israeli attack on Lebanon in 2006 and during the Israeli attack on Gaza in August 2014.

Religious activism

The YouTube postings of the film *Innocence of Muslims*, in September 2012, ignited angry protests from all over the Muslim world, including Egypt, triggering the Egyptian authorities to order the arrest of seven US-based Egyptian Christians allegedly involved in the film production. The protests can be seen as a form of Islamic activism in which religion provides the ideological basis for collective action. Chapter 6 by Ahmed Al-Rawi discusses online responses to the incidents of the burning of the Quran on the anniversary of the 9/11 attacks, which led to massive protests in several Muslim countries. The discussion sheds new light on the way Arab social media users reacted towards these incidents. Deborah Wheeler's Chapter 7 looks at the forms of resistance on social media sites and how these media provide small acts of opposition to authoritarian regimes in the MENA region, in an attempt to redefine power relationships. One of her examples is the Saudi No Woman, No Drive video on YouTube posted by a Saudi young man in the USA. We return to the same example in Chapter 11 where Gilbert Ramsay and Sumayah Fatani argue that many such podcasts produced by professional Saudi companies have a unified agenda conforming to traditional Islamic channels in Saudi Arabia.

It was also after the 9/11 attacks that Arab Muslim communities in the Western diaspora came under scrutiny for their support of any action or actors in their homelands, financial or propagandist, thereby questioning their loyalty and degree of integration within Western societies. Several chapters in this volume focus on such communities in Europe: in Chapter 8, Dalia Yousef and Rasha Abdulla explore how European Muslims (with a special focus on British Muslims) utilize the Internet in handling their hybrid identities, and how the different online platforms reveal the diverse perceptions within the same social and religious groups. Drawing upon social identity theory, case studies of European and British Muslim online representations are tackled as major models for analysis, with historical and theoretical propositions recalled and reconsidered throughout. Primary and secondary sources are used in studying offline and online contexts. Khalil Alagha resumes this discussion in Chapter 9 with the results of his fieldwork amongst a sample of Arab youth in the UK, exploring their perception of their cultural and religious identities, influenced by the recent upheavals in their homelands. Khalil Rinnawi expands on this exploration in Chapter 10, about Arab communities in Berlin – how they use transnational Arab media, and how this impacts on their sense of cultural and religious identities.

Mediated Islamic practices

Thanks to the advance of media technology, Muslims across the world have been linked up via the World Wide Web; indeed, the media provide a space for cultural interaction, which includes religious practices as part of the cultural discourse (Hoover, 2006). The media then can serve as a two-edged sword: on the one hand, they can influence public perception of other religions and therefore address people's biases and stereotyping of those religions; and on the other, they can help foster a dialogue between religions and encourage better understanding of other religious groups. Online engagement and discussions continue to articulate one's religious identity through the subjective narratives of members of these religious communities. New media can indeed provide an alternative platform to mainstream media, in which traditional media professionals, such as journalists, act as gatekeepers. Peter Mandaville (2001b, 169), for one, argues that the Muslim *ummah* has emerged as a reimagined community in which its members engage in discussions through mediated communication across geographical boundaries, and that 'we need to understand these media as spaces of communication in which the identity, meaning and boundaries of diasporic communit[ies] are continually constructed, debated and reimagined'.

Online engagement between diverse religious groups has, on the one hand, a significant bearing on the authority of religious establishments in that new media may undermine traditional religious authorities that provide an alternative platform for rival groups and ideologies, such as the case in Saudi Arabia. It was particularly after the 9/11 attacks that the Saudi religious authorities felt their primordial position as the sole decision makers weaken; they had to bear their share of responsibility for breeding the fundamentalists behind the attacks (Mellor, 2016). Clerics such as the Saudi Salman Al-Oudah changed position after the 9/11 attacks; from being a supporter of Osama Bin Laden, Al-Oudah denounced al-Qaeda's practices of killings in the name of Islam (Wright, 2012). On the other hand, the new media may also be used to reinforce religious authority within society. The Committee for Propagating Virtue and Preventing Vice in Saudi Arabia, which serves as a religious police force, set up its own public relations (PR) department in the aftermath of the 2001 accident when a fire broke out at a girls' school in Mecca, killing 15 students; at the time, it was reported that the religious police had not only slowed down rescue operations because the girls inside the burning building were not wearing their black body coverings, but also stopped the girls from leaving the blazing building (Mellor, 2016).

The contributions by Gilbert Ramsay and Sumayah Fatani shed more light on the new Saudi media, arguing that they have helped to promote the reformist agenda of the Saudi regime rather than represent a vehicle for criticism of the establishment. They argue that the freedom promised by the new media is surprisingly subjected to the Saudi regime's modernization projects and not so much to the activists' own agenda. On the other hand, Mohammed Ibahrine's Chapter 12 argues that new and social media serve as a new platform to challenge the status quo. Focusing on the role played by social media, particularly Twitter, in the religious lives of Saudis, Ibahrine argues that Saudi religious leaders' authority has been questioned by the advent of digital technology.

The religious authorities are amongst those who have been profiled in transnational satellite television as well as new and social media, and are the so-called 'new preachers' or the 'new generation of preachers' who mainly appeal to the middle and upper-middle classes, such as the Egyptians Moez Masoud and Amr Khaled – the latter being one of the most influential Sunni Muslim televangelists whose televised sermons have attracted a large audience across the Arab region, particularly among young people. Khaled proudly compared his efforts to those of traditional scholars, who, in his view, had not done enough to mobilize the youth towards developmental projects and reforms, or, as he put it in a television interview with Al Jazeera (Arabic), 'We have a problem in the Middle East with traditional scholars who talk about faith … Faith for what, to build what? Open channels for Muslim youth, for their dreams and their ideas for development through faith' (quoted in Echchaibi, 2012, x). Khaled's social media accounts are avidly followed by an audience of thousands, and his website has been launched in several languages, addressing Muslims both inside and outside the Arab region. His rise to fame triggered a debate about the phenomenon of the so-called new preachers who blurred the borders between religious and material worlds (ibid.).

In Chapter 13, Nermeen Alazrak and Alamira Samah Saleh also examine the new televangelists and their impact, particularly on young Egyptian audiences, by drawing on focus groups as well as a survey of 400 Egyptian university students from two state and two private institutions.

The Internet has undoubtedly provided a new platform for the dissemination of religious discourses: the number of forums and discussions about Islam as a life guide has greatly increased – for example, the prominent Islam Online website, launched in 1997 and based in Qatar, included forums on various topics such as politics, economics and family matters. New digital technology, Roxanne Marcotte argues in Chapter 14, challenges the traditional sites of Islamic knowledge, namely mosques, religious circles and Islamic courts. Muslims can now participate in live, online sessions with religious scholars and read *fatwa* about diverse life issues, worldwide. Marcotte's illustration of *fatwa* therefore epitomizes Islamic religious authority by intersecting legal theory and social practice. Mona Abdel-Fadil examines Islam Online in Chapter 15, particularly the 'problems and answers' section in this online forum, in order to demonstrate the negotiations of the religious-secular boundaries of Islamic identity, and how this section of the forum serves as an intellectual hub for counselling professionals producing Islamic solutions to real-life problems. Finally, there has been sporadic scholarly attention to the way Muslim media professionals make use of Islamic ethics in their work. Mohammed-Ali Abunajela and Noha Mellor's Chapter 16 examines the link between media and Islam, taking Al Jazeera Arabic's coverage of the Muslim Brotherhood in Egypt as a topical example. The discussion aims to illustrate how Arab journalists reconcile their religious (Islamic) ethics with their professional code of practice.

The underpinning theme of the contributions in this volume is to illustrate how global media and cyberspace can serve as a place for contestation, deliberation and even cyberwar, in which offline conflicts are extended online. Seen in this light, new and social media are not only the pivotal constituents for understanding contemporary tensions by Muslims across the world, but also the plurality of responses to local and global issues on an easily accessible, inclusive and worldwide information platform.

References

Abu Zeid, Nasr Hamid (1994) *Critique of the Religious Rhetoric (Naqd el Khitab el-Deeni)*. Cairo: Sina Publishing (in Arabic).
Al Jazeera Arabic (2004) *Al Sharia and Al Hayat*, episode broadcast on 20 November (in Arabic).
Arthur, Chris (1996) *Media, Meaning and Method in the Study of Religion*. Leeds: British Association for the Study of Religions Occasional Paper No. 16.
Ash-Sheeban, Ibrahim (2015) 'Rokn el Hiwar attracts 5000 followers to Islam via the Internet', *Al-Riyadh*, 17 March, www.alriyadh.com/1030700 (in Arabic).
Bawer, Bruce (2006) *While Europe Slept. How Radical Islam is Destroying the West from Within*. New York: Broadway Books.
Bawer, Bruce (2009) *Surrender: Appeasing Islam, Sacrificing Freedom*. New York: Doubleday Publishers.
Browne, Nathan J., Hamzawy, Amr & Ottaway, Marina (2006) *Islamist Movements and the Democratic Process in the Arab World: Exploring Gray Zones*. Working paper, Carnegie Endowment, 8 March, carnegieendowment.org/2006/03/08/islamist-movements-and-democratic-process-in-arab-world-exploring-gray-zones/2cvu.
Brubaker, Rogers (2005) 'The "diaspora" diaspora', *Ethnic and Religious Studies*, 28(1): 1–19.
Bunt, Gary R. (2003) *Islam in the Digital Age: e-Jihad, Online Fatwas and Cyber Islamic Environments*. London: Pluto Press.
Bunt, Gary (2009) *iMuslims: Rewiring the House of Islam*. Chapel Hill, NC: University of North Carolina Press.
Campbell, H. (2005) *Exploring Religious Communities Online: We are One in the Network*. New York: Peter Lang Publishing.
Choueiri, Youssef M. (1996) 'The political discourse of contemporary Islamist movements', in Abdel Salam Sidahmed & Anounshirvan Ehteshami (eds) *Islamic Fundamentalism*. Boulder, CO: Westview.
Cohen, Robin (1997) *Global Diasporas*. London: UCL Press.
Coughlin, Con (2014) 'How social media is helping Islamic State to spread its poison', *The Daily Telegraph*, 5 November, www.telegraph.co.uk/news/uknews/defence/11208796/How-social-media-is-helping-Islamic-State-to-spread-its-poison.html.
Dawson, L. & Hennebry, J. (2004) 'New religions and the Internet', in L. Dawson & D. Cowan (eds) *Religion Online: Finding Faith on the Internet* (pp. 166–186). New York: Routledge.
Echchaibi, Nabil (2012) 'Foreword', in Pradip Ninan Thomas & Philip Lee (eds) *Global and Local Televangelism*. Basingstoke: Palgrave Macmillan.
El-Ouseimi, Turki B.A. (2000) *How to Serve Islam Using the Internet*. Riyadh: Dar el Maarij (in Arabic).
Esposito, John (2000) 'Political Islam and the West', *JFQ*, Spring, pp. 49–55.
Hadden, J.K. & Cowan, D.E. (2000) *Religion on the Internet: Research Prospects and Promises*, Vol. 8, Religion and the Social Order. New York: Elsevier.
Hall, Stuart (1990) 'Cultural identity and diaspora', in J. Rutherford (ed.) *Identity: Community, Culture, Difference*. London: Lawrence and Wishart.
Hamid, Shadi (2014) *Temptations of Power: Islamists and Illiberal Democracy in a New Middle East*. Oxford: Oxford University Press.
Hashem, Ali (2014) 'The Islamic State's media warfare', *Al Monitor*, 22 October, www.al-monitor.com/pulse/originals/2014/10/islamic-state-media-strategy-propaganda-iraq-syria.html#ixzz3Hvv5e0UX.
Helland, C. (2000) 'Online-religion/religion-online and virtual communities', in J. Hadden and D. Cowan (eds) *Religion on the Internet: Research Prospects and Promises* (pp. 205–223). New York: JAI Press.

Helland, C. (2004) 'Popular religion and the World Wide Web', in L. Dawson and D. Cowan (eds) *Religion Online: Finding Faith on the Internet* (pp. 30–36). New York: Routledge.

Hoover, Stewart (2006) *Religion in the Media Age*. London and New York: Routledge.

Hoover, Stewart M. and Venturelli, Shalini S. (1996) 'The category of the religious: the blindspot of contemporary media theory?' *Critical Studies in Mass Communication*, 13, pp. 251–265.

Huntington, S.P. (1993) 'The Clash of Civilizations?' *Foreign Affairs*, 72(3).

Hutchings, T. (2010) 'The Internet and the Church: an introduction', *The Expository Times*, 122(1), pp. 11–19.

Jenkins, Richard (2004) *Social Identity*. London: Routledge.

Jenkins, S. (2008) 'Rituals and pixels. Experiments in online church', *Heidelberg Journal of Religions on the Internet*, 3(1), pp. 95–115.

Mandaville, P. (2001a) *Transnational Muslim Politics: Reimagining the Ummah*. London: Routledge.

Mandaville, P. (2001b) 'Reimagining Islam in diaspora: the politics of mediated community', *International Communication Gazette*, pp. 169–186.

McPhee, S. (2005) *Muslim Identity: The European Context*. Sussex Migration Working Paper no. 34. University of Sussex, www.sussex.ac.uk/migration/documents/mwp34.pdf (accessed 24 November 2008).

Mellor, Noha (2014) 'Religious media as a cultural discourse: the views of the Arab diaspora in London', in Ehab Galal (ed.) *Arab TV Audiences: Negotiating Religion and Identity*. Frankfurt: Peter Lang.

Mellor, Noha (2016) 'Religious ideologies and news ethics: the case of Saudi Arabia', in Yoel Cohen (ed.) *Spiritual News: Reporting Religion around the World*. New York: Peter Lang.

Polletta, Francesca & Jasper, James M. (2001) 'Collective identity and social movements', *Annual Review of Sociology*, 27, pp. 283–305.

Power, F.C. (2004) 'Moral self in community', in D.K. Lapsley & D. Narvaez (eds) *Moral Development, Self and Identity* (pp. 47–64). Mahwah, NJ: Lawrence Erlbaum Associates.

Roy, O. (1994) *The Failure of Political Islam*. London: I.B. Tauris.

Stein, Ewan & Volpi, Frédéric (2014) 'Islamism and regime change in the Middle East and North Africa: looking beyond the Arab uprisings', in E. Stein et al. (eds) *Islamism and the Arab Uprisings*, www.casaw.ac.uk/wp-content/uploads/2014/04/Islamism-and-the-Arab-Uprising-June-2014-Ewan-Stein-Report.pdf.

Weaver, Matthew (2010) 'Angela Merkel: German multiculturalism has "utterly failed"', *The Guardian*, 17 October, www.theguardian.com/world/2010/oct/17/angela-merkel-german-multiculturalism-failed/print.

Weber, Max (1947) *The Theory of Social and Economic Organizations*. Translated by A. Henderson and R. Parsons. New York: Oxford University Press.

Wellman, B. (2011) 'Studying the Internet through the ages', in M. Consalvo & C. Ess (eds) *The Handbook of Internet Studies* (pp. 17–23). Chichester: Blackwell Publishing Ltd.

White, Robert A. (2007) 'The media, culture, and religion perspective', *Communication Research Trends*, 26(1).

Wright, Robin (2012) 'The Middle East: they've arrived', in R. Wright (ed.) *The Islamists Are Coming. Who They Really Are*. United States Institute of Peace.

PART I
The rise of political Islam

1
LEGITIMATE SINGULARITIES
Ennahdha in search of plural identities?

Ratiba Hadj-Moussa and Samar Ben Romdhane

Introduction

In 2011, Tunisia experienced major shifts in its political structure during what is widely called the Arab Spring. The Tunisian Islamist party Harakat Ennahdha (Renaissance Movement) was a surprising element in the period following the popular uprising in the country. Its strong return to Tunisia's public scene amazed many observers, disoriented a certain number of Tunisians who thought it was dead, and mobilized civil society members opposed to its political positions. After the return from London exile of its leader Rached Ghannouchi on 30 January 2011, the party was elected to the National Constituent Assembly (ANC) by universal vote with 41.0% of the seats (Storm, 2014, 199). Criticism of Ennahdha has continued unabated, even when the party started governing Tunisia by allying itself with two other parties, the Democratic Forum for Labour and Liberties (Ettakatol) and Congress for the Republic (CPR). The fear that the decade-long civil war in Algeria, a close neighbour, would spill into Tunisia, the emergence of a supposedly spontaneous Islamist generation, together with serious political events in Egypt and Libya, made many see Ennahdha as the party of danger. This forced Ennahdha to create and propagate a renewed image of the party, while crafting a liberal view of Tunisian society.

In this chapter, we seek to provide an interpretation of the ways in which the party and its supporters have used social media to disassemble and give their own vision of being Tunisian, as well as how they bring to the foreground the identity issues at work in Tunisian society. The Ennahdha party has been called into question, has been challenged by its political opponents and has been rejected by a large part of 'civil society', who see it as fatal to freedom. This position, which emerged among Tunisian elites during the Bourguiba and Ben Ali regimes, has created the spectre of an alien party, by its values and practices, which has haunted post-revolutionary Tunisia. Ennahdha raises thus the issue of the place of religion in the political life of a country in the process of establishing the rules of democracy, and this within a regional and global context where there is a mostly combative view of Islam.

We will begin by giving a brief historical context of the Islamist movement in Tunisia, better to establish how articulated the themes of the debate are in defining the political organization of the nation – particularly what legislation will better protect civil liberties, citizen rights and obligations, the place of religion in the public sphere, and the foundations of the values and identities in Tunisian society. Then we will draw a map of media policy in Tunisia, in which to place our analysis of Ennahdha and how the party uses media in relation particularly to stakes and themes such as women, nationality, Islam and the Arabic language.

Ennahdha: a Tunisian party

In her recent book on Tunisian Islamists, Labat (2013) categorically rejects, from the first pages of the introduction, the 'moderation' that 'Western countries' ascribe to the Ennahdha party. Why, she wonders, was the party able to get such a high number of votes even though it is 'intrinsically anti-democratic' (ibid., 10)? Leaving aside the socio-anthropological explanation that could clarify such election results, Labat implicitly reduces it to the manipulation carried out by the Islamists. In fact, like many other authors trying to examine the Islamist presence and the issues it raises in Tunisia, this author subscribes to the idea that (all) Islamists are 'intrinsically' anti-democratic, and that they are a product of an elsewhere yet to be named. Although the issue of democracy is at the heart of the theoretical study and description of contemporary Muslim societies, touching upon daily practices, we will treat it here only tangentially. We will explore its general contours, and only in relation to the themes developed in this text. We will also touch on some traits of the Tunisian Islamist movement, while stressing its links and relations with other Tunisian political parties.

Although some authors writing on the Tunisian post-revolution period tend to situate Ennahdha in an antagonistic relationship to other so-called democratic or secular parties, others insist on its influence on and anchoring in Tunisian society. Michel Cameau and Vincent Geisser (2003) have retraced these links, however, without purporting a cause-and-effect relationship to the Muslim wing affiliated with Ben Youcef, one-time comrade-in-arms to Bourguiba and later an opponent, who left in his wake the so-called Islamo-Destourian group. These links were facilitated by the official creation of the Association for the Safeguarding of the Quran (1967), to which many functions were given, including the training of imams (Cameau & Geisser, 2003, 277). The association was short-lived as the Bourguiba regime quickly understood the danger it posed. The Tunisian Islamist Movement (MIT) was created in 1979, but not in isolation in Tunisian political culture. It shared many elements with the Destourian Socialist Party (PSD, 1964–88), the party then in power: social and geographical elitism in recruitment, membership dominated by the educated middle class, and an organizing model requiring monopoly and unanimity (ibid., 184, 295). Furthermore, the movement took its inspiration, in terms of action and training of its members, from left-wing groups (Khiari, 2003, 133; Cameau & Geisser, 2003, 343–344; Cesari, 2013), and, like the latter, drew most of its members from the academic milieu. From within the PSD, the state party, there were insistent calls for the movement leaders to join it and influence its politics. These calls by the '*passeurs*' (ibid., 274), who were at the core of the regime, echoed the desire for Islam by the Tunisian people.[1]

Realizing the popularity of the movement, the powers that be persecuted its militants. Later, the overthrow of Bourguiba in 1987 offered the movement the opportunity to become a party, and it was legalized in 1988, nine years after its creation (Storm, 2014, 95). However, again this was short-lived, as Ben Ali's regime quickly realized, following the 1988 legislative elections in which Ennahdha members ran as independent candidates, that the party was a real threat due to its growing popularity (Ferrié & Santucci, 2006, 15). The party was banned and its militants, leaders and their families became the target of systematic persecution that pushed them either to exile or to prison,[2] or else to join other groups such as the Tunisian League of Human Rights. The Ben Ali regime had by then started improving the social fabric, and the civil war in Algeria contributed further to solidify the image of 'fundamentalist danger' that Western nations willingly and encouragingly accepted (Khiari, 2003, 7).

For us, it seems important to highlight not so much the electoral moments as the sociological structure within which Ennahdha operated, and which let us better explore how it played in the Tunisian political landscape, how it was anchored in Tunisia's society and how it constructed identities. Many authors restrict their study to the transactions and functions of political structures and ignore the threads between political players, the cultural dynamics that inspire them, as well as the continuity and affiliations that make up the 'social substratum' (François & Neveu, 1999, 21) of Tunisian political culture. This does not mean that Ennahdha does not have its own specificities – on the contrary – but we must study it as a product of Tunisian society where it coexists on anthropological grounds with other political movements and groups. We must also abandon 'methodological spontaneism', which might look at this party without taking the long-term view, and also might ignore all the degrees of complexity of its place in Tunisian society. Khiari (2003),[3] who has a perceptive reading of Ennahdha, shows that the party revisited its central themes to adapt to political modernity, that it committed to secularization out of necessity, and that it always preferred to choose a legalistic position that allowed it at the end of the day to avoid the label of 'Islamic terrorism'.

One of the elements that highlighted its association with conservative and reactionary movements, and made it appear divorced from the values of Tunisian society at large, was the party's adoption of an 'ambivalent' posture positioning it as both a political party and a social movement working to bring morality to society (Allal & Geisser, 2011; Cameau & Geisser, 2003, 309). As we will see later, this ambivalence sometimes caused conflicts between different arguments put forth by the party. By giving predominance to the second element to the detriment of the first, it gave adversaries opportunities to criticize it and to reveal its 'double-speak'. However, it seems that the Islamization[4] of society remained vague and went beyond the party itself, inasmuch as thousands of its supporters and sympathizers acted with and without it. Finally, the Islamization of the state seems now to be off the table, not only because the party has renounced imposing Shari'a law in the new Tunisian Constitution (January 2014) but also it has taken firm positions, albeit not promptly enough according to its adversaries, vis-à-vis the Salafists and the jihadists, which it sees as destabilizing factors.

After this brief presentation, let us now return to the question asked at the beginning of the present chapter by Labat, and others, regarding the apparent contradiction between the success of Ennahdha in the 2011 elections and its acknowledged lack of democratic convictions. This question is quite interesting, as it draws out the dividing line between the so-called secular people and the Islamists,[5] while simultaneously identifying democracy with women's rights and other major themes of the political debate. Quite often, the accusation of a lack of democracy flung at the party was associated with women's rights violations. Ennahdha was unable to convince its adversaries, despite focusing on equality between men and women or insisting on the inalienable gains made by women. To quell all scepticism and criticism regarding its purported wish to take power, it withdrew after finishing its task of bringing to term the new constitution, then took up the causes of youth and women's issues for its second public party convention in Rabat in 2013. As we will see later in the analysis section, this is emphasized by the party. During the 2011 election, it enabled 48 women to be elected (out of a total of 89 members of parliament), becoming thus the party with the highest female representation. Although it targets the political arena in its work to persuade voters of its importance and modernity, Ennahdha has turned to others, its *alter*, and the world outside.

The media: censorship and freedom

Our second contextualization, which will situate better and render clearer the arguments put forth by Ennahdha concerning Tunisianess, comes from the media. A lot has been written on the role of the media in the revolution, and we do not want to add an umpteenth interpretation, when in-depth ground research on audience, public and usage is still to be done. Our contextualization will briefly describe the period preceding the revolution and will provide a cursory look at media practices by Ennahdha, and then will show how the party situated itself in the post-revolutionary period in relation to major identity themes.

The Tunisian media, as in other Maghreb countries, have been in a straitjacket since independence despite a façade of some openness allowing some breaches in this sphere. From independence (1956), the Tunisian authorities have ruled with an iron fist the print media (Rugh, 2004) and television. In Tunisia, audio-visual policies and regulatory agencies seem to have, at first blush, the public interest at heart. However, upon reading the provisions of the policies, and looking at the organizations created to apply them, as Mostefaoui (1995) and Chouikha (2005–06) point out, the field is in fact closed off from media professionals as well as from public participation. Satellite television, which emerged in the late 1980s in Tunisia,[6] was also under control as Tunisians were compelled to ask beforehand for permission to access it, and were encouraged to request it collectively (Dahmen, 2001; Hadj-Moussa, 2012, 2015). However, this control became obsolete in the late 1990s to early 2000s, when individual antennae started invading urban spaces and the marketplace, thus skirting the type of surveillance carried out by the regime. According to our research during the 2000s, satellite television only became widely popular towards the second half of the 1990s, and only after 2001 did people truly adopt this type of television, starting directly with digital television.

The first group to have access to satellite television was the urban upper and middle classes. According to Khiari (2003, 51), by its choice of consumption and its values, a large part of this class supported the Ben Ali regime. While the regime continued fully to censor independent newspapers that were a nuisance, and continued to control the entry into national territory of foreign press critical of the regime, it released its grip somewhat and allowed various private radio and television stations, duly keeping them under control. Dahmen (2001; see also Chouikha, 2005–06) clearly shows links with Gulf countries' business interests. They made perfunctory attempts at openness in private audio-visual projects, whereas private television stations such as Hannibal TV (2005) were run by people close to the regime. Despite the reality of censorship, as we have mentioned before (Hadj-Moussa, 1996), following field work in Algeria, satellite television and other television channels let viewers see new realities, thus opening the way to new criticism by television viewers (Hadj-Moussa, 2003).

We do not claim that criticism did not exist before – far from it – but these television stations confirmed and validated it. Due to their transnational character, these stations made local criticism by ordinary people tangible, while for structural reasons allowing them to seep out. Starting in 2003, in parallel with this apparently controlled internal breach, the opposition created its own satellite channels, El Hiwar (The Debate, 2003), El Mustaquila (The Independent) and El Zeitouna (The Olive, or Olive Tree), which broadcast a few hours a week for Tunisians both in Tunisia and in the diaspora.

In terms of the Internet, this is where the regime carried out stronger censorship. Caught in a double bind of wanting to be the most innovative country in the domain, both in Africa and in the Arab world, and of wanting to protect itself from the unavoidable opening up that the Internet creates, the regime controlled the Internet cafés, called '*publinets*',[7] trying especially to cut off access to troubling websites (Trabelsi, 2001). This led to Tunisian web surfers becoming experts at circumventing obstacles and doing proxy searches. Called by Tunisians 'Amar 404' – and immortalized by committed singer Bendir Man – the message 'Error 404 Not Found', which appeared when access to forbidden websites was denied, showed the regime's fervour in tracking down 'deviant' users (see the campaigns by Amnesty International in support of ordinary users). In a parallel development, and this time inside the country, mobile phone ownership and use showed a phenomenal breakthrough, not taken much into account due to a paucity of research.

Although dominated by the political powers, the Tunisian communication structure was not limited. Many initiatives came about, often from outside the country, from political parties and ordinary citizens in all types of media: creation of satellite television stations, web-based radio stations, Facebook pages and blogs. The Ennahdha party joined in, but broadcasting Islamic ideas and adopting supposedly Muslim behaviours did not always go together.

Before focusing on Ennahdha and its use of cyberspace, we want to mention that, during the Ben Ali era, Islamist ideas did not come exclusively from Ennahdha. During our fieldwork in Tunisia before the revolution, we met women who had worn the hijab since 1988, some younger ones who had worn it between two and four years, while still others wished to wear it but could not due to their professional activities in public institutions with a strict ban on covering up.

Many television viewers listened to radio stations that broadcast the Quran by satellite television or watched shows broadcast by religious satellite television stations – the majority – and were thus influenced to varying degrees. Although we cannot compare these stations to the reduced number of broadcasts by Ennahdha's television station, El Zeitouna, the content of which was essentially political, the general values defended by Ennahdha were broadcast frequently, somewhat by default, by the foreign satellite television channels, bêtes noires of the Ben Ali regime. Moreover, the events of the first decade of the 2000s, which saw the region aflame, also fed anti-American sentiments and a marked rejection by lower and poor middle classes of the '*dimocratiyat el gharb*' (Western democracy). However, until 2011, the party had a weak media hold in the Tunisian national space, although Arab satellite television stations – especially Al Jazeera – never stopped interviewing regime opponents, including general Islamist movement members. Some nuance must be taken with this lack of access, as we know little about the grassroots use of mobile telephones, the medium that experienced the most remarkable expansion.

In 2011, the party re-launched its newspaper, *El Fajr*, which had been banned for 20 years, and reinforced its image and presence in the national and international realms by strengthening or launching its Facebook pages. Given the importance of media convergence in the events of the popular uprising, one would have expected the party and its supporters to be active on the web to convince, persuade and define the prescriptive nature of the values they defend, in particular seeing as many authors have indicated that Ennahdha was very active online. Puchot writes in citing an academic: 'Islamists have become masters in the use of social networking sites ... Ennahdha is supported by many dozens of information websites in Arabic ... and the Ennahdha blogosphere is by far the most active today in Tunisia' (Puchot, 2012, 201). As for Labat, she indicates that the American State Department 'has put means at the disposal of En Nahdha, namely in terms of electronic equipment ... On top of having gotten a comprehensive telephone network, En

Nahdha did also get an IT tool with all the data (at the En Nahdha headquarters in Montplaisir, a floor is dedicated to IT services)' (Labat, 2013, 51).

Now that the famous fictional and virtual character 'Amar 404' is thought to be dead and with him cyber censorship and Internet surveillance, Tunisians are getting mad at another virtual character of a different type. This new invisible character who emerged to feed a well-publicized 'media debate' is what Tunisians call, rightly or wrongly, 'Ennahdha's electronic militia'. When one of the co-authors of this chapter (S. Ben Romdhane) visited the headquarters of Ennahdha in Montplaisir in 2012, she found two students, daughters of Ennahdha militants, who had the task of managing the Ennahdha Facebook pages. One of them, with a degree in Arabic language and civilization, introduced herself as a replacement for Mohamed Nejib Gharbi (an Ennahdha Executive Board member): 'I don't have training in communications but my father is an Ennahdha member who was jailed for many years.' Thus Ennahdha practises its retributory justice.

Moreover, our research on Tunisian Islamist blogs in Arabic and French revealed that they are relatively fewer compared to blogs and pages of their adversaries. We noted that the 'shares', 'likes' and 'views' were sometimes reduced; even the tweets by Ennahdha's leader are very seldom retweeted.

In parallel with investment in mobile telephone services, YouTube is one of the privileged media, either in terms of series embedded in Facebook pages or unrelated to them. Our hypothesis is that the audio-visual aspect of YouTube made it the medium that could reach a larger number of people, because it resembles television and also the information provided is similar to oral exchanges and the radio format. Facebook pages remain the most active support as they offer the following technical functions: cut and paste of articles found on the web, the ability to have in one's message a hypertext link to an information site or YouTube video. The practice of producing online discourse is what this chapter proposes to examine under the rubric of shaping or constructing identities.

Data and method

The goal set up by this research is to understand how Ennahdha produces its discourse on identities, while ensuring its digital visibility on the web, and in particular, how it responds to its detractors. To achieve this goal, we adopted discourse analysis as a research methodology that focuses on both content and context of Ennahdha's online discourse related to identity issues. As there exists a plethora of data related to identity construction within social media, we carried out a sampling of selected discourse. We concentrated our analysis on three criteria that were chosen for being representative, for being controversial, and for how much they circulated in social network sites (messages produced by one user then forwarded by another). In this chapter, we will cite three extracted Facebook videos and one Facebook status. The extracts were published during the transitional period representing the ruling of the troika alliance – more specifically, between December 2011 and October 2014, when presidential and parliamentary elections were held.

A distinctive feature of this period was its effervescence and vigorous debates on a large number of issues, causing extensive dissension in public opinion. In this article, we focus on the issue related to the various conceptions of being Tunisian. In fact, Tunisia's public scene, and especially social media, experienced during this transitional period a proliferation of social media productions including as a fundamental element the construction of a collective identity.

This selection was essential due not only to the large numbers of different social media platforms as well as the large amount and complexity of shared data but also to our interests in exploring 'how' Ennahdha used its arguments. In fact, the online discourse 'universe' linked to Ennahdha has a large scale and range of Facebook pages and groups, of national and international newspapers, and blogs that are anti-Ennahdha or have a highly critical position towards the party. Sometimes these websites are renowned for their verbal aggressiveness, even rudeness (e.g. the name of a Facebook group, '*nahdhaoui ya haoui*' – Ennahdha the non-virile).

As shown in Figure 1.1, our data sources include five types of Facebook page: the Ennahdha party official pages; regional pages (some more active than others – for example, 'Facebook Ennahdha Bizerte'); an international Facebook page in English and another in French (Ennahdha France); pages of media close to

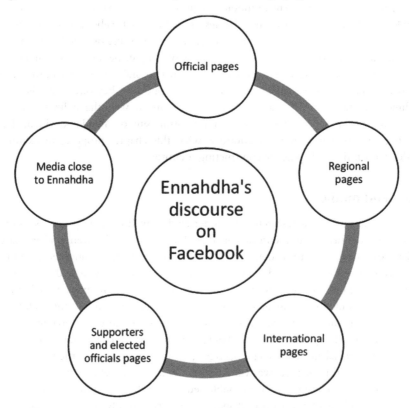

FIGURE 1.1 Data sources

Ennahdha (the weekly *El Zeitouna,* El Zeitouna TV and Al-Moutawasset); and pages of elected officials and those of supporters of Ennahdha.

Messages posted on the official pages of Ennahdha tend to be informative and mention the daily and public activities of the party. The Ennahdha Tunisia page offers minimal information, especially during the debates on the constitution (December 2011–January 2014). As for the pages of media close to Ennahdha, they amply re-exploit information taken from reports in traditional media. Contrary to Facebook pages of elected officials of other parties, the messages posted on pages of Ennahdha elected officials establish a clear separation between their public and private lives: formal language and photos, no posts divulge family activities or informal photographs.

The discourse in the online universe linked to Ennahdha focuses on themes close to the party's political identity, namely its religious orientation considered sometimes incompatible with the government of a modern state. The issue of secularism and the separation of state and religion are areas where the party stumbles in its attempts to persuade. The other major themes debated are women, language and the diaspora/binationality – all debates on identity. The issue of women is an important one here, as it is the link to modernity and openness that made Tunisia the Arab country where the status of women is the most advanced. Conversely, language and diaspora/nationality are the dyad that shows the anchoring of Tunisia in Arabity. These are all central and symbolic issues.

Tunisian women: between Islamic ethics and emancipation

The question of women's autonomy is a central issue, and an important element of the popular consensus sought to accede to power. It is often reduced to a polarity: oppression/liberation. The discourse by the Islamist party on this subject attempts to detach it from this binary position and proposes a representation of gender cut off from all formalism (imposing a model), a representation that nevertheless remains workable in the Islamic discourse on gender and women. There is an attempt to find a balance between being faithful to Islamic ethics and liberating women. This is perhaps the reason why, when the matter is women, the issue of type of clothing often arises in the discourse of Ennahdha's members of parliament.

In his statute of 2 October 2014, Deputy Habib Khedher, general rapporteur of the constitution, published a message in reaction to a statement by Beji Kaid Sebsi,[8] leader of Nidaa Tounes (created in 2012) and then candidate in the presidential election, who stated: 'She is only a woman', in response to statements by Deputy Speaker of the ANC Meherzia Laabidi, who accused his party of having collaborated with the old regime.

> He dared to defy sister Meherzia Laabidi and behind her all Tunisian women. Our sister does not need to be defended as people know how militant she is … To the women of my nation, who are fellow humans and pairs

[*chakaikou*] to men, I tell them: 'This thing coming from where it comes does not surprise us.'

(Our translation)

Mentioning Meherzia Laabidi as a 'sister' is a specificity of Islamic discourse, according to which the fraternity relation is based on faith, whereas the term *chakaikou* (fellow human) links it to religious discourse, specifically to a hadith[9] affirming equality between men and women. This discourse strategy serves to refute criticism focused around the controversial article 28 that gave women 'complementary roles ... in the family'.

A video shared on YouTube for Women's Day (celebrated on 13 August in Tunisia) shows demonstrators chanting '*l'mra ettounsya mahichi mahrzya*' (the Tunisian woman is not Meherzia). What is targeted with Meherzia Laabidi is her veil. Despite how concise this slogan is, it focuses the debate on women and shows that often it is addressed through clothing. Meherzia Laabidi, who according to this slogan embodies 'the other woman', the Islamic one, and personifies the threat to women's rights, reacts by rejecting uniformization and focusing on one sole mode.

> Never did I say that Tunisian women resemble me. Never. We started a revolution to shed this single model. Tunisian women are a varied and diverse lot. There are some women with whom I share ideas, and there are others whose ideas I don't share. There are some who wear a head covering, others who don't cover their head. You know what unites us? Love for Tunisia.[10]

Thus, at a rhetorical level, the Ennahdha party positions itself as a modern party that takes on the challenges of its time, such as contesting conformism and being open to a plurality of individual choices, including the choice of deciding. This response corresponds to what Ducrot (1983) calls a 'polemic negation', and constitutes an excellent illustration of a reactive position that tries to create consensus within difference. This discourse strategy suggests a resolutely pluralistic definition of the identity of Tunisian women, and takes into account the multiplicity of identities, experiences and real life, with or without a veil. In fact, if in the majority of Ennahdha videos women are veiled, they also appear without a veil. Thus appears a position that demonstrates that there are no clothing behaviours and codes that will be imposed on Tunisian women: the veil is neither imposed nor forbidden. The party can in this way assert to Tunisians that it is able to articulate its political and cultural identity as a religious party while preserving the gains of the republican tradition. This explains why the Justice and Development Party in power in Turkey was often approvingly quoted by candidates to the legislative elections of October 2014.[11] In the same vein, a post on 8 September 2014 on the Ennahdha official international Internet page affirms that 'Tunisia can build on its capacity to reconcile between different political, social and religious beliefs to reach a political consensus that respects the society's pluralism'.

Moreover, this openness to individual choice attempts to reject – while pointing a finger at – the repressive practice of the Ben Ali regime, which, in the name of freedom accorded to women by law, excluded veiled women from public service, educational institutions and the media, and exercised police pressure on those who wore a veil on the street (Ben Salem, 2010). The Ben Ali regime (as did Bourguiba before) instrumentalized women to 'make them a simple decoration on the image it projected both domestically and abroad'.[12]

However, plurality does not mean forgetting the 'self' or 'one's personality' in the anthropological sense of the term, and this is what undermines the plurality that is so vaunted and claimed. Asked during the same interview her opinion on Amina Femen, who took a photograph of herself bare-breasted and posted the image on the web, saying, 'My body belongs to me, and is not the source of anyone's honour', M. Laabidi responded:

> You know what saddens me in this whole affair of Amina Femen? It's that she says: my body belongs to me. As for me, I say to her: girl [*ma fille*], I want your conscience to belong to you, your mind to belong to you ... So, does your conscience belong to you? And this, I say to each and every Tunisian woman.

In our opinion, we must anchor this comment by Meherzia Laabidi less within the framework of two opposing arguments, one that denounces sexism and the social status quo supported by an act of disobedience and another that defends a moralizing attempt, where conscience becomes the prerequisite to maintain one's integrity to think and avoid following Western feminism, where emancipation succeeded when women were able to practise the demand of 'my body belongs to me' (Tahon, 2010, 226). In this relationship of the body to the conscience, one of the factors at play goes beyond Amina Femen and concerns all Tunisian women. This generalizing taints the social scene with a conservative moral approach to women's rights and proposes an identity where the individual and collective expressions distance themselves from one of the rights women claim in the West.

This discourse implicitly refers to the moral principles of Islam that question the liberal use of women's freedom in terms of their body. The speech[13] by Souad Abderrahim, minister of women's affairs, called on social media 'the Tunisian Sarah Palin' for her condemnation of single mothers, 'foreign to Tunisian Arab-Muslim society', claims that one cannot talk of freedom in absolute terms: 'Freedom must be anchored and framed by customs, traditions and the respect of morality.'

'I have chosen to be solely Tunisian': binationality versus revolutionary authenticity

At the end of the Ben Ali regime, many opponents were able to return to Tunisia to represent their compatriots remaining abroad. The ANC has among its ranks about 30 people in this category, with about 20 of them binational citizens. When the deputies were debating the new constitution in the ANC, the speech around binationality targeted particularly Meherzia Laabidi. Our first example is a televised debate in French, broadcast on YouTube,[14] between M. Laabidi and Abdelaziz Mzoughi, a member of the Nidaa Tounes party (legalized in 2012), one year after the first elections for the Constituent Assembly that took place on 23 October 2011. As we have suggested previously, Ennahdha is *de facto* at the intersection of issues at the heart of political life in Tunisia since the revolution. This is the case with binationality, an identity theme if there is one that spells out the origin, indeed the authenticity of people.

In his response to the journalist on the issue of Ennahdha's accomplishments in the past year, Mzoughi answers, but by shifting his response, starting thus a polemic discourse that is, according to Amossy and Burger, 'a counter-discourse aim[ing] to discredit a target within a polarized presentation' (Amossy & Burger, 2011, 18). Thus, Laabidi is described by her opponent as a 'piece of an enormous machine' that 'has no power', and he adds, 'I think that Madame Laabidi doesn't represent Tunisian women. First of all, she is French. She has dual nationality. Ennahdha should have had the good taste of naming someone who lives in Tunisian reality … [Laabidi is shown smiling] So she doesn't represent Tunisian women and even veiled women don't see themselves at all in her'. In this polemic discussion, certain rebuttals are barely articulated and even deliberately ignored, but 'binationality' constitutes a centrepiece that is impossible to avoid. First, the response by the Ennahdha representative to her opponent draws out 'the target', that is to say herself, in an unjustly segregated group, to wit 'emigrants that bring in more money than … tourism'. Second, within binationality there are degrees of identity affiliation: 'I am binational and I am Tunisian before being … I am even more Tunisian than you, due to my emotions and involvement. And I am not the only one. In our Assembly, there are more than 20 … binationals.'[15]

This debate on binationality and on single nationality – 'I could have been a binational like you, but I chose to be only Tunisian' (Mzoughi) – anchors identity in a physical space and leaves little space for diaspora or exile experiences. The implications are threefold. The first, although implicit in the body of work on this theme, is a new reality that emerges: the diaspora as a political issue and player in the Tunisian context. The second is that Ennahdha exists beyond the territorial 'physicality'. However, that does not make it foreign, as its members were the regime's main targets and victims. Suffering is their bounty of war. The third implication, and certainly the most central, is related to the revolutionary legitimacy that flows from the 'physicality' or the presence in Tunisia and fidelity to the nation.[16] By the *ad hominem* criticism (Masara, 2011) targeting Laabidi on her double allegiance, built on a fixed and utilitarian concept of 'nationality', there is an *ad rem* argument thrown at the Ennahdha party – a party that was able to take advantage of a revolution already underway. From whence the question posed to Laabidi, 'Where were you on 14 January?' and the statement, almost a scream, 'Me, I was here on 14 January!' (Abdelaziz Mzoughi).

While the issue of binationality was raised to Ennahdha in relation to the party representatives during the period of debate on the constitution, it was raised again during the recent legislative elections (autumn 2014), but it seems to come this time from debate within the party. One can retrace the questions that enlivened the debate in the campaign speeches of Ennahdha's representative in the 'France 1' district (northern France), Saida Ounissi, broadcast on the Facebook page of Ennahdha France. One of the new candidates, Ounissi is part of what is generally called the 'second generation', although she 'was born in Tunisia',[17] as she herself states to underline that she belongs, to parents who were Ennahdha political refugees. In addressing Tunisians in France, in Tunisian Arabic and in French, she uses the same references that Laabidi uses with regards to binationality. Namely, on the one hand, precedence of 'being Tunisian' over other things: 'For all Tunisians abroad, I tell you, you are Tunisians above all …' and 'Tunisia belongs to all Tunisians without distinction'. On the other hand, the continuity that exists between the 'here' and the 'there', bringing forth new players and a diaspora identity turned towards the country of origin.

Tunisianess

'Tunisia has her own personality', Bourguiba used to say, but has this personality remained stable and rigid? Is it not being renegotiated at present? As Lanneau (1986, 10) writes, 'It is when a society feels threatened in its very existence, when it is disorganized, when its own regulation mechanisms are rendered defective by new modes of organization, either planned or already implemented, that it reacts to preserve them'. In this section, we want to highlight a link in the rebuilding of Tunisianess, namely the issue of language and religion raised by Islamists. Despite the inherent bond that exists between Islam and the Arabic language, we distinguish between the reference to religious belonging and ethno-linguistic belonging. In fact, this very issue was debated during the writing of the constitution.

On Ennahdha's Facebook pages, what is published, including comments by supporters, is essentially written in Arabic, especially in comparison to the other web pages where French dominates. Habib Khedher, an Ennahdha deputy mentioned earlier, is undeniably the most remarkable example of an attachment to the Arabic language, and this through the calm rhythm of his interventions, the pure and perfect articulation of the language he uses, his clear intonation and formal tone. Khedher's Facebook pages and his other online publications highlight the high value he gives to literary Arabic over dialect Arabic, the purity of the Arabic language being for him the most efficient defence against what party leader Rached Ghannouchi calls 'linguistic pollution': 'We are Arabs and our language is the Arabic language, we have become Franco-Arabs. This is linguistic pollution. We encourage learning all languages, especially the most alive, without losing our identity. If one cannot be proud of one's language, one cannot be proud of one's homeland.'[18]

For Islamists, the Arabic language is the pivot of Arabity. It is the source of Tunisianess, especially when in the public realm, such as the Constituent Assembly, deputies talk to each other in French. The Arabic language becomes a *sui generis* element, one that ought to remain unquestionable. However, the literary Arabic language is never the only element that is claimed, as its strength rests in being a support for other identity categories, such as Ennahdha Deputy Sanaa Haddad enumerated, when she spoke during the proceedings in the Constituent Assembly against the polarization marking the debate between secular and Islamic deputies: 'As for me, I am a Tunisian woman, a modernist who follows *salaf* [Muhammad and his companions]. I admire my flag and I hold my Quran sacred.'

Two videos on YouTube (with more than 75,000 views each) ensure that in social media networks this excerpt of Haddad's speech is widely known. The parliamentarian produces what Orvar Löfgren (1989) calls an 'identity check list' consisting of a nationality, a flag, a tradition and a holy book. This statement has attracted attention due to its emotional charge, seen in the deputy's tears, and puts together without any apparent contradiction the flag, the Quran, the *salaf* and modernity. Much of the time, which is the first meaning of the term 'modern', Islamists are thus both modern and Muslim. The challenge was to import modernity and to integrate it into *salaf* without associating the terms Islamist – 'backward' tradition. At the same time, identifying with the nation ('I admire my flag') and giving value to the faith ('I hold my Quran sacred') gives this statement an Islamic flavour that balances out the secular reference to the nation.

Identity symbols such as the Quran and the mosque, which are at the foundation of a belief in a common origin, i.e. Islamic culture, are frequently used in the videos shared on Ennahdha's web pages. Thus, in the Islamist movement, the relationship between politics and religion is at the level of culture – that is, of values shared by individuals and not just in the connections between the state and religion. This hierarchy of identity values that give prominence to religion goes beyond the party. It places Ennahdha in a reactive position and in a delicate balance, but does not affect the stability given to believers by their relationship with religion.

Conclusion

By its presence on social media, the Ennahdha party brings forth great tension in its identity list. The party's search for consensus, the fact that it keeps reiterating that there is freedom of choice for individuals, as well as its insistence on women's freedom and autonomy, make it a modern player and let it participate in political actions. However, this modern identity is incessantly superimposed onto a reference, or rather a series of references – Quran, religion, *salaf*, Arabic language – while no thought is given to the problematizing of the modern and Muslim dyad.

Notes

1 A result of the 'popular consultation' initiated by the regime in 1970 (Cameau & Geisser, 2003, 274).
2 The number of Islamists thrown in prison varied between 15,000 and 30,000.

3 See Marks, 2013.
4 One realizes how much this term confuses and gives the impression that Tunisian society was not already Islamized. However, the Islamization we mention here touches on the voluntary shaping and proselytizing of society.
5 These shifts represent a certain continuity with the discourse of the fallen regime, in that they implicitly construct voters as necessarily accepting secular theses, forgetting immediately afterwards the complexity of the relationships of people not only to politics but also to Islam.
6 For its history and use in the three Maghreb countries, see Hadj-Moussa, 2012.
7 The interpretation that the users of *publinets* played a significant role in the revolution (Haugbolle & Cavatorta, 2012, 164) still remains largely to be proven. The controls that the *publinets* were under resulted in the fact that in Tunisia in 2010 there were fewer 'than 3 out of 10,000 people [using them] whereas the ration was three times higher already in Morocco and Algeria in 2002' (Lecomte, 2014, 31).
8 The current president of Tunisia.
9 This report could be found in the collection of hadith compiled by Imam Abu 'Isa at-Tirmidhi, hadith 113.
10 Comment by Ms. Laabidi concerning Femen: www.shemsfm.net/fr/video/meherzia-la abidi-commente-le-slogan-la-femme-tunisienne-n-est-pas-meherzia-et-parle-d-amina-fe men_45590.
11 Here is what Saida Ounissi, head of the France 1 list, says to her voters (in Tunisian Arabic): 'Turkey has become an example in the progressive world because it has been taken [governed] by competent people (in French) who fear God' (www.youtube.com/ watch?v=wI8PzXE_-M0).
12 'Speech by sister Kalthoum Badreddine during Women's Day', www.youtube.com/wa tch?v=eFT9zFX6dfE (Nahda channel). In this 12-minute speech, the 'equality between Tunisian men and women' enshrined in the new constitution is mentioned at least 20 times, so as to highlight Ennahdha's contributions.
13 Statement by Souad Abderrahim on the issue of single mothers, www.facebook.com/ video/video.php?v=299321146744557.
14 Debate between Ms. Laabidi and Abdelaziz Mzoughi, www.youtube.com/watch?v= eiBCRxXNpQs,
15 This criticism takes various forms and is on different media. In the programme 'Politica' broadcast by Radio El Jawhara, and re-broadcast by the Ennahdha channel, Ms. Laabidi is interviewed and answers questions from the listeners. A satirical excerpt, using different discourse genres, journalistic, musical, etc., and giving a portrait of Ms. Laabidi, presents her thus: [Voice of a journalist] 'Meherzia Laabidi is a *female politician of Tunisian origin*. Let us see what she says: [a voice imitating Ms. Laabidi saying in English, a reference to her training in translation] 'My name is Meherzia. I …' This sentence has as background music *La Marseillaise*, the French national anthem. This indirect criticism of binationality is lightened and defused by its humorous dimension but also by the 'politician who must accept criticism', according to the interviewee.
    www.youtube.com/watch?v=etOREP1FnHk. See also the rap song, created by Meherzia Laabidi: www.youtube.com/watch?v=vUdlabnB1vc.
16 We do not elaborate this important point, which merits further development.
17 Saida Ounissi's interview, www.youtube.com/watch?v=gF3h5RGMhdY.
18 For Rached Ghannouchi's position on the Arabic language, see: www.lefigaro.fr/fla sh-actu/2011/10/26/97001-20111026FILWWW00438-ennahda-notre-langue-c-est-l-a rabe.php.

References

Allal, Amin & Geisser, Vincent (2011) 'La Tunisie de l'après-Ben Ali. Les partis politiques à la recherche du "peuple introuvable"', *Culture et Conflits*, 83(3), pp. 18–25.

Amossy, Ruth & Burger, Marcel (2011) 'Introduction. La polémique médiatisée', *Semen*, 31, pp. 7–24, semen.revues.org/9072.
At-Tirmidhi, ImamAbu Isa (1999) *Jami at-Tirmidhi*. Riyad: Dar as-Salaam.
Ben Salem, Maryam (2010) 'Le voile en Tunisie. De la réalisation de soi à la résistance passive', *Revue des mondes musulmans et de la Méditerranée*, 128, December, remmm.revues.org/6840 (accessed 27 January 2012).
Cameau, Michel & Geisser, Vincent (2003) *Le syndrome autoritaire. Politique en Tunisie de Bouguiba à Ben Ali*. Paris: Presses de Sciences Po.
Cesari, Jocelyne (2013) *The Awakening of Muslim Democracy. Religion, Modernity, and the State*. New York: Cambridge University Press.
Chouikha, Larbi (2005–06) 'L'audiovisuel en Tunisie: une libéralisation fondue dans le moule étatique', *L'Année du Maghreb*, pp. 549–558.
Dahmen, Zouha (2001) *Sphère publique et logiques de l'action communicationnelle en Tunisie. De la presse d'opinion aux chaînes de télévision transnationales*. PhD dissertation, Université Grenoble III – Stendhal, UFR Sciences de l'Information et de la Communication, (Vol. I & Vol. II).
Ducrot, Oswald (1983) 'Opérateurs argumentatifs et visée argumentative', *Cahiers de Linguistique Française*, 5, pp. 7–36.
Ferrié, Jean-Noël & Santucci, Jean-Claude (2006) *Dispositifs de démocratisation et dispositifs autoritaires en Afrique du Nord*. Paris: CNRS.
François, Bastien & Neveu, Érik (1999) 'Espaces publics mosaïques. Acteurs, arènes et rhétoriques, des débats publics contemporains', in F. Bastien & É. Neveu (Eds) *Espaces publics mosaïques. Acteurs, arènes et rhétoriques, des débats publics contemporains* (pp. 13–58). Rennes: Presses Universitaires de Rennes.
Hadj-Moussa, Ratiba (1996) 'Les antennes célestes, les émirs – apparatchiks et le peuple: L'espace public en question', *Anthropologie et sociétés*, 20(2), pp. 129–155.
Hadj-Moussa, Ratiba (2003) 'New media, community and politics in Algeria', *Media, Culture and Society*, 25, pp. 451–469.
Hadj-Moussa, Ratiba (2012) 'Sur un concept contesté. La sphère publique arabe est-elle soluble dans les médias?', *Anthropologie et Société*, 36(1–2), pp. 161–180.
Hadj-Moussa, Ratiba (2015) *La télévision par satellite au Maghreb et ses publics, Espaces de résistance, espaces critiques*. Grenoble: Presses Universitaires de Grenoble.
Haugbolle, Rikke H. & Cavatorta, Francesco (2012) '"Vive la grande famille des médias tunisiens". Media Reform, Authoritarian Resilience and Societal Responses in Tunisia', *The Journal of North African Studies*, 17(1), pp. 97–112.
Khiari, Sadri (2003) *Tunisie: Le délitement de la cité. Coercition, consentement, résistance*. Paris: Khartala.
Labat, Séverine (2013) *Les islamistes tunisiens. Entre l'État et la mosquée*. Paris: Demopolis.
Lanneau, G. (1986) 'Identités régionales, milieux urbains et ruraux', in P. Tap (Ed.) *Identités collectives et changements sociaux production et affirmation de l'identité: colloque international, Toulouse, septembre 1979*. Paris: Privat, pp. 189–192.
Lecomte, Romain (2014) 'Au-delà de la "révolution 2.0". Analyse du cyberactivisme tunisien', *Moyen-Orient*, 21, pp. 30–35.
Löfgren, Orvar (1989) 'The nationalization of culture', *Ethnologia Europaea*, 19(1) pp. 5–24.
Marks, Monica (2013) *Convince, Coerce, or Compromise? Ehnnahda's Approach to Tunisian Constitution*. Doha: Brookings Doha Center.
Masara, Karina (2011) 'À qui profitent les dialogues des sourds. La question de l'action dans la polémique entre mondalistes et Altermondialistes autour de la pauvreté', *Semen*, 31, semen.revues.org/9111.
Mostefaoui, Belgacem (1995) *La télévision française au Maghreb: Structures, stratégies et enjeux*. Paris: L'Harmattan.

Puchot, Pierre (2012) *La révolution confisquée. Enquête sur la transition démocratique en Tunisie.* Paris: Sindbad.

Rugh, William A. (2004) *Arab Mass Media. Newspaper, Radio, and Television in Arab Politics.* London: Praeger.

Storm, Lise (2014) *Party Politics and the Prospects for Democracy in North Africa.* Boulder, CO: Lynne Rienner Publishers.

Tahon, Marie-Blanche (2010) 'Les artisanes de l'intermonde', in *Sociologie de l'intermonde. La vie sociale après l'idée de société*, (pp. 221–235). Louvain: Les Presses de l'Université de Louvain.

Trabelsi, Anouar (2001) *Insertion et appropriation d'internet en Tunisie. D'une acclimatation sociotechnique dans les pays du sud.* PhD dissertation, Sciences of Information and Communication, Université de Grenoble III.

2

SOCIAL MEDIA AS A NEW IDENTITY BATTLEGROUND

The cultural comeback[1] in Tunisia after the revolution of 14 January 2011

Noureddine Miladi

Introduction

The Arab Spring revolutions, which started in Tunisia in December 2010 and culminated on 14 January 2011 with a regime change that ousted the country's dictator, marked an historical turn in consolidating people's sense of national identity and the significance of what it is to be Tunisian. Mobile phones, blogs, YouTube, Facebook pages and Twitter feeds have empowered university students, social and political activists, along with other marginalized citizens with a platform for free debate. Also they have provided a virtual space for debates about religious identity and the negotiation of the cultural history of the country.

By analysing the content of various social media network sites and homepages of religious activists as well as civil society organizations, this chapter discusses the cultural comeback in Tunisia after the revolution. It examines cultural and religious debates mediated by social media and investigates how the question of Tunisia's cultural identity and historical claims are being manifested and negotiated. It looks at the extent to which this growing virtual social media sphere has become an ideological battleground between religious groups and secularists: a reflection of the rutted transition phase that the country has been going through.

The struggle for religious identity in Tunisia after the revolution

The struggle for religious identity and authority in the North African region goes back a few centuries. The tension had always been between a locally adapted North African Islamic tradition that is guided by the Maliki Fiqh[2] (School of Islamic Jurisprudence) and other influences including the Salafi movement[3] (used sometimes interchangeably with the word 'Wahhabi'), originating from Saudi Arabia. Back to the early 18th century, there had been resistance from Al-Zaytouna's[4] scholars in Tunisia to the attempts of Wahhabi[5] scholars to spread their school of thought. While North African traditional Islamic teachings propound an Islam that is coherent and consistent with the local environment, and draws from the teachings of Imam Malik, al-Ghazali in addition to the influence of the Sufi movement, Salafism advocates a more rigid version of Islam. The Wahhabi scholars tend to ignore the cultural specificities and the importance of context in applying Islamic teachings. They mainly view Islam as purely understood through a literal interpretation of the Quran and Sunnah, the practices of the Sahaba (Prophet's companions) and the Tabi'een (first two generations of early Muslims). Due to their rigid approach to religious teachings and their refusal to compromise their interpretation of Islam in various parts of the Muslim world, the followers of the Salafi School have always been likely to face imminent confrontation with both civil and state institutions. In most of the cases, 'Salafism, in both its violent and non-violent forms, represents a rebellion against local Islamic traditions and practices and their relationship to political systems', argues Malka (2014, 1).

However, it can be argued that the reasons why such groups have gained certain popularity, for instance, in Tunisia are threefold: first, the total media control under the regimes of Habib Bourguiba[6] and Ben Ali, which aimed at homogenizing the Tunisian culture and its political thought. Through the centralization of the religious establishment, President Habib Bourguiba, also called *al-Mujahid al-Akbar* (greatest *mujahid*), had a total monopoly on media output relating to modernism, educational reform, women's emancipation, religious and political discourse, and every other aspect of governance. During his rule, and every day for over 40 years, before the main news programme at 8.00 pm, the state channel (Tunisia TV) used to broadcast the *Taujihaat al-Rais* (directions/speeches of the president). Such speeches constituted the trend of thought that characterized political life and the political and religious discourse enforced on the Tunisian population.

Second, being the leader of the country, who claimed to be elected for life, Bourguiba ruthlessly excluded every potential competitor for the country's headship including the religious leadership/authorities of Al-Zaytouna Mosque and the Tunisian National Union of Workers. Al-Zaytouna educational and religious institution had served for centuries as a centre of learning and a multi-disciplinary university offering religious as well as secular subjects such as mathematics, chemistry and astronomy in addition to *fiqh*, history and Quranic studies. More importantly, 'Karaouine (in Morocco) and Al-Zaytouna (in Tunisia) sat at the crossroads of the medieval Islamic, Christian, and Jewish worlds, and they were instrumental not only in transmitting advanced scientific knowledge to Europe but also in promoting Maliki Islam' (Malka, 2014, 2). The era of Bourguiba's rule meant a complete subjugation of all forms of political, intellectual and religious dissent and the suppressive containment of all forms of diversity. The continued total absence of a well-informed religious authority during the reign of Ben Ali, who succeeded him, has led to an evident vacuum in the country, which was ultimately occupied during the 1990s onward by preachers from abroad via satellite TV channels.

Third, one may also argue that the violent tendency of such groups (sometimes called the *al-Salafiya al-Jehadya*) is due to the failure of the ruling regimes over the last few decades to partly contain them, but also their deficiency in building a multicultural society, a multi-party political system and promote the right of minority groups to thrive. In fact, the state media since the independence of Tunisia in 1956 have been solely in the service of the regime and its political elite. Both Bourguiba and Ben Ali (the only two presidents who ruled Tunisia from 1956 to 2011) have exploited all mass media outlets to advance their parties' ideologies and they ruthlessly marginalized any religious or political groups that had the potential to influence society. Their version of cultural, political as well as economic development is solely based on channelling all media outlets in promoting the only official ideology of the ruling regime. This version of governance has obviously proven deficient since the beginning of the 1970s. Yet the country had to wait until the revolution of 14 January 2011 for a regime change to take place.

The aftermath of this political landmark in the modern history of Tunisia has meant that debates on religious authority intensified with the development of the Internet as a form of mass dissemination empowering such groups as the Salafis (followers of the Salafi group). Since then, the fever of cultural confrontation has surfaced more on the social scene on various occasions and in various contexts. Followers of the Salafi groups, who were suppressed and many of them jailed under the reign of Ben Ali, have found following the revolution a fertile ground for religious activism and membership recruitment.

The palpable influence of satellite TV preachers on Tunisian young generations has been evident since 2003, with the emergence of young people wearing long beards and long dresses (most known as part of the Salafi movement dress code) – a sight not common among the Tunisian traditional/religious dress style. However, Ben Ali's government response to this growing phenomenon was twofold: on the one hand, it attempted to suppress its growth by jailing its leaders after successive waves of arrests; on the other hand, it set out to promote the regime's version of cultural Islam, which focuses on the outer look rather than the substance. Folkloric groups and traditional music bands of certain Sufi trends were generously funded by the government in an attempt to channel the religious revivalism spreading mainly among college and university students to these traditional forms of Islam. Moreover, the regime employed, all the way through, a systematic way of incarcerating the leadership and activists of moderate Islam (from the Ennahdha party) and prevented them from accessing public institutions, the religious space (mosques) as well as public media.

Since the revolution there has been a consensus among the political elite and a large part of the civil society organizations to fight extremist groups who employ hate speech and violent means. The troika government (three-party coalition) formed after the elections of 23 October 2011 took the matter of religious extremism very seriously. Not least the Tunisian Army and security forces waged a war against the jihadists in various parts of the country, especially those taking refuge in al-Shaanbi Mountains. However, saying this, one may also argue that there has been silence regarding the extremist tendencies from fundamentalist secularists who control a sizeable part of the media, especially the public service outlets like TV, radio and newspapers. Moreover, scores of intellectuals and 'experts' who had sustained the dictatorial regime of Ben Ali for 23 years seem unable nowadays to accept cultural as well as ideological differences in the public domain.

New platforms for mediated cultural identities

Part of the literature regarding online identity construction suggests that the use of social media networks by online groups strengthens their social and emotional ties, attracts more community members and increases their circle of friendship (Ellison et al., 2007). Boyle and Johnson (2010), in their study of online communities in university and college environments, argue that students' networks and social interactions get cemented and are normally stronger in the online environment when students already know each other offline. The online self is presented in a way aligned with the offline self, i.e. a representation of the real self in the everyday environment. To certain youth groups in Tunisia, online interaction is in fact a continuation of their offline encounters (Miladi, 2015). Mosques, universities, colleges and public spaces represent thriving spheres of religious and social engagement. Lectures, talks, debates and sometimes fights that take place in the physical space also find their way to the virtual world. However, not everything expressed in those online and offline spaces is accepted by mainstream society. This evolving notion of identity manifestation invokes nowadays certain practices that do not align with the cultural identity of the mainstream. For them the notion of identity is a process of negotiation with the social environment and no longer a matter of acceptance and affiliation to a specific community. The online environment, especially social media networks, has facilitated the creation of virtual communities and virtual identities.

It is worth noting that the articulation of a common identity among the Tunisian youth has nowadays diverse sources:

> In localized face-to-face interactions, identity is constructed under a unique set of constraints. The presence of the corporal body in social encounters prevents people from claiming identities that are inconsistent with the visible part of their physical characteristics (e.g., sex, race, and looks), and the shared knowledge of each other's social background and personality attributes renders it difficult for an individual to pretend to be what he or she is not.
>
> *(Zhao et al., 2008, 1817)*

However, the national identity as suggested by some scholars is becoming a fluid and changing concept in the core of its formation expressions of language, culture, ideology, history and memory. In its complex form a nation is described as 'a group of people who feel they are a community bound together by ties of history, culture and common ancestry' (Kellas, 1991, 3). The Internet is probably the most influential one. Contrary to previous generations who were brought up through family values, an education system and religious teachings, nowadays satellite TV and online environments seem the most influential spaces of interaction about identity and opinion formation.

Over the last decade the use of social media networks has steadily gained momentum among youth and political activists in Tunisia. Their proliferation came to fruition with the explosion of the Tunisian revolution, which brought about a regime change on 14 January 2011. Human rights and political activists, civil society organizations and marginalized groups found in the Internet a priceless resource for various reasons. Before and after the Tunisian revolution, young people have been the most likely users of social media networks. The revolution was reportedly aided by Facebook and Internet activism. On the eve of the revolution, Facebook users in Tunisia had reached 3 million. That figure has been steadily growing for the obvious reason of the new freedoms that Tunisians entertain. According to the Arab Social Media Report, Facebook user penetration in the Arab region is 42.1%[7] of the total population.

Contrary to old media, social media networks have been instrumental in aiding the social and political changes that the country is witnessing. First, the Internet has provided a networking opportunity at a very cheap cost. Second, it is probably the most effective way to exchange information (text, sound, picture and video footage). Third, there is the potential impact on public opinion both locally and internationally. In addition to the above-mentioned players in this virtual sphere, new players seem also to be fully benefiting from the new technologies. Scores of religious activists, especially those defined by the government as 'extremist groups', have adopted the Internet as a:

> tactical response which has turned into a strategic choice and an effective tool to break the censorship placed on them and the global war on terror waged on their affiliates on the ground since the 11 September 2001 attacks. The physical constraints that such groups have been facing in the real world have pushed them to an expansion in the virtual sphere, in an organized and systematic and structured manner. The aim has been to recuperate the losses from an unbalanced war they have been facing in conventional battlefields [such as Afghanistan, Iraq, Somalia, Syria, etc.].
>
> (Zran, 2008, 86)

Studies relating to identity construction and religious engagement on social media have focused on self-presentation, especially when most of the users tend to keep their identity anonymous in the online environment. Numerous studies from various cultural and geographic contexts found that users of all age groups, namely the youth, engage in role-play and most of the time hide their real gender, age or geographic location. While engaging in sophisticated discussions in the online world, they may also use a different social status to fit in with like-minded users in the online environment. This is probably due to the feeling of security and lack of accountability while being anonymous online. However, what is evident is that discussions on Facebook pages, for instance, do give the impression that users feel empowered by the new democratic transformation that has circumvented all forms of control on free speech and congregation. Also, it seems clear from online interactions that various forms of Tunisian identity do not necessarily constitute components of young people's personal identity. Certain aspects of their personal identity are in fact in contrast with the Tunisian mainstream religious school of *fiqh*, which is the Maliki School.

Online visual components and the expression of personality

As part of their identity expression, certain religious groups (such as the Tunisia Islamic Front, Ansar al-Sharia and Al Salafia Al Jihadia in Tunisia) tend to use explicit visual elements (photos/pictures, cultural attire, etc.) to boost their propaganda campaigns. Such practices reveal a wish among the Salafi groups to show off their cultural pride as belonging to a specific 'pure' school of thought. Also, such tendencies reflect loyalty and allegiance to a particular sheikh (religious leader) or a sect, most often from abroad. Via social media networks such groups are creating sophisticated cyber-environments to extend their influence in society. Such environments do reflect the growing sphere of activities available in real life for such groups after the revolution. Mosques, community centres and Quranic clubs have in fact been transformed into strongholds for those groups, where they disseminate their teachings. This is in tune with Mitchell's (1995) and other researchers' argument that, owing to the technological developments, subcultural groups in society have created for themselves online communities, something nearing cyberscapes, which transcend the geographic, age and other limitations faced in real life.

So the adaptation of subcultural groupings in Tunisian society is not unique among other religious groups or minorities from around the word. Leonardi (2003) argues in his study that Latino migrant minorities in the USA, for instance, adapt quickly and efficiently to the new technologies as they resourcefully employ mobile phones and Internet networks to stay in touch and build their own networks inside and outside the USA. Facebook provides users with a variety of activities that are advantageous and convenient for promoting their views and ideologies. This proposition extends the influence of such groups and their recruitment potential especially among the youth. Their operation, in other words, is no longer geographically based but spreads its net through a complex, sometimes unmeasured scope of effect.

The expression of identity among a few activists, namely those preaching 'extremist' religious tendencies, is characterized by total anonymity, a deliberate form of interaction that reveals nothing about their physical characteristics, name, age, colour, ethnic background, institutional affiliation, etc. By doing so, such online actors operate free from any of the above constraints and more significantly from any form of accountability for the content they circulate on their pages. 'This combination of disembodiment and anonymity', argue Zhao et al. (2008, 1817), 'creates a technologically mediated environment in which a new mode of identity production emerges'. In a fully anonymous online world, extreme views, citing hatred and deviance go most of the time unpunished, with damage that may be significant to social stability. As a result, the impact of those anonymous pages of Salafi or jihadi groups can be significant since much of its material does not promote understanding, coexistence or social harmony.

One would appreciate in this context the various studies that have claimed during the last two decades that global media have negatively affected local cultures and marginalized minority identities through the creation of a global trend of consciousness. However, what is also evident from the developments due to the use of social media is that such technologies have in fact empowered minority groups from all strata of society and created influential virtual cultural cyberspaces. Such spaces are not only serving their designated members but also extending their outreach to the wider society. Part of this influence is evidently due to the new openness and freedom that came with the revolution – particularly during the first two years in which the country witnessed an unrestricted and unregulated free speech environment both online and offline. Scores of statements made in gatherings, on TV, radio debates and social media networks go unchecked and the instigators are unaccountable.

In this evolving environment, one of the groups that emerged soon after the revolution was Ansar al-Sharia, founded by Seifallah Ben Hassine (known as Abu Iyadh al-Tunsi). The group emerged in the poorer quarters of the capital Tunis and has spread to various parts of the country. One of its media outlets is al-Qayrawan Media Foundation. In its publications the group openly rejects the democratic process and calls it the 'idol of democracy', referring to it as a polytheistic act against the will of God. The group also openly condemns the Ennahdha party for its 'violation of monotheism', and calls its leader, Rached Ghannouchi, a 'heretic' for being part of this process. The group further considers any other opinion that contradicts theirs a 'pollution' of the Islamic faith.

Moreover, Ansar al-Sharia is probably one of the Salafi groups that has managed to harness social media effectively to disseminate its ideology to the wider society. Although the general feel of the postings from the Ansar al-Sharia group on Facebook[8] is related to reminders and joining what is good and forbidding what is bad, the tendency seems to be to promote hard-line preachers and extremist views in interpreting the teachings of Islam. The content of those pages can be classified into three main categories: 1 reminders about the importance of following the Prophet's Sunnah (i.e. his example); 2 support of jihadi groups for their wars in various parts of the Arab and Muslim world; and 3 attacks on secular figures and groups that oppose their opinions and teachings. Some of the postings, as an illustration of the above, include: 'Oh Allah take care of the coward tyrants, Oh Allah do not grant them any supremacy, and do not let them achieve their goals'.[9] Other content is related to general advice for believers, such as 'whoever says there is no God but Allah and Mohammad is his messenger as his last words before he dies will go to Paradise'. Other postings are about glorifying jihad, which read, for instance:

'if the Jihad in the sake of Allah is terrorism, I am the first terrorist'. Other posts are supplications, such as 'O Allah make my tomb a guardian from Paradise and do not make it a hole from Hell fire', 'O Allah I entrust you with my heart, so please do not fill it with anyone else apart from you', 'Oh Allah your victory', 'Oh Allah grant me your pleasure and Paradise'.[10]

Another Facebook page run by a similarly minded group is called 'Group for the fight against tyrants', which had 3,813 likes by 27 September 2014. Its profile picture is a black flag with the caption 'There is no God but Allah and Mohammad is his messenger'. It is obvious that this group is an offshoot of the Ansar al-Sharia, which has attempted to diversify its presence on social media networks. The group posts a map of Africa and the Middle East with highlights in black signifying the regimes most corrupt in the region,[11] which may also signify that those are potentially their primary targets.

Performing identity online: the cultural comeback

Worthy of mention is that some of the above-mentioned groups do not explicitly endorse violence but promote a radical interpretation of the Islamic teachings. In attempting to enforce their radical teaching, Ansar al-Sharia threatened various artists and secular figures. However, as alluded to above, the origin of such groups is not necessarily a home-grown phenomenon but mainly grew out of the influence of satellite TV religious preachers, especially those with extreme Salafi tendencies. Their daring ambitions in wanting to change society by force have various manifestations. One of those was on 28 November 2012 when Ansar al-Sharia students took hostage the Dean of Manouba University in the capital Tunisia after he decided to ban the *niqab* (veil cover for women). Events started when two face-veiled students, Iman Melki, 20, and Faten Ben Mahmoud, 21, who seem to be from the Ansar al-Sharia group refused to take off their face veils in class and during exams. In support of the two students the Ansar al-Sharia group occupied the university until 24 January 2012.

In an attempt to theorize this phenomenon it is maybe of relevance to pin this on the works of the French sociologist Pierre Bourdieu (1986), who argued that social capital emerges through people's interaction in society and via the relationship that is created through this network of interaction. He defines social capital as the 'aggregate of the actual or potential resources which are linked to possession of a durable network of more or less institutionalized relationships of mutual acquaintance and recognition' (ibid., 248). The complex framework of communications technology that is currently in existence has expanded the outreach of religious groups. The oral communication among Tunisians, which is traditionally confined to word of mouth in the Arab culture and thrives in public spaces like cafés, town squares, mosque gatherings, clubs and neighbourhoods, has nowadays been expanded in scope to unlimited virtual spaces. The terrain of influence, which extends beyond the immediate geographical location, is no longer watched and controlled by the police apparatus, but is seemingly encouraged as part of the thriving scene of a new democratic society.

Persepolis and the clash of cultural values

One of the significant events that stirred cultural and religious controversies during the last few years was the airing of the animated programme *Persepolis* on the independent TV channel Nessma. This French film was directed by Marjane Satrapi and Vincent Paronnaud and released first on 25 December 2007 in the USA. The storyline was created from Satrapi's novel (*Persepolis*) and centres around the story of a little Iranian girl who grows up after the Iranian revolution. After its release, the film was met with an outcry in a few Muslim countries. It was, for instance, banned in Iran and Lebanon as it was seen as abusive of Islamic religious teachings. In Tunisia, the film was first shown on 7 October 2011 when the TV channel Nessma decided to air it. Given that the mainstream Islamic ethos forbids the depiction of God in any shape, the content was considered a violation of the religious creed of 99% of the population, as it portrays the image of God through one of the characters in the film. This event instigated anger and heated debate on TV, radio and in the print media about freedom of expression versus veneration of the sacred. Also, it prompted animated discussion on social media networks between religious activists and secularists. Angry protestors congregated in front of the Nessma TV station to express their resentment and demanded the trial of its owners.[12] Faced with mounting pressure from the public, Nabil Karoui, the owner of Nessma, subsequently had to make an unreserved apology to the Tunisian public before being tried in a Tunisia court for 'violating sacred values' and 'disturbing public order', after which he was fined 2,400 dinars (US$1,550).

Considering the above, what was significant about this event was the timing of showing this film. The final week of the election campaign for the first ever democratic elections in Tunisia was considered very sensitive. While candidates as well as the Tunisian public had been waiting for this historic festival, the programme was seen as a 'provocation' because it spoilt the festive mood in the country. It also instigated an atmosphere of cultural clash, which therefore led to distracting the public concern towards a chaotic web of controversial issues. Nabil Karoui (the channel's owner) reflected some of the threats he received through social media networks: 'After we aired "Persepolis" on Friday, there were messages posted on Facebook calling for Nessma to be torched and our journalists to be killed'.[13] Many of the responses on Facebook were anonymous, and originated from individuals as well as groups. In response to this event and others after the revolution, the Salafi groups have become increasingly vocal in Tunisia. Activists on Facebook use nicknames for affiliation to the Salafi movement, for instance, 'Ines Um Naim Assalafiya', 'Ines Assalafiya', 'Umayma assalafiya', 'Shayma Salafiya or 'Assalafiya ala Minhaaj annubuwah' (Salafi on the path of the prophethood), to hide their true identity and whereabouts (although some users may mention on their pages their cities/towns of origin). Others use group names like 'Ahlusunnah waljamaa biwilayat Nabeul', 'Ahlul-hadith Ghar almilh, Bizerte', 'Kun salafiyan filhayat', among many others. However, regardless of the names/nicknames being used, such discussions clearly have channelled the debate towards confrontation and the non-acceptance of unchecked freedom of expression to be tolerated in the country.

Contrary to the above discourse, the Ennahdha Islamic party, which was leading the coalition government at the time, trod very carefully in response to this very controversial debate. Its media office as well as its communication channels remained cautious in taking a balanced response. During that period, the party had been entirely in support of freedom of expression, but equally considered the screening of *Persepolis* as blasphemous. Ghannouchi, along with other key figures, was for decades a victim of suppression and prevented from any political participation. Therefore, since the revolution Ennahdha has been advocating free speech but that which respects the sacred, especially the beliefs and symbols of Islam, which are embraced by almost 99% of Tunisians. The party has also been active on social media networks from the early weeks of the revolution as platforms to convey its views to local and international public opinion. Its main homepage, Ennahdha.tn, and Facebook pages for Ghannouchi, for instance, have been considered official and credible sources for its vision of society and current affairs. Other active pages run by its members and supporters have also mushroomed in the last few years. Some have teamed up under the umbrella of Ittihad Kulluna ma' Harakat Ennahdha (union of pages all of us are with the Ennahdha movement). The overwhelming discourse on Ennahdha websites is respect for the law and the right to free expression, but Ennahdha sees freedom as a precious value that should also come with social responsibility. Therefore, journalists should not abuse the faith or denigrate the identity of a group of people under the pretext of freedom of expression.

One may argue that all of the above postulates the dynamics of cultural and political change in a country long controlled by a dictatorship, but such claims seem to overlook significant nuances vis-à-vis the dramatic changes in the political as well as the media scenes in Tunisia. 'The image of an authentic, homogeneous and tolerant Tunisian Islam is contrasted with the innovative plurality of fervent or even radical Muslim discourses that upset the original balance in the country and threaten to undermine Tunisian identity' (Ubachs, 2013).

Social media and the active user-generated content producers

The unprecedented developments in computer-mediated communications have transformed our perception of the user or consumer of Internet content. Reference to Internet use in Tunisia among adults tells us that content production and active interaction in the social media networks is an overwhelming practice among various age groups. The new participatory culture seems to characterize the current interactivity. As noted above, an analysis of the social media networks of some religious groups reveals that users are largely active in producing content in terms of brief comments, sayings, short articles, video clips and pictures. Also, in most of the cases they tend to circulate content from other users or other Internet sites. Such active users challenge the traditionally held assumption of Internet users/

audience as mere consumers, and credit them with the power of producing and generating content (Leadbeater, 2008; Gee & Hayes, 2011).

Pan-Arab media can be seen as important players in the thriving religious revival in Tunisia. After the explosion of satellite TV in the mid-1990s, followed by the emergence of the power of the Internet, such spaces have become contested arenas between various religious schools of thought. The obvious impact of such scholars as Sheikh Yousuf Al-Qaradawi, Ayidh Al-Qarni and Hamza Yousuf, among others, is a case in point. Also the influence of religious channels such as Iqraa, al-Risala and al-Majd in Arab societies is also very evident in this line of argument.

As noted above, and through the exposure to myriad religious teachings, religious activists develop their identity and cultural affinities, some of which are through the influence of overseas preachers. More importantly their online interactions also lead to the development of their online identities. This social community online goes beyond daily interaction with people in real life, and by doing so, participants engage in more honest and open discussions about every aspect of their cultural identity.

Social media and the decentralized religious authority

This chapter extends the above line of research to the role of social media networks and homepages in an attempt to understand the extent to which religious authority has become decentralized in a country embracing a democratic transition. I noted earlier in this chapter that the explosion in technological development has aided religious activists to take advantage of this space in an unprecedented manner. As argued by Marks (2013), the Internet has become a decisive tool that amplifies the popularity of *Salafi jihadism* among marginalized Tunisian youth. Traditionally, Tunisia's religious authority in terms of *fatwa* (religious ruling) and other decrees comes from the grand imam or the mufti (religious judge) of the country. Now not only is the Internet changing how people exchange religious teachings but they themselves have potentially been transformed into influential authorities over the religious discourse being circulated. Among many things, the understanding of authority is shifting dramatically from the hands of the well-established and experienced religious leaders, creating new axes of power, the Internet sheikhs. A plethora of religious websites nowadays provide a platform of engagement and a challenge to the established authority, hence flattening the traditional religious power centres.

Consequently, and contrary to the hegemonic classes (in Gramscian terms) such as intellectuals and other organized power structures in society who traditionally represent cultural and other forms of dominance, I would argue that religious groups in Tunisia have emerged as the new centres of influence in society. They certainly do not possess intellectual leadership, but they could prove influential in changing the youth culture and establishing an eccentric trend from the mainstream. As suggested by Berger and Luckmann (1991: 137), such groups represent a new reality, which 'includes the power to determine the decisive socialization processes'. A case in point was the attempt to enforce certain norms of dress and behaviour among university students at the University of Manouba (Tunis) and other public spaces in the country.

Conclusion

During the last few years, the initiatives to articulate a moderate yet efficient alternative to what has been perceived as 'religious extremism' in the region have become undoubtedly urgent. The development of the so-called *Dai'sh* or 'Islamic State' is an illustration of how urgently this alternative must be sought in the Arab region. This chapter has explored ways in which online interaction among Tunisian religious groups may affect their cultural identities and the religious discourse being circulated after the revolution. I have also argued in this chapter that the advent of satellite TV and social media networks has transformed the long-assumed approach of identity production. The scope of freedom available after the revolution has allowed the youth to become more active in the realization of their identity as an existential foundation. Amidst this sophisticated development, the mediascape has proven an effective tool in the formation of the self via a self-gratification process. Also, new technologies have extended the spaces of influence for the circulation and negotiation of religious discourse in Tunisia after the revolution. Such unprecedented conditions have led to the emergence of a multiplicity in religious authorities and the absence of a unified establishment able to earn an overwhelming legitimacy among the populace. However, while there is insight into the interaction of religious groups online as they negotiate and reproduce their religious and cultural affinities, it would be equally important to find out how these groups develop after a certain period of time and establish themselves as recognized authorities. A longitudinal interaction with social media will probably be of social interest as the attitude of such groups may change over time, due to circumstances or political or economic variables.

On another note, during the last few decades there has been a great deal of discussion regarding the emergence of Islamic groups. Among most of the research centres, academic quarters and policymaking bodies this phenomenon has been given various terminology such as 'Islamic extremism', 'political Islam', 'radical Islam', 'Islamic fundamentalism', 'Islamism', 'Islamists', 'Islamic terrorism', etc. The reasons for the development of such groups, including the challenges they pose, has been attributed most of the time to various problems that the Arab and Muslim world has been witnessing, but to some it has been considered a sign of a renewed clash of civilizations. I argued in this chapter that, contrary to the claim that these groups emerged as part of a de-Westernization project in the region, in fact they have gained credibility due to the absence of a thriving civil society in the Arab world that is willing to open up the opportunity for freedom of expression and organization and accommodate diverse ideological and religious differences. Various dictatorships in the region not only have been considered stumbling blocks towards modernization and development but also constitute total failures even in their attempts to develop their countries economically, politically and technologically following the Western liberal model.

In conclusion, it is worth emphasizing that at the centre of religious reform in Tunisia is the revival of its historical and religious institutions and the transformation of its religious establishment into an independent state body free from political and ideological tensions. Al-Zaytouna Mosque is in fact central in this reform, as it still represents a national symbol of knowledge and guidance. The potential influence of this significant establishment is crucial, on the one hand in providing a doctrinal as well as spiritual compass for Tunisians, and on the other hand standing as an authority in countering and pacifying what can be regarded as 'religious extremism'.

Notes

1 By cultural comeback we mean the transformative environment that has emerged after the revolution of 14 January 2011. After decades of suppression of free speech regarding religion, culture and politics, this new era has been witnessing thriving debate and conflicting inputs from all strata of society about what makes Tunisian identity.
2 The Maliki School of *fiqh* (Islamic jurisprudence/law) is named after Imam Malik Bin Anas who lived in Medina, Saudi Arabia (711–795 AD). His seminal book *Al-Muwatta* is one of the greatest sources of Islamic jurisprudence.
3 The Salafi movement is a religious trend within Islam that identifies itself with the 'As-Salaf as-Salih' (early pious generation of Muslims). Although there are various derivations nowadays of what is known as 'Salafi' groups, with different leaders, the movement was originally named after Sheikh Mohamed Abdulwahab (1703–92).
4 Al-Zaytouna Mosque is the oldest mosque in Tunisia (after the Mosque of Okba bin Nafee in Kairawan). It was built around 703 and remained for centuries a centre for learning. Al-Zaytouna Mosque also used to be called Al-Zaytouna University as it taught theology and sciences to students from various parts of the world.
5 The Wahhabi movement is named after Sheikh Mohamed Abdulwahab (1703–92) and is a reformist movement that seeks the revival of Islam based on pure monotheism. Also called the 'Salafi' movement or 'Salafists'.
6 Habib Bourguiba was the first president of Tunisia, who ruled the country from 1956 until 1987 after a coup by the then Prime Minister and Minister of the Interior Zein Elabideen Ben Ali.
7 'Citizen Engagement and Public Services in the Arab World: The Potential of Social Media', Arab Social Media Report, www.arabsocialmediareport.com/News/description.aspx?NewsID=16&PriMenuID=15&mnu=Pri (accessed 26 September 2014).
8 Ansar al-Sharia in Tunisia (Facebook page in Arabic) أنصار الشريعة بتونس, www.facebook.com/profile.php?id=100005290153679&fref=ts (accessed 27 September 2014).
9 Ibid.
10 Ibid.
11 Group for the fight against tyrants, www.facebook.com/pages/%D9%81%D8%B1%D9%82%D8%A9-%D9%85%D9%83%D8%A7%D9%81%D8%AD%D8%A9-%D8%A7%D9%84%D8%B7%D9%88%D8%A7%D8%BA%D9%8A%D8%AA/268108893340329?ref=profile.
12 'Protesters attack TV station over film Persepolis', BBC News, 9 October 2011.
13 'Tunisian Salafists attacks TV station for screening film on Iran revolution', *Al-Arabia News*, 9 October 2011, english.alarabiya.net/articles/2011/10/09/170965.html (accessed 30 September 2014).

References

Berger, L.P. & Luckmann, T. (1991) *The Social Construction of Reality: A Treatise in the Sociology of Knowledge*. London: Penguin Books.

Bourdieu, P. (1986) 'The forms of capital', in J. Richardson (ed.) *Handbook of Theory and Research for the Sociology of Education* (pp. 241–258). New York: Greenwood.

Boyle, K. & Johnson, T.J. (2010) 'MySpace is your space? Examining self-presentation of MySpace users', *Computers in Human Behaviour*, 26, pp. 1392–1399, dx.doi.org/10.1016/j.chb.2010.04.015.

Crisis Group (2013) *Tunisia: Violence and the Salafi Challenge*, Crisis Group Middle East/North Africa Report No. 137, 13 February, www.crisisgroup.org/~/media/Files/Middle%20East%20North%20Africa/North%20Africa/Tunisia/137-tunisia-violence-and-the-salafi-challenge.pdf.

Ellison, N., Steinfield, C. & Lampe, C. (2007) 'The benefits of Facebook "friends": social capital and college students' use of online social network sites', *Journal of Computer-Mediated Communication*, 12(4), pp. 1143–1168.

Fabio, M. (2013) 'Salafism in Tunisia: an interview with a member of Ansar al-Sharia', www.jadaliyya.com/pages/index/11166/salafism-in-tunisia_an-interview-with-a-member-of.

Fabio, M. & Francesco, C. (2013) 'The emergence of Salafism in Tunisia', www.jadaliyya.com/pages/index/6934/the-emergence-of-salafism-in-tunisia.

Gee, J. Paul & Hayes, E. (2011) *Language and Learning in the Digital Age*. Abingdon: Routledge.

Kellas, J.G. (1991) *The Politics of Nationalism and Ethnicity*. Houndmills: Macmillan Press Ltd.

Leadbeater, C. (2008) *We-Think. Mass Innovation, Not Mass Production*. London: Profile Books.

Leonardi, P. (2003) 'Problematizing "new media": culturally based perceptions of cell phones, computers, and the Internet among United States Latinos', *Critical Studies in Media Communication*, 20, pp. 160–179.

Malka, H. (2014) 'The struggle for religious identity in Tunisia and Maghreb', CSIS, May, csis.org/publication/struggle-religious-identity-tunisia-and-maghreb (accessed 27 September 2014).

Marks, M. (2013) 'Youth politics and Tunisian Salafism: understanding the jihadi current', *Mediterranean Politics*, 18(1), pp. 104–111.

Miladi, N. (2015) 'Alternative fabrics of hegemony: city squares and street graffiti as sites of resistance and interactive communication flow', *Journal of African Media Studies*, 7(2), pp. 129–140.

Mitchell, D. (1995) 'There's no such thing as culture: toward a reconceptualization of the idea of culture within geography', *Transactions of the Institute of British Geographers*, 20, pp. 102–116.

Sivan, E. (1985) *Radical Islam: Medieval Theology and Modern Politics*. New Haven and London: Yale University.

Ubachs, F. (2013) 'Tunisia's religious opposition', Centre for Religion, Conflict and the Public Domain, 11 September, religionfactor.net/page/2/ (accessed 30 September 2014).

Zhao, S., Sherri, G. & Jason, M. (2008) 'Identity construction on Facebook: digital empowerment in anchored relationships', *Computers in Human Behavior*, 24, pp. 1816–1836.

Zran, J. (2008) 'Terrorism and the Internet: faces of a virtual public opinion', in *Media and Public Opinion* (pp. 77–101). Tunis: Institute of the Press and Sciences of Communication and Konrad Adenauer Stiftung (in Arabic).

3

ONLINE AESTHETICS OF MARTYRDOM

A study of the Bahraini Arab Spring

Magdalena Karolak

The Internet fostered the emergence of online forms of commemoration of death. These practices, thanks to the growth of Internet users around the globe, have become more and more commonly performed by groups and individuals and they include, among others, 'the construction of a digital afterlife, commemorative communities of grief and remembrance, interaction in guest books, digital candles and commentary fields on digital memorials' (Lagerkvist, 2013, 1). Online forums dedicated to such practices have also recently witnessed growing popularity among social movement actors worldwide who sought to preserve memories of killed protesters and to expose the brutality of the security forces (Askanius, 2013). In addition, such commemorative websites proved to play an important role in fostering shared emotions and rallying people for collective action (Olesen, 2013).

This chapter seeks to analyse the practices related to the commemoration of martyrdom in the aftermath of the Bahraini Arab Spring in February 2011. Similarly to other countries in the Middle East and North Africa region affected by popular upheavals, Bahraini anti-government activists used social media initially to mobilize protesters. Yet, as the unfolding events precipitated violent confrontations between the anti-government movement and the security forces and led to loss of life on both sides, social media began to serve as sites of commemoration of death. Given the strong religious commitment underlying the activism of the anti-government movement, dedicated websites serve not only for grieving but also for celebrating martyrdom. Consequently, we observe the emergence of online aesthetics of martyrdom. Such online practices became, in turn, also visible among the pro-government supporters who seek to commemorate online the martyrdom of their fellows, most often, security forces on duty. This chapter seeks to examine such online commemoration of martyrdom in Bahrain in relation to the Arab Spring events, its aesthetics and its functions.

Theoretical background

Commemoration of past events touches upon the subject of collective memory. Halbwachs (1980 [1950]) highlighted the fact that collective memory, i.e. an image of past events, binds individuals together into groups such as families, social classes and, ultimately, a nation; the latter link was suggested already a century before by Renan (1990 [1882]). Indeed, a community exists as such thanks to a shared perception of the past, present and future events that transcend the individuals linking their lives to those of their predecessors and their successors in a meaningful way and thus providing a common point of reference for individual actions (Berger & Luckmann, 1966, 120). A community in order to survive and continue in the future must have a collective memory. Consequently, within a nation, professional agents are employed in inscribing the community in 'sites of memory' through language, but also in physical forms through creation of monuments, archives, memorials, changing street names, and so on (Nora, 1989). Commemoration of past events in the present is, however, not a process of simple recollection but rather that of recreation: 'the past is not preserved but is reconstructed on the basis of the present' (Halbwachs, 1980, 40; see also Bartlett, 1932, 213) and memories may be altered, forgotten or erased when aspects of social life change. Collective memory is in constant evolution, hence its fluidity (Nora, 1996, 3). Theorists also note that commemoration is as important as forgetting. Indeed, collective amnesia plays a fundamental role as nations seek to erase some events such as violence committed against other groups (Renan, 1990) and those that 'could separate individuals' in the community (Halbwachs, cited by Connerton, 1989, 38).

The role of media in creation of collective memory is primordial (Anderson, 1991; Sturken, 1997; Shandler, 1999, among others). The Internet revolutionized our approach to collective memory by fostering a 'digital memory culture', which is a quest for 'capturing, storing, retrieving and ordering' memories (Garde-Hansen et al., 2009, 5). This phenomenon, often referred to as 'memory boom' (Winter, 2006), has clear political ramifications as marginalized groups seek formal recognition of their memories (which are in sharp contrast to the official collective memories) through treaties, restitution, compensation, etc. Indeed, the access to digital technologies may revert the control of a society's memory, which is always characterized by the hierarchy of power and bears on the questions of legitimation (Connerton, 1989, 1). The groups that are involved in politics of recognition, i.e. those that hardly have any institutional bases on which to make their claims (Hobson, 2003), may transfer their struggles onto the digital environment to make themselves seen and seek acknowledgment of their collective memories there.[1] Negated by the official discourses and, consequently, not having the possibility of taking on physical forms, the 'sites of memory' of marginalized groups may permeate now in the virtual world.

The aesthetics of death offer a particular venue to examine the processes of commemoration. Zelizer stressed the fact that images, rather than words, are 'an effective mode of relay about the past and a key vehicle of memory' (Zelizer,

2001). As a result, photographs very often become 'the primary markers of memory itself' (ibid.). Nonetheless, research on the portrayal of Western aesthetics of death in the media shows that such imagery is controversial due not only to the sensitivity of the audience, but also to the negatively perceived voyeurism that violates the privacy and dignity of the deceased. Consequently, the media often prefer to present about-to-die images rather than images of the actual death (Zelizer, 2010). Nonetheless, another approach to visualization of death exists, one that exposes death and dying in minute, graphic details. It permeates in the memories of individuals who were present at the time of tragic events and who share their traumatic memories in public domains. It becomes a moral duty for such individuals to expose these events as wrongdoing and to show the suffering and the injustice that the community wishes to erase from the collective consciousness (Ashuri, 2011, 106). Consequently, the audience may be compelled to watch such graphic scenes of death in order to bear witness and to act upon them. The latter provides a powerful tool for community mobilization as 'suffering in common unites more than joy does [...] Griefs are of more value than triumphs, for they impose duties, and require a common effort' (Renan, 1990, 19). Such is the case of recent protest movements that brand their killed protesters as martyrs[2] and expose their deaths online in full detail, thus putting on those who remain the duty of carrying out the political project of the movement. Such traumatic events can be brought to the collective consciousness through ritualized re-enactments (Connerton, 1989, 69).

Social media and the Arab Spring

The uprising in Bahrain in February 2011 forms part of popular upheavals in the region commonly known as the Arab Spring. Bahraini opposition, disappointed with the limits of political liberalization reforms carried out in the early 2000s, resented the lack of power sharing, economic hardships and naturalization of foreigners, and, above all, alleged sectarian and ethnic[3] discrimination. Following examples of other Arab nations, Bahraini activists occupied the central area of the capital Manama, the Pearl Roundabout, on 14 February. Despite the initial success in generating a widespread occupy movement, activists suffered a blow when the authorities cleared the roundabout on 17 February. The efforts to retake the area led to several casualties among the protesters, but ultimately the authorities withdrew on 19 February. The following weeks brought unsuccessful negotiations and radicalization of the opposition groups. The arrival of GCC Peninsula Shield forces deployed from Saudi Arabia on 14 March marked the end of the occupation of Pearl Roundabout. The opposition movement was confined to suburban districts where it continues activism. Despite the non-denominational character of the movement, Shias formed a majority of the activists and the uprising was often understood in sectarian terms.

The Bahraini opposition movement is an example of groups referred to as those involved in politics of recognition. Its version of history has remained within the community passed on from one generation to another that counters official narratives (Louër, 2008). The Arab Spring confirms this pattern. The opposition sought to commemorate the events by opening a Revolution Museum depicting the protests and their casualties. However, the displays angered the authorities, which closed down the installation within two days of its opening. As a result, social media began to serve as an archive for their version of history, which is marked by the tortured and killed community members.

The important role played by social media in Bahraini society during and in the aftermath of the Arab Spring is worth exploring. Socialbakers, a company providing social media network statistics, assessed that, among the top ten most popular Facebook sites in Bahrain in 2013 in the media category, five included spontaneous anti-governmental social media. The importance of social media during and in the aftermath of the Arab Spring explains why they may provide valuable evidence for analysis.

This research aims to assess how social media are employed in commemoration of the Arab Spring events in Bahrain. Given the confrontational character of the events, the analysis focuses on the functions martyrdom plays in upholding memories of various groups and what duties it carries on to the group members. In addition, the aesthetics of commemoration will be discussed. Most importantly, the research examines how such 'sites of memory' function in an online environment and what is their relation to physical spaces. The analysis is based on a sample of web pages created anonymously and in direct connection to the Arab Spring events in Bahrain, which maintain a focus on the commemoration of martyrdom. A search in commercial engines with different combinations of keywords 'Bahrain', 'Revolution', 'Arab Spring', 'February 14th', 'Facebook' and 'Twitter' allowed me to create a list of websites pertinent to the Arab Spring. The latter included Bahrain-wide opposition and pro-government websites and district opposition websites. From the sample, I chose websites based on their relevance to the subject of martyrdom and the popularity ranking measured by the overall number of followers and the number of 'likes' (Jin et al., 2011). The results of the search were then limited to include the most popular websites, shown in the Appendix.

Edy (2006) noted that, in order to study collective memory of a troubled past, framing provides a useful tool for analysis. Frames are defined as 'schemata of interpretation that enable individuals to locate, perceive, identify, and label occurrences within their life space and the world at large' (Snow et al., 1986, 464). Retrieving frames from texts and visual content of the Bahraini Arab Spring-related social media constitutes the first step of this research. For the purpose of analysis, I chose to use qualitative content analysis, which concentrates on the text itself, complemented by discourse analysis, which concentrates on understanding 'the meaning of social reality for actors' (Hardy et al., 2004, 19). Secondly, in order to analyse a high volume of visual content, I adopted Barthes's (1961) semiotic theory. Barthes suggested that the analysis of images should extract their denotations, which are their literal meanings, and their connotations, which are the meanings that are suggested or implied by the sign (the image). The latter are of special interest to this research. Consequently, Barthes's six connotative procedures will be applied in the analysis, as follows: 1 trick effects (fake photographs and, with modern technology, digital-image editing with Photoshop); 2 pose (of the person/people); 3 objects (the choice and the arrangement of objects in the photo); 4 photogenia (techniques of lighting, exposure and printing, which also can be applied in digital-image editing); 5 aestheticism (references to artistic styles); and 6 syntax (arrangement of photos in a series). The latter may be complemented by the volume of photographs with similar connotative messages that set the general impression of the web page. Barthes's classification of connotative procedures is useful as it allows us to take into account modern digital-image editing techniques.

The initial overview of the results shows that the opposition groups engage in martyrs' commemoration online to a much higher extent than the pro-government groups do. Consequently, the anti-government groups display a higher volume of graphic content (drawings, collages, illustrations, etc.) and videos produced for the purpose of martyrs' commemoration. As far as the pro-government groups are concerned, online commemorations use mostly photographs without any software editing. The differences in the aesthetics stem from the fact that online activism serves specific purposes that are not equally shared by the groups involved in conflict, and the aesthetics of martyrdom support these particular goals. Given the fact that pro-government groups are in the position of domination, the commemoration takes more modest forms and its purposes are limited in comparison to the opposition groups. Furthermore, the opposition groups transfer collective rituals from physical spaces to their representation in online spaces as it occurs also with other protest movements (see Askanius, 2013).

Remembering as a duty

For both the opposition groups and the pro-government supporters, online commemoration of martyrs plays, to begin with, a role in engraving their lives and their sacrifice in the collective consciousness. As a result, online visual imagery aims at preventing the community from forgetting these exceptional individuals and their sacrifice for the good of the community. Martyrs' sacrifice is highlighted, to begin with, by contrasts. The martyrs' photos alive and happily engaged in daily activities such as spending time at home with their families or going about their daily lives are juxtaposed with the horrific images of their dead bodies. The images of death are explicit: photographs of bodies sewn after autopsy, detailed visual accounts of injuries, mutilated bodies and funerals form part of these online commemorations. The focus on the body is not accidental, as observed by Das: 'because violence annihilates language, [and] … terror cannot be brought into the realm of the utterable […] It invites us to constitute the body as the mediating sign between the individual and society, and between past and present' (cited in Humphrey, 2002, 8).

The websites offer users the opportunity to write their condolences or their prayers for the deceased under the commemorative photographs. The religious messages dominate such forums, for instance, 'A nice young guy I will pray for his soul goes to the paradise' (security forces website post). The anti-government groups' websites also focus closely on the families of the martyrs. The vivid expressions of their grief in morgues and during funerals while paying a last farewell to the deceased present viewers with a very emotional account of the pain that the families suffer. Such depictions do not appear on the pro-government websites. These differences may be due to the fact that expressing deep grief publicly is part of the mourning aesthetics of Muharram among Shias, while it is non-existent to this extent among the Sunnis.

In addition, websites display exact places where the martyrs died, and often such photographs or videos were taken at the time of their deaths. Freshly spilled blood stains the pavement around the martyrs' bodies. The comments to such imagery clearly state the purpose of remembrance: 'Will not forget you, O martyr [...] the first anniversary of the martyrdom of Ahmed Farhan [...] who was shot by the Peninsula Shield fault of Al Khalifa and Al Saud' (an opposition website title), or 'We Will Never Forget Our Martyrs may الله grant them place in *jannat* (AMEEN)' (pro-government group title).

Online portals remind their followers about the anniversaries of martyrs' deaths; thus through yearly celebrations martyrs acquire an eternal status in the community. While for the pro-government groups those are simple reminders on online forums such as '1st Death Anniversary of Our 2 SSFC Policemen' accompanied by photos of the martyrs, for the opposition groups the celebrations become ritualized performances taking place in the community and then documented online. The celebrations of martyrs' birthdays and the anniversaries of their deaths are marked in the opposition districts by visiting their families. Photos and videos portray handing bouquets of flowers and certificates to martyrs' families and speeches at gatherings dedicated to these individuals. Such visits mirror the official visits of the Bahraini authorities to the families of the security forces martyrs. During gatherings in opposition communities, portraits of martyrs adorn the banners and flags around the district and clothing of those taking part in commemoration. The commemoration of martyrdom becomes a ritualized performance, with community members taking the stage to invoke the martyr's life and death on stage. In addition, commemoration is considered a religious duty, practised during religious festivals: 'There were also visits to the graves of the faithful martyrs on the occasion of Eid al-Fitr, a renewal of the pledge to the fulfillment of them [the martyrs]. Gatherings for joint visits of the families of the martyrs, the wounded and prisoners on the occasion of Eid al-Fitr, [were performed] in many Bahraini revolution towns and cities.' It is clear that through such efforts martyrs continue to be a vital part of the community of the living.

Furthermore, martyrdom is celebrated in the opposition districts through mourning marches that also include carrying symbolic coffins for the memory of particular martyrs who fell in other areas of Bahrain. The moments of death are thus constantly present as a reminder of the duty that lies upon the living. As a result, the commitment of one's life to the cause is not a vain effort but becomes part of the collective memory of a shared trauma. In addition, the martyrs' names become permanently engraved in the collective consciousness of the opposition groups as inhabitants unofficially rename streets and roundabouts after them. Social media are used to conduct online polls among the community members to decide what name the street and other landmarks should carry. These names, stemming from the place where a martyr or martyrs were killed, become a daily reference for the inhabitants of the area and are asserted in online references as real.

Ultimately, the opposition communities not only remember but also consolidate, in turn, a sense of loyalty towards their martyrs: 'We will stay faithful to our martyrs' and 'We promise the martyrs and their families that we are moving on the same path', proclaims a website. Indeed, loyalty to the martyrs implies loyalty to the goals for which they fought. As a result, the communities organize marches and closures of streets under the names of martyrs: 'the rebels [...] blocked the Martyr Husam Roundabout in the memory of his martyrdom' or 'the crowd gathered in the middle of the street to offer a eulogy of the hero martyr Hussein Jaziri and then proceeded towards the Martyrs' Square'. It is important to highlight that 'rituals and practices of commemoration must be seen as constitutive part of the political project to construct and cultivate a specific interpretation of the past in the present' (Endres & Lauser, 2011, 123). They project the community forward to the expected victory that is to be achieved thanks to the martyrs' efforts, as will be explored below.

Both the opposition and the pro-government groups see the importance of remembering their martyrs (Table 3.1). However, the difference in online aesthetics stems from the position of dominance of the pro-government groups, which thanks to institutionalized means of commemoration do not require elaborate rituals to keep up the memory and the political message of their martyrs. Consequently, the commemorations among the anti-government groups take the form of ritualized performances that are archived online and motivate them to continue their future struggle.

TABLE 3.1 Comparison of the functions of the Internet for remembrance

Opposition groups	*Pro-government groups*
Inscribing the martyr in the history of the community	Inscribing the martyr in the history of the community
Preserving details of the martyr's death	Preserving details of the martyr's death
Offering condolences and celebrating the anniversaries of martyrs' deaths	Offering condolences and celebrating the anniversaries of martyrs' deaths
Documenting ritualized performances of remembrance	–
Renaming city landmarks	–
Fostering collective activism under martyrs' names	–

Cementing the community of the righteous

The narratives of martyrdom, no matter the cultural region and the historical era, have been used as divisive forces and have served to create a clear boundary between the community and those who oppose it (Swanson, 2001, 121; Mock, 2012, 161; Papadakis, 2003, 254; De Spiegeleer, 2004). Such is also the function of martyrdom narratives in Bahrain, for both the opposition groups and the pro-government supporters. As a result, martyrs are markers of deep communal divisions:

> Martyrdom tends to be a group phenomenon, drawing strength from a collective identity and representing serious cultural divisions within the state. In contrast to the hero, who is the product of a consensus society where the quality and worth of the heroic act is undisputed, the martyr is the offspring of a community at war with itself. Such societies are unable to agree whether the martyr's death should be praised as the highest service that can be rendered God or humanity, be dismissed as pointless folly, or be branded as the proper punishment reserved for traitors.
>
> *(Smith, n.d.)*

Given the fact that martyrdom is subject to conflicting interests and interpretations of reality, martyrs are often used to elevate the community so it acquires a 'righteous' status opposing those who killed the martyrs and who are therefore considered the 'wicked'. In the context of Bahrain, the latter are clearly mentioned as guilty parties: 'the martyr was run over by the Al Khalifa terrorist forces' (an opposition title), or at times contain a clear message addressed to the perpetrators, as this slogan of the opposition website proclaims: 'For Those Who Killed Our Martyrs [...] Our Motto To You: GET OUT !! [of our country]' (an opposition title). It is clear that commemoration of martyrs, similarly to collective memories in general, 'achieve a kind of perfection unattainable by either real life [...] They resolve ambiguous events and complex characters into simple, moral tales populated by heroes, villains, and fools' (Edy, 2006, 204). As a result, each community claims through their martyrs an absolute degree of righteousness that removes any possibility of doubt for their actions overall. Consequently, even though both sides of the conflict committed killings, references to such events and feelings of guilt never appear voiced online. On the contrary, the opposition recalls the rightful path of its martyrs: 'Martyr Ali Al-Samaheeji['s] story asserts the rightfulness of [the martyr's] struggle.' The pro-government groups, on the other hand, claim righteousness through an alleged inscription on the face of the dead policeman: 'MashaAllah check out this pic [...] The name of our Holy Prophet (PBUH) "Muhammad" is clearly shown on the face of our Martyr Mahmood Fareed after he died in a bomb blast in ekar.' A holy name shown through the bruise on the martyr's cheek confirms that he supported the right side of the conflict.

The circumstances of death may also be used to confirm who upholds the right values. Indeed, Islamic theologians who debated the conditions of martyrdom concluded that '[t]he true martyr is distinguished by his or her pure intentions, especially during the time just prior to death' (Cook, 2007, 36). This characteristic is visible when Bahraini pro-government forces accuse the anti-government groups of killing a policeman by detonating a bomb while he was praying and such an act puts into question the perpetrators' religiosity. As a result, the security forces post a slogan – 'Our faith is stronger than your bombs' – which excludes the opposition from the group of rightful believers. The anti-government groups also refer to religious ideals to support their martyrs' cause. A website displays the last words written by a child before he was killed in clashes, which are a prayer, confirming the martyr's devotion to God. Such black and white divisions impact the interpretation of events. A disputed case of the death of a protester, Ali Faisal Al Akrawi, is attributed to the security forces among the opposition groups, while the pro-government groups claim he died when planting an explosive, which blew up, tearing his limbs apart, hence killing him. The fact that the martyr died undisputedly carrying explosives earns him among the opposition members a title of '*mujahid shahid*', i.e. a warrior martyr.

The reference to the out-groups as 'thugs' among the pro-government groups or 'mercenaries'[4] among the opposition reflects their disconnection from the righteous citizens, whether based on the claims of their criminal behaviour or oppression of Bahrainis by foreigners. This high level of righteousness is acquired through martyrs' devotion to the country. An opposition drawing depicts this connection in a drawing with blood drops spilling out of a red rose and taking ultimately the shades of the Bahraini flag. Nonetheless, both pro- and anti-government groups claim patriotism as their motivation, and both use the slogan 'Ready to die for Bahrain'. Yet, for the opposition groups patriotism equates with fighting for the rights of the citizens. In another drawing, for instance, a bloody hand of the martyr grabs the word freedom, marking it as the ultimate goal of the Bahraini opposition.

The strengthening of community bonds through martyrdom is especially visible in the Bahraini opposition communities that find themselves under threat. Opposition activities are portrayed online as including all inhabitants, with no distinction of age or gender.[5] Consequently, children, the elderly and women may acquire the status of martyrs. It is interesting to note that the concept of martyrdom has been extended to include unborn children. Websites display foetuses aborted in times of confrontation with security forces, thus making them participants in the struggle as well. The graphic depictions of foetuses', infants' and children's martyrdom aim at supporting the division between the 'righteous' and the 'wicked' as martyrdom of these innocent creatures marks the security forces as the 'villains'. Indeed, ultimately, through the acts of martyrdom, '[t]he rational organizational arrangements for opposing the enemy are energized by martyrdom. The sacrificial act converts economic and political conflict into sacred conflict and so drives it toward the pursuit of goals at any cost' (Klausner, 1998).

Rectifying the past wrongs through further resistance

This function of martyrdom refers to the historical predicament of the Shia populations overall and to their continued political struggle. Despite the fact that the concept of martyrdom also exists among Sunnis, it holds an important place in Shia narratives (Moghadam, 2007). It has been engraved in Shia history since the inception of the Sunni–Shia split. The martyrdom of Hussein and his followers at the battle of Karbala is the central event in Shia history and it is relived through the events in Bahrain. A verse of a poem referring to Bahrain asserts, for instance, a repetition of the same pattern: 'The tragedy of Karbala came back again / In every era, Yazid will reappear / He wishes Hussein's death by tyranny.' Another user confirms: 'Bahrain has embodied for us Karbala, Hussein.' This perception of current events through the 'Karbala paradigm' results in a time collapse.

This sentiment shared by Shias centres on the idea of religiously motivated martyrdom for the revolutionary cause. The heroic attitude of the opposition members and their adherence to martyrdom ideals is portrayed as supported by strong religious beliefs: 'God has taught us through Hussein how to be oppressed [and] we are victorious.' The historical narratives are so powerful that they motivate the living: 'our steadfastness stems from the land of Karbala'; protesters wave black banners with inscription calling on Hussein during demonstrations. Death for the revolutionary cause is understood as following in Hussein's footsteps, instantly granting the deceased access to paradise. The connection between the day of Ashura (a day marking Hussein's martyrdom) and the revolution is depicted in the Ashura gallery tents set up in various districts during Muharram. Martyrs' pictures are placed in the tent. A symbolic coffin in memory of the martyrs occupies its centre. The inscription above the tent juxtaposes 'Ashura approach and revolution'.

Martyrdom, despite the sadness of the loss for the martyr's survivors, is ultimately a happy event allowing the believer to reach Hussein. Consequently, graphics and online forums pay their respects to the martyrs by congratulating them on their success: 'congratulations to the happy martyr for this outcome and this victory'; 'a hero martyr for whom God's bounty [awaits]'. In addition, martyrs' families encourage others online to continue their struggle: 'Message from father of the martyr: do not fear imprisonment.' It comes as no surprise that some opposition activists wear clothing and facemasks marking their readiness to die. Inscriptions referring to martyrdom ('with our martyrs'; 'I love jihad'; 'I am the next martyr') written on the foreheads of participants and on their T-shirts or shrouds signal their commitment to the revolutionary cause, as documented in online forums. The pro-government social media, on the contrary, refrain from any references to jihad.

This defiant attitude is supported by the motif of blood that permeates the online graphics. Blood is often used as background for the graphics depicting the district activities. Photographs of freshly spilled blood are also archived online. In one photograph, the blood of a martyr spilled on the ground is labelled with his name, and activists soak red tulips and Bahraini flags in it. Bloodstains and blood drops motivate the participants to further activism as online logos proclaim: 'Blood of our martyrs – our future'; 'Blood of martyrs fuels resistance'; 'Martyrs' blood – our strength'; or 'Martyrs fuel our revolution'. Spilled martyrs' blood that appears over and over again is a reminder of the duty left on those alive to continue the martyrs' efforts and to achieve victory. Indeed, martyrs' blood opens the path to follow: 'Your blood [referring to the martyr] we saw dripping on the ground is the only light to illuminate the path for each free man and free woman in the world until they get rid of tyrants' control by uniting under one God and not accepting humiliation.'

This function of martyrdom holds an important place for the Shia populations in Bahrain. As a result, the aesthetics of martyrdom use elements of the portrayal of martyrdom shared among Shias elsewhere such as red tulips or red roses to symbolize martyrdom and white doves[6] to symbolize the soul of the martyr (Marzolph, 2003).

Coping with traumatic events

For the opposition groups the depictions of martyrdom play a role in helping the community cope with the trauma caused by the Arab Spring events. As a result, turning oppression into spectacle becomes a natural way of reliving and commemorating recent events and engraving them in the collective memory. The spirit of martyrdom has a liberating dimension, as is proven by video hyperlinks posted on the websites. Among the many links found, I chose two videos that are the most representative of these ideas.

In the first theatrical representation, revolutionaries carry out the body of a martyr in a coffin and lay it in front of the public in the square. The body is covered with a Bahraini flag. Once on the ground, the martyr comes back to life and stands up. From under the flag, he reveals the usual white shroud used for burying the deceased, but his shroud is covered in red stains, marking a martyr's death. Animated, the martyr lights up a torch in a burner shaped like the Pearl Roundabout. The torch symbolizes the flame of self-determination. He passes it on to a young revolutionary, pointing out the cells of a prison where other revolutionaries are kept. The prisoners represent the various professions of detainees. There is a student, a doctor, a member of a football team and a young protester. The young revolutionary proceeds to the prison and bends the bars of the cells with ease, freeing his comrades. The group marches together through the streets of the town, carrying the flame. Crowds line the street to honour this procession and the revolutionary spirit is bestowed upon all. Through this scene, it is clear that victory comes through death. The spirits of the martyrs open the gates to freedom. It is their sacrifice that upholds the revolutionary spirit, guiding the living in the right direction. With their martyrdom, it is clear that there is no withdrawing from the fight for freedom.

The second video opens with a night-time view of three symbolic graves dug in the soil. They are covered with Bahraini flags and a picture of a martyr is placed on each one of them. A man dressed in a white shroud symbolizing the next martyr is seen sitting reading the Quran next to the grave. Suddenly, a hand rising from the grave passes him a lit torch. The torch illuminates the man's path as he takes it to the village. On his arrival crowds greet him waving Bahraini flags and he takes to the stage with the torch, rallying the crowds to continue the revolution. The torch of self-determination and its passage from the martyrs' graves to the community illuminates the path they ought to take in order to reach their goal. Martyrs through their sacrifice pave the way for the community.

The videos are filmed with professionalism and edited online with titles and dates of filming. It is clear that such elaborate rituals are developed to cope with traumatic events of the Arab Spring uprising. When performed in the communities, they are recorded, edited and posted on the websites to form an archive that documents the continuity of the political struggle. Strombon noted that 'one way out of the historical predicament of weakness and insecurity is to create a perception of a strong collective self in the present, a group that would be better fit to cope with aggression and domination if exposed to it' (Strombon, 2010, 84). Through the promotion of defiant attitudes even in the face of death and ritualized celebration of martyrdom, which promise ultimate victory, the opposition communities cope with the disappointment of the Arab Spring outcomes in Bahrain, while keeping their hopes alive for the future.

Conclusion

The aesthetics of martyrdom depicted on the social media of the pro-government and anti-government groups in Bahrain strike by their explicit graphic content. Such portrayals clearly serve to mobilize the viewers to witness the atrocities and lay on their shoulders a duty to act upon viewing them. The new media play multiple functions among these communities separated by their political loyalties. On the one hand, the social media keep the memories of martyrs alive in the collective consciousness and allow community members to cope with their losses by grieving online in what Cook calls 'cyber graveyards' (Cook, 2007, 170). On the other hand, they cement the community around what is perceived as the righteous path, which is supported by religious ideals and by the sense of patriotism. As a result, this phenomenon creates a split between the Sunni pro-government supporters and the Shia opposition groups, and another cleavage between the Bahraini opposition and the foreign communities who serve in the security forces. Nonetheless, social media play additional functions for the opposition groups who are in the position inferior to the dominant power. They form a digital archive of revolutionary activities, as the virtual world is the only public form such commemoration may take. Consequently, websites are maintained with great care, providing daily detailed updates, whether textual or pictorial. They include graphics created for the purpose of mourning and videos of commemorative rituals. Martyrdom is placed in the centre of the political project. It questions the legitimation of the current political system. Martyrs continue their daily presence among the community through commemorations of their anniversaries and through theatrical re-enactments. While forming a vital part of Shia beliefs, martyrdom motivates the living to continue the revolutionary struggle for which the martyrs sacrificed their lives. Martyrdom has a liberating dimension for the martyr who reaches Hussein and for the living for whom he opens the path to victory. The online aesthetics testify to the importance of martyrdom for the opposition communities and we agree with Cook (2007, 170) that martyrdom is in large part advertisement; in the case of Bahrain, an advertisement for the political struggle against the monarchy. Given the fact that the pro-government groups dominate the current political system, their aesthetics of martyrdom are simple and are displayed in large part through photographs.

Appendix

TABLE 3.2 Bahrain-wide anti-government websites

Name	URL	Number of likes[7]	Language	Description
14 February Revolution in Bahrain	www.facebook.com/TrueRoyalDemocracy	92,095	Arabic	Pressing for political reforms; news about the continued protest struggle
14 February Youth Coalition	www.facebook.com/Coalition14th	65,235	Arabic	The official page of the 14 February Youth Coalition[8]
Feb 14 Media Network	www.facebook.com/14Feb.Media	62,558	Arabic	Diffusion of news about the protest activities backtracked to 1954; emphasis on martyrdom
Bahrain Media	www.facebook.com/Occupy.Bahrain	82,115	Arabic	Diffusion of news about the protest activities; general news (IT); anti-sectarian stance
Occupy Bahrain	www.facebook.com/Occupy.BH	52,574	English	Reaching out to the international community for support; inspired by the Occupy movement
Bahrain	www.facebook.com/social.bh	44,910	Arabic, rarely English	Site devoted to up-to-date information about protest activity and rallying for continued activism
Bahrain Voice	www.facebook.com/bahrainvoice	44,525	Arabic	Diffusion of news about the protest activity
Pearl Martyrs Magazine	www.facebook.com/lula1Lshohada2?fref=photo	12,325	Arabic	Promotion of martyrdom figures

TABLE 3.3 Facebook opposition district websites[9]

URL	Number of likes	Geographic area
www.facebook.com/akbar.sitra	10,471	Sitra
www.facebook.com/HrktShbabStrtSitraYouthMovement	2,562	Sitra
www.facebook.com/Sitraa.Media	16,550	Sitra
www.facebook.com/KarzakkanNews	17,351	Karzakkan
www.facebook.com/karbabad	3,500	Karbabad
www.facebook.com/juffair.media?ref=stream	5,863	Juffair
www.facebook.com/SaarTV	5,664	Saar
www.facebook.com/SBR.TV	11,248	Barbar
www.facebook.com/ahrar.3ali	13,928	Aali
www.facebook.com/AaliNews	14,760	Aali
www.facebook.com/HrktAhrarJdhfsAhrarMovementJidhafs	3,645	Jidhafs
www.facebook.com/ManamaOnline	23,786	Manama
www.facebook.com/ManamaFeb1	7,168	Manama
www.facebook.com/SamaheejVoice	7,768	Samaheej
www.facebook.com/jannousanNews	2,326	Janusan
www.facebook.com/Malkiya.network	7,376	Malkiya
www.facebook.com/AbusaibaMedia1	7,700	Abu Saiba
www.facebook.com/KarranahNews	9,004	Karranah

TABLE 3.4 Bahrain-wide pro-government websites

Name	URL	Likes/followers	Language	Description
7areghum (incenders)	twitter.com/7areghum	107,172	Arabic	Support of the government; denouncing the opposition; anti-Shia rhetoric
Special Security Force Command of Bahrain (SSFC)	www.facebook.com/SSFCBH	65,738	English, rarely Urdu	Supporting the government and the special security forces; providing information about events in the country
Knights of Bahrain Movement	twitter.com/FRSAN_ALBAHRAIN	38,159	Arabic	Defence of the Arab identity and monarchy
First Breaking news Page (love Your Gvt and Safra)	www.facebook.com/pages/First-Breaking-News-Page-love-You-Govt-and-Safra/446576968716326	41,901	English, rarely Urdu	Supporting the government and the security forces; denouncing the opposition as 'terrorists'; providing the latest news from the country
Bahrain Defense Group	twitter.com/BHRdefense	23,773	Arabic	Anti-Shia rhetoric; discrediting the opposition groups
Defend Bahrain	www.facebook.com/D.Bahrain	24,247	English	Defending Bahrain's reputation 'against regional and international conspiracies'; supporting the monarchy; providing information from the country
Bahraini Security Forces	www.facebook.com/pages/Bahraini-Security-Forces/624833434211051	12,980	English	Supporting the security forces; providing news from the country; denouncing the opposition as 'terrorists'
Martyrs of Bahrain	www.facebook.com/WeWillNeverForgetOurMartyrsBahrain	10,138	English, rarely Urdu	Promotes the security forces martyr figures

Notes

1 As proved very successful by the Zapatista rebellion.
2 The concept of martyrdom is shared by the protest movements no matter their location; see Askanius (2013) for European protest movements, but also refer to the Arab Spring movements in Tunisia, Egypt, etc.
3 Khuri (1980) lists the following groups: tribal Sunnis represented by the ruling Al Khalifa family, rural Arab Shias (*Baharna*), urban Sunnis of Persian origin (*Hawala*), urban Sunnis of non-tribal Arab origin (*Najdi*), and urban Shias of Arab origin. In addition, Bahrain is also home to a more recent migrant Shia population of Persian descent (*Ajam*). These cleavages often determine political allegiances.
4 The term 'mercenary' is used by oppostion groups to denote foreigners employed in the security forces in Bahrain.
5 Compare with Cook (2007, 33–36) on the debates about the extension of conditions of martyrdom.
6 The martyrs' souls are said to have the shape of white birds also in the Sunni tradition (Bonner, 2006, 75).
7 As of 20 May 2014.
8 Various youth anti-government networks gathered under the umbrella of the 14 February Youth Coalition.
9 The phenomenon of district websites is not significant among pro-government groups.

References

Anderson, B. (1991) *Imagined Communities: Reflections on the Origin and Spread of Nationalism*. New York: Verso.
Ashuri, T. (2011) 'Joint memory: ICT and the rise of moral mnemonic agents', in M. Neiger, O. Meyers & E. Zendberg (Eds) *On Media Memory: Collective Memory in a New Media Age* (pp. 104–116). New York: Palgrave Macmillan.
Askanius, T. (2012) 'DIY dying: video activism as archive, commemoration and evidence', *International Journal of e-Politics*, 3(1), pp. 12–25.
Askanius, T. (2013) 'Protest Movements and Spectacles of Death: From Urban Places to Video Spaces', in Nicole Doerr, Alice Mattoni & Simon Teune (Eds) *Advances in the Visual Analysis of Social Movements*, Research in Social Movements, Conflicts and Change, Vol. 35. Emerald Group Publishing Limited, pp. 105–133.
Barthes, R. (1961) 'The photographic message', in S. Sontag (Ed.) *A Barthes Reader* (pp. 194–210). New York: Hill and Wang.
Bartlett, F. (1932) *Remembering: A Study in Experimental and Social Psychology*. Cambridge: Cambridge University Press.
Berger, P.L. & Luckmann, T. (1966) *The Social Construction of Reality: A Treatise in the Sociology of Knowledge*. London: Penguin Books.
Bonner, M. (2006) *Jihad in Islamic History: Doctrines and Practice*. Princeton, NJ: Princeton University Press.
Connerton, P. (1989) *How Societies Remember*. Cambridge: Cambridge University Press.
Cook, D. (2007) *Martyrdom in Islam*. Cambridge: Cambridge University Press.
De Spiegeleer, Ch. (2004) 'The blood of martyrs is the seed of progress: the role of martyrdom in socialist death culture in Belgium and the Netherlands, 1880–1940', *Mortality: Promoting the Interdisciplinary Study of Death and Dying*, 19(2), pp. 184–205.
Edy, J.A. (2006) *Troubled Pasts: News and the Collective Memory of Social Unrest*. Philadelphia, PA: Temple University Press.

Endres, K. & Lauser, A. (2011) 'Contests of commemoration: virgin war martyrs, state memorials, and the invocation of the spirit world in contemporary Vietnam', in K. Endres & A. Lauser (Eds) *Engaging the Spirit World, Popular Beliefs and Practices in Southeast Asia* (pp. 121–143). New York: Berghahn Books.

Garde-Hansen, J., Hoskins, A. & Reading, A. (2009) *Save as Digital Memories*. Basingstoke: Palgrave Macmillan.

Halbwachs, M. (1980 [1950]) *The Collective Memory*. Translated by F.J. Ditter, Jr and V.Y. Ditter. New York: Harper Colophon Books.

Hardy, C., Harley, B. & Phillips, N. (2004) 'Discourse analysis and content analysis: two solitudes?' *Qualitative Methods*, 2, pp. 19–22.

Hobson, B. (2003) *Recognition Struggles and Social Movements*. Cambridge: Cambridge University Press.

Humphrey, M. (2002) *The Politics of Atrocity and Reconciliation: From Terror to Trauma*. London: Routledge.

Jin, X., Wang, C., Luo, J., Yu, X. & Han, J. (2011) 'LikeMiner: a system for mining the power of "like" in social media networks', *Proceedings of the 17th SIGKDD International Conference on Knowledge Discovery and Data Mining*.

Khuri, F.I. (1980) *Tribe and State in Bahrain*. Chicago, IL: The University of Chicago Press.

Klausner, S.Z. (1998) 'Martyrdom', in R. Wuthnow (Ed.) *Encyclopedia of Politics and Religion* (pp. 494–497). Washington, DC: Congressional Quarterly, Inc, www.cqpress.com/incon text/terrorism/links/epr_martyrdom.html (accessed 15 September 2015).

Lagerkvist, A. (2013) 'New memory cultures and death: existential security in the digital memory ecology', *Thanatos*, 2(2).

Louër, L. (2008) *Transnational Shia Politics, Political and Religious Networks in the Gulf*. New York: Columbia University Press.

Marzolph, U. (2003) 'The martyr's way to paradise: Shiite mural art in the urban context', *Ethnologia Europaea*, 33(2), pp. 87–98.

Mock, S. (2012) *Symbols of Defeat in the Construction of National Identity*. Cambridge: Cambridge University Press.

Moghadam, A. (2007) 'Mayhem, myths, and martyrdom: the Shia conception of jihad', *Terrorism and Political Violence*, 19(1), 125–143.

Nora, P. (1989) 'Between memory and history: les lieux de mémoire', translated by Marc Roudebush, *Representations*, 26, pp. 7–25.

Nora, P. (ed.) (1996) *Realms of Memory: Rethinking the French Past*, trans. by Arthur Goldhammer. New York: Columbia University Press, vol. 1.

Olesen, T. (2013) '"We are all Khalid Said": visual injustice symbols in the Egyptian revolution, 2010–2011', in N. Doerr et al. (Eds) *Research in Social Movements, Conflicts and Change: Advances in the Visual Analysis of Social Movements* (pp. 3–26). Bingley: Emerald Publishing Group Ltd.

Papadakis, Y. (2003) 'Nation, narrative and commemoration: political ritual in divided Cyprus', *History and Anthropology*, 14(3), pp. 253–270.

Renan, E. (1990 [1882]) 'What is a Nation?', trans. by M. Thom, in H.K. Bhabha (Ed.) *Nation and Narration* (pp. 8–22). London and New York: Routledge.

Shandler, J. (1999) *While America Watches: Televising the Holocaust*. New York: Oxford University Press.

Smith, L.B. (n.d.) 'Martyrs', *Encyclopedia of Death and Dying*. www.deathreference.com/ Ke-Ma/Martyrs.html (accessed 15 September 2015).

Snow, D.A., Rochford, E.B., Worden, S.K. & Benford, R.D. (1986) 'Frame alignment processes, micromobilization and movement participation', *American Sociological Review*, 51, pp. 464–481.

Socialbakers (2013) 'Facebook Statistics', www.socialbakers.com/facebook-statistics/bahrain (accessed 1 June 2013).

Strombon, L. (2010) *Revisiting the Past: Israeli Identity, Thick Recognition and Conflict Transformation*. Lund: Media-Tryck.

Sturken, M. (1997) *Tangled Memories: The Vietnam War, the AIDS Epidemic, and the Politics of Remembering*. Berkeley, CA and Los Angeles, CA: University of California Press.

Swanson, M.N. (2001) 'The martyrdom of Abd al-Masih, superior of Mount Sinai, Qays al-Ghassani', in D. Thomas (Ed.) *Syrian Christians Under Islam: The First Thousand Years* (pp. 107–130). Leiden: Brill.

Winter, J. (2006) *Remembering War: The Great War between Memory and History in the Twentieth Century*. New Haven, CT: Yale University Press.

Zelizer, B. (2001) *The Voice of the Visual in Memory*, www.sas.upenn.edu/folklore/center/ConferenceArchive/voiceover/voice_of_the_visual.html (accessed 1 September 2014).

Zelizer, B. (2010) *About to Die: How News Images Move the Public*. Oxford: Oxford University Press.

4

REREADING JIHADI TEXTS

Between subalternity and policy discourse

Andrew Hammond

The rise to prominence of the Islamic State organization in the context of weakened central state power and contestation in Syria and Iraq has revived the issue of the Islamic caliphate, its historical role and its putative desirability among Muslims. The organization started life in the post-war turmoil of Iraq in 2003 under the leadership of Abu Mus'ab al-Zarqawi, a Jordanian who associated himself with the Arab Islamic revolutionary nexus centred around Osama bin Laden in Afghanistan (al-Qa'ida). Zarqawi channelled both the nationalist and religious sentiments of Sunni Muslim Iraqis as well as Arab and non-Arab Sunni Muslims who joined their cause, and was even prepared, despite the sectarianism of the movement, to concede status to Muqtada al-Sadr's Shi'ite Mahdi Army.[1]

Their enemy was a foreign occupier and Shi'i Iraqis considered as native informants who had facilitated the colonial enterprise for their own advantage as a community within Iraqi society, and existing anti-Shi'i discourse was lifted from Wahhabi Salafism to be deployed by Zarqawi in the conflict.[2] At the same time, Baathist figures from the former regime, including officers from the disbanded Iraqi army, were reckoned to be working with Zarqawi. These diverse, seemingly contradictory strands continued as the organization morphed in stages into the Islamic State in Iraq and the Levant (ISIL) and then the Islamic State (IS). Reports said Baathist military commander Izzat Ibrahim al-Duri had constituted a paramilitary force through his connections within the Naqshbandi Sufi order and was cooperating with the Salafists in the project to reconstitute the nationalist-Islamist resistance as ISIL.[3] Joining the Syrian civil war, it used its base in Raqqa in northeast Syria to seize control of Mosul and other Sunni towns in north and north-west Iraq in June 2014, renaming itself the Islamic State and declaring its leader, Abu Bakr al-Baghdadi, as *khalifa*, or caliph. The caliphate was an Islamic political institution that ceased to be important in Sunni Islam with the entrenching of the legal traditions in the Abbasid period but was employed as a title conferring nominal pan-Islamic legitimacy by the Ottoman sultans, particularly in the empire's final stages, before Kemal Ataturk ended the office in 1924 (Al-Rasheed et al., 2012).

As this brief history indicates, the rise of IS and its nature is more nuanced than much of the discussion around the movement suggests. Of the dozens of media articles, think tank papers and book publications on the topic since the caliphate declaration, two themes emerge: the IS attempt to encapsulate an ancient Islamic essence that challenges every Muslim to take a stance on its claims, and IS as a departure in Islamic political theory that portends a new stage in the history of Muslim sensibility and action.[4]

This chapter aims to examine how elements of the IS phenomenon, rather than representing innovations in Islamic tradition, reproduce familiar themes that have evolved in the modern jihadist tradition, and to ask whether debate has not overly focused on questions of ideology to the detriment of social and political analysis. I will refer to a series of jihadist texts, starting with Egyptian Muslim Brotherhood ideologue Sayyid Qutb's *Ma'alim Fi'l-Tariq* (Milestones), published just before his execution in 1966; *Jihad, al-Farida al-Gha'iba* (Jihad, the Neglected Obligation) by Abd al-Salam Farag, a member of the Jihad group that assassinated Anwar Sadat in 1981; the letters composed by Juhayman al-Utaybi, who led the group that seized the Meccan Grand Mosque in 1979; Jordanian religious scholar Abu Muhammad al-Maqdisi's *Millat Ibrahim* (The Religion of Ibrahim, 1984) and *al-Kawashif al-jaliyya fi kufr al-dawla al-Sa'udiyya* (The Obvious Proofs of the Infidelity of the Saudi State, 1989); al-Qa'ida leader Ayman al-Zawahiri's *Fursan fi Rayat al-Nabi* (Knights Under the Banner of the Prophet, 2001); and speeches by IS leader al-Baghdadi.

Defining Salafism

First, some words on terminology. Salafism, Islamism and political Islam are contested, even confused terms upon which there is no consensus in the scholarly literature. The history of Salafism can be separated into two broad parts, in which different strands within the Islamic intellectual tradition intertwine. In the first, the notion of *al-salaf al-salih*, the exemplary first generations of Muslims, was invoked by puritanical trends within the Hanbali legal rite. Ibn Taymiyya (1263–1328), an Arab religious scholar from Harran in today's south-east Turkey, and his followers, formulated their ideas in the context of Crusader and Mongol invasion of Muslim territories (Hanafi, 2014, 137).

However, *Salafiyya* did not yet exist as a recognized designation, an idea, an abstract noun, while trends that appear Salafi in nature made themselves felt in Ottoman Istanbul, in the criticisms of Sufism of Imam Birgivi Mehmed Efendi (c.1522–73) and the Kadizade movement, which campaigned against Sufi influence in 17th-century Istanbul (Ocak, 2012, 293–299; and Zilfi, 1986).[5] The Kadizadelis were not necessarily opposed to speculative theology (*kalam*), while Sufi followers of Andalusian philosopher Ibn Arabi (1165–1240) who believed in the monistic theosophy termed *wahdat al-wujud* in fact shared Ibn Taymiyya and Hanbalism's aversion to *kalam* and some even praised Ibn Taymiyya's position (El-Rouayheb, 2015). There were also Hanbali figures who were Sufi (Voll, 1972). Ibn Taymiyya's ideas were developed, however, by the Saudi-Wahhabi movement in the 18th-century Arabian Peninsula. Preacher Muhammad ibn 'Abd al-Wahhab (1703–92), in alliance with dynastic ruler Muhammad ibn Saud (d.1765), embarked on a mission to purify Islam from the polluting beliefs and practices Ibn Taymiyya had called out. In the eyes of most Wahhabi scholars the Ottoman state was illegitimate for failing to prevent such popular practices, while Istanbul looked on the Wahhabis with similar alacrity, but a modus vivendi saw each accommodate the other through the rest of the 19th century.

Salafiyya's entry into Islamic discourse came at the hands of the intellectuals of the late 19th and early 20th centuries, who grappled with the question of why Europe had managed to eclipse Muslim society in science, technology, and political and military power. They invoked the spirit of the first Muslims, but while they internalized some of the critique of the Wahhabi-Taymiyya tradition – in particular its attitude towards Sufi practices – they did not generally adopt its legal and theological prescriptions and retained links with Sufism at least at the intellectual level. The political movement these reformers inspired, the Muslim Brotherhood, would define itself in 1938 as 'a Salafiyya message, a Sunni way, a Sufi truth' (Mitchell, 1969, 14). Of the leading figures of this Muslim Reform movement, Jamal al-Din al-Afghani (1738–1897), Muhammad 'Abduh (1849–1905) and Rashid Rida (1865–1935) (and perhaps we should add Brotherhood founder Hassan al-Banna), Rida developed links with the Saudi-Wahhabi state, which had been revived in 1902 under the leadership of Abd al-Aziz (Ibn Saud), viewing it as a vanguard movement challenging Western imperialism. The result, as Hamid Redissi has argued, was a revamping of Wahhabism's image from a radical sect on the margins to 'a precursor of the fundamentalist spirit' (Redissi, 2008, 173).

By the 1970s Salafism had decisively shifted to an ideological approach identified with Wahhabism. It no longer signified an effort to engage with modernity but, as Oliver Roy argues, now indicated the notion of repelling ideas emanating from non-Muslim civilizational blocs rather than of how to internalize or manage them (Roy, 2004, 233). While Wahhabism claimed Salafism, 'Islamism'/'political Islam' filled the remaining semantic space covering the range of Sunni and Shi'ite groups operating in a competitive political field across the Islamic world, a distinction Islamists welcome since it serves their claims to represent a 'moderate' aesthetic.[6]

This transformation can be put down to several factors: the financial power behind Saudi Wahhabism following the structural shifts in the energy market of the mid-1970s, the Brotherhood and Turkish Islamic activists moving into electoral politics in the 1970s and 1980s, and the Saudi-Wahhabi instrumentalization of jihad in Afghanistan in the 1980s. The political Islamists were engaged in a model of political activism, one that sought to achieve 're-Islamization' after the interruption of colonialism but which reconceptualized lines of religious and political authority in a manner that privileged laymen over the *ulama* who had been the traditional gatekeepers of the classical sources and that favoured working with electoral legislative systems that superseded the *Shari'a* courts, in which the *ulama* had adjudicated, as the locus of action to ensure *Shari'a*-based sanctification of politics and society. While Salafism empowers the *ulama*, the Islamists were laymen who invoked *Shari'a* through the legislative action of elected assemblies.

Salafism today can be divided into three blocks, following the schema adopted in Roel Meijer's collection *Global Salafism: Islam's New Religious Movement* (2009): political Salafism, quietist Salafism and jihadi Salafism. The first, sometimes termed *al-Salafiyya al-Tanẓimiyya* (organized or activist Salafism), supports some level of involvement in national political processes (as seen in Kuwait, Bahrain, Egypt and the Saudi Ṣaḥwa movement). The second, *al-Salafiyya al-'Ilmiyya* (scholastic Salafism), in rejecting political activity, is an appealing ideology to governing powers in its theory that rebellion against a Muslim ruler is illegitimate. This categorization remains imperfect in that the lines are often blurred. Quietist Salafists have engaged in jihad against non-Muslim foes (Afghanistan), while some have crossed over into the activist, political arena (Egypt). Different branches of Brotherhood thought have influenced both the jihadists and the political activists, and the principle of *takfir* creates a constant tension between the quietist and jihadist imperatives of the Salafi-Wahhabi tradition.

Jihadi Salafism

As for jihadi Salafism (*al-salafiyya al-jihadiyya*), it is concerned with the conditions that justify insurrection against a Muslim or non-Muslim ruler, which may or may not involve declaring the Muslim ruler to be outside Islam (*takfir*). In *Milestones* Sayyid Qutb engaged in extensive discussion of jihad but, rather than declare directly that the Egyptian ruler was non-Muslim, he used the categories of *jahiliyya* (pre-Islamic 'age of ignorance') and *hakimiyya* (sovereignty of God) to imply that the state was such, since it was not the province of Shari'a but subject to the post-Shari'a political and legal constructs of modernity moulded in the hands of Europeans. Qutb's ideas were critically developed by a number of jihadist activists in the milieu of religious politics in Egypt and Saudi Arabia in the 1970s and 1980s.

Farag's *The Neglected Obligation* sought to make clearer the duty to wage jihad for the purpose of removing the ruler and applied Ibn Taymiyya's thinking on *takfir* and jihad (while he does not mention Qutb directly, he cites Ibn Taymiyya at length), bringing in the concept of the near and the far enemy. Removing the ruler (the near enemy) becomes the obligation: 'The rulers of this age are apostates (*fi ridda 'an al-islam*), educated at the table of colonialism, whether that of the Crusaders, the Communists or the Zionists' (Farag, 1982, 6). For this reason they have failed to follow the divine plan for Muslim society through adopted Western political and legislative systems. For Farag, establishing an Islamic state within the framework of the caliphate was advocated by the Prophet as a divine order and it is a duty for every Muslim to see this through. An 'Islamic awakening' (*sahwa islamiyya*) would enable this to take place despite the 'coups that put people in power against the will of the people' (Farag, 1982, 3–4). As Kepel noted in his study of Egyptian jihadist groups of the 1980s, Farag's was a rejection of paths chosen by others in Egypt, specifically the Brotherhood's decision to work with the system, the Islamic groups that functioned openly on university campuses, and the withdrawal (modelled as analogous to the Prophet's decision to quit Mecca for Medina) from society of Shukri Mustafa's Jama'at al-Muslimin, the Society of Muslims (which rejected all dealings with the modern state – it was dubbed by Egyptian media al-Takfir wa'l-Hijra).

Juhayman al-Utaybi's writings deal with these themes differently. His main concern is the question of loyalty to the ruler, which he rejects without viewing *takfir* of the ruler as necessary. In '*al-Imara wal-bay'a wal-ta'a*' (The State, Allegiance and Obedience) he says Al Saud are not fit to rule since they are not from the Prophet's Quraysh tribe, and while the state is *kafir* (infidel), he says he cannot speak for individuals within it. His group, *al-Jama'a al-Salafiyya al-Muhtasiba* (JSM), shared much in common with Shukri Mustafa's, rejecting service in government institutions while objecting to their use of *takfir*. Nasir al-Huzaymi, a companion of Juhayman at the time, relates in his account of the period how members of Mustafa's group would reside with them in Medina and discuss these questions. Their confusion over how to respond to the Egyptians' argument led them to seek a meeting with Nasir al-Din al-Albani, the Salafi hadith scholar who was a major intellectual inspiration behind the group (Al-Huzaymi, 2011, 48).[7] Albani's ideas rejecting partisan adherence to any of the major Sunni legal schools (*tamazhub*) were central to Juhayman's thinking; Juhayman also developed apocalyptic arguments regarding the coming of the Mahdi, and it was this, once Juhayman believed he had located this figure (Muhammad al-Qahtani, a group member from Riyadh), that gave the impetus for insurrectionary action. Juhayman was also innovative in framing the concept of *al-wala' wa'l-bara'*, meaning loyalty (*wala'*) to the religion of Ibrahim – a term that implies a primordial Islam – and disavowal (*bara'*) of the ways of polytheists, who in his model were Al Saud (Wagemakers, 2009).

These various strands within jihadi Salafism came together in the writing of religious scholar Abu Muhammad al-Maqdisi. A Palestinian-Jordanian born in 1959, he became familiar with Juhayman's ideas through the circle of sympathizers who left for Kuwait after the mosque siege, then spent some years in Medina before travelling to Pakistan, before returning to Jordan in the 1990s where he has been imprisoned on numerous occasions for his views. In his 1984 book *Millat Ibrahim*, he takes Juhayman's ideas forwards by merging his *al-wala' wa'l-bara'* with the ideas on *takfir* that Juhayman had avoided, but he also references Qutb in attacking Muslim rulers for following man-made rather than Shari'a-based laws. The Saudi state 'deceives people through encouraging *tawhid*' in terms of warring against Sufism, visiting graves, sorcery, etc. while ignoring the implications of *tawhid* in its foreign or domestic policies (Al-Maqdisi, 1984, 40). Like Farag, he cites Ibn Taymiyya and Ibn Abd al-Wahhab at length, citing each around two dozen times, as well as Qutb (three times) and Juhayman (once). The *ulama* have been duped into cooperating with illegitimate regimes via organizations such as the

Saudi-based World Muslim League, he writes (ibid., 160). He does not discuss the caliphate as an ideal Islamic system. In *al-Kawashif al-Jaliyya*, however, Maqdisi explicitly declares Al Saud as infidels, while the caliphate is discussed in general terms as a desirable outcome.

Maqdisi's influence was considerable in the next stage of the jihadi tradition. Transforming *al-wala' wa'l-bara'* from 'a tool to increase religious strictness and piety into a revolutionary ideology that is incumbent upon every Muslim' (Wagemakers, 2009, 95), Maqdisi's programme forms the general framework within which jihadi Salafism came to operate as it developed under the al-Qa'ida rubric in Afghanistan and then via al-Zarqawi's activities in post-2003 Iraq (Maqdisi engaged in a public dispute in 2004 with Zarqawi over atrocities against Shia Iraqis). Al-Qa'ida texts, via its two leading figures, Osama bin Laden and Ayman al-Zawahiri, are many and they appear more clearly to render the theological subordinate to the political. The caliphate features heavily in Zawahiri's *Knights*, but it could almost be read as a Third World anti-imperialism text. Trained as an eye doctor, Zawahiri is no religious scholar. He cites Ibn Taymiyya once in a shortlist of early shaykhs he praises (without specifying their Shari'a specialization as *ulama*); Ibn Abd al-Wahhab does not feature at all, while Saudi-Wahhabi Shaykh Muhammad bin Ibrahim Al al-Shaykh is listed among contemporary *ulama* worthy of praise (Al-Zawahiri, 2001, 175). Qutb, on the other hand, is mentioned 14 times in the text as a seminal figure in the revolutionary jihad movement: 'Sayyid Qutb's call for *tawhid* and complete submission to the rule of God (*hakimiyyat Allah*) and sovereignty of the divine programme (*al-manhaj al-rabbani*) was and remains the spark for the Islamic revolution against the internal and external enemies of Islam, who are replenished day after day' (ibid., 12). Zawahiri gives a history of the Islamic movement (*al-haraka al-islamiyya*) in which Egypt plays a central role: Egypt is where he dates its beginning in 1966 (Qutb's death) and he implies, without saying directly, that Egypt would be the most appropriate location for a new caliphate. In a section dedicated to demonstrating British perfidy he gives the example of Britain preventing Egypt's Ottoman governor Muhammad Ali from marching on Istanbul in the 1830s to replace weak Ottoman sultans (ibid., 100). The danger in Muhammad Ali's adventure for the British was that 'he could establish a strong Arab state in Egypt or he could march on Istanbul to reinvigorate the Ottoman caliphate' (ibid., 101).

He also includes among his citations a popular and important work by Muhammad Hassanayn Haikal, the Egyptian journalist, historian and one-time confidante of Nasser.[8] Zawahiri offers the view that Britain's solution to the problem of a horizontal reconstitution of power between Constantinople, Egypt and the Levant was the project to create a Jewish state in Palestine (Zawahiri, 1981, 103). Through such historical argument he leads to the conclusion, that Muslims need to find a liberated territory to use as a base for the two key aims: 'returning the caliphate and ejecting the invaders from Islamic territories' (ibid., 242).

If we look at Baghdadi's speeches, the political themes are strikingly similar. Several days before Baghdadi's famed public sermon in a Mosul mosque in July

2014, he issued a voice recording marking the beginning of the fasting month of Ramadan, in the immediate aftermath of the group seizing Mosul and declaring itself a caliphate. Notably, the speech does not engage discussion of the 'end of days' theme,[9] despite its considerable presence in IS English language recruitment and mobilization publication *Dabiq*, but rather focuses on two elements: exhortations to engage in jihad during Ramadan, citing the Quran and hadiths in support of that position; and decrying injustice faced by Muslims around the world. Indeed, Baghdadi's location of the IS fight in the discourse of oppression suggests the tradition of anti-imperialist Third World-ism is at least one framework for understanding the movement's motivations. The dominant emotion he evokes is revenge for historical injustice that came with Western expansion in the colonial era. He problematizes the nation-state itself and takes issue with Western discourse on terrorism, which he sees as part of a hypocritical epistemology of neo-imperialist control.

> Indeed the Muslims were defeated after the fall of their caliphate.[10] Then their state ceased to exist, so the disbelievers were able to weaken and humiliate the Muslims, dominate them everywhere, plunder their wealth and resources, and rob them of their rights. And they accomplished this by attacking and occupying their lands, placing their treacherous agents in power to rule the Muslims with fire and iron, and spreading dazzling and deceptive slogans such as: civilization, peace, co-existence, freedom, democracy, secularism, Baathism, nationalism and patriotism, among other false slogans. Those rulers continue striving to enslave the Muslims, pulling them away from their religion with those slogans. So either the Muslim pulls away from his religion, disbelieves in God and disgracefully submits to the manmade polytheistic laws of the East and West, living despicably and disgracefully as a follower, by repeating those slogans without will and honour, or he lives persecuted, chased and expelled, to end up being killed, imprisoned, or terribly tortured, on the accusation of terrorism.
>
> (Baghdadi, 2014a)

This sense of righting an historical wrong was illustrated by the statements and videos accompanying the caliphate declaration. Thus IS claimed it had smashed the 'borders of humiliation' and broken the 'idol' (*sanam*) of the British-French lines drawn up during and after the First World War. Videos showed non-belligerents passing through former checkpoints without passports amid commentaries citing it as a victory over America.[11]

Islamist responses to IS

Echoing his criticism of Zarqawi, Maqdisi focused on IS' violent conflict with other Salafi jihadists in Syria and its breach with al-Qa'ida (Al Jazeera, 2014).

Abu'l-Mundhir al-Shinqiti, a prominent scholar on an informal body of *ulama* organized by Maqdisi, issued an influential *fatwa* rejecting the caliphal announcement (Al-Shinqiti, 2014).[12] Its central contention was that the Taliban had already established an Islamic emirate under Mullah Omar, which had obtained the oath of fealty from al-Zawahiri, that IS leader al-Baghdadi had given his fealty to Zawahiri. He argued that there was a distinction between the legal qualifications for *khilafa* and its political understanding. As long as an entity led by an individual had been declared to meet the legal standards, it was incumbent upon Muslims to recognize this, even if it was not possible to bring all Muslims within the purview of this *khilafa* for political reasons or if the emirate was no longer functioning or locked in protracted conflict. In other words, Mullah Omar is the legitimate caliph-in-waiting, and therefore possessor of what he termed *al-imama al-'uzma* (the great leadership of the community) so Baghdadi's announcement is void since he is the leader of one *imara* (emirate) under the aegis of a greater project begun by Mullah Omar. The opinion also noted that Baghdadi's announcement came in the context of Muhajideen internecine conflict, which means that Omar's death, announced by the Taliban in 2015, does not ease IS' case. Maqdisi was jailed again in 2014 after he denounced as apostates Arab rulers who joined non-Muslims in 2014 to fight IS.[13] The caliphate was denounced by state-backed Sunni, Brotherhood, Wahhabi and other Salafi jihadi scholars and groups.[14] The Global Federation of Muslim Scholars headed by Yousef al-Qaradawi, the Qatar-based scholar close to the Muslim Brotherhood, said IS had not sought the opinion of a wide range of Muslim scholars.[15]

State Wahhabism's denouncements are interesting in three ways: they came at the prompting of the Saudi government, they were moderate in tone, and they aimed to assert Wahhabi authority over the Salafi tradition within the Saudi realm without addressing how Muslims under IS rule should respond. The Grand Mufti Shaykh Abd al-Aziz Al al-Shaykh issued his first commentary in July 2014. Its first point of concern is that IS wasted energies in fighting Sunni Muslim warriors in Syria and used excessive methods; the text cites its use of *takfir* only once and IS is referred to as simply *firqa*, a sect among the sects of the Islamic whole.[16] He expresses concern that some youth in Saudi Arabia have declared allegiance to IS and calls on them to listen to the state's *ulama*, then cites hadith material to reinforce his point that zeal for religion (*ghuluww fi din*), which is welcome, should not lead to losing one's life in suicide operations abroad or engaging in 'slaughter with knives' (beheading).[17] Following a public rebuke from King Abdullah, who was shown on state television telling assembled *ulama* to provide guidance regarding the question of extremism, the shaykh began referring to the group as outside Islam, a 'Jahiliyya gang' ('*assaba jahiliyya*').[18] Most of such statements were issued in response to jihadist attacks inside the country, usually against Shi'i targets.[19] Responding to a questioner, the Mufti exhorted Saudis against giving the oath of fealty to anyone other than *wulaat al-amr* (the rightful guardians), an opinion directed solely towards Muslims of Saudi Arabia.[20] In other words, little was said to address IS claims within its own territories in Iraq and Syria.

Rereading jihadism

Socio-political readings of jihadism become less fashionable the closer they impinge upon contemporary realities. The context of mass repression in Nasser's totalitarian state is expounded uncontroversially in any standard description of Sayyid Qutb's writing. His jihadism is granted its political context without contestation. Nasser's Egypt was also locked in political conflict with Western nations and moved in non-aligned and Soviet circles, thus there were few barriers in public political discourse to scholarship elaborating on its dysfunctional aspects. Qutb's memory has been blessed with scholarship that allows examination not only of the religious ideological elements of his thought but also of the socio-political milieu that helped produce it. However, jihadism that developed after him has not fared quite so well.

History is written by victors and material that does not conform to the victor's narrative usually finds itself marginalized or even forgotten. This has been the major challenge of the field of early Islamic history, and it is compounded by the fact that the victor's conceptualization of the past transforms with the evolution of society, religion and politics. In the case of jihadi Salafism, its history has been written by those it challenged and failed to defeat. Jihadism is presented in Western narrative as a series of violent eruptions informed by ancient patrimony and inherently incapable of building a future. Orientalist depictions that reduce a complex and diverse historical and intellectual tradition to a word, 'Islam', barbaric and retrograde in connotation, further complicate the picture. Movements of a similar revolutionary nature have been subject to revisitations and reframings – Wahhabiyya itself comes to mind, rescued in the early 20th century by the efforts of Rashid Rida and post-9/11 by a considerable propaganda effort focused on Western academic institutions.[21] One notes here Stephen Walt's useful alternative discussion of IS as a revolutionary movement.[22]

Juhayman's revolt has been discussed consistently in terms of the Ikhwan revolt of the 1920s against the compromises of Abd al-Aziz in the process of state building and his securing British imperial support for the project.[23] It is depicted that way in a recent account of the events by Nasir al-Huzaymi, a one-time companion of Juhayman who in Al-Huzaymi's telling was an 'ideological extension' (Al-Huzaymi, 2011, 161) of the Ikhwan, obsessed by his Utaybi tribal origins and set on revenge for the repression of the Ikhwan (ibid., 61, 86–91). Al-Huzaymi is a Saudi national who began recounting his experiences in the Saudi daily *al-Riyadh* in 2003, and, while there is no reason to question the historical detail of his account, its presentation within the sphere of Saudi public discourse must be taken into consideration. Al-Huzaymi is no dissident. In his book he is careful to point out at numerous points that he disagreed with Juhayman over taking control of the mosque and over his theory of the Mahdi, and thus broke with him (ibid., 64).[24] Yet Al-Huzaymi still manages to indicate, albeit without detail, that Juhayman was interested in establishing 'a just state' (*dawlat 'adl*)[25] and may be considered a 'revolutionary' (ibid., 161). Juhayman composed 14 pamphlets in all, which circulated through Saudi mosques in 1978–79 (ibid., 136), but they were printed in Kuwait at the printing press of the leftist *al-Tali'a* newspaper, which was impressed by the fact that their author was someone on the run from Saudi security forces (ibid., 66).

The first of these works is in many ways the most enlightening in terms of Juhayman's inspirations. Titled '*Raf' al-iltibas 'an millat man ja'alahu allah imaman li'l-nas*' (Ending confusion concerning the path of those whom God set as a guide for people), it provided the framework for Maqdisi's seminal jihadist tract *Millat Ibrahim*.[26] In this text, Juhayman can be seen challenging the political conceptualization of modernity as received by the West, as his predecessors in the jihadi literature had done, as well as the power dynamics of a tyrannical system. He states at the outset that he seeks to clarify the nature of the religion of Ibrahim in order to demonstrate 'the difference between truth and falsehood and show that it is contrary to what some people claim concerning Islam as a religion of "civilization" (*hadara*);[27] thus they mix East with West, act like them [Westerners] and live among them'.[28] This warning is primarily directed to the *ulama* and their followers, whom he divides into three groups: those who focus on combatting Sufism, visiting graves and other such heretical innovations (core state Wahhabi teachings);[29] those whose concern is hadith studies and who object to dogged championing of one or another legal school (a reference to his mentor Albani); and those obsessed with challenging communism and who seek to dominate government positions (the Muslim Brotherhood). His objection to the first two groups is that they only direct their attention to people 'with no authority' while staying silent on those who have power yet 'destroy the religion of God'. He gives as an example the application of *hadd* penalties to the weak (*da'if*) but not the powerful (*qawiyy*), while these *ulama* give themselves the excuse that they are weak and incapable of creating change. As for the third group, they are engaged in a political project to 'control thinking' (*tahkim al-afkar*) and belittle those who engage in the real work of combatting polytheism and innovation, and for that reason they accept positions as bureaucrats, preachers, teachers, soldiers and experts rather than combat the infidels as the Prophet did, no matter the cost. This willingness to suffer for a higher principle is the essence of the 'religion of Ibrahim'.

Rather than an argument lodged in religious ideology, Juhayman's discourse here is one of social justice. '*Al-Imara wal-bay'a wal-ta'a*' (The State, Allegiance and Obedience)[30] continues with this theme. It starts with the invocations of Quranic verse 30, sura 26 (which cites the Prophet Dawud being established as a *khalifa fi'l-ard*), warning those who have been shown the right path but veer away from it, and he follows up with a prophetic hadith instructing the *'a'ima* (the imams) that they must judge according to the book of God. In other words, he says, the leaders of God's community must 'rule the people fairly and not follow their whims'. His concern is not only those who hold power in the sense of Al Saud or any other ruler, but the religious classes (*al-mutadayyina*) who have been humiliated and corrupted by power. They have fallen into extremes: that of the Saudi religious police (the Committee for the Promotion of Good and Prevention of Vice), who take on the mantle of monks rejecting the world and wanting others to do the same; and that of the *ulama* who work with state institutions. In the Saudi state, 'the *khalifa* is the one who imposes himself on [Muslims] and then they are obliged to give him their loyalty'; further, this ruler is not from the Quraysh. He takes the example of Abd al-Aziz bin Baz, one of the most respected religious scholars who in 1993 became Grand Mufti: the Saudi rulers 'take from him and his knowledge what suits them, but they would not hesitate to contradict him if he faced them with what is right (*al-haqq*), and he knows this well'. Juhayman then cites a prophetic hadith that in the last analysis excuses Bin Baz; if a Muslim is in a position that does not allow him to speak out against *munkar* then at least he should condemn it 'in his heart, which is the weakest choice'.[31]

It is of note that in this pamphlet Juhayman cites the eschatological hadith regarding Dabiq, which IS has utilized to recruit non-Arabs (its Arabic-language journal is in fact centred at Naba, the news, not appealing to the apocalypse at all).[32] The hadith suggests that a Muslim army will defeat the army of Rum (probably intended as Byzantium) and then march on Constantinople, after which Jesus returns and defeats the Anti-Christ. Dabiq is a plain north of Aleppo where early Arab/Muslim armies would gather before campaigns against the Byzantines. Juhayman's point in citing this is that it should be a means of sustenance to those facing injustice today to know that in the long run victory will be theirs. His conclusion is that many of today's rulers do not deserve the oath of loyalty (*bay'a*) or obedience (*ta'a*). In other words, the text discusses how one should deal with an unjust situation, when to stay silent, when to speak, when to withdraw from the scene entirely.

In their review of the Juhayman material, Hegghammer and Lacroix argue that Juhayman's movement represented a form of 'rejectionist Islamism' that was intellectually and organizationally separate from other trends of the period, 'characterized by a strong focus on ritual practices, a declared disdain for politics, and yet an active rejection of the state and its institution' (Hegghammer & Lacroix, 2007, 104). They look at rejectionist beliefs regarding the Saudi state's concessions to modernity, including elements such as carrying identity cards and passports, which denoted loyalty to an entity other than God, unusual positions on ritual such as wearing sandals while praying and removing the *mihrab* from mosques, which caused a split with the JSM (ibid., 107–109). They also discuss in detail at Juhayman's apocalyptic thinking on the Mahdi, which was outlined mainly in '*Fitan wa akhbar al-Mahdi wa nuzul 'Isa 'alayhi'l-salam wa ashratu'l-sa'a*' (Turmoil and Reports of the Mahdi, the Coming of Jesus, Peace Be Upon Him, and Portents of the Last Hour), and conclude that the texts in general, with their 'relatively monotonous religious language', 'do not reveal a particularly clear political doctrine' (ibid., 111). They allow that the JSM, whose creation in the mid-1960s Bin Baz had blessed, was a result of a religious establishment fearful of rival ideological currents and the dislocations of rapid modernization, while Juhayman's radical faction was more driven by 'ideology and charismatic leadership than by structural socioeconomic and political factors' (ibid., 115).

It can be argued, however, that the dislocations of the period were more considerable, culturally and economically, than this analysis implies. Abdullah al-Ghaddami captures them well in his study of the religious debates that were unleashed by Juhayman's action, *Hikayat al-Hadatha* (The Story of Modernity). He points to shifts in Saudi urban topography as large cities were developed on an American model of wide streets and boulevards – 'urban spaces devoid of any humanity' (Al-Ghaddami, 2004, 177) – while oil wealth changed the country's economic profile almost overnight (ibid., 164). Further, Saudi Arabia's political structure and foreign policy framework were produced in the crucible of US political and military support – a dynastic system that the US government, determined to protect its Aramco investment, helped prevent from opening up to leftist and Arab nationalist elements, allowing Prince Faisal and some of his brothers to remove King Saud in 1964 and establish the depoliticized authoritarian model that has lasted now for nearly five decades with Western support.[33]

Alternative views

In his seminal study, *The Prophet and Pharaoh: Muslim Extremism in Egypt*, Gilles Kepel is forthright in arguing that jihadist zealots were motivated by the poverty and hopelessness of a post-colonial police state. Reading their texts closely, Kepel presents a comprehensive analysis of the jihadi phenomenon up to that point in Egypt. The genesis of Qutb's ideas is clear. A writer of fiction and literary criticism, Qutb began to engage in political writing from 1949 with ten works, eight of them concerning Islamist doctrine and written after 1951 when he joined the Brotherhood. The Brotherhood, Kepel writes, perceived early on the totalitarian character of the military regime because it suffered in its concentration camps, leading Qutb to engage in a comprehensive critique of the modern state in terms of the classical Islamic tradition whose conceptual language a generation of devotees subsequently sought to develop. In other words, 'the language and categories adopted by Qutb and his emulators captured the suffering, frustration, and daily demands of certain components of that society' (Kepel, 1985, 27). Qutb believed the prison guards, torturers, rulers and those who failed to challenge them had forgotten God; only the imprisoned Brothers were true Muslims (ibid., 28–29, 61). Like Lenin's *What is To Be Done?*, Qutb intended *Milestones* as a manual for the vanguard who would lead an Islamic resurrection (Qutb, 1979, 9).[34]

One reader inspired by Qutb was Shukri Mustafa. While Mustafa was tried and put to death with his followers in 1977 for the murder of a former government minister, Kepel says state media made sure to present the group's ideology and practices in as ludicrous a light as possible, ensuring that Mustafa was seen as an 'insane criminal' in rejecting state employment or involvement in the education system and arguing, as he did at his trial, that the Prophet did not approve of learning to write unless it had a clear purpose (Kepel, 1985, 78). Kepel places this thinking in the context of the socio-economic conditions of millions of people who struggled to obtain an education, find government employment and then get married and set up home in the corrupt failing Egypt of the 1970s. Their choice was withdrawal, stylized as prophetic *hijra*. With a prosaic sympathy that perhaps stands in contrast to the neo-conservative turn he took in the wake of 9/11, Kepel sees the group as 'the lost children of a Third World independent state who were convinced, in effect, that life was intolerable' (ibid., 90); they were outcast victims of 'disorientation at the painful changes wrought by modernity' (ibid., 90). Mustafa's was an 'impassioned revolt of the poor, the disinherited, and the hopeless' (ibid., 102). Aggregating data regarding the jihad group that assassinated Sadat and the Military Academy group that attempted an earlier military coup, Kepel notes they were largely from the newly constructed districts of rural migrants around Cairo, 'children of the rural exodus' who found the city incapable of providing them with the keys to modernity (ibid., 218). 'They are the living symbols, and their numbers are massive, of the failure of the independent state's modernization projects', Kepel writes (ibid., 218).

Kepel's humanization of the 'Islamic militant' was in harmony with the spirit of the times. It not only was a challenge to the modernization theory regarding development outside the Western world that infused the spirit of scholarship across a variety of disciplines, but it also came just as Edward Said's questioning of the Western intellectual tradition of representation of the Arab and Muslim Other in *Orientalism* (1978) was rippling its way through the academe. In 1982 Ranajit Guha also launched his Subaltern Studies project, which aimed to reconsider the role of non-elites in the process of social and historical change and disentangle self-serving discourses of power. If history could be written not only from the perspective of 'the working class', in which Marxist historians had long engaged, but also from that of the urban poor, peasantry, slum dwellers, unemployed, bandits, slaves or gypsies, then there was no reason why scholars could not problematize and deconstruct the category of Muslim extremist too.

Two decades before Kepel's study came the publication of Frantz Fanon's last work, *The Wretched of the Earth* (1961). Written in the heat of decolonization's historical moment, it presented a raw analysis of the mentalities produced by colonialism and the pathologies of the post-colonial regime. While Fanon based his writing largely on the Algerian experience, which was particularly bitter, reading it today casts in sharp relief the failure of national elites to realize the national project in the Middle East region. Jihadism, lashing out at both Farag's near and far enemies, is one of the earliest and most enduring signs of that failure. The national project, whether republican Arab nationalist or consumerist Gulf monarchy, remains forever on hold and to be continued, as if the moment has been hanging unfulfilled since 1961, allowing us to stretch Fanon's descriptions of dysfunction over five decades in time. In the decolonized state, there was/is 'a masked discontent, like the smoking ashes of a burnt-down house after the fire has been put out, which still threaten to burst into flames again' (Fanon, 2001, 59); violence was/is a 'cleansing force' that frees the native from inferiority complex, despair and inaction (ibid., 74); as the decadent national bourgeoisie became manager for Western enterprise the country became/becomes the 'brothel of Europe' (ibid.,

123); native intellectuals, 'wonder-struck before the history of today's barbarity', sought/seek solace in the past (ibid., 169). In their particular response to the superiority complex of empire, its client regimes, and discursive frameworks that have 'ridiculed, demonized, declared inferior and irrational' (Sardar, 2008, vi), perhaps it could be said that in the hands of jihadist movements this epistemic violence has produced a transmogrified Islam intended to provoke the West's ultimate civilizational horror. If IS has delved into the obscure corners of hadithology to justify sexual slavery, mediatized beheadings (in which Zarqawi engaged before) and other forms of gory death, it has also internalized the stereotype and returned it to sender in the most lurid form.

A third voice to be considered in a rereading of jihadism is that found in Fawaz Gerges's *The Rise and Fall of Al-Qaeda* (2011). An attempt to inject sobriety into analysis of the phenomenon during the al-Qa'ida era, Gerges writes that exaggeration and notions of Islamic exceptionalism had taken grip of what became an industry. 'Evidence and reality no longer matter in a world built on perception and illusion. Every plot and incident is viewed as an affirmation of al-Qaeda's invincibility and reach: to the American leadership bin Laden and his successors appear to be 100 feet tall,' he said (Gerges, 2011, 192). The militants' lack of a popular base was made apparent by the Arab uprisings, while domestic and transnational jihadists proved to be their own worst enemies with indiscriminate violence that 'alienated ordinary Muslims in Egypt, Algeria, Iraq, Lebanon, Saudi Arabia, Indonesia, and elsewhere' (ibid., 204). The 'terrorism narrative' of the West living under constant and imminent threat becomes then an institutionalized self-fulfilling prophecy among policymakers, government officials and the general public. Al-Qa'ida became an industry, creating in the USA, for one, a security bureaucracy of some 854,000 people, while 'most scholars of the Middle East have avoided discussion of the War on Terrorism, either fearful or suspicious of the politics involved' (ibid., 23). The response to the challenge of terrorism became an 'ideology of its own' (ibid., 23). We could say that IS is different in that it manages territory, resources and state structures, but beyond ungoverned space and conflict zones of opportunity there is no reason to believe it would be capable of winning any more adherents than al-Qa'ida.

Conclusion

The jihadi tradition has developed since Sayyid Qutb through a dialectic that deploys a series of concepts and external discursive traditions, including *takfir*, jihad, caliphate, apocalyptica, *al-wala' wa'l-bara'*, Arab nationalism, anti-imperialism. Rather than a radical departure, IS deals with the same material but, like those before it, engages with it in its own way: it uses eschatological arguments for recruiting and mobilization in Syria, and disputes with al-Qa'ida over the caliphate, while engaging in the same Salafi legalistic paradigm as Maqdisi and other scholars in the Saudi-Wahhabi Salafi orbit. However, discussion of jihadism has heavily focused on radicalization as a security issue and questions of ideological creed and practice, opening the way to arid debates over how 'Islamic' IS is or is not, which assumes there exists notionally an absolute standard by which a complex historical tradition such as Islam can be judged, and to reductive polemics that serve political agendas ('IS expresses Sunni disenfranchisement, therefore Assad "must go"').

Social readings of foundational jihadi texts with a less bellicose approach that goes beyond the exotica of Islamic theology have become decidedly unfashionable. This is possibly the result of the fusing of state and media narratives in the context of globalization, such that discourses emerging from Western power centres are today capable of taking an immediate hegemonic grip on the global imagination in a way that was not possible before. This reduces the space to think about an issue like jihadism away from the policy sphere.[35] It is possibly no coincidence too that, while incisive investigations of jihadism have been attempted in Egypt, a country whose leadership and social crises are easily problematized by media and government, this is less the case for Saudi Arabia, where judicious treatment by Western allies and regime arguments of cultural exceptionalism have left its citizens prey to the discursive matrix of religious obscurantism. There remains too what Gayatri Chakravorty Spivak, writing in 1988, termed the 'interested desire to conserve the subject of the West, or the West as subject' (Spivak, 1988, 271): obsessive attention to the utter otherness of the jihadist allows countries of 'the West', in the warzone of global economy and political will, to continue defining themselves as a civilizational package that is, if nothing else, everything the jihadist is not.

The intense global and Western interest in figures like Juhayman and Baghdadi is such that it is impossible to get to these figures, so drowned in policy discourse have they become. In her essay 'Can the subaltern speak?' Spivak suggested that, even if historical inquiry could get at the truth of an event, colonialism and discourses of representation make it impossible. Others such as Fanny Colonna have suggested that even the presence of an historical actor's voice can be impossible to disentangle from the cacophony of narratives surrounding a contested post-colonial arena such as that of Algeria (Colonna, 2003). There is no reason for us not to understand Juhayman as a subaltern, a non-elite actor who challenged political tyranny and social injustice, but can we reach him? As we have seen, Juhayman left his own accounts; they are not unmediated in that they were dictated and edited by two of his companions, but his words allow us to attempt an ideological understanding of his actions (Atwan, 2015).[36] Kepel's study of Egyptian movements of the 1970s rejected a view of 'atavistically backward fanatical terrorists' (Kepel, 1985, 224) through reading their texts as more than just a manual for violent action. Through approaches like those of Kepel, Fanon and Gerges, I suggest that it can be possible to recover alternative readings of jihadist movements, one of the more enigmatic products of the post-colonial order.

Notes

1 Fighters were directed not to attack the Sadrists during the 2005 Iraqi elections. See 'Iraq Qaeda says to spare anti-U.S. Sadr group – Web', Reuters, 19 September 2005.

2 Pakistan also has its sectarian texts and voices, but there has been little study of its role in the genealogy of sectarianism in contemporary Arabic religious discourse. See Zaman (2012, 27) for the role of Jam'iat al-Ulum al-Islamiyya.
3 IS operative Abu Bakr al-Janabi gives an account of this cooperation (English and Arabic): worldanalysis.net/14/2014/06/abu-bakr-al-janabi-leader-state-baathification-islamic-reveals-realities-feel/ (accessed 17 November 2015).
4 See for example, Graeme Wood, 'What ISIS really wants', *The Atlantic*, March 2015, who argued ISIS 'derives from coherent and even learned interpretations of Islam' but is run by psychopaths; and Jessica Stern and J.M. Berger, *ISIS: The State of Terror*. London: William Collins, 2015, who looked at the group's use of apocalyptic discourse. Michael Weiss and Hassan Hassan, *ISIS: Inside the Army of Terror*. New York: Regan Arts, 2015, typical of the think tank community, sought to explain the group's rise as a function of Assad regime manipulation.
5 See Ocak (2012, 293–299); and Zilfi (1986).
6 While the term 'Islamism' has its origin in French Orientalist tradition as a calque on *Christianisme*, 'Islamist' spread in the wake of the Iranian Revolution in 1979. Its use in Arabic may go back to Nasserist-era debates between Qutbists and the Brotherhood leadership over how to designate themselves and the post-colonial regime. See Ramadan, 1998, 27–28, 439–440.
7 Al-Huzaymi says Ibn Taymiyya's *Kitab al-Iman* was introduced as a teaching manual to contextualize the ideas of *takfir* being pressed by Shukri Mustafa's followers.
8 *Al-Mufawwadat al-Sirriyya bayn al-Arab wa Isra'il: al-Imbratoriyya wa'l-dawla al-yahudiyya*. Cairo: Al Shurouq, 1996.
9 His closing words referring to Rum, 'This is my advice to you; if you hold to it, you will conquer Rum and own the world, if God wills', possibly refer to the hadith in question. He cites the apocalypse gathering place in Dabiq in one speech released in December 2015; see al-Naba 11, 17.3.1437, pp. 2–3.
10 He appears to mean the Rashidun or the Abbasid caliphs, thus discounting the Ottoman (a modern Salafi approach), since in his video sermon in Mosul he refers to the caliphate as 'lost for centuries' (Baghdadi, 2014b). A later sermon attacked the Saudi regime as a facilitator of Western imperialism (Baghdadi, 2014c).
11 See Abu Mohammed al-Adnani's declaration, 29 June 2014, www.youtube.com/watch?v=bA_h_J1I_9A (accessed 15 November 2015). Also 'Da'ish tu'lin isqat al-hudud al-sanam', *al-Nahar*, 29 June 2014, www.annahar.com/article/146329-%D8%AF%D8%A7%D8%B9%D8%B4-%D8%AA%D8%B9%D9%84%D9%86-%D8%A7%D8%B3%D9%82%D8%A7%D8%B7-%D8%A7%D9%84%D8%AD%D8%AF%D9%88%D8%AF-%D8%A7%D9%84%D8%B5%D9%86%D9%85-%D9%81%D9%8A-%D8%AF%D9%8A%D9%88.
12 'I'lan al-khilafa fi-l-mizan al-shar'i', Almaqreze.net, 18 July 2014.
13 'Jail, jihad and exploding kittens', *The Economist*, 1 November 2014. The first edition of ISIL's caliphate-era journal *Dabiq* makes reference to *millat Ibrahim*, in a possible attempt to appeal to Al-Maqdisi (*Dabiq*, 1, pp. 20–25).
14 See 'Egypt's top religious authority condemns Islamic State', Reuters, 12 August 2014, www.reuters.com/article/2014/08/12/us-iraq-security-egypt-mufti-idUSKBN0GC1BN20140812; several days later the Saudi Mufti spoke, 'Grand Mufti: IS is Islam's "enemy No. 1"', *Saudi Gazette*, 20 August 2014, www.saudigazette.com.sa/index.cfm?method=home.regcon&contentid=20140820215352.
15 'Prominent scholars declare ISIS caliphate "null and void"', *Middle East Monitor*, 5 July 2014.
16 Al-Qa'ida insurgents in Saudi Arabia were referred to as *al-fi'a al-dalla* (the errant group).
17 'Fitnat al-khilafa al-'iraqiyya al-maz'uma', Assakina website, 27 July 2014, www.assakina.com/fatwa/49687.html (accessed 4 November 2015).
18 'Ha'yat kibar al-'ulama fi al-sa'udiyya: tafjir masjid al-mashhad fi najran dani"', *al-Quds al-Arabi*, 27 October 2015. 'It isn't a state, it's a gang, and it is isn't Islamic, it's Jahili,' it said.
19 Statement in *al-Riyadh*, 29 September 2015, www.alriyadh.com/1086543 (accessed 3 November 2015).

20 Assakina website, 15 November 2014, www.assakina.com/fatwa/57298.html (accessed 3 November 2015).
21 For example, Natana Delong-Bas, *Wahhabi Islam: From Revival and Reform to Global Jihad*. Cairo: The American University in Cairo, 2005. For academic funding, see the US Department of Education's 2012 foreign gifts report, which lists all external funding since the 1980s to US academic institutions: studentaid.ed.gov/es/sites/default/files/fsa wg/datacenter/library/ForeignGift04052013.xls (accessed 15 November 2015). The site www.foreignlobbying.org lists PR agency payments.
22 Stephen Walt, 'ISIS as Revolutionary State: New Twist on an Old Story', *Foreign Affairs*, November/December 2015.
23 See for example Rif'at Sayyid Ahmad, *Rasa'il Juhayman al-'Utaybi, qa'id al-muqtahimin li'l-Masjid al-Haram bi-Makka*. Cairo: Madbuli, 2004.
24 He says that rehabilitation and not brute force was the best way to deal with militant zealotry, which has echoes of the government's policy of *munasaha* since 2006 in dealing with Saudi adherents of al-Qa'ida.
25 Ibid., 163.
26 Hegghammer and Lacroix translate *milla* as community but I think the sense is more path/religion. The introduction to this Juhayman text is used as a foreword to Maqdisi's *Millat Ibrahim*.
27 Maqdisi's translator uses 'modernistic religion'; *hadara* is being used in the sense of modern and Western.
28 It can be read here: www.muslm.org/vb/showthread.php?291249-%D8%B1%D9%81% D8%B9-%D8%A7%D9%84%D8%A7%D9%84%D8%AA%D8%A8%D8%A7%D8%B3-% D8%B9%D9%86-%D9%85%D9%84%D8%A9-%D9%85%D9%86-%D8%AC%D8%B9 D9%84%D9%87-%D8%A7%D9%84%D9%84%D9%87-%D8%A5%D9%85%D8%A7%D 9%85%D8%A7%D9%8B-%D9%84%D9%90%D9%84%D9%86%D8%A7%D8%B3.
29 Al-Huzaymi says this was aimed at the Salafi tradition in Egypt of Ansar al-Sunna al-Muhammadiyya, but this may be a means of avoiding stating that it targeted mainstream Saudi state Salafism (106–107).
30 It can be read here: www.islamist-movements.com/25726.
31 For a discussion of Bin Baz's relationship with the Saudi leaders, see Steinberg, 2005.
32 *Sahih Muslim*, (41/9(6924): 'The last hour (*al-sa'a*) will only come when the Rum come to A'maq [intended location unclear] or to Dabiq ...'
33 See Robert Vitalis, *America's Kingdom: Mythmaking on the Saudi Oil Frontier*. Stanford, CA: Stanford University Press, 2007.
34 He uses the word *ba'th*, which Michel Aflaq had already used for the Arab secularist party of the same name, while the word was to give way in Islamist discourse to *sahwa* (awakening).
35 It has become de rigueur even for scholars to punctuate discussions of ISIS with clarifying comments of disapproval for its acts, as if there would be doubt about this otherwise.
36 For more on Baghdadi, see Abdel Bari Atwan, 'A Portrait of Caliph Ibrahim', *The Cairo Review of Global Affairs*, Fall 2015.

References

Al-Baghdadi, Abu Bakr (2014a) Sermon (audio), 2 July, soundcloud.com/user989329471/ 7hvtjxvebgbv (an English translation of part of it can be found here: ia902501.us.archive. org/2/items/hym3_22aw/english.pdf).
Al-Baghdadi, Abu Bakr (2014b) Sermon (video), 4 July, www.youtube.com/watch?v= -SZJMMdWC6o.
Al-Baghdadi, Abu Bakr (2014c) Sermon (audio), 13 November, www.youtube.com/watch? v=siVpGHPQ3nY.
Al-Ghaddami, Abdullah (2004) *Hikayat al-Hadatha*. Casablanca: al-Markaz al-Thaqafi al-Arabi.

Al-Huzaymi, Nasir (2011) *Ayyami ma' Juhayman: Kuntu ma' al-Jama'a al-Salafiyya al-Muhtasiba*. Beirut: Arab Network for Research and Publishing.
Al Jazeera (2014) 'Maqdisi yantaqid i'lan al-khilafa wa yuhajim tanzim al-dawla', 29 September, www.aljazeera.net/news/arabic/2014/7/1/%D8%A7%D9%84%D9%85%D9%82%D 8%AF%D8%B3%D9%8A-%D9%8A%D9%86%D8%AA%D9%82%D8%AF-%D8%A5%D 8%B9%D9%84%D8%A7%D9%86-%D8%A7%D9%84%D8%AE%D9%84%D8%A7%D9% 81%D8%A9-%D9%88%D9%8A%D9%87%D8%A7%D8%AC%D9%85-%D8%AA%D9%8 6%D8%B8%D9%8A%D9%85-%D8%A7%D9%84%D8%AF%D9%88%D9%84%D8%A9 (accessed 31 January 2016).
Al-Maqdisi, Abu Muhammad (1984) *Millat Ibrahim (The Religion of Ibrahim): And the Calling of the Prophets and Messengers*. Amman: At-Tibyan Publications.
Al-Maqdisi, Abu Muhammad (1989) *Al-Kawashif al-jaliyya fi kufr al-dawla al-Sa'udiyya*. Minbar al-Tawhid wa'l-Jihad.
Al-Rasheed, Madawi, Kersten, Carool & Shterin, Marat (2012) 'Introduction', in M. Al-Rasheed et al. (Eds) *Demystifying the Caliphate*. London: Hurst.
Al-Shinqiti, Abu'l-Mundhir (2014) 'I'lan al-khilafa fi'l-mizan al-shar'i', *Almaqreze.net*, 18 July, justpaste.it/kil-mon (accessed 31 January 2016).
Al-Utaybi, Juhayman (1978a) 'Fitan wa akhbar al-Mahdi wa nuzul 'Isa 'alayhi'l-salam wa ashratu'l-sa'a'.
Al-Utaybi, Juhayman (1978b) 'Raf' al-iltibas 'an millat man ja'alahu allah imaman li'l-nas'.
Al-Utaybi, Juhayman (1978c) 'Al-Imara wal-bay'a wal-ta'a'.
Al-Zawahiri, Ayman (2001) *Fursan fi rayat al-nabi*. Minbar al-Tawhid wa'l-Jihad.
Atwan, Abdel Bari (2015) 'A portrait of Caliph Ibrahim', *The Cairo Review of Global Affairs*, Fall, www.thecairoreview.com/essays/a-portrait-of-caliph-ibrahim/.
Colonna, Fanny (2003) 'The nation's unknowing other: three intellectuals and the culture(s) of being Algerian, or on the impossibility of subaltern studies in Algeria', in James McDougall (Ed.) *Nation, Society and Culture in North Africa* (pp. 155–170). Frank Cass.
Dabiq, Issues 1–11.
Farag, Abd al-Salam (1982) *Al-Jihad: al-farida al-gha'iba*. Amman.
El-Rouayheb, Khaled (2015) *Islamic Intellectual History in the Seventeenth Century: Scholarly Currents in the Ottoman Empire and the Maghreb*. Cambridge: Cambridge University Press.
Fanon, Frantz (2001) *The Wretched of the Earth*. London: Penguin.
Gerges, Fawaz (2011) *The Rise and Fall of Al-Qaeda*. New York: Oxford University Press.
Hanafi, Hasan (2014) 'Al-Salafiyya wa-l-'Ilmaniyya', in Ahmet Kavas (Ed.) *Tarihte ve Günümüzde Selefilik* (pp. 135–156). Istanbul: Ensar Neşriyat.
Hegghammer, Thomas & Lacroix, Stephane (2007) 'Rejectionist Islamism in Saudi Arabia: the story of Juhayman al-'Utaybi revisited', *International Journal of Middle East Studies*, 39(1).
Kepel, Gilles (1985) *The Prophet and Pharaoh: Muslim Extremism in Egypt*. London: Al Saqi Books.
Mitchell, Richard P. (1969) *The Society of the Muslim Brothers*. London: Oxford University Press.
Ocak, Ahmet Yaşar (2012) *Perspectives and Reflections on Religious and Cultural Life in Medieval Anatolia*. Istanbul: Isis Press.
Qutb, Sayyid (1979) *Ma'alim Fi'l-Tariq*. Cairo: Dar Al-Shurouq, sixth edition.
Ramadan, Tariq (1998) *Aux Sources du Renouveau Musulman: D'al-Afghānī à Ḥassan al-Bannā un Siècle de Réformisme Islamique*. Paris: Bayard Editions/Centurion.
Redissi, Hamadi (2008) 'The refutation of Wahhabism', in *Kingdom Without Borders: Saudi Arabia's Political, Religious and Media Frontiers*. London: Hurst.
Roy, Olivier (2004) *Globalized Islam: The Search for a New Ummah*. London: Hurst.
Sardar, Ziauddin (2008) 'Foreword', in F. Fanon, *Black Skin, White Masks*. London: Pluto.

Spivak, Gayatri Chakravorty (1988) 'Can the subaltern speak?' in Cary Nelson & Lawrence Grossberg (Eds) *Marxism and the Interpretation of Culture*. Urbana: University of Illinois Press.

Steinberg, Guido (2005) 'The Wahhabi ulama and the Saudi state', in Paul Aarts & Gerd Nonneman (Eds) *Saudi Arabia in the Balance*. London: Hurst.

Wagemakers, Joas (2009) 'The transformation of a radical concept: al-wala' wa-l-bara' in the ideology of Abu Muhammad al-Maqdisi', in Roel Meijer, *Global Salafism: Islam's New Religious Movement* (pp. 81–106). London: Hurst.

Voll, John O. (1972) 'The non-Wahhabi Hanbalis of eighteenth-century Syria', *Der Islam*, 49, pp. 277–291.

Zaman, Muhammad Qasim (2012) *Modern Islamic Thought in a Radical Age*. Cambridge: Cambridge University Press.

Zilfi, Madeline C. (1986) 'The Kadizadelis: discordant revivalism in seventeenth-century Istanbul', *Journal of Near Eastern Studies*, 45(4), pp. 251–269.

5

FRIDAY *KHUTBA* WITHOUT BORDERS

Constructing a Muslim audience

Ehab Galal

Introduction

On 3 August 2012, it was announced that a special room for persons with impaired hearing would be opened in the grand mosque of Al-Medina, providing a TV screen on which the Friday *khutba* would be interpreted into sign language. This individualizing and universalizing step reflects an increasing awareness of everyone's right to access Friday prayers, and an opportunity to form their own opinions with regard to their content. People from all walks of life are increasingly able to access and follow the same Friday sermon, worldwide, through modern technology such as satellite TV, the Internet and social media. The access to mediated Friday prayers not only universalizes the messages, but also allows Muslim audiences to become acquainted with preachers from all parts of the Muslim world (Galal, 2014); despite this development, however, research into the Friday *khutba* is still considerably limited.

The screen-mediated Friday sermon has become an inevitable issue to explore, not only due to its far-reaching potential, both locally and transnationally, but also because of its accessibility to Muslim audiences and the composition and rhetoric of the *khutba* through the possible influence that this new communication technology can have. The media have started not only to take over a part of religious communication with the development of new technology and marketing strategies, but also to offer a virtual space for practising Islam: a space that is potentially transnational in its capacity to be broadcast more or less anywhere (Kraidy & Khalil, 2009; Lynch, 2006; Mandaville, 2001). The transnational potential raises a range of questions. Does the *khutba* acquire new functions through the new ways of its mediation? Does the *khutba* message change due to the potentially wider access that audiences have to Arab Muslim satellite TV and YouTube, for instance? How can the *khutba* be explored as part of a transnational Arab Muslim public sphere?

The aim of this chapter is to suggest an analytical approach to the study of mediated *khutba* through satellite TV, which takes into account the programme's relationship with local and international audiences. Three aspects that influence this relationship, and hence the space being offered to audiences, will be of particular interest. First, the *khutba* is broadcast as a programme in itself by most Arab state and some private channels, in competition with other media such as YouTube and Facebook. This is a result of political and religious interests of state or religious institutions and organizations that are behind specific channels, on the one hand, and individuals who personally upload sermons on YouTube on the other. Second, television production adds a particular visual aspect and meaning to the *khutba* by delivering the event in a certain manner. Third, the content of the *khutba* positions the audiences in specific ways and thus creates a particular space.

The presentation of some facts about the broadcasting of *khutba* on Arab satellite television will be made, in the first instance, followed by an introduction to an analytical and theoretical approach regarding transnational television and its relationship with audiences, and third, an analysis of examples of these *khutba* from Sharjah in the United Arab Emirates (UAE), Egypt, Saudi Arabia, Kuwait, Qatar, Algeria, Libya, Sudan and Yemen, broadcast during two armed conflicts in the Middle East that have produced wide media coverage, namely the Israeli attack on Lebanon in 2006 and the Israeli attack on Gaza in August 2014. By choosing cases that both involve the same adversary, Israel, and with the Arab Spring in between, the purpose is to draw attention to the development and potential changes that have influenced the *khutba* during exceptional events such as war. Including the struggle against Israel in both cases gives a better understanding of possible changes due to new configurations of global and Islamic politics. The historical long-term conflict with Israel makes it possible to demonstrate how this relationship is addressed by preachers according to particular circumstances of the period in question.

Khutba al-Juma'a on Arab satellite television

The spread of satellite technology has blurred the boundaries between which channels are national and which ones transnational (Alterman, 1998). The launching of the first Islamic channel, Iqraa, in 1998 encouraged more private channels, among which around 135[1] so-called Islamic satellite channels have since been introduced. While most of the Arab states' television stations broadcast the Friday *khutba*, the private channels are generally more reluctant, especially commercial private satellite channels; not even the privately owned Islamic satellite channels are overly keen to broadcast the *khutba*. Those that do are also the most popular, such as Iqraa and two other Sunni Saudi-owned private Islamic channels, Al-Resaleh and Al-Majd. All three broadcast the *khutba* from Saudi Arabia, either from Mecca or Al-Medina. Well-known Egyptian Islamic channels, with close ties to Saudi Arabia, transmit the *khutba* delivered by the channels' religious main figures such as Al-Rahma TV's Mohammed Hassan and Al-Naas TV's Mohammed Hussain

Yacoub. Shi'a channels such as Al-Kawther, Ahl-Albyt, Al-Anwar and Al-Mustafa often transmit from Shi'ite holy places, for instance, Karbala in Iraq. These Sunni and Shi'a channels are all characterized by their popularity among Arab audiences compared to other Islamic channels, and by being financially well established, either as part of larger media consortia or as individual channels – they all have close relations with political and wealthy elites.

State channels that broadcast the *khutba* and transmit them via satellite mainly represent secular Arab states, with the exception of Lebanon and Syria before the Arab Spring 2011. The Arab states have increasingly attempted to legitimize their form of religious discourse and practices during the past 40 years of the Islamic awakening, in order to outdo the discourses of Islamic movements. A result of this process of Islamization has been a massive increase in the number of mosques and *zawayya* (prayer rooms without a pulpit) being created, for example, on the ground floor of private properties. This explosion in the number of mosques and *zawayya* has made it impossible for states such as Egypt to meet the demand for trained, qualified imams from Al-Azhar, making it more difficult for the state to monitor what is being disseminated in the name of Islam; thus, the transmission of the *khutba* by state channels can be understood as an attempt to spread their understanding of the 'right' concepts of Islam to more people, by using modern satellite technology. The choice of broadcasting these sermons may be seen simultaneously as the state's support of the idea that the *khutba* is legitimate only within a specific religious sphere, represented here by the mosque, and TV transmission's adaptation to people's desire to gain access to this religious sphere through electronic media.

The *khutba* on these state television channels is an example of what Sami Zubaida has called 'compartmentalization' of different aspects of the modern individual's life in the public secular sphere. Religion has become isolated from the transmission of movies, entertainment, children's programmes and so on – separate aspects, separate programmes (Zubaida, 2005, 444). This is supported by the fact that religion has not had a predominant place on Arab TV either before or now; most Arab countries have limited the representation of religion in national media, for example, as late as 2002, when Islam was flowering in Egypt, religious programming on the eight Egyptian national TV channels took up no more than 5% of their transmissions (Galal, 2003). Lila Abu-Lughod describes this separation between secular and religious spheres as a natural consequence of secular state building after obtaining national independence (Abu-Lughod, 2005): arguably, a way of putting religion in its proper place.

The *khutba*, previously intended for the local or national public, now has a worldwide audience through being broadcast by satellite TV. The choice that audiences currently have to pick and choose their preferred programmes from a plethora of different channels, from media of different countries, and in different languages, is limitless. Transmission of the *khutba* by national, state-owned satellite channels illustrates their participation in the struggle to define the transnational Muslim public. The three largest, privately owned Saudi Islamic channels (Iqraa, Al-Majd and Al-Resaleh) are not alone in broadcasting religious programmes: the

British English-language 'Islam Channel' also broadcasts its *khutba* in English from Saudi Arabia, as do some of the state satellite channels periodically in the Gulf countries.

Wider audiences have become the strategic target for many more competing religious, political and commercial interests (cf. Eickelman & Anderson, 1999): Iqraa transmits its English and Arabic TV channels to most parts of the world through 13 different satellite providers. Some 134 or more other Islamic Arab channels transmit mostly through NileSat, Arabsat and the privately owned Noorsat, along with state and commercial satellite channels. While the Islamic satellite channels define their objective as promoting a universal Islam and transnational *Ummah* (Muslim nation) identity (Galal, 2012), on the one hand, state-owned channels might have other, more national objectives behind their transmission of the *khutba*, on the other. The question is whether the *khutba* in practice reflects these differences. Does the transmission of the *khutba* serve national, transnational or other purposes? An attempt at answering these questions will be made by analysing some of the *khutba* broadcast on different satellite channels during two periods of armed conflicts in the Middle East. From 12 July to 14 August 2006, an armed conflict between Hizbollah in Lebanon and the Israeli army led to more than 1,000 mainly civilian Lebanese being killed and the Lebanese infrastructure being damaged (Harb, 2009). On 8 July 2014, Israel initiated a military operation against Hamas in the Gaza Strip and was met by rocket attacks by Hamas. The following seven weeks of conflict resulted in thousands of people, mainly Gazans, being killed (Bratchford, 2014). As in any other war, the media became a propaganda machine used in the struggle of legitimacy (Harb, 2009). Also, the mediated *khutba* took part in this struggle.

The *khutba* that have been selected were broadcast in August 2006, during the peak of the Israeli–Lebanese war, and in August 2014, when the war between Israel and Gaza was at its peak. This case material can be considered exceptional, since it is taken from the periods of conflict that represented a strong symbolic value in the Arab and Islamic world, due to the role that Israel played in them; consequently, these case studies are characterized by intensity, which, according to Helle Neergaard, offers rich information and manifests the intensive phenomena involved (Neergaard, 2007, 28). These examples therefore offer concentrated samples of how transnational topics are covered and ascribed meaning across different national and religious divides; furthermore, by choosing sermons from different countries and in different years, it is possible to identify potential variances and similarities across time and place. The choice of different countries will uncover correspondence with, or inconsistencies between, preachers in the conservative Gulf countries and more liberal religious countries like Egypt and Algeria. The chosen sermons are between 20 minutes and about an hour and a half long. Those from 2006 were all broadcast on state satellite channels from Algeria, Libya, Yemen, Sharjah, Egypt (ESC1), Sudan, Abu Dhabi, Qatar and Kuwait. The transmission from Abu Dhabi TV, however, was the *khutba* from Mecca, while the analysed sermons from 2014 were broadcast on Egyptian, Jordanian and Saudi state satellite channels, and one *khutba* was broadcast on the Egyptian On-TV, a privately owned, secular satellite channel.

I begin with a brief introduction to the analytical and theoretical concepts of the *khutba*'s relationship with its transnational audience, prior to the general analysis.

How to explore *khutba al-jum'a* on satellite television

The Friday prayer has, since the time of the Prophet, had a double function of religious ritual and political forum. Both in the Qur'an (*Al-Jumu'a*, The Day of Congregation, 62: 9) and in the Hadith,[2] it is possible to find statements on the special significance of *Youm al-Jum'a* (Friday) (Abdel Haleem, 1990, 36–40). The word *Jum'a* comes from the root *Jama'a* – 'to gather', consequently, Friday is considered the weekly holiday when friends and family gather together.

Abdel Haleem describes how the Friday prayer and sermons initially had two parallel functions: first, it was prayer and preaching used by the authorities as an opportunity to bring together the people, to disseminate their political goals and convince people about their merits; second, it was to explain the religion and its rules. During the Prophet's time, the sermons included, among other things, *Al-Mu'aamalaat* (how to deal with each other), *Al-Akhlaaq* (morality) and *Al-'Ibaadaat* (dedication, sacrifice) (Abdel Haleem, 1990). The mosque had many functions in addition to the framework of religious ceremonies or rituals, including a political function, as it was linked to education, law and social welfare (Gaffney, 1994). Modern states, however, have increasingly had an interest in making the mosque a place only for rituals (Gaffney, 1994), incorporating services, education and so on into centralized bureaucracy. Besides introducing general education and social services, the Arab states have had different motives of supporting this development, such as secularization and control of the religious establishment. However, the states' general lack of being able to provide education and social services has strengthened the success of Islamic groups, such as Salafi movements and the Muslim Brotherhood, as alternative providers leading to reinvention of the mosque as a complex social, political and religious space (cf. Mahmood, 2011).

Gaffney's (1994) analysis of a series of sermons simultaneously shows that they each, in their own way, contain political messages. The Islamic groups have particularly been a contributing factor to increased politicization of Friday sermons and the mosque's role in society; consequently, the Friday sermons have become a battleground for religious and political authority (Gaffney, 1994). A particular interest of existing research has been whether the Friday sermons are a conservative instrument to keep people in a religious, political and social status quo, or an instrument for change; until recently, in that context, nothing much has been said on religious programming, even less on the *khutba*; where it has, it has mostly been seen as an obstacle for the development of a civic public (Al-Hroub, 2006). There has been little elucidation or in-depth discussion – with a few exceptions – on whether religious programming should have any other kind of distinct influence on the development of an Arab Muslim civic public (Galal, 2009b; Sætren, 2010). It is considered more profitable here to explore the competing civic public, of which Arab national television in general, and Arab transnational television in particular, are co-producers, rather than the tendency to measure the extent of a civic public by comparing it to those in Western countries. It is far from clear how the Friday sermons operate as a political instrument in a religious form; therefore, in order to identify some of the complexities that exist in the transmission of Friday *khutba*, an investigation will be made into how the sermons discursively construct *al-Ummah* and the Islamic community.

The *khutba* is an excellent empirical illustration of how a differentiated media system is currently taking place in the Arab world, compared to the 1990s. Satellite channels have entered into the global media landscape and illustrate that liberalization and globalization of the media does not necessarily result in a uni-directional media flow, but rather uncovers an increased cultural, religious and political complexity.

Positioning theory (Harré & van Langenhove, 1999) is used in order to analyse the content of the programmes and their relationship with their audiences: by exploring how each programme positions its audience, the researcher obtains access to the programme's preferred interpretation and the subject position it offers to its audiences; however, it does not mean that audiences necessarily interpret it accordingly; from this perspective, the *khutba* are analysed as identity discourses promoted by the preacher. The presented discourse(s) of identity may well interfere with, stand in contrast to, or be subordinate to others: how the intersection between religious, ethnic, national and other identities are presented is of analytical interest.

The *khutba* is initially a one-way communication through which the religious authority tells the audiences what to think and what to believe; in the process, the preacher appropriately addresses particular audiences in order to make them identify with the message, talking within a specific storyline in which a certain normative order is projected. The normative order proposed in the *khutba* is mainly constructed through two kinds of discursive process: 1 by offering the audiences a specific position as a righteous Muslim; and 2 by rhetorical re-descriptions of Muslim history and events, presenting them as social and religious icons. The positioning of the Muslim as part of one imagined Muslim community is visually strengthened through the transmission of the *khutba*, which focuses on picturing the common prayer of many people and reflects the inclusiveness and universality of the Muslim community. The paradoxical nature of this claimed universality of the Islamic message, the bounded time and place, and the politically and historically embedded message, is another relevant feature to examine.

The subject positions offered by the preacher to Muslim audiences shall be pinpointed in the following analyses of the sermons broadcast in 2006 and 2014, and how the narratives were presented as part of the normative Islamic order and part of a current political and social order. The exploration of the positions held by subject audiences and the rhetorical re-descriptions will help to identify to whom the *khutba* were addressed and, more specifically, how these sermons constructed the normative order of the Muslim public.

Different *khutba*, different proposed Muslim subject positions

These cases of periods of armed conflict have deliberately been selected as they could arguably be considered exceptional. The incentive behind this choice is to be able to demonstrate the different storylines produced in response to events that intensively mobilized transnational feelings and political reactions in a global setting. The selection of these two particular cases, which have the emotional potential to lead the transnational Arab Muslim public in the same direction, offers the possibility of being able to identify how different paths are constructed and authorized by the preachers.

The various channels practised diverse methods for the transmission of the *khutba*; most countries broadcast the *khutba* every Friday with the same few preachers such as those from Sudan, while countries like Egypt, and, to a lesser degree, Algeria, presented successive preachers on Fridays; in Egypt, moreover, the place of the *khutba* typically changed between different mosques, often chosen due to their position vis-à-vis a local project or current event. Two ideal preachers seem to have been represented in August 2006 and in less uniform versions in 2014: first, the *'Alim*, who represent scholarly, state-sponsored, institutional Islam; and second, the *Mujaheed*, who represent the mission-oriented defenders of the faith (Gaffney, 1994). They both represent the state and are also trained scholars, which means that the *Mujaheed* on state satellite channels also have another role in non-governmental mosques, such as those who officiate on private, Salafi, Islamic satellite channels (Al-Rahma and Al-Naas), or on social media. Private or transmitted recordings of these often self-appointed preachers are popular uploads on YouTube and Facebook. This distinction between state imams is relevant due to their different delivery styles, storylines and the normative order of their *khutba*.

The findings of the analysis of sermons from August 2006 and 2014 are presented in the next section: in 2006, all the preachers generally seemed to refer to the war in Lebanon, although in different storylines. The picture is more blurred regarding Gaza in 2014, as shall be seen below.

The *'Alim* universalizing the Muslim *Ummah*

State channels that broadcast *khutba* of the *'Alim* type on 4 August 2006 were Sharjah, Egypt, Saudi Arabia and Kuwait. In 2014, the same kind of *khutba* was transmitted by Saudi Arabia, while the Egyptian Al-Azhar sheikh appeared to be giving a more hybrid speech on the Egyptian state channel. The commonality of these types of *khutba* lay in their presentation of a topic related to war and conflict, and to the state of the Muslim people, at that time, but did not give special attention to the current wars in Lebanon or Gaza, except as a reference point. They referred to the Prophet Mohammed instead, and how he responded in times of war and conflict: a war narrative inscribed in a storyline of universal Muslim history.

The *khutba* is a long prayer of praise, the essence of which is worshipping God and referring to the Prophet and what he said and what he did. The message is that those who worship God will be saved by Him; they will not experience anything evil or bad, but will live in peace. The subject position offered by these preachers was to be a pious Muslim: pray, pay *zakat*,[3] follow God's wishes and not to engage in the forbidden (*haram*[4]). This, according to the preacher, was the only way out of the misery being suffered by Muslims at the time.

The *khutba* from Sharjah had the title 'The Islamic civilization in peace and war'; without mentioning Lebanon by name, the main message to Muslims was 'be patient'. The preacher gave several examples from the time of the Prophet, who was frequently encouraged by his followers to attack their enemies, but he refused; instead, he told them to be patient and to pray to God and continuously pay their *zakat*. The preacher also referred to the rules of war: *wa qaatilou fi sabil Allah al-lazi yuqaatilounakum. Allah la yuhibbu al-Mu'tadiyn* (fight for God against those who fight you, and do not attack because God does not love those who attack). The closest reference to the Lebanese war was when he identified Muslims as different from those who, at the time, killed women and children and burnt down trees and houses. The *khutba* from Kuwait emphasized the importance of piety and prayers.

The *khutba* broadcast from Abu Dhabi (and transmitted from the Ka'aba in Saudi Arabia) was very similar. The suffering of the Muslim *Ummah* was presented in general terms such as catastrophes, suffering and fire. The only solution was to practise what is written in the Book (Qur'an) and to follow the Prophet. The subject position of the Muslim was to be pious before it was too late, but also to help and support each other, the Lebanese people and the Palestinians; however, no advice was given on how to help the people in need. The *khutba* transmitted by Egyptian state TV emphasized Muslims' unity; despite belonging to different peoples and tribes, Muslims had to be good, righteous and united. He referred to the period of the Prophet and spent some time reflecting on the split of Muslims into different religious schools, which divided them, and disrupted and weakened the Muslim nation. The Egyptian preacher was not very specific but briefly mentioned the Muslim brothers in Lebanon, Iraq and Afghanistan.

The Saudi *khutba* by Sheikh Abd al-Rahman al-Sudis was broadcast on 15 August 2014 and focused on Muslims who, in the name of Islam, violently attacked, kidnapped or terrorized other Muslims and non-Muslims alike. As in the 2006 sermons of the *'Alim* type, al-Sudis mainly referred to historical events and the time of the Prophet in order to criticize the infidels among Muslims. One of many examples he gave was *al-khawarij*,[5] which was established after the death of the Prophet. He argued that the story repeated itself and warned against such Muslim groups:

> They have destroyed pure Islam's tolerant image. And they do that in the name of religion. Those who do not know anything about Islam believe that everything coming from current days' *al-khawarij* is Islam. In reality Islam is innocent and has nothing to do with their behaviour. We are enormously sad because of the violence and misinterpretation. Human lives have no value to

them. They are bloodthirsty. They kill innocent people. They destroy everything, human beings and nations. They do not listen to anybody. Not even to God who has forbidden killing. God forbade extremism.

Without explicitly referring to specific groups, the preacher talked about terrorism. When he referred to the violence in Palestine, Gaza and Levantine countries, it was most of all an implicit reference to the threats against the Saudi state, but he also explained that it was a war against humanity. He stressed that terrorism may be committed by groups, organizations as well as nations, the last one being the most dangerous, but he did not specify whether he was talking about Hamas, ISIS (Islamic State in Iraq and Syria), Israel or Syria. The Saudi *khutba* positioned the Muslims as either true believers, knowing their religion, or as infidels or terrorists who misrepresented Islam. He especially addressed the Muslim youth and asked them to 'wake up', reject the false believers and their violence, and work towards dialogue. He thus positioned the youth as particularly receptive to extremism.

The storyline and proposed Muslim subject positions are very similar in these five *khutba*, with the exception of the Saudi one from 2014, in which it was inscribed within a Muslim nation as the spiritual religious community, the *Ummah*, defined by its historical and religious roots at the time of the Prophet. The past, present and future of the Muslims are interconnected through the storyline and normative order of the *khutba*. The references to war, implying the war in Lebanon, conflicts, catastrophes, internal struggles among Muslims, were presented as *fitna* (chaos). The *fitna* of the present was explained by the lack of patience, justice and fairness in conflict, gratitude and prayer, or, as in the Saudi *khutba* from 2014, as lack of education and knowledge. All values were inscribed in the normative order by referring back to the time of the Prophet, when the Muslims were prospering. The link to the past explains the situation of today and the possibilities of tomorrow, by encouraging the Muslims to follow the teachings of the Prophet; if the Muslims followed the normative order presented according to this *khutba*, the Muslim nation would have peace, prosperity and progress.

The message fitted the transnational broadcasting theme, because it addressed all Muslims as equal members of the Muslim nation; by ignoring, or at least displacing, the suffering of specific national groups of Muslims such as the Lebanese in 2006 and Palestinians in Gaza in 2014, it became a generalized theme for all Muslims. No one had a specific responsibility, particularly for severely affected groups such as the Lebanese and Palestinians, which, according to the preacher, only needed attention at a general level; hence, the Muslim subject position in these *khutba* is universalized and detached from modern historical, political or social contexts. There were some brief references to current events, but the preacher repeatedly used the language of the Qur'an and Hadith: it is up to the individual Muslim to combine this Muslim subject position with a political, national, ethnic, gender or consumer identity of the day – the *khutba* could have been appropriate for any historical moment.

The hybrid *khutba*

The *khutba* from Qatar in 2006 and from Egypt in 2014 separated themselves from the others by producing a less abstract enemy, despite the similarities with the above-mentioned *khutba*. The Qatari preacher referred to the fierce Jewish attacks and the Zionist disruption of peace. He also constructed the Jewish enemy as being cowards, not being able to stand up to the righteous people, and he warned against forgetting the Palestinians, which was what the Zionists wanted Muslims to do. However, despite this much more political discourse compared to the '*Alim khutba*, the solution was the same as the Kuwaiti *khutba*: prayer and entreating God to help the brothers in need.

The *khutba* by the Al-Azhar Sheikh Ahmed Omar Hashim, on 1 August 2014, consisted of two parts: the first was a long evocation of Muslims to remember the virtues of Ramadan, the month of fasting that had just finished. Virtues like mercy, forgiveness, good works, helpfulness, honesty and prayer were highlighted and presented as the basic values of the Muslim *Ummah*. The sheikh praised dialogue and respect for opposing opinions, thus avoiding violence and conflict. The second part, which took eight minutes (compared to 15 minutes for the first part), addressed the global Muslim *Ummah* and Arab and Muslim leaders:

> Oh, all Arab and Muslim state leaders living in East and West, you should know that your countries will be eaten by your enemy, and the international Zionists are attacking your brothers in Palestine, smashing the country, killing the people. You will be asked about this when facing God at the day of Judgment, if you do not confront the danger, stop the enemy, and if you do not unite and leave the rift you live with behind you, and stop slaughtering each other. The Prophet and the Qur'an have warned you.

Despite this clear identification of the enemy, the solution was the virtues of the first part of the sermon: peaceful dialogue, prayers and solidarity. In this case, the subject position is not, in substance, very different from the '*Alim* type.

The revolutionary *khutba*

The four *khutba* broadcast by Algeria, Libya, Sudan and the Yemen on 4 August 2006, and the one broadcast by Jordanian television on 8 August 2014, underpinned the Muslims' position in a global field of power struggles. Not only was the enemy clearly specified, but also the nation-states seemed to play a larger role than in the '*Alim khutba*.

The Algerian *khutba* was the most complex, with many references made to historical and present-day figures and events; citations from the Qur'an and Hadith were minimal. The key message was not that different from the former, emphasizing the need for Muslims to stand united. The preacher supported his statement by referring to the Qana massacre of 1996, in which more than 50 Lebanese were killed, including many children. He also referred to the second Qana massacre on 30 July 2006, in which 28 civilians were killed, of whom 16 were children (Human Rights Watch, 2006). He blamed Western democracies and the United Nations for not condemning the killings by pointing out their double standard when it involved Israel. Britain was also blamed for acknowledging Israel in 1948, and Israel for being the 'evil tumour' in the Muslim nation. Stressing the right to fight for one's freedom, he questioned the Western definition of terrorism. He mentioned the Algerian fight against the French colonizers, and the legacy of colonialism. This 'being colonized' experience was later repeated, giving the situation in Gaza and Lebanon as an example:

> Our ancestors lived more than 100 years under colonial power. That is why we know what colonial power means. Or in better words: the destructive power of the colonial power. The Arab land is under occupation.

The new colonial powers were, first and foremost, the USA and Israel, to which the preacher continually referred. The heroes, on the other hand, were the freedom fighters. By using the term 'freedom fighters', he takes part in the discursive struggle over in this case the contested term of freedom fighters, who from another, for instance Israeli, perspective would be 'terrorists' (Jenkins, 2003). He ended his speech by encouraging the Muslims to support their brothers in Lebanon with money.

The *khutba* from Libya, Sudan and the Yemen were quite similar. The Libyan preacher introduced his *khutba* with more traditional quotations, but then specifically criticized the Zionist attacks on Lebanon and Palestine in particular, and the present-day crusaders in general, but the greatest enemy was the Zionists. The *khutba* from Sudan attacked the Jews, while positioning the Muslims as the only freedom fighters of the day. The *khutba* from the Yemen was similar to the Algerian one by presenting the Zionists, the Americans and British as the enemy. The Yemeni preacher first blamed 'the enemy' for dividing the Muslims into factions, which had led to conflicts between different schools and movements within Islam, then continued with a long rhetorical appeal to the Muslim *Ummah*:

> Oh, the Muslim *Ummah*, your blood is pouring and your honour violated in Palestine and Lebanon. It is a religious duty as a Muslim to support the Muslim brothers in the victory. Oh, the Muslim *Ummah*, your brothers in Palestine are being slaughtered, and your Muslim brothers in Lebanon have been defeated. What are you doing? Oh, the Muslim Nation, the slaughtering is intensifying. Your children and women are being attacked in both Palestine and Lebanon. What are you doing? Oh, you, leaders of Muslim states, the Muslim countries are being destroyed and the rights of Islam's children have been stolen. What are you doing? Oh, the Muslim *Ummah*, it is time for *jihad* with your life, money, help and prayers. It is a duty of all Muslims, where are they, the *mujahideen*?[6]

The appeal continued, but became more specific by referring not only to the Hadith but also to the plight of the Yemeni people, who, as the people of wisdom, should support and help people in need. The appeal ended by asking the Yemenis to donate money, food and clothes, and to pray, followed by the information that the president had made the process easy by opening a bank account for that purpose.

The storyline in the *khutba* by the Jordanian Sheikh Ahmed Shahrory on 8 August 2014 constructed the enemy as not only the Zionists and Western countries, but also Arab countries and their pan-Arab and nationalist ideologies that had weakened the Muslim *Ummah*. He directly addressed the Egyptian people and asked them to remember that they were Muslims, Arabs and Egyptians, and should support the freedom fighters, and not the Jews against fellow Muslims.[7] Gaza was depicted as an almost ideal Muslim state. The preacher had found security, little crime, civilization and order in Gaza a few years earlier, because Gaza was led by people who believed in and practised God's way, he argued. Gaza had achieved what many other Arab capital cities had not. The message was to fight and work:

> God's victories are not won by lying on the sofa. It is achieved by confrontation and work. In order to achieve victory, God's *sunnah*[8] tell the Muslims to be patient, to accept killings, wounding, destruction, miseries and martyrs.

The storylines and subject positions of the Muslim in these five *khutba* are similar, but due to the different narratives they vary more than the *'Alim khutba*. The Algerian, Libyan, Sudanese, Yemeni and Jordanian *khutba* all construct the Muslim nation as a colonized and wrongly persecuted community. The Algerian *khutba*, however, inscribes this colonization into modern history of Western colonization, while the Libyan inscribes it in the history of the Crusaders as the Christians' persecution of the Muslims. The Sudanese *khutba* inscribes the war as part of an ongoing battle between the Jews and the Muslims, while the Yemeni *khutba* concentrates on the Israeli–Arab conflict of modern times. The Jordanian *khutba* from 2014 turns the victim (Gaza) into a model Muslim state; furthermore, mutual disagreements and interests between different Arab Muslim countries are highlighted at the expense of the Zionists: by constructing different storylines, the various *khutba* also illustrate diverse subject positions.

All five *khutba* position the Muslim audience as members of the Muslim *Ummah* and therefore are also responsible for, or are part of, what was occurring in Lebanon and Gaza. The conflicts in Lebanon and Palestine were not discussed as exceptional cases, but as generalized conflicts with 'the Other', the aggressor, creating a lack of internal Muslim unity – an imagined Muslim transnational community is crystallized as the natural 'Us'. National particularities in the Algerian, Yemeni and Jordanian *khutba*, however, were also at play; in the first two (Algerian and Yemini) the references to national belonging were explicit, whereas in the Jordanian *khutba*, nationality stood in the way of the Muslim *Ummah*, as Egyptians were not addressed in order to mobilize the Egyptians as Egyptians, but rather as fellow Muslims. The result was that Muslims were positioned not only as members of the *Ummah*, but also as subjects of nation-states.

The solution in the first four *khutba* was to donate money and to pray, even though the freedom fighters were praised; only in the Jordanian *khutba* was war presented as a necessary evil, but neither the individual Muslim nor Arab leaders were directly encouraged to undertake this course of action; instead, they were urged to protest and to support the Muslim brothers in Lebanon and Palestine.

The local *khutba*

State satellite channels and privately owned ones may choose to broadcast Friday *khutba*, as mentioned at the beginning of this chapter, which illustrates what appears to be an increasing complexity. One of the latest is On-TV, a privately owned Egyptian satellite channel, which represents another tendency in the *khutba* to veer away from the evocation of the global Muslim *Ummah* towards a more local, national positioning of the audiences. On-TV broadcast a *khutba* from a tent, arranged as a mosque and placed in the middle of the new Suez Canal project on 29 August 2014. It was inaugurated by the Egyptian President Al-Sisi under huge media coverage. The *khutba* was, first and foremost, an attempt to mobilize a high work ethic, not only in the name of Islam, but also in the name of the nation – 'Our religion is a religion of work', the preacher argued. The *khutba* contained two parts: worship and promoting the nation. Referring to the Qur'an and the Prophet, the preacher presented work as an Islamic duty, and the hard-working man as loved by God. The preacher turned from a general exposition to the workers involved in the Suez Canal project, and asked them to work hard for the benefit of the nation and, ultimately, to receive appreciation on the Day of Judgment. The audiences were clearly addressed as citizens who needed to give their best in order to fulfil their duty, not only as Muslims but also as Egyptian nationals. Being Muslim and being members of the nation converge, thus postponing the duty towards the greater Muslim community – *Ummah* – to the Day of Judgment. No mention was made of Gaza or any other current conflicts in the region.

Conclusion

The analysed *khutba* appear in accordance with political and religious discourses in the Arab world, without having changed much as ritual in form or function. The *khutba* is still informative, mobilizing and spiritual in different combinations, and functions as proof to the believer of the link between the religious historical past and the political present and future. There are also distinct differences: the *khutba* that are able to mediate the most generalized Muslim subject position are the sermons that are least political, while those that refer to concrete enemies and nationalities risk positioning Muslims in their particularities at a higher level; therefore, in the contexts of transnational media, if the preacher wishes to address the whole of the Muslim community within the same speech, a high degree of abstract reasoning is required for this purpose – consequently, the narrative of the Prophet works as a reference point. The more particular the Muslim position becomes, especially in accordance with specific state politics and despite the repetitive invocation of the Muslim *Ummah*, the more concrete the sermon. In broad terms these differences are present in both 2006 and 2014. The sermons from 2014, however, appear to have an increased focus on internal conflicts among Muslims, while the positioning of the Zionist and the West as the enemy receives less attention. The internal conflicts may be presented as abstract or concrete, and between Muslim factions or Muslim countries. The point is that this focus creates other subject positions on offer to the audience: they are now asked not only to identify themselves as a universalized category of Muslim, but also to take a position against other Muslims. The sermons in 2014 seem less preoccupied with the concrete events in Gaza than their preoccupation with Lebanon in 2006. Part of the explanation is the development in the Arab world, after the Arab Spring, which has left the countries with individual problems and challenges. Hence, the focus on Islam on the global scene that followed 11 September 2001 and the Danish cartoon crisis has moved into an increasing emphasis on internal aspects that have been further strengthened by Hamas's challenge of the Sunni Islam authority of Saudi Arabia and Egypt. Hizbollah, on the other hand, as a Shi'a movement, is not considered a real rival to Sunni states in the same way as Hamas. It appears, furthermore, that the increasing complexity of, and competition between, satellite and digital media leads to less universalization and more diversity.

Notes

1 From Itihad iza'at al-Dewwal al-'Arabiya (2013).
2 Hadith refers to the record of the traditions or sayings of the Prophet Mohammed (Speight, 1995).
3 Muslims with the financial means are obliged to give a certain percentage of their wealth as *zakat* (2.5% of net worth, deducted annually). It is a form of charity, almsgiving, donation or contribution, but, contrary to these, *zakat* is a formal duty (Al-Shiekh, 1995, 366).
4 *Haram* means 'forbidden' or 'taboo' and evokes constraint; an act deemed *haram* is one forbidden (Reinhart, 1995, 101).
5 *Al-khawarij* ('exiters') is the name of the third major sectarian grouping in Islam, with Sunni and Shi'a as the other two. It traces its beginning to a religious–political controversy over the Caliphate between 656 and 661 (Williams, 1995).
6 *Mujahideen* is a term used for Islamic freedom fighters or holy warriors. The term has been used for guerrilla fighters in Afghanistan among others (Roy, 1995).
7 Egypt took on the not always popular role of mediator between the Israelis and Hamas in Gaza during the conflict, trying to negotiate a ceasefire (Dorsey, 2014).
8 The term *sunnah* connotes 'established customs, precedent, the conduct of life, and cumulative tradition', most often referring to the Prophet Mohammed's *sunnah* (Nanji, 1995, 139).

References

Abdel Haleem, M.D. (1990) *Khutbat al-Jum'a wa al-Itisaal bi al-Jamaahir*. Cairo: Maktabat al-Angelo al-Masriyya.
Abu-Lughod, L. (2005) *Dramas of Nationhood: The Politics of Television in Egypt*. Cairo: The American University in Cairo Press.

Al-Hroub, K. (2006) 'Satellite media and social change in the Arab world', in *Arab Media in the Information Age* (pp. 89–119). The Emirates Center for Strategic Studies and Research.
Al-Shiekh, A. (1995) 'Zakat', in J.L. Esposito (Ed.) *The Oxford Encyclopedia of the Modern Islamic World* (pp. 366–370). New York: Oxford University Press.
Alterman, J.B. (1998) *New Media, New Politics? From Satellite Television to the Internet in the Arab World*. Washington, DC: The Washington Institute for Near East Policy.
Bratchford, G. (2014) 'Visualizing a society on the brink: Gaza and Hebron', *Journal of Arab & Muslim Media Research*, 7(2 & 3), pp. 145–162.
Dorsey, J. (2014) 'The Cairo talks: mediation or end game in the Gaza war?' *The World Post*, www.huffingtonpost.com/james-dorsey/the-cairo-talks-mediation_b_5665333.html (accessed 23 February 2015).
Eickelman, D.F. & Anderson, J.B. (eds) (1999) *New Media in the Muslim World. The Emerging Public Sphere*. Bloomington, IN & Indianapolis, IN: Indiana University Press.
Gaffney, P.D. (1994) *The Prophet's Pulpit. Islamic Preaching in Contemporary Egypt*. Los Angeles, CA: University of California Press.
Galal, E. (2003) 'Islam via satellite', in L.P. Galal and I. Liengaard (Eds) *At være muslim i Danmark* (pp. 93–107). Copenhagen: Anis.
Galal, E. (2009a) 'Yusuf al-Qaradawi and the new Islamic TV', in B. Gräf and J. Skovgaard-Petersen (Eds) *The Global Mufti: The Phenomenon of Yusuf al-Qaradawi* (pp. 149–180). London: Hurst.
Galal, E. (2009b) *Identiteter og livsstil på islamisk satellit-tv. En indholdsanalyse af udvalgte programmers positioneringer af muslimer* (Identity and Lifestyle on Islamic Satellite-Television: A content analysis of selected programmes' positioning of Muslims). PhD thesis, University of Copenhagen.
Galal, E. (2012) 'Modern Salafi broadcasting: Iqra'a channel (Saudi Arabia)', in K. Hroub (Ed.) *Religious Broadcasting in the Middle East* (pp. 57–79). London: Hurst.
Galal, E. (2014) 'Audience responses to Islamic TV: between resistance and piety', in E. Galal (Ed.) *Arab TV-Audiences. Negotiating Religion and Identity* (pp. 29–50). Frankfurt: Peter Lang.
Hall, S. (2006) 'The West and the rest: discourse and power', in R. Maaka and C. Andersen (Eds) *The Indigenous Experience: Global Perspectives*. Toronto: Canadian Scholars' Press.
Harb, Z. (2009) 'The July 2006 war and the Lebanese blogosphere: towards an alternative media tool in covering wars', *Journal of Media Practice*, 10(2–3), pp. 255–258.
Harré, R. & van Langenhove, L. (1999) 'Introducing positioning theory', in R. Harré & L. van Langenhove (Eds) *Positioning Theory: Moral Contexts of Intentional Action* (pp. 14–31). Malden: Blackwell Publishers.
Hjarvard, S. (2009) 'Ustabile forbindelser: Medier i en globaliseret verden', in E. Galal & M. Thunø (Eds) *Globale medier i verdens brændpunkter: religion, politik og kultur* (pp. 9–22). Copenhagen: Museum Tusculanum Press.
Human Rights Watch (2006) *Israel/Lebanon: Qana Death Toll at 28 International Inquiry Needed into Israeli Air Strike*. www.hrw.org/news/2006/08/01/israel/lebanon-qana-death-toll-28 (accessed 7 November 2015).
Itihad iza'at al-Dewwal al-'Arabiya (2013) *Al-Bath al-Fada'iy al-'Arabi: al-Taqrir al-Sanawi 2012–2013*. Tunis: Arab States Broadcasting Union.
Jenkins, P. (2003) *Images of Terror. What We Can and Can Not Know about Terrorism*. New York: Aldine de Gruyter.
Kraidy, M. & Khalil, J.F. (2009) *Arab Television Industries*. London: Palgrave Macmillan.
Lynch, M. (2006) *Voices of the New Arab Public. Iraq, Al-Jazeera, and Middle East Politics Today*. New York: Columbia University Press.
Mahmood, S. (2011) *Politics of Piety: The Islamic Revival and the Feminist Subject*. Princetown, NJ: Princeton University Press.

Mandaville, P. (2001) *Transnational Muslim Politics. Reimagining the Umma.* London: Routledge.

Mellor, N., et al. (2011) *Arab Media Globalization and Emerging Media Industries.* Cambridge: Polity Press.

Nanji, A.A. (1995) 'Sunnah', in J.L. Esposito (Ed.) *The Oxford Encyclopedia of the Modern Islamic World* (pp. 136–139). New York: Oxford University Press.

Neergaard, H. (2007) *Udvælgelse af cases i kvalitative undersøgelser.* Frederiksberg: Samfundslitteratur.

Reinhart, A.K. (1995) 'Haram', in J.L. Esposito (Ed.) *The Oxford Encyclopedia of the Modern Islamic World* (p. 101). New York: Oxford University Press.

Roy, O. (1995) 'Afghan Mujahidin', in J.L. Esposito (Ed.) *The Oxford Encyclopedia of the Modern Islamic World* (pp. 174–175). New York: Oxford University Press.

Sætren, J.E. (2010) *Two Narratives of Islamic Revival: Islamic Television Preaching in Egypt.* PhD thesis, The University of Bergen.

Speight, R.M. (1995) 'Hadith', in J.L. Esposito (Ed.) *The Oxford Encyclopedia of the Modern Islamic World* (pp. 83–87). New York: Oxford University Press.

Williams, J.A. (1995) 'Khawarij', in J.L. Esposito (Ed.) *The Oxford Encyclopedia of the Modern Islamic World* (pp. 419–420). New York: Oxford University Press.

Zubaida, S. (2005) 'Islam and secularization', *Asian Journal of Social Science*, 33(3), pp. 438–448.

PART II
Religious activism

6

THE ONLINE RESPONSE TO THE QURAN-BURNING INCIDENTS

Ahmed Al-Rawi

Introduction

The controversies surrounding the Quran-burning incidents began on social media. Terry Jones's proposal to burn 200 copies of the Quran was first announced on Twitter but turned within a couple of months into an international crisis. Jones suggested burning the Muslims' holy book on the anniversary of the 9/11 attacks in 2010, calling it 'Int Burn a Koran Day', then he rallied support in order to 'bring to awareness to the dangers of Islam and that the Koran is leading people to hell', as he claimed. In July 2010, Jones bragged in one of his tweets that his Facebook followers had reached 500 (Gerhart & Ernesto, 2010). On 25 July, Jones used YouTube to attract more followers. In the video clip, he held the Quran and stated: 'This book is responsible for 9/11' (Weaver, 2010). By September 2010, Jones had more than 16,000 followers on Facebook (Hill, 2010).

It seems that international media attention gave Jones a great deal of publicity as over 150 media outlets from all around the world interviewed him (Alvarez, 2011). Several international figures, including US President Barack Obama and US Foreign Secretary Hillary Clinton, denounced the attempt and called for the cancellation of the idea. For example, President Obama mentioned that the act would be a 'recruitment bonanza for al-Qaida'. Jones did cancel the plan, but he changed his mind later when he conducted a trial of the Quran, after which he burnt a copy on 20 March 2011. Jones burnt the Quran once more on 29 April 2012 as a protest against the arrest of a Christian pastor by the Iranian government.

The Quran-burning incidents led to numerous street protests, mostly in Afghanistan and Pakistan. The former country witnessed intense violence as tens of people were killed and hundreds injured due to these incidents. On Facebook there were hundreds of thousands of oppositional groups that rejected Jones's proposal (Hill, 2010). There are still numerous Arabic Facebook pages that are active such as 'Millions of Muslims against Burning the Quran' (over 22,000 followers and created in 2011), and 'Together Against Burning the Quran' (over 20,000 followers and created on 14 September 2010). Due to the high degree of controversy he generated, Terry Jones in the end had '300 death threats, mostly via e-mail and telephone, and had been told by the F.B.I. that there was a $2.4 million contract on his life' (Alvarez, 2011).

Another important incident that was highlighted on YouTube was the burning of the Quran by a group of US soldiers stationed at Bagram Air Base in Afghanistan, in February 2012. The incident occurred after a group of US soldiers wanted to dispose of copies of the Quran that were either torn or desecrated by prisoners. The action prompted the US president to apologize. Again, protests erupted and people were killed due to this incident.

In this regard, social media helped Jones achieve international fame (Lidsky, 2011, 5) as other Quran-burning incidents did not receive the same kind of worldwide attention. Some of these incidents include the US soldiers' desecration of the Quran at Guantanamo Bay in 2005, the details of which were published in *Newsweek* in May 2005 (CBC News, 2005), or when members of a Baptist Church in Kansas burnt the Quran in Washington in 2008 (Weaver, 2010). Indeed, social media proved instrumental in spreading anti-Islamic sentiments (Mosemghvdlishvili & Jansz, 2012) in relation to other incidents like Geert Wilder's Fitna film (Van Zoonen et al., 2010; *WikiIslam*; Larsson, 2007).

Theoretical background

Media and religion are closely linked. Almost 64% of Americans have used the Internet for religious or faith activities (Hoover et al., 2004). However, the academic study of religion and the media is still under-researched, though they both play major roles in human society (Stout & Buddenbaum, 2002, 5), and this includes the study of online media (Campbell, 2010).

Empirical studies on the link between social media and Islam are few, and most of them are limited to Islamic blogs, websites and forums (Bunt, 2000, 2003, 2009; El-Nawawy & Khamis, 2009). The focus of the previous studies was mostly on e-jihad, and the role of YouTube was rarely mentioned, despite its popularity and wide public reach. Bunt does make passing references to YouTube, but with no elaborate discussion. For example, he refers to '*Ummah* Films', which offer entertainment outlets in an acceptable Islamic manner and mentioned that they 'gave an outlet to a number of speakers on popular issues via YouTube and other film sites, which generated interest through populist and at times humour[ou]s approach to contemporary issues' (Bunt, 2009, 50–51). Here, *Ummah* is a reference to the assumed Islamic nation regardless of the linguistic and ethnic diversity and geographic locations of Muslims.

Among the important issues discussed in the above studies is the concept of *Ummah* on the Internet, which is also termed 'virtual *Ummah*' or 'online *Ummah*', with a special focus on Muslim communities living in the diaspora (Mandaville,

2001, 2003; Roy, 2004; Lawrence, 2002). Indeed, the Internet has unified many Muslims from around the world in spreading their messages and consuming and producing Islamic materials. It seems that the '[d]istributive and networked technologies are helping Muslims to forge and sustain distanciated links reminiscent of the umma concept. These forces are ... contributing to the development of a wider Muslim public sphere' (Mandaville, 2001, 190). Jon Anderson (2003) claims that the first Muslim bloggers were students who studied at Western universities who managed to create online communities for Muslim students' associations and uploaded religious texts online. The virtual *Ummah* constitutes what Benkler (2006) calls the 'networked public sphere' or what Castells terms the 'global network society' or the 'global public sphere', which is 'built around the media communication system and Internet networks, particularly in the social spaces of the Web 2.0, as exemplified by YouTube, MySpace, Facebook, and the growing blogosphere' (Castells, 2008, 90).

In the case of the Arab world as it is elsewhere, governments, major corporations and some religious authorities own mainstream media channels and control the flow of news and messages, while the majority of people are left without a channel to voice their hopes, frustrations and fears. Hence, social media networks function as an alternative media channel. Mandaville (2001) argues that the new Muslim intellectual often challenges the authority of his government and the mosque, and situates himself in 'spaces which institutionalized forms of politics cannot reach' and 'online media helped him to achieve' (ibid., 190). Further, as the Internet crosses borders and allows people from different places to be interconnected (Papacharissi, 2002; Volkmer, 2003), these channels started to make up the foundations of the global public sphere by enhancing and strengthening the link among people sharing the same political or religious convictions (Castells, 2001; Dahlberg, 2007; Calhoun, 2004), especially that these alternative media channels like Twitter, Facebook and YouTube provided the platform for self-expression (Price & Cappella, 2002). As a result, Muslims from all over the world began sharing views and opinions on different issues relevant to their religion, including *fatwas* and basic guidance.

In this study, the focus is on online audiences, as many previous studies relied on audience surveys and interviews with newsreaders to understand the way they frame events and issues like risk from science (Hornig, 1992) and the welfare state (Feldman & Zaller, 1992; Sotirovic, 2000). Matthew Nisbet mentions the importance of studying framing in social media, which marks a shift from traditional studies that are limited to the 'transmission model of traditional news framing effects to a more interactive, social constructivist, and "bottom up" model of framing'. In this way, ordinary citizens become 'active contributors, creators, commentators, sorters, and archivers of digital news content' (Nisbet, 2010, 75). Constantinescu and Tedesco (2007, 444) recommend including 'the Internet as a resource for quantitative research on audience frames', as the frames transmitted by the online public are usually done through social media. Further, and in relation to Entman's assumption of audiences' counter-framing, Cooper refers to frames used by some news bloggers who sometimes talk 'back to power' with the way they often oppose and criticize the dominant news frames. As indicated above, despite the fact that the influence of these frames might be weak, it is important to highlight their meanings, intentions and types by which 'an ordinary citizen question[s] the veracity of factual assertions in the news products, [and] ... he or she could problematize the interpretations of facts routinely packaged with straight news reporting' (Cooper, 2010, 136). Groshek and Al-Rawi (2013) call audience frames used on social networking sites 'user generated framing', while I refer to it as 'computer-mediated framing' (Al-Rawi, 2014), and Meraz and Papacharissi (2013) call it 'networked framing', which basically 'aggregates the actions of the crowd in an organic, ad hoc manner', in order to sustain and amplify certain messages in the online information flows. In this study, I argue that computer-mediated framing in relation to issues dealing with Islam functions as a bottom-up flow of information, which mostly attempts to provide alternative messages that counter the stronger information flows coming from some Western mainstream media outlets and/or some authoritative political powers in the region. This is done because YouTube offers a venue for those who are voiceless or under-represented in politics and/or mainstream media, as explained above.

Finally, it is relevant to discuss briefly the impact Muslims living in the diaspora have on strengthening the global public sphere that makes up the basis of the virtual *Ummah*. Karim argues that diasporic communities living in the West are among the most active members in producing cultural content. 'There appears to be an attempt by diasporic participants in cyberspace to create a virtual community that eliminates the distances that separate them in the real world ... Time and space are seemingly held in suspension in this effort to reconstitute the community and to exchange cultural knowledge held in the diaspora' (Karim, 2007, 273). It seems that Muslims living in the diaspora feel an urge to assert their identities and religious beliefs amid what some view as a threat to their core convictions. Olivier Roy argues that Islamic revival, or 're-Islamization', in Europe and North America results from the efforts of Westernized Muslims to retain their faith and identity in a non-Muslim context. Social media networks are used by many Muslims in the diaspora for religious and faith-related issues that serve to keep them closely connected with other followers in their home countries and elsewhere.

YouTube and the global public sphere

In recent years, YouTube has become the most popular video platform online since it delivers two out of every five videos viewed around the world (Burgess & Green, 2009). In October 2011, there were about 1.2 billion people aged 15 and older watching 201.4 billion videos online, globally (comScore, 2011). Statistics published by YouTube reveal that more than 800 million unique users watch clips on YouTube every month, amounting to more than 3 billion hours of video clips. Almost every minute, 72 hours of video are uploaded online, and by 2011 YouTube had over 1 trillion views, equivalent to 140 views for each person in the world (YouTube Statistics, 2012). According to a study conducted by the Pew Research Center's Project for Excellence in Journalism in 2012, YouTube has become a news source for most people around the globe. The study, which lasted 15 months from January 2011 to March 2012, concluded the following:

> Citizens are creating their own videos about news and posting them. They are also actively sharing news videos produced by journalism professionals. And news organizations are taking advantage of citizen content and incorporating it into their journalism. Consumers, in turn, seem to be embracing the interplay in what they watch and share, creating a new kind of television news.
>
> *(Journalism.org, 2012)*

Based on statistics offered by Alexa, YouTube ranks number three worldwide in terms of its usage. The percentage of YouTube global visitors from the Arab world in relation to worldwide viewership is as follows: Saudi Arabia (1.5%), Egypt (1.0%) and Algeria (0.7%). In Saudi Arabia and Algeria, YouTube is ranked the second most visited website, which is the highest ranking worldwide (Alexa, 2012). Douai and Nofal assert that 'YouTube and social media have grown more popular, and gained more legitimacy because they are perceived to be autonomous from their authoritarian states, unlike the mass media landscape' (Douai & Nofal, 2012, 269).

YouTube's role in enhancing the public sphere and political activism is very significant since it is a platform for disseminating messages due to the easy manner of uploading and editing video clips and comments (Jarrett, 2010; Thorson et al., 2010; Christensen, 2007). Based on an empirical study on YouTube comments, religion seems to be the most discussed topic, unlike music, comedy, how to and style categories (Thelwall et al., 2011). Strangelove asserts that a 'considerable number of video bloggers on YouTube engage in debates over religion. Some of the larger areas of debate are focused on evolution, abortion, atheism, Scientology, Mormonism, Christianity, and Islam' (Strangelove, 2010, 148). Unfortunately, many of these debates can develop into heated discussions, which often involve insults and curses. Burgess and Green call it the flame war or 'YouTube drama', which occurs when a 'flurry of video posts clusters around an internal "controversy" or an antagonistic debate between one or more YouTubers', which 'can sometimes be based around controversial debates (especially religion, atheism, or politics)' (Burgess & Green, 2009, 97).

Aside from flaming, which involves swearing and the use of obscene language that seems to be very common among YouTube and other social network users (O'Sullivan & Flanagin, 2003; Alonzo & Aiken, 2004; Crystal, 2001), the online disinhibition effect needs to be discussed here, which sheds light on some of the reasons behind online flaming. The disinhibition effect 'releases deeper aspects of intrapsychic structure, that it unlocks the true needs, emotions, and self attributes that dwell beneath surface personality presentations' (Suler, 2004, 324). However, first we need to mention briefly some of YouTube's social networking behaviour that is linked to the disinhibition effect. Lange's ethnographic study reveals that

YouTube manifests two types of relationships among the youth in relation to social network behaviour. The first one is the 'publicly private' behaviour in which the video posters' identities are disclosed but content access is limited to the public. On the other hand, the 'privately public' behaviour indicates that YouTube content is widely shared and accessible, but personal details of the posters are often limited (Lange, 2007). Since the identities of the posters are mostly hidden or are 'privately public', they seem to be freer in expressing their views. Suler (2004) identifies six factors that lead to the disinhibition effect: dissociative anonymity, invisibility, asynchronicity, solipsistic introjection, dissociative imagination, and minimization of authority.

Two of these factors are of relevance here, especially the dissociative anonymity and solipsistic introjection. The former refers to the kind of behaviour manifested when 'people have the opportunity to separate their actions online from their in-person lifestyle and identity, they feel less vulnerable about self-disclosing and acting out' (Suler, 2004, 322). On the other hand, solipsistic introjection is a psychological condition in which '[p]eople may feel that their mind has merged with the mind of the online companion. Reading another person's message might be experienced as a voice within one's head, as if that person's psychological presence and influence have been assimilated or introjected into one's psyche' (ibid., 323). Many comments analysed in this study seem to fall within these two concepts. In relation to the dissociative anonymity factor, some YouTube commenters who regularly insult Islam and the Quran seem to act based on the fact that they remain anonymous; otherwise, they would be punished in many Arab societies, which prohibit insulting the Prophet of Islam and/or his family members (Associated Press, 2012). For instance, a Saudi journalist, Hamza Kashgari, was once accused of insulting Mohammed in one of his public tweets; as a result, he was forced to flee Saudi Arabia to Malaysia, from where he was later deported to his home country. Kashgari's tweet generated over 30,000 angry responses and many death threats (BBC, 2012). The journalist later apologized and asked for forgiveness. Others who were less restricted in revealing their identities have received threats, as will be shown below; most of the anti-Islam comments were made by Arab Christians living in the diaspora and/or atheists. In his study on religion and YouTube, Theobald rightly observes:

> Despite the dynamic nature of the medium, the quality of interfaith relations online, particularly on YouTube, is neither new nor revolutionary, but, instead, reflects the centuries of animosity that characterised dialogue among the pious in the years before the nineteenth century. Historically, contact between the advocates of different religions typically resulted in a battle for souls; conversion was the aim, ridicule or polemic the method, apologetics the defence.
> *(Theobald, 2009, 326)*

In connection to solipsistic introjection, when some YouTube users call for jihad against America or the West, many others follow the same line of thought by encouraging war and conflict.

This chapter attempts to answer the following research questions:

1. What were the issues discussed in the comments posted by Arab YouTube users with regard to the Quran-burning incidents?
2. What is the tone of the YouTube videos posted in relation to the Quran-burning incidents?
3. What is the demographic distribution of the YouTube commentators and those who posted video clips?

Previous studies of the digital sphere

There are few studies that deal with Arabs' online responses to controversial issues related to Islam. For example, Douai and Nofal (2012) studied the Arab readers' online responses on Al Arabiya.net and Al Jazeera.net towards the banning of minaret building in Switzerland and the Ground Zero mosque controversy in the USA. The study investigated 4,539 comments and categorized them as either 'support', 'opposition' or 'neutral'. The study revealed that 43% of Al Arabiya's online readers opposed the Swiss government's minaret ban, while 33% of them supported the decision. The remaining 24% of readers were neutral. As for the Al Jazeera online readers, 20% opposed the ban, while 56% supported it and the remaining 24% were neutral. In relation to the Ground Zero mosque controversy, 39% of Al Arabiya's online readers supported the construction of the mosque, while 35% rejected the idea and 26% of the online readers expressed neutrality. Regarding Al Jazeera readers, 59% supported the idea of building the mosque, while 20% opposed it and 21% had neutral views (ibid.).

Furthermore, Rasha Abdulla studied 752 message boards that dealt with Arabs' reaction to the 9/11 attacks, on three Arab portals: Masrawy, Islam Online and Arabia. Her study concluded that 43.1% of the respondents condemned the attack, while 30.2% gave a justification behind it and somehow approved it (Abdulla, 2007, 1072). The remaining responses (26.7%) contained various other reactions. Conway and Mcinerney (2008) analysed 50 jihadi videos on Iraq, uploaded by 30 YouTube users. They also studied 1,443 comments posted by 940 commenters and provided self-proclaimed demographic details on the users like their age and geographic location, as well as other relevant information like number of views, ratings, and number of comments. The study revealed that the majority of posters are under 35 years old and most resided in the USA.

The choice of using Arabic is related to the fact that it is widely used not only in the Arab world but elsewhere in the world, with over 250 million speakers. The majority of Arabic speakers are Muslims, and the Quran, the Muslims' holy book, is in Arabic. It is assumed that more reactions towards the Quran-burning incidents will be found among Arabic speakers. A webometric analyst tool was used to analyse the video clips and comments (Thelwall, 2009). Moreover, detailed information on the video posters and the commenters was collected to help understand the demographic variations and other variables such as sex, age and location. The study employed two different keyword searches in Arabic alone to ensure that the video clips were posted by Arabic speakers.

The two Arabic search terms used, 'Quran burning' and 'Mushaff (Book) burning', yielded a total of 972 video clips with over 14,600 comments. However, the actual number of video clips analysed was 328 and 4,293 comments because the remaining ones were unrelated to this study. For example, there are hundreds of video clips on burning the Quran due to accidents that occurred in Iraq, Bahrain and elsewhere in the Arab world. Tens of video clips were uploaded on burning the Quran in Bahrain by government forces where the Shiite opposition accused the Sunni-led security forces of being behind the accident. Besides this, tens of other videos were uploaded on protests organized by the followers of an Iraqi Shiite leader, Mahmood Al-Sarkhi, who accused the ayatollahs in Najaf of being responsible for burning copies of the Quran during the assaults against his office in southern Iraq.

First, a preliminary study following the inductive framing approach was conducted, which included examining over 450 comments and 40 video clips in order to find the most dominant issues used in the comments as well as the classification of video clips' genres. A thorough examination of the most recurrent themes covered in the comments was conducted by focusing on any patterns that were later linked to the overreaching ideas. This was done by first identifying the framing and reasoning devices, after which the main issues were determined (Van Gorp, 2010, 94–103). The identification of the frames or main issues included examining the use of metaphors, exemplars, catchphrases and depictions (Gamson & Modigliani, 1989; Tankard, 2003), as well as the use of 'keywords, stock phrases' and 'sentences that provide thematically reinforcing clusters of facts or judgments' (Entman, 1993, 52). The inductive framing stage yielded six main issues that were frequently used in the comments (Al-Rawi, 2015; 2016): 1 pro-Islam; 2 neutral towards Islam; 3 threats and calls for jihad; 4 curses and insults against Terry Jones and/or America; 5 anti-Islam; and 6 others (unrelated to the Quran-burning incidents). In relation to the video clips' genres, five main types were identified: 1 copy and paste/edit from TV and other sources including TV news reports; 2 public speech, sermon or demonstration; 3 street protests; 4 chants, songs, poems made specifically because of the incidents; and 5 testimonials. These issues and types of video clips were previously found to be prominent in two other studies conducted by the researcher on the Mohammed cartoons incident on YouTube, and an online protest against the *Innocence of Muslims* film on Facebook (Al-Rawi, 2015). Regarding the two studies, two coders worked independently to analyse over 10% of the data investigated (Wimmer & Dominick, 1994, 173). Cohen's Kappa, which accounts for 'chance agreement', was employed since the data coded were nominal (Lombard et al., 2002), and the test that was conducted by SPSS 11.5 for Windows indicated a 'substantial' agreement (Landis & Koch, 1977, 165) in the two studies. For the Facebook study, the agreement was .756 (Cohen's Kappa), while the research on YouTube produced a score of .689 for YouTube comments and .750 for the videos.

Reactions to burning the Quran

The comments investigated in this study included those written in Arabic, Latinized Arabic and English. Of the 4,293 comments analysed, the study revealed that the majority N=1,407 (32.77%) were unrelated or irrelevant. The second highest percentage of comments N=926 (21.56%) were either curses and/or insults against Terry Jones, the US soldiers from Bagram Air Base, or America. Neutral or moderate comments consisted of 17.09% (N=734), while positive responses in which the commenters praised Islam and its holy book made up 13.09% (N=562). As for lethal threats and calls for jihad against America and the West as a reaction towards the Quran-burning incidents, there were not as many as expected, with N=107 constituting 2.49% of the responses. Finally, anti-Islam comments made up 12.76% of the response (N=548) (see Figure 6.1). It was expected that many commenters would call for economically boycotting America, similar to the case of the Danish cartoon controversy, but there were only four such references in all the comments analysed.

In relation to the tendencies of the video clips, the analysis is based not only on the visual and textual content of the clips themselves but also on their descriptions and titles following a framing analysis approach. Of the 328 videos studied, the majority were pro-Islam N=236 (71.95%), which in total received N=13,411 likes and N=942 dislikes from YouTube users. As for neutral or moderate videos, they constituted 21.95% (N=72), which received N=296 dislikes and N=467 likes, while anti-Islam clips were few in number N=20 (6.09%), which collectively received N=3,554 dislikes and N=209 likes.

Since there were several Quran-burning incidents, the study revealed that the topic of Terry Jones got the highest amount of attention with 62.80% of the clips (N=206), while the issue of US soldiers at Bagram Air Base who burnt the Quran received 23.47% (N=77) of the attention. Finally, other minor incidents that happened in the West by unknown people constituted 13.71% of the clips (N=45), including a proposed one that erroneously happened in Denmark and was linked to the Mohammed cartoon controversy. As for the video clip genres, the highest number of clips were copied/pasted (edit) from other sources such as TV news

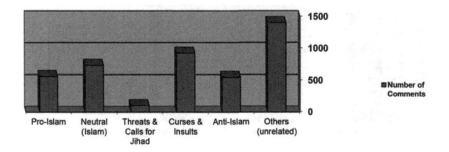

FIGURE 6.1 Comment tendencies

48.78% (N=160), followed by others like chants/songs/poems specifically made due to the Quran-burning incidents 24.69% (N=81). Religious sermons, public speeches or personal demonstrations of burning the Quran (or Bible or cross in a couple of cases) made up 17.07% (N=56), while street protests were 6.70% (N=22) and testimonials were 2.74% (N=9).

In relation to the gender differences of the posters, the majority were males in both the video clips and comments. The latter category had 67.29% (N=2,889), while females made up only 13.58% (N=583). As for the video posters, males constituted 84.45% (N=277), while females were only 6.70% (N=22). Regarding the self-proclaimed geographic location of the posters, the study showed that the largest percentage of comments came from Saudi Arabia 28.62% (N=1,229), followed by the USA 11.50% (N=494) and Egypt 10.99% (N=472). As for video clip posters, the highest percentage came from Egypt 26.52% (N=87), followed by Saudi Arabia 8.84% (N=29) and the USA 8.84% (N=29) (see Tables 6.1 and 6.2).

Finally, in relation to age distribution, the highest percentage of comments and video clips was posted by the age groups 19–24 and 25–29. As for the highest concentration of posters based on their age, the highest percentage of video clip uploads was among 27-year-olds (N=13), 23-year-olds (N=12), and 28-year-olds (N=11). As for the commenters, the highest number of posts were made by people who are 22 years old (N=191), 32 years old (N=175) and 28 years old (N=156).

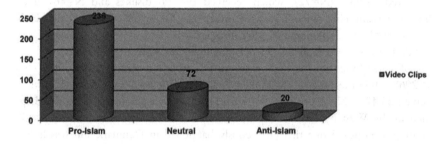

FIGURE 6.2 Tendencies noted in video clips

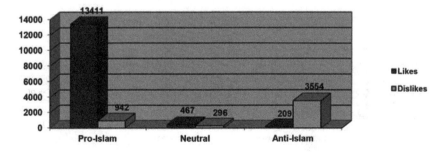

FIGURE 6.3 YouTube users' reactions to the videos

TABLE 6.1 Top 15 self-proclaimed geographic locations of comment posters

Geographic location	No. of comments
1 Saudi Arabia	1,229
2 USA	494
3 Egypt	472
4 Kuwait	141
5 United Arab Emirates	122
6 Morocco	119
7 Algeria	87
8 UK	81
9 Germany	79
10 Iraq	78
11 Canada	64
12 France	55
13 Yemen	50
14 Afghanistan	38
15 Israel/Palestine	32

TABLE 6.2 Top 10 self-proclaimed geographic locations of video clip posters

Geographic location	No. of video clips
1 Egypt	87
2 Saudi Arabia	29
2 USA	29
4 Morocco	26
5 UK	17
6 Algeria	13
7 Germany	9
8 Canada	8
9 Qatar	7
10 France	4

Discussion and conclusion

As stated earlier, burning the Quran created a great deal of controversy in the Islamic world. Many Muslims felt that their respective governments did not take decisive and adequate steps to 'make' America and/or Terry Jones refrain from burning their holy book; thus, they resorted to online media to voice their feelings. In this sense, YouTube functioned as a platform for the global public sphere that constitutes what is known as the virtual *Ummah*. The audience frames about this issue managed to spread due to the lack of government control over this online platform. Based on the findings of this study, the video clip and comment posters come from countries across the globe with obvious concentration in the Middle East, North America and Western Europe. This finding is similar to that of a previous study carried out on the anti-Islamic Fitna film, as most of the videos were posted from the Netherlands, USA and UK (Zoonen et al., 2010, 254). The Saudi-run programme Assakina Campaign for Dialogue, which is supervised by the Saudi Ministry of Religious Affairs, conducted its own study on Al-Qaeda-affiliated websites and revealed that the organization was trying to recruit Muslims in the diaspora. Some 38% of those who got involved with Al-Qaeda's ideas online are Muslims living in Europe and Northern America, while 9% are from the Arab Gulf region. The study revealed that about 90% of those who interacted tended to use insults, curses and accusations during their dialogue instead of relying on sound religious texts (Assakina, 2012).

To answer the first research question, the majority of comments carried angry tones, especially curses and insults against America, Jones or US soldiers 21.56% (N=926), followed by neutral 17.09% (N=734), pro-Islam 13.09% (N=562) and anti-Islam comments 12.76% (N=548). In relation to curses, online flaming has been widely used by the majority of the posters cited above, mostly due to the nature of the issue and anonymity YouTube provides. The discussion on the solipsistic introjection effect is relevant here since there has been a trend wherein one type of post encourages or generates similar ones – e.g. curses and insults or calls for jihad against America. Reading the kind of insults and curses that many Arab YouTube users posted, one user commented on the CNN interview with Jones, saying: 'If the interviewer [Sanchez] reads the Muslims' comments on YouTube, he would immediately change his stance [on Islam]'. Further, many highly pejorative terms and expressions were used such as the words 'pig' and 'dog', which were found in over 90 and 200 contexts, respectively. These negative expressions were mostly directed at Jones, the US soldiers and others whose views opposed those of other posters. For instance, one YouTube user, who seemed reasonable in discussing the Quran issue, expressed his surprise with the kind of angry responses posted, stating: 'Why some are upset with burning of the Quran? Don't we sometimes burn an old torn paper ... This is what this pig has done thinking that he would demean the Quran or enrage us. Instead, we felt pleased because we didn't want the Quran to remain in his filthy hands.' Another YouTube user described his anger, saying: 'Let Allah curse them and shake the ground beneath them and dry the blood in their veins.' Finally, most of the insults found in this study contained highly obscene language, which was observed in other contexts and topics on YouTube (see, for example, Lindgren, 2011).

To answer the second research question, the majority of video clips were pro-Islam 71.95% (N=236), followed by neutral or moderate videos 21.95% (N=72) and finally anti-Islam clips 6.09% (N=20). This was expected as most of the video clips and comments were posted by Arab Muslims who mostly wanted to defend their religion. One of the most popular pro-Islam videos was an edited CNN interview with Terry Jones that was conducted by Rick Sanchez. The footage was translated into Arabic and edited with a subtitle that read: 'This film shows the interview with the cursed man who wants to burn our holy Quran – Source: CNN.' There were many versions of this interview, but one in particular (MWHW2yi4dhM) got over 3,360,068 views (10,878 likes/462 dislikes).

As part of the imagined conflict, some pro-Islam videos include those that claim that the fires that spread in California in 2010, which coincided with the Quran-burning controversy, were caused by God as a punishment against America for its attempt to burn the Quran (e.g. 4EHgeMIIe50, 3bpEiXT-Ia8 and a8OFqO-QuT3w). These three clips alone were so popular that they generated over 700,000 views. However, most of the comments that accompanied the clips were critical of the videos as they discarded them and strongly discredited the claim made.

Also, there were some violent reactions on YouTube that seemed to be supported by Al-Qaeda. For instance, there were over ten video clips that showed Osama Bin Laden's aide, Ayman Al-Zawahiri, calling for jihad and threatening America as a reaction against the US soldiers' burning of the Quran in Afghanistan. Al-Qaeda group posted several messages inciting violence against US forces (e.g. P4GZSWE5hfA). President Obama's prediction that the Quran-burning incidents would empower Al-Qaeda was somehow true, as many posts praised the militant organization and/or Al-Zawahiri's speech and showed great respect for this man, which is evident from the titles they gave him (e.g. Sheikh, Mujahid, hero, etc.). Other reactions included sending implicit threats to burn Christian symbols (gvKvCFRCbqg) or urinating on Bibles (MUzmw3Q_l0o) and/or burning the cross (WsM8MLqXbEw).

Some YouTube users resorted to other methods to protest the burning of the Quran. Several hackers posted clips bragging about their achievements; for instance, one person claimed that he had hacked into a US server (3lYlbwHS1o4), while another hacker mentioned that a virus had been sent to the USA, which infected several computers (IkMifFGqt78). Finally, a group of Syrian hackers calling themselves 'Angel Hackers' took pride in hacking into six American servers (I2I25iXUtR8). It seems that this kind of behaviour is an expected reaction to controversial issues similar to what happened during the Mohammed cartoon controversy when over 600 Danish websites were defaced (Carr, 2010, 187).

To answer the third research question, most of the comments and video clips were posted from Saudi Arabia (28.62% for comments; 8.84% for video clips) and Egypt (10.99% for comments; 26.52% for video clips); however, diasporic communities living in the West were also important, especially those residing in the USA (11.50% for comments; 8.84% for video clips). Moreover, the Quran-burning incidents seem to attract the attention of various cyber-communities that share the same beliefs and sentiments. In this context, the sectarian dimension was very evident in the discussions that were generated. For example, many Shiites regularly accuse Sunni Wahhabis and Salafists of distorting the image of Islam for their extremist views. On the other hand, many Sunnis accuse Shiites of being engaged in religious practices that are alien to Islam, which only divided the Muslim *Ummah* and created schism. In fact, YouTube has become a venue for what we term 'the

Arabs' virtual civil war' among Sunnis and Shiites. The hate speech, insults and prejudice are so widespread that one finds such references in many YouTube clips even if the topic is irrelevant. One YouTube user expressed his astonishment at the type of hate speech he found in the comments he was reading, saying: 'The funny thing is that this man [Jones] insulted Islam, while the comments here are only about [insults] between Sunnis and Shiites.'

At the same time, many Arab Christians and atheists – especially those living in the diaspora – found the topic of burning the Quran a good chance to attack Islam and its holy book. As indicated earlier, many diasporic communities that live in the West are very active online in their attempt to keep the link with their homeland. However, the feedback sent by such communities might sometimes be very critical. For example, an Egyptian man posted a video in which he publicly insulted Islam, its Prophet and the Quran. As a result, one video clip was uploaded under the title 'Wanted: Dead or Alive because of burning the Quran' (wZU89etd6OE). Further, a couple of video clips were posted by an Egyptian Coptic who allegedly wanted to burn the Quran (1G33yrEsc-s); the man is part of the so-called Coptic CPR Government in Exile, in Frankfurt, Germany.

To sum up, the Quran-burning incidents, which mostly started on social media sites, led to violent reactions on the streets but were also reflected online. The video clips and comments posted on YouTube revealed the popular sentiments about this important issue, which attracted a great deal of attention from various cyber-communities within the global public sphere that meet to discuss a vital topic related to their core beliefs. The anonymity offered by YouTube gives some posters a liberating feeling, which empowers them to discuss many taboos that are banned by mainstream media – e.g. jihad and blasphemy. Due to its visual and textual features, YouTube attracts more online users than many other social network sites, which makes it an ideal venue for the virtual Islamic *Ummah* but also enhances its division along sectarian lines.

References

Abdulla, R. (2007) 'Islam, jihad, and terrorism in post-9/11 Arabic discussion boards', *Journal of Computer-Mediated Communication*, 12(3), pp. 1063–1081.

Alexa: The Web Information Company (2012) 'YouTube', www.alexa.com/siteinfo/youtube.com.

Alonzo, M. & Aiken, M. (2004) 'Flaming in electronic communication', *Decision Support Systems*, 36(3), pp. 205–213.

Al-Rawi, A. (2014) 'Framing the online women's movements in the Arab world', *Information, Communication & Society*, 17(4), pp. 1–25.

Al-Rawi, A. (2015) 'Online reactions to the Muhammed cartoons: YouTube and the virtual Ummah', *Journal for the Scientific Study of Religion*, 54(2), pp. 1–30.

Al-Rawi, A. (2016) 'Facebook as a virtual Mosque: Reactions against the Innocence of Muslims Film', *Culture and Religion*, 17, pp. 1–23.

Alvarez, L. (2011) 'Koran-burning pastor unrepentant in face of furor', *The New York Times*, 2 April, www.nytimes.com/2011/04/03/us/03burn.html.

Anderson, J. (2003) 'The Internet and Islam's new interpreters', in D. Eickelman & J. Anderson (Eds) *New Media in the Muslim World* (pp. 45–60). Bloomington: Indiana University Press.

Aouragh, M. (2011) *Palestine Online: Transnationalism, the Internet and the Construction of Identity*. London: I.B. Tauris.

Assakina (2012) *A Special Study by Assakina: Terrorists' Websites Lose their Scientific Glamour*. 30 July, www.assakina.com/news/news3/17085.html.

Associated Press (2012) 'Bahrain court jails man over Muhammad wife insult', 13 August.

BBC (2012) 'Saudi detained in Malaysia for insulting Prophet tweet', 10 February, www.bbc.co.uk/news/world-asia-16977903.

Benkler, Y. (2006) *The Wealth of Networks: How Social Production Transforms Markets and Freedoms*. New Haven, CT: Yale University Press.

Bunt, G. (2000) *Virtually Islamic: Computer-Mediated Communication and Cyber Islamic Environments*. Cardiff: University of Wales Press.

Bunt, G. (2003) *Islam in the Digital Age: e-Jihad, Online Fatwas and Cyber Islamic Environments*. London: Pluto Press.

Bunt, G. (2009) *iMuslims: Rewiring the House of Islam*. Carolina, NC: University of North Carolina Press.

Burgess, J. & Green, J. (2009) *YouTube: Online Video and Participatory Culture*. Cambridge: Polity Press.

Calhoun, C. (2004) 'Information technology and the international public sphere', in D. Schuler & P. Day (Eds) *Shaping the Network Society: The New Role of Civil Society in Cyberspace* (pp. 229–251). Cambridge, MA: MIT Press.

Campbell, H. (2010) *When Religion Meets New Media*. London: Routledge.

Carr, J. (2010) *Inside Cyber Warfare: Mapping the Cyber Underworld*. Sebastopol, CA: O'Reilly Media Inc.

Castells, M. (2001) *The Internet Galaxy*. Oxford: Oxford University Press.

Castells, M. (2008) 'The new public sphere: global civil society, communication networks and global governance', *The Annals of the American Academy of Political and Social Science*, 616, pp. 78–93.

CBC News (2005) 'U.S. admits abuses to Qur'an in Guantanamo', 4 June, www.cbc.ca/news/world/story/2005/06/03/quran050603.html.

Christensen, C. (2007) 'YouTube: the evolution of media', *Screen Education*, 45, pp. 36–40.

comScore (2011) 'More than 200 billion online videos viewed globally in October', 14 December, www.comscore.com/Press_Events/Press_Releases/2011/12/More_than_200_Billion_Online_Videos_Viewed_Globally_in_October.

Constantinescu, A. & Tedesco, J. (2007) 'Framing a kidnapping: frame convergence between online newspaper coverage and reader discussion posts about three kidnapped Romanian journalists', *Journalism Studies*, 8(3), pp. 444–464.

Conway, M. & Mcinerney, L. (2008) 'Jihadi video and auto-radicalisation: evidence from an exploratory YouTube study', *Intelligence and Security Informatics*, 5376, pp. 108–118.

Cooper, S. (2010) 'The oppositional framing of bloggers', in P. D'Angelo and J. Kuypers (Eds) *Doing News Framing Analysis: Empirical and Theoretical Perspectives* (pp. 135–155). London: Routledge.

Crystal, D. (2001) *Language and the Internet*. New York: Cambridge University Press.

Dahlberg, L. (2007) 'The Internet, deliberative democracy, and power: radicalizing the public sphere', *International Journal of Media and Cultural Politics*, 3, pp. 47–64.

Douai, A. & Nofal, H. (2012) 'Commenting in the online Arab public sphere: debating the Swiss minaret ban and the "Ground Zero mosque"', *Journal of Computer-Mediated Communication*, 17, pp. 266–282.

El-Nawawy, M. & Khamis, S. (2009) *Islam Dot Com: Contemporary Islamic Discourse in Cyberspace*. London: Palgrave Macmillan.

Entman, R.M. (1993) 'Framing: toward clarification of a fractured paradigm', *Journal of Communication*, 43(4), pp. 51–58.

Feldman, S. & Zaller, J. (1992) 'The political culture of ambivalence: ideological responses to the welfare state', *American Journal of Political Science*, 36, pp. 268–307.

Gamson, W.A. & Modigliani, A. (1989) 'Media discourse and public opinion on nuclear power: A constructionist approach', *American Journal of Sociology*, 1–37.

Gerhart, A. & Ernesto, L. (2010) 'Pastor's Koran-burning threat started with a tweet', *The Washington Post*, 11 September, www.washingtonpost.com/wp-dyn/content/article/2010/09/10/AR2010091007033.html.

Groshek, J. & Al-Rawi, A. (2013) 'Public sentiment and critical framing in social media content during the 2012 US presidential campaign', *Social Science Computer Review*, 0894439313490401.

Hill, E. (2010) 'Quran row feeds media frenzy', *Al Jazeera*, 10 September, www.aljazeera.com/indepth/features/2010/09/2010910123534220284.html.

Hoover, S., Schofield, C. & Rainie, D. (2004) *Faith Online*. Pew Internet and American Life Project, 7 April, www.pewinternet.org/~/media//Files/Reports/2004/PIP_Faith_Online_2004.pdf.pdf.

Hornig, S. (1992) 'Framing risk: audience and reader factors', *Journalism & Mass Communication Quarterly*, 69(3), pp. 679–690.

Jarrett, K. (2010) 'YouTube: online video and participatory culture', *Continuum: Journal of Media & Cultural Studies*, 24(2), pp. 327–330.

Journalism.org (2012) 'YouTube & news: a new kind of visual news', 16 July, www.journalism.org/analysis_report/youtube_news.

Karim, H. (2007) 'Media and diaspora', in Eoin Devereux (Ed.) *Media Studies: Key Issues & Debates* (pp. 361–379). London: Sage.

Landis, J. Richard & Koch, Gary G. (1977) 'The measurement of observer agreement for categorical data', *Biometrics*, 33(1), pp. 159–174.

Lange, P. (2007) 'Publicly private and privately public: social networking on YouTube', *Journal of Computer-Mediated Communication*, 13(1), pp. 361–380.

Larsson, G. (2007) 'Cyber-Islamophobia? The case of WikiIslam', *Contemporary Islam*, 1(1), pp. 53–67.

Lawrence, B. (2002) 'Allah on line: the practice of Islam in the information age', in S.M. Hoover and L.S. Clark (Eds) *Practicing Religion in the Age of the Media: Explorations in Media, Religion, and Culture* (pp. 237–253). New York: Columbia University Press.

Lidsky, L. (2011) 'Incendiary speech and social media', *Texas Tech Law Review*, 44(1), pp. 1–18.

Lindgren, S. (2011) 'YouTube gunmen? Mapping participatory media discourse on school shooting videos', *Media Culture Society*, 33(1), pp. 123–136.

Lombard, M., Snyder-Duch, J. & Bracken, C. (2002) 'Content analysis in mass communication: assessment and reporting of intercoder reliability', *Human Communication Research*, 28(4), pp. 587–604.

Mandaville, Peter (2001) *Transnational Muslim Politics: Reimagining the Umma*. London: Routledge.

Mandaville, P. (2003) 'Communication and diasporic Islam: a virtual ummah?' in Karim H. Karim (Ed.) *The Media of Diaspora* (pp. 135–147). London: Routledge.

Meraz, S. & Papacharissi, Z. (2013) 'Networked gatekeeping and networked framing on #Egypt', *The International Journal of Press/Politics*, 18(2), pp. 138–166.

Mosemghvdlishvili, L. & Jansz, J. (2012) 'Framing and praising Allah on YouTube: exploring user-created videos about Islam and the motivations for producing them', *New Media & Society*.

Nisbet, Matthew (2010) 'Knowledge into action: framing the debates over climate change and poverty', in Paul D'Angelo & Jim Kuypers (Eds) *Doing Framing Analysis: Empirical and Theoretical Perspectives* (pp. 43–83). New York: Routledge.

O'Sullivan, P. & Flanagin, A. (2003) 'Reconceptualizing "flaming" and other problematic communication', *New Media and Society*, 5(1), pp. 69–94.

Papacharissi, Z. (2002) 'The virtual sphere: the Internet as a public sphere', *New Media & Society*, 4, pp. 9–27.

Price, V. & Cappella, J. (2002) 'Online deliberation and its influence: the electronic dialogue project in Campaign 2000', *IT & Society*, 1(1), pp. 303–329.

Roy, Olivier (2004) *Globalized Islam: The Search for a New Ummah*. New York: Columbia University Press.

Sotirovic, M. (2000) 'Effects of media use on audience framing and support for welfare', *Mass Communication & Society*, 3(2–3), pp. 269–296.

Stout, D. & Buddenbaum, J. (2002) 'Genealogy of an emerging field: foundations for the study of media and religion', *Journal of Media and Religion*, 1, pp. 5–12.

Strangelove, Michael (2010) *Watching YouTube: Extraordinary Videos by Ordinary People*. Toronto: University of Toronto Press.

Suler, J. (2004) 'The online disinhibition effect', *CyberPsychology & Behavior*, 7(3), pp. 321–326.

Tankard, James W. (2003) 'The empirical approach to the study of media framing', in Stephen D. Reese, Oscar H. Gandy & August E. Grant (Eds) *Framing Public Life: Perspectives on Media and Our Understanding of the Social World*. London: Routledge.

Thelwall, M. (2009) *Introduction to Webometrics: Quantitative Web Research for the Social Sciences*. San Rafael, CA: Morgan & Claypool.

Thelwall, M., Sud, P. & Vis, F. (2011) 'Commenting on YouTube videos: from Guatemalan rock to El Big Bang', *Journal of the American Society for Information Science and Technology*, 63(3), pp. 616–629.

Theobald, S. (2009) 'Faith, interfaith, and YouTube: dialogue, or derision?' *Literature & Aesthetics*, 19(2), pp. 326–342.

Thorson, K., Ekdale, B., Borah, P., Namkoong, K. & Shah, C. (2010) 'YouTube and proposition 8', *Information, Communication & Society*, 13(3), pp. 325–349.

Van Gorp, B. (2010) 'Strategies to take subjectivity out of framing analysis', in P. D'Angelo & J. Kuypers (Eds) *Doing News Framing Analysis: Empirical and Theoretical Perspectives*. London: Routledge.

Van Zoonen, L., Vis, F. & Mihelj, S. (2010) 'Performing citizenship on YouTube: activism, satire and online debate around the anti-Islam video Fitna', *Critical Discourse Studies*, 7(4), pp. 249–262.

Volkmer, I. (2003) 'The global network society and the global public sphere', *Development*, 46(1), pp. 9–16.

Weaver, M. (2010) 'Qur'an burning: from Facebook to the world's media, how the story grew', *The Guardian*, 10 September, www.guardian.co.uk/world/2010/sep/10/quran-burning-how-the-story-grew.

Wimmer, R. & Dominick, J. (1994) *An Introduction to Mass Media Research*. California: Wadsworth.

YouTube Statistics (2012) 'YouTube statistics', www.youtube.com/t/press_statistics.

7

WORKING AROUND THE STATE

The micro-demise of authoritarianism in a digitally empowered Middle East

Deborah L. Wheeler

> Technology and globalization has put power once reserved for states in the hands of individuals ... Technology is empowering civil society in ways that no iron fist can control ... The upheaval of the Arab world reflects the rejection of an authoritarian order that was anything but stable, and now offers the long-term prospect of more responsive and effective governance.
> *(Excerpts from President Barack Obama, West Point Commencement Address, 28 May 2014, www.washingtonpost.com/politics/full-text-of-president-obamas-commencement-address-at-west-point/2014/05/28/cfbcdcaa-e670-11e3-afc6-a1dd9407abcf_story.html)*

President Obama's observations about new media use empowering Arab civil society in ways 'no iron fist can control' reveal more about American optimism, potentially, than they do about Arab society, especially when considered in light of recently enhanced state brutality in Syria, Egypt and Gaza, where collectively more than 162,850 citizens were killed between 2011 and 2014 (Surk, 2014; Edroos, 2014; and Michael, 2011). This chapter, however, grounds President Obama's observations in three case studies of Middle Eastern social media use, which, in limited ways, give powers once reserved for states to individuals in their demand for better governance. I call this process of using communication technologies to resist bad governance, 'working around the state' (Wheeler, 2009).[1]

The story of enhanced state power in the digital age is not surprising. Especially in authoritarian contexts, the Internet has been used by the state for 'propaganda purposes' and 'surveillance', by 'paying bloggers to spread propaganda and troll social networking sites looking for new information on those in the opposition' (Morozov, 2011, xiv, xv). What is surprising, however, is that citizens in authoritarian contexts have effectively used the Internet to enhance their political and social agency in spite of the risks. Why, when the chances of success are so limited, and the costs for taking on the authoritarian state are so potentially life threatening, do Middle Eastern citizens resist, as demonstrated vividly by the Arab Spring revolutions and the case studies examined below. In order to answer this question, three kinds of digital resistance are considered: 1 digital disclosure to confront bad governance; 2 people-to-people diplomacy; and 3 social media for social change. In all three of these examples, we see 'new avenues of political change, through autonomous capacity to communicate and organize', which take place 'beyond the usual methods of [...] political control' (Castells, 2012, 21).

In other words, as argued below, people in the Middle East use social media to resist because they can. Digital media multiply the forms in which resistance can occur, replicate the avenues through which resistance can be expressed, and pool and intensify the results of small acts of defiance into big, potentially transformative waves. With social media, a one-click raindrop turns into a Facebook like, viral video, hashtag flood. Communicative acts, as examined in more detail below, are agentive. In other words, 'media have become the social space where power is decided' (Castells, 2007, 238). Moreover, if 'discontentment or grievance' are matched with 'the attitude that people are able to change things if they become involved in politics, then political action becomes more likely' (Spaiser, 2012, 126). Social media play a role in mobilization because they 'provid[e] easier access to political action for [...] people who have reached the point of being motivated to act' (Spaiser, 2012, 126).

A loss of control over what the public knows, says and does is a force for change in the Middle East, and new media tools play a role in this process. As David Faris argues, social media uses 'make it difficult for regimes to cover up news stories or events that are deemed threatening to government control' (Faris, 2013, 29). Middle Eastern governments in the past have 'depended so heavily on their ability to dominate and control the public sphere' (Lynch, 2012, 11). Thus, the growing presence of new media access and use in the Middle East can replicate and multiply disruptions to state control. As Faris has illustrated in a case study of social media networks in Egypt, 'certain kinds of information – if shared by all citizens – might be damaging to the long-term viability of the system' (Faris, 2013, 29). A recent study by Madar Research in the United Arab Emirates (UAE) states that Internet penetration in the Arab world is set to surge to 51% by 2017, which is 3% above the projected global average for Internet connectivity worldwide (Basit, 2014). Will this increasingly wired region see citizens demanding 'more effective and responsive governance' (Obama, 2014)? The following cases suggest yes, and illustrate how and why.

This analysis builds on the work of three scholars, who examine micro-forms of political and social change. Jeffrey Goldfarb's *The Politics of Small Things* locates the groundwork for revolution in Poland within the oppositional imaginations and practices of the artist/theatre communities (Goldfarb, 2006). Goldfarb's work encourages us to look for political resistance and change in unusual places, and also asks that we not underestimate the power of small forms of opposition. He encourages us to realize that 'there are smaller, less grand ways to combat powerful wrongs' (Goldfarb, 2006, 3). Asef Bayat's *Life as Politics: How Ordinary People*

Change the Middle East highlights how just living, and refusing to be invisible, is a blow to the authoritarian state, by fostering an active citizenry, even if this mobilized public is not collectively expressed, but rather exists in 'individual and quiet direct action' (Bayat, 2010, 58). Last, but not least, *Small Media, Big Revolution* by Annabelle Sreberny-Mohammadi and Ali Mohammadi, which examines the role of new media tools in the Iranian revolution, encourages scholars to think of revolutions 'in terms of communications' because of 'the amazing potential power of the media to foster change' (Sreberny-Mohammadi & Mohammadi, 1994, xix). Thus, this chapter looks at small acts of opposition to authoritarian states, using social media as a new public sphere in which communicative acts strive to redefine power relationships and to encourage civic engagement in the service of better governance.

Why we should care about new media

Three recent examples of 'working around the state' with new media tools highlight political engagement that is challenging power arrangements in the Middle East in, albeit subtle, individual, indirect ways. With these cases of working around the state as illustrations, scholars and policymakers are encouraged to consider the power and implications of new media practices in the Middle East. The main message of this chapter is that new media micro-empowerments enable ordinary citizens to disrupt the status quo, thus neutralizing the effects of authoritarian rule in small ways, even if the effects of such disruptions are hard to sustain and hard to measure, as explored more completely below.

The bottom line up front: the military has a firmer grip on Egyptian politics than ever before; Iran and Israel still sabre rattle daily; and women in Saudi Arabia still cannot drive without risking punishment. At the same time, however, the capacity of citizens to work around such entrenched power structures, to challenge the effects of bad governance and authoritarianism at work in their everyday lives, suggests an enhanced citizen capacity for disruptive behaviour. Whether or not the status quo will be reshaped beyond individual life and digital practices is indeterminate. Direct causation of significant institutional change as a result of individual acts of quiet new media resistance is difficult to prove in the amorphous, web-like world of digital empowerment.

These examples of working around the state illustrate new forms of power relationships in the making, where in spite of authoritarianism, and high costs for overt opposition, Middle Eastern citizens remain active in expressing their demands for change. The cumulative effects of confronting leviathan are still emerging, but citizens in the Middle East are increasingly unwilling to accept bad governance, a lack of opportunity, marginalization and to express deference to the state. The declining capacity of states in the region to offer enough patronage to enough citizens to keep the masses loyal spells uncertainty for state–society stability even in oil-rich nations (Springborg, 2012). In the cases that follow, we see that new media technology use, especially in authoritarian contexts, levels the playing field between state and society to small degrees, and thus provides evidence to support President Obama's West Point words.

Whistle-blowing to resist corruption in the digital age

The Middle East is not a region known for its transparency but, through the use of social media, citizens in the region are exposing corruption and bad governance in the quest for social and political change. According to Transparency International, '[n]ot a single country in the region figures in the top half of the world in terms of public accountability, as measured in terms of access to information or holding leaders accountable for their actions' (Transparency International, n.d.).

Social media usage is enabling Middle Eastern citizens to press for more accountable government by 'demanding reform through social empowerment' (Bertolt et al., 2010, 265). Social media give citizens the power to disclose bad governance by leaking stealth video (Khalid Said, Egypt), distributing secret documents (Manning and Snowden; WikiLeaks has disclosed aspects of bad governance in the Middle East even if Snowden and Manning are not citizens of the region), Twitter campaigns (Turkey), and public allegations and rallies (Kuwait former MP Barak's mobilizations against corruption). In the words of Turkish Prime Minister Recep Erdogan, '[t]his thing called social media is currently the worst menace to society' (Vick, 2014). Erdogan's words represent a state on the defensive and are uttered in response to two recent events: 1 whistle-blowers using social media tools to expose his alleged corruption (Associated Press, 2014); and 2 leaked audio footage on YouTube, which implicated Turkey in secret plans to attack Syria (Barden, 2014).

In response to the public's criticism, Erdogan shut down Twitter. In response to the leak of war plans to attack Syria, the prime minister shut down YouTube. The Freedom Foundation in response downgraded Turkey's media freedom to 'not free'. Efforts to control social media expression have tarnished Turkey's reputation abroad and have done little to calm public mobilization. The vice president of the European Commission called Erdogan's social media crackdown 'another desperate and depressing move' (Barden, 2014).

The costs for Turkey could be high, for as former U.S. Ambassador to Turkey James Jeffreys observes, '[b]y banning Turkish social media, the government is running the risk of exiling itself from the global economy' – a risk Turkey cannot afford, since its 'success has been based on integrating into the global economy' (Barden, 2014). By intervening in executive-level politics, using social media disclosures, the Turkish public resists government policies – including corruption, and a proposed war against a neighbour. Through social media use, we see Turkish citizens become 'informed, participatory, critical, expressive, ethical, and creative', and through such practices, 'individuals make democratic society a reality' (Simsek & Simsek, 2013, 132).

The public campaign to resist bad governance and corruption has been highly animated in Egypt, before, during and after the Arab Spring revolution, which deposed former President Housni Mubarak. For example, in the first week of

October 2013, a citizen of Egypt 'worked around the state' to disclose a behind-closed-doors meeting with senior staff, regarding the military government's emerging media strategy. During the meeting, an anonymous participant took a stealth video of General Sisi admitting that new media tools were empowering citizens. After the meeting, the anonymous video was uploaded to YouTube (www.youtube.com/watch?v=WB9MVTR02YE). In the video, General Sisi instructs his officers to prepare for an increase in public and parliamentary oversight of the military. For as the General states, '[t]he revolution has dismantled all the shackles that were present – not just for us, not just for the military, but for the entire state' (Kirkpatrick, 2011). This disclosure reveals both public resistance to military oppression, and the state's view of increased citizen empowerment.

Social media, which give citizens the power to capture the Egyptian state behaving badly, provide transparency where none is expected. Notable moments where Egyptian citizens worked around the state using social media include Khaled Said, who, in 2010, videotaped and posted online 'Egyptian police officers sharing profits after a drug bust' (Eltahawi, 2010) – an act of resistance for which he paid with his life (Ungerleider, 2010). Faris highlights other social media campaigns to confront bad governance in Egypt, including analysis of 'the sexual harassment scandal of October 2006; the torture scandal of January 2007; the Sudanese refugee crisis of 2006; and the Al-Qursaya Island takeover attempt of 2007–8' (Faris, 2013, 23). In all of these examples we see that Egyptian social media were used to expose bad governance. These examples illustrate what it means to 'experience the Middle Eastern state' at its worst (Rudolph & Jacobsen, 2006, vii); as a manifestation of 'pathology and failure' that 'direct[s] attention to the possibilities of civil society' (ibid., x). In the Middle East, resistance channels are multiplied and amplified through new media, and, in this sense, social media create 'new tools' that enabled citizens 'to accomplish political goals that had previously been unachievable' (Howard & Hussain, 2013, 18). In Egypt, a dictator was deposed, even if Sisi's Egypt calls into question the revolutionary nature of change.

In the summer of 2014, a Twitter-wielding public bent on exposing bad governance besieged another Middle Eastern state – Kuwait. Mobilizations and citizen demands for more accountable governance in Kuwait stem from the 2006 campaign to oppose the appointment of an ailing emir. Public protests during these early stages of Kuwait's Orange Revolution, supported by both opposition politicians and the youth movements, collectively called for political reforms and an end to corruption. Encouraging further public resistance, the end results of this social media-fuelled mobilization were a change of head of state, and a reform of Kuwait's electoral district lines. Subsequent protests and mobilizations have resulted in increased government salaries, investigations of corruption, and even resulted in the dismissal and reappointment of a new prime minister.

The most recent phase of Kuwait's political reform movement exploded with mass rallies in June 2014. The immediate cause of this round of Kuwait's summer protests was the government's detainment of opposition leader former MP Musallam al Barak. Barak is a former member of parliament who obtained more votes for a parliamentary seat than any other politician in Kuwait's history. He is the symbol and figurehead of a protest movement that demands an end to corruption and an elected government to strengthen Kuwaiti democracy. Barak is no stranger to the Kuwaiti justice and incarceration system. He is vulnerable – especially now that he is no longer a member of parliament and thus no longer receives parliamentary immunity. Barak forfeited his chances for continued representation in parliament when the opposition movement boycotted the 2012 elections, in protest against the emir of Kuwait's unilateral 'reform' of Kuwaiti electoral law. Opposition politicians argued that the emir's reforms made it more difficult for their candidates to win seats.

In the summer of 2014, the presence of an active opposition, riot police, tear gas, rubber bullets, revoked citizenship for some participants, including two former MPs, Abdullah al Barghash and Ahmad Jabr al Shemmeri, illustrate the degree to which Gulf countries are not immune to the political transformations sweeping the Middle East. Kuwait's active opposition movement, under the leadership of Barak, worked collectively to expose an alleged 'coup plot that could implicate members of the ruling al-Sabah family of attempting to overthrow the monarchy's government' by assassinating the crown prince (Kholaif, 2014).

Barak also called into question the independence of the Kuwaiti judiciary, and risked jail time for his vocal opposition to several government officials including the former speaker of the parliament, Jassim al Khorafi, and another member of the ruling family, for alleged misuse of public funds. His detention in July 2014 led thousands of Kuwaitis to mobilize in protest, the end result of which was his release from detention. The struggle to expose corruption through leaks of video and government documents continues, as does the Kuwaiti government's 'iron-fist' approach to calming the oppositional public. With each crackdown on citizens, Kuwait risks increased public explosiveness. The state has fostered a citizenry that expects a five-star lifestyle, and that was raised on a political culture that used constitutional law and an active, freely elected parliament with limited legislative powers, to distinguish itself among Gulf neighbours as being 'more democratic' than anyone else in the region. Information and communication technologies helped the Gulf nation resist Iraqi occupation in 1990, and thus post-liberation were distributed widely within society as a form of national self-preservation. As the population grows, the demands on state coffers stretch beyond sustainable limits, for salaries, subsidies, housing and health care, matched by increasingly networked and vocal publics, undeterred in their capacity to protest bad governance, the stability of this emirate is shaken. Regime loyalists label Barak and the public opposition he encourages as against the Constitution and Kuwaiti culture. Those who continue to benefit from the regime patronage are unlikely to join the protest movement, and render Kuwait an increasingly divided society, with an uncertain future. In the words of Kuwaiti journalist Muna Al-Fuzai, 'Kuwait is passing through a very delicate time these days with regards to corruption and misuse of power. If the situation isn't controlled and resolved peacefully, consequences can be negative and unpredictable' (Al-Fuzai, 2014). Reflecting on the summer 2014 protests, Al-Fuzai observes, 'when police began to use teargas ... on the protesting civilians, we saw a new chapter in Kuwait's history' (ibid.). She predicts, 'I think more people will join the opposition – simply because the circle of corruption is becoming bigger and getting out of control' (ibid.).

People-to-people social networking to resist warmongering states

We see a second case of Middle Eastern citizens using social media to work around states when on 14 March 2012, tired of the threats and escalations to war, citizen diplomat Ronnie Edry, an Israeli graphic designer, shared a message on Facebook with the people of Iran, 'Iranians we will never bomb your country. We ♡ you' (www.facebook.com/israellovesiran?ref=profile). A letter, addressed to the Iranian public, accompanied the poster. The letter stated:

> To the Iranian people. To all the fathers, mothers, children, brothers and sisters. For there to be a war between us, first we must be afraid of each other, we must hate. I'm not afraid of you; I don't hate you. I don t even know you. No Iranian ever did me no [sic] harm. I never even met an Iranian ... Just one in Paris in a museum. Nice dude. I see sometime[s] here, on the TV, an Iranian. He is talking about war. I'm sure he does not represent all the people of Iran. If you see someone on your TV talking about bombing you, be sure he does not represent all of us. I'm not an official representative of my country. I'm a father and a teacher. I know the streets of my town, I talk with my neighbors, my family, my students, my friends and in the name of all these people, we love you. We mean you no harm. On the contrary, we want to meet, have some coffee and talk about sports. To all those who feel the same, share this message and help it reach the Iranian people.
>
> *(www.youtube.com/watch?v=mYjuUoEivbE)*

With one simple poster, and message, Ronnie worked around the Israeli and Iranian states to make an effort at peace in the face of war. His efforts illustrate that '[t]he international, person-to-person relationships made possible by Web 2.0 technologies constitute, to a great degree, an increasing and substantial new domain for public diplomacy' (Payne et al., 2011, 42).

The message worked. Within days of posting his plea on Facebook, citizen diplomats in Iran responded with their own cries for peace and cooperation. The return messages were equally transformative, constructing people-to-people peace opportunities one click at a time (edition.cnn.com/2012/03/19/world/meast/israel-iran-social-media/index.html?hpt=hp_c1).

In an interview with CNN, Ronnie Edry explained that he started this campaign 'to talk directly to Iranians to see whether there really was anything to fight about' (Said, 2012). A TED talk on Edry's Facebook movement has gone viral, with over 1.8 million views (www.ted.com/talks/israel_and_iran_a_love_story). One observer explains that the peace movement Ronnie Edry created illustrates '[a] new dawn where individual people are forging friendships and alliances in the face of the politicians' (Hetzer, 2013). Hetzer sees Edry's movement as part of the Arab Spring, because the Arab Spring 'is a movement based upon open communications among common people', whereby 'an opportunity to make changes at the grassroots level' emerges (Hetzer, 2013).

Based on the success of the Facebook campaign, Ronnie and his team created a nongovernmental organization to collect and channel the peace messages into action, Peace Factory (thepeacefactory.org). Peace Factory is a movement based upon the principle of working around the state to end war. Social media are the platforms on which peace work takes place, under the slogan 'Peace, it's viral' (thepeacefactory.org/facebook/). More specifically,

> Peace starts with the people, one person at a time. Today it's easier than ever to connect and reach out to one another. We can talk, we can meet, and we can start a new friendship without even leaving our homes just by the click of a button. One new person, one new connection. Peace is when we see and treat each other as people. All we have to do is talk.
>
> *(thepeacefactory.org/facebook/)*

An article in *The New Yorker* summarizes the promise of working around the state with citizen-to-citizen social media tools. Ruth Margalit observes:

> The Israel-Iran group, apart from the colorful photos and catchy slogans, really hasn't *said* much so far; its organizers haven't put forth a cohesive agenda nor have they lobbied the Israeli or Iranian governments to tone down their threats. Yet to ignore the campaign would be to sadly, gravely miss the point: a new grassroots force seems to have found a unified voice in the unlikeliest of places.
>
> *(Margalit, 2012)*

Since Margalit's 2012 observation, Peace Factory has escalated its action agenda to work around the state of war in the Middle East by providing workshops, expanding social networks for peace, launching campaigns to encourage Israeli voters to 'vote for peace', and encouraging meetings between Israelis and Iranians in neutral locations. According to Edry, '[w]ith every new person that joins our community we are moving one step forwards making the hope for peace in the Middle East a reality' (thepeacefactory.org/about/). The Israel Loves Iran Facebook movement, as well as Edry's Peace Factory efforts, demonstrate 'that people – citizens – today are increasingly driving global events' (Sonenshine, 2013).

The Saudi women's driving campaign, 'No Woman, No Drive', no longer

A third case of using social media to work around the Middle Eastern state is unfolding in Saudi Arabia. The Saudi women's driving campaign is based upon a demand for increasing women's self-sufficiency. Transport for Saudi women costs large sums of capital, and reduces incentives for women to work outside the home. Saudi Arabia is the only country in the world where women cannot legally drive. One woman I interviewed in Riyadh in January 2014 noted that the cost of transportation (having to hire a driver) meant that she was 'actually paying to work' (interviewed January 2014 at the residence of the US ambassador to Saudi Arabia).

With the 26 October women's driving campaign and 'Women2Drive' (www.facebook.com/SaudiWomenSpring/info), we see Saudi women 'working around the state' with the use of new media tools to publicize their defiance and demands for change. The 26 October Saudi women's driving campaign (www.oct26driving.com) includes, in addition to women physically driving in the kingdom, a website hosting uploaded videos of women driving in the kingdom, photographs, an online petition and a comments board. The petition demands:

> In the midst of these regional and international developments and what is going on in the modern world of innovations in various fields of economics, society and culture, we as part of this total sum of humanity declare our ambition to develop and change for the betterment of ourselves and our homeland. As we find no clear justification for the government to ban adult female citizens who are able to drive a car from doing so, we call for the need to provide appropriate means to conduct driving tests for female citizens who want to be issued permits and that the government issue licenses for those women who do pass the driving test. And if female citizens do not pass the driving test then a driving license should not be issued to them, so that they are equal to men in this regard. Hence the ability to drive will be the only standard, regardless of the gender of the citizen.
>
> *(www.oct26driving.com/?page_id=44)*

By using the Internet to distribute their call for change, the Woman2Drive movement has gained wide recognition in the global media (www.youtube.com/watch?v=WcIojGwyZYo) and also garnered a complex web of supporters, crossing gender, social class and national boundaries. For example, in one video posted during the campaign, a woman driving in Saudi Arabia receives a 'thumbs up' from some male drivers who pass her (www.huffingtonpost.com/2013/10/16/saudi-women-defying-drivi_n_4103375.html). Women2Drive makes active use of Twitter (twitter.com/W2Drive/) and Facebook (www.facebook.com/SaudiWomenSpring).

One of the best-known responses to the campaign, responsible for raising global awareness, is the 'No Woman, No Drive' video. A satire by Hisham Fageeh, Fahad al-Butairi and Alaa Wardi, the YouTube video 'No Women, No Drive' has gone viral (www.youtube.com/watch?v=aZMbTFNp4wI), achieving more than 13 million views since it was posted on 26 October 2013. The video pokes fun at the driving law, to commemorate the Saudi women's day of resistance, and especially critiques a Saudi cleric's claim that women who drive put their reproductive organs at risk. The video temporarily achieved 'top video' status on Reddit. In light of the social media campaign to support women's quest for change, *The Guardian* newspaper described the 26 October women's driving campaign as '[t]he best organized social campaign ever seen in Saudi Arabia' (Black, 2013).

While opposition to the Saudi state's driving laws by women is not new (the first public driving campaign occurred in 1990), and emerged prior to the country's first Internet connection (1994), public awareness of the movement both locally and globally has increased, given the amplification of calls online for change. Moreover, given global attention on the issue and increasingly widespread resistance within the kingdom, the Saudi state's willingness to crack down is on the wane. For example, one of the participants, Tamador Alyami, expressed surprise and satisfaction at working around the state when she observed,

> One of the traffic policemen saw me and didn't stop me. I was scared, but when he just drove by and went away, I felt so happy, so reassured and more determined than ever to go out on the 26th.
>
> *(Jamjoon, 2013)*

The cost to re-impose the status quo is high, perhaps impossible, as trumping state power increases citizen determination for change. New media practices and texts provide windows into political negotiations at the grassroots, on issues that matter both locally and globally, like the Saudi women's driving campaign. In January 2014, a Saudi colleague confided, 'I predict that women will be able to drive within the next 5 years' (conversation, 24 January 2014, Doha, Qatar). Moreover, one of the participants in the Women2Drive movement, Naseema al Sada, observes: 'More people around the country seem to be warming up to the cause' (Byrnes, 2014).

Women's use of social media for empowerment goes well beyond the Saudi driving campaign. For example, in 2012, a Saudi woman used YouTube to resist harassment by a *mutawah* (religious police working for the committee for the promotion of virtue and protection against vice – see Figure 7.1) in a mall. The woman was wearing red nail polish, and the *mutawah* considered this to be sexually suggestive and a violation of public morality. The woman fought back, accusing him of sexual harassment and calling him a pervert for noticing her nail polish. She told him to leave her alone because she had rights, and King Abdullah had forbidden *mutawah* officers from harassing citizens in public. She threatened that, if he did not leave her alone, she was filming the whole encounter and the footage was going straight onto the Internet (the encounter is available here: www.al-monitor.com/pulse/originals/2012/al-monitor/imagined-heroism-of-the-saudi-na.html). In the end, the Saudi government chastised the religious police officer, and the woman's act of defiance became one more sign of women's empowerment and change in the kingdom. One commentator observes:

Saudi Arabia is not a country known for its women shouting, 'I am free' and posting YouTube videos of themselves being assertive and defiant toward Committee members. The woman remained invisible in the clip while her phone camera followed the Haya agent and his comrades as they turned their backs and disappeared into the crowd of shoppers. Little did they know that the video of their encounter with this woman would draw hundreds of thousands of tweets and generate dozens of articles in the Arab and international press. The woman rocketed to fame as YouTube views topped one million. She is known now as the hero of the clip entitled '*Fatat al-Manakir*,' or 'The Nail Polish Girl'.

(Al-Rasheed, 2012)

A formal institutionalization of women's empowerment in Saudi Arabia occurred in January 2013, when King Abdullah granted women one fifth of the seats on the Shura Council. The Shura Council acts in an advisory role to the king on issues of public policy and security. It is the highest political office the general public can achieve. The members of the assembly can propose draft laws to the king, but only the latter has the power to legislate. Represented in the council are the nation's 'best and brightest', including doctors, lawyers, engineers, professors, retired civil

FIGURE 7.1 Committee for the Promotion of Virtue and Prevention of Vice Headquarters, Riyadh, Saudi Arabia
Source: Photo by Deborah L. Wheeler, 11 January 2013

servants, military officers and business leaders. Two of the women appointed are highly accomplished ruling family members. In the current Shura, 70% of members have PhDs, 50% of which are from US universities. While restrictions on women (including driving, and society telling them what they must wear or not wear in public) remain severe, having women on the Shura Council may give women the opportunity to create change from within the government for the first time in the country's history. Some of the challenges that remain for women in Saudi Arabia include not being able to 'travel, work, study abroad, marry, get divorced or gain admittance to a public hospital without permission from a male guardian' (Al-Shihri, 2013).

The Academy Award-nominated film *Wajda*, made by a female Saudi filmmaker and screened at embassies in Riyadh in order to qualify for the Academy Awards (2013), epitomizes the situation of Saudi women. The film suggests that the bar is very high for women's empowerment, since institutions responsible for a woman's life and livelihood, all the way down to the family and primary school level, impose collective definitions of how a woman should act to guard her honour and reputation. One of the rules is that women should not allow men to hear their voices, including laughter, and that girls are not allowed to ride bikes, to protect their virginity. The main character, Wajda, however, uses a Quran recitation contest as a way to resist these conservative interpretations of women's public conduct. The film suggests that, using Islam as a vehicle, women can carve out pathways to empowerment. In this same way, women in the Saudi Shura Council may find ways to use Islam in their redefinition of women's everyday life opportunities, from engaging in sports (Al Jazeera, 2014), to working in retail shops (Wharton School of Business, 2014), to driving a car (Byrnes, 2014), and participating in governance (Al-Ahmadi, 2014; Shaqiran, 2014). Social media give Saudi women a public platform on which to organize, and with this tool they 'have become more engaged in political and civic actions, playing a critical, leading role in the rapid and historical changes sweeping the region' (Arab Social Media Report, 2011).

Conclusion

While citizen resistance to bad governance intensifies with the diffusion and use of social media, the short- and long-term effects remain murky at best. Since, as Manuel Castells observes, 'few institutional systems can last long if they are predominantly based on sheer repression' (Castells, 2007, 238), we may expect authoritarian states to be on the losing side of this battle with citizens, especially in an era of shrinking state resources, growing populations, global increases in the costs of grain and food imports, and volatility in oil markets, matched with explosive public spheres throughout the Middle East. Civil wars, insurgencies, capital flight, refugee crises, terrorism, and ecological breaches of sustainable food, water and energy demands all spell challenges for political stability in the region. The contexts in which digital resistance occurs are increasingly fragile. As Howard and Hussain observe, however, 'it is not clear if the popular demand for change will result in new sustainable political institutions' (Howard & Hussain, 2013, 3). In the meantime, we can watch the digital games people play and look for signs of lasting change, even in small forms. For what we could be witnessing is 'a zone of independent cultural and political action that is part of a society-wide reinvention of the political culture' of the Middle East, similar to what Jeffrey Goldfarb observed in Poland before the collapse of communism (Goldfarb, 2012, 2). If so, social media may be the vehicle for increased resistance and greater effects on power relations over time, as more people have access, increased agency and voice.

Note

1 I owe this phrase to Phillip Howard, who served as editor of the volume in which the 2009 piece was published. He said the process my work described in that chapter was best characterized as 'working around the state' (Wheeler, 2009). The term has proven very useful as citizen digital activism to trump state power in small ways has intensified.

References

Al-Ahmadi, Hanan Bint Abdal-Rahim (2014) 'Shura Council membership opened new opportunities for women', *Al-Sharq al Awsat*, 12 July, www.aawsat.net/2014/07/article55334168.

Al-Fuzai, Mona (2014) 'Freedom of expression', *Kuwait Times*, 6 July, news.kuwaittimes.net/freedom-expression/.

Al Jazeera (2014) 'Saudi Arabia moves to allow girls to play sports in school', Reuters, 9 April, america.aljazeera.com/articles/2014/4/9/saudi-arabia-movestoallowgirlstoplaysportsinschool.html.

Al-Rasheed, Madawi (2012) 'Imagined heroism of the Saudi "nail polish girl"', *Al-Monitor*, 30 May, www.al-monitor.com/pulse/originals/2012/al-monitor/imagined-heroism-of-the-saudi-na.html.

Alshaer & Salem (2013) 'Arab world on-Line: trends in Internet usage in the Arab region', in *Arab Social Media Report*. Dubai: Dubai School of Government. www.dsg.ae/en/Publication/Pdf_En/4242013110171851000000.pdf.

Al-Shihri, Abdullah (2013) 'Saudi King Grants Women Seats on Advisory Council', Associated Press, 11 January, bigstory.ap.org/article/saudi-king-grants-women-seat-top-advisory-council-first-time.

Alterman, Jon (1998) *New Media, New Politics? From Satellite Television to the Internet in the Arab World*. Washington, DC: Washington Institute for Near East Policy.

Arab Social Media Report (2011) 'Role of social media in Arab women's empowerment', in *Dubai School of Government: Arab Social Media Report*, November, www.arabsocialmediareport.com/UserManagement/PDF/ASMR%20Report%203.pdf.

Associated Press (2014) 'Opposition leader calls for corruption probe into Prime Minister Recep Tayyep Erdogan', 25 February, www.cbsnews.com/news/opposition-leader-calls-for-corruption-probe-into-turkey-pm-recep-tayyip-erdogan/.

Ayash (1998) *The Information Revolution and the Arab World: Its Impact on State and Society*. Abu Dhabi: ECSSR.

Barden, Andrew (2014) 'Turkey blocks YouTube after Syria incursion plans leaked', Bloomburg, 28 March, www.bloomberg.com/news/2014-03-27/turkey-blocks-youtube-after-leak-of-syria-incursion-planning.html.

Basit, Abdul (2014) 'Arab web users to double: UAE at forefront', *Khalij Times*, 28 May, www.khaleejtimes.com/biz/inside.asp?xfile=/data/uaebusiness/2014/May/uaebusiness_May413.xml&section=uaebusiness.

Bayat, Asef (2010) *Life as Politics: How Ordinary People Change the Middle East*. Stanford, CA: Stanford University Press.

Bertolt, John C., Jaeger, Paul T. & Grimes, Justin M. (2010) 'Using ICTs to create a culture of transparency: e-government and social media as openness and anticorruption tools for societies', *Government Information Quarterly*, 27, pp. 264–271.

Black, Ian (2013) 'Saudi Arabia's women hold day of action to change driving laws', *The Guardian*, 25 October, www.theguardian.com/world/2013/oct/25/saudi-arabia-women-action-driving-laws (accessed 9 August 2014).

Byrnes, Mark (2014) 'Driving in Saudi Arabia as a woman', *CityLab*, 1 April, www.citylab.com/politics/2014/04/driving-saudi-arabia-woman/8771/ (accessed 10 August 2014).

Castells, Manuel (2007) 'Communication, power and counter-power in the network society', *International Journal of Communication*, 1, pp. 238–266.

Castells, Manuel (2012) *Networks of Outrage and Hope: Social Movements in the Internet Age*. Cambridge: Polity Press.

Coy, Peter (2011) 'Youth unemployment bomb', *Bloomberg Businessweek*, 2 February, www.businessweek.com/magazine/content/11_07/b4215058743638.htm (accessed 10 December 2012).

Edroos, Faisal (2014) 'Palestinian and Israeli fatalities since the start of Israel's military offensive in Gaza', *Al Jazeera Gaza Blog Live*, 16 August, live.aljazeera.com/Event/Gaza_Blog (accessed 17 August 2014).

Eltahawi, Mona (2010) 'Generation Mubarak/Generation Facebook', *Huffington Post*, 25 June, www.huffingtonpost.com/mona-eltahawy/generation-mubarakgenerat_b_625409.html (accessed 13 March 2014).

Emirates Center for Strategic Studies and Research (ECSSR) (1998) *The Information Revolution and the Arab World: Its Impact on State and Society*. Abu Dhabi: ECSSR.

Faris, David (2013) *Dissent and Revolution in a Digital Age: Social Media, Blogging and Activism in Egypt*. London: I.B. Tauris.

Fekete, Emily & Warf, Barney (2013) 'Information technology and the Arab Spring', *Arab World Geographer*, 16(2), pp. 210–227.

Fleck, Fiona & La Guardia, Anton (2003) 'Internet a tool of British imperialism, says Mugabe', *The Telegraph*, 11 December, www.telegraph.co.uk/news/worldnews/africaandindianocean/zimbabwe/1449172/Internet-a-tool-of-British-imperialism-says-Mugabe.html.

Gladstone, Rick (2014) 'Saudi Arabia: online chats between sexes denounced', *The New York Times*, 30 May, p. A11.

Global Voices (2002) 'Threatened voices: Zouhair Yahyaoui', threatened.globalvoicesonline.org/blogger/zouhair-yahyaoui.

Goldfarb, Jeffrey C. (2006) *The Politics of Small Things: The Powers of the Powerless in Dark Times*. Chicago, IL: University of Chicago Press.

Goldfarb, Jeffrey C. (2012) *Reinventing Political Culture: The Power of Culture versus the Culture of Power*. Malden, MA: Polity.

Hetzer, Jim (2013) 'Power of one: Ronny Edry creates Israel ♡ Iran image', *Examiner.com*, 3 January, www.examiner.com/article/power-of-one-ronny-edry-creates-israel-iran-image-1.

Howard, Phillip N. & Hussain, Muzammil M. (2013) *Democracy's Fourth Wave? Digital Media and the Arab Spring*. Oxford: Oxford University Press.

Jamjoon, Mohammad (2013) 'Saudi Arabia issues warning to women drivers, protesters', *CNN*, 23 October, www.cnn.com/2013/10/24/world/meast/saudi-arabia-women-drivers/.

Jaspal, Rusi & Cinnirella, Marco (2010) 'Media representations of British Muslims and hybridised threats to identity', *Contemporary Islam: Dynamics of Muslim Life*, 4(3), pp. 289–310.

Kalathil, Shanthi & Boas, Taylor (2003) *Open Networks, Closed Regimes: The Impact of the Internet on Authoritarian Rule*. Washington, DC: Carnegie Endowment for International Peace.

Kholaif, Daliah (2014) 'Kuwait strips dissidents' citizenship', *Al Jazeera*, 22 July, www.aljazeera.com/news/middleeast/2014/07/kuwait-strips-dissidents-citizenship-2014722112037525983.html.

Kirkpatrick, David (2011) 'Tunisian leader shaken as riots hit rich hamlet', *The New York Times*, 14 January, www.nytimes.com/2011/01/14/world/africa/14tunisia.html?pagewanted=all.

Lacroix, Stephane (2011) 'Comparing the Arab revolts: is Saudi Arabia immune?' *Journal of Democracy*, October, 22(4), pp. 48–59.

Lynch, Marc (2012) *The Arab Uprising: The Unfinished Revolutions of the New Middle East*. New York: Public Affairs.

Margalit, Ruth (2012) 'Israel loves Iran on Facebook', *The New Yorker*, 23 March, www.newyorker.com/online/blogs/culture/2012/03/israel-loves-iran-on-facebook.html.

Michael, Maggie (2011) 'Egypt: at least 846 were killed in protests', *Washington Times*, 19 April, www.washingtontimes.com/news/2011/apr/19/egypt-least-846-killed-protests/?page=all.

Morozov, Evgeny (2011) *The Net Delusion: The Dark Side of Internet Freedom*. New York: Public Affairs.

Payne, Gregory, Sevin, Efe & Bruya, Sara (2011) 'Grassroots 2.0: public diplomacy in the digital age', *Comunicàcao Publica*, 6(10), pp. 45–70, cp.revues.org/422.

Obama, Barack (2014) 'West Point commencement address', 28 May, West Point, NY, www.washingtonpost.com/politics/full-text-of-president-obamas-commencement-address-at-west-point/2014/05/28/cfbcdcaa-e670-11e3-afc6-a1dd9407abcf_story.html.

Rudolph, Lloyd & Jacobsen, John Kurt (Eds) (2006) *Experiencing the State*. Oxford: Oxford University Press.

Said, Samira (2012) 'Peace minded Israeli reaches out to everyday Iranians via Facebook', *CNN*, 21 March, edition.cnn.com/2012/03/19/world/meast/israel-iran-social-media/index.html?hpt=hp_c1.

Saunders, Doug (2004) 'What changed Libya? Not Iraq, but IRC', *The Globe and Mail* (Canada), 11 December, p. F3.

Shaqiran, Fahad Bin Suliman (2014) 'Shura Council membership opened new opportunities for women', *Al-Sharq al Awsat*, 12 July, www.aawsat.net/2014/07/article55334169.

Shirky, Clay (2011) 'The political power of social media: technology, the public sphere and political change', *Foreign Affairs*, February, 90(1), pp. 28–41.

Simsek, Eylem & Simsek, Ali (2013) 'New literacies for digital citizenship', *Contemporary Educational Technology*, April, 4(2), pp. 126–137.

Sonenshine, Tara (2013) 'People-to-people engagement: cultures, history, and mutual understanding through public diplomacy', Remarks at the US Islamic World Forum, Doha, Qatar, 9 June, www.state.gov/r/remarks/2013/210431.htm#.

Spaiser, Viktoria, Luna-Reyes, Luis & SoonAe Chun (2012) 'Empowerment or democratic divide? Internet based political participation of young immigrants and young natives in Germany', *Information Polity: The Journal of Government and Democracy in the Information Age*, 17(2), pp. 115–127.

Springborg, Robert (2012) 'The precarious economics of the Arab Spring', *Survival: Global Politics and Strategy*, December 2011–Jan. 2012, 53(6), pp. 85–104. www.iiss.org/en/publications/survival/sections/2011-2760/survival–global-politics-and-strategy-december-2011-january-2012-a43c/53-6-08-springborg-9350.

Sreberny-Mohammadi, Annabelle & Mohammadi, Ali (1994) *Small Media, Big Revolution: Communication, Culture and the Iranian Revolution*. Minneapolis, MN: University of Minnesota Press.

Sunstein, Cass (2001) *Republic.com*. Princeton, NJ: Princeton University Press.

Surk, Barbara (2014) 'Death toll in Syria's war tops 160,000 activists', *Huffington Post*, 19 May, www.huffingtonpost.com/2014/05/19/syria-war-death-toll_n_5353021.html.

Theodoulou, Michael (2003) 'Proliferating Iranian weblogs give voice to taboo topics', *Christian Science Monitor*, 23 June.

Thurow, Lester (1998) 'Information-communications revolution and the global economy', in *Information Revolution and the Arab World: Its Impact on State and Society* (pp. 11–35). Abu Dhabi: ECSSR.

Transparency International (n.d.) 'Middle East and North Africa: archive site', archive.transparency.org/regional_pages/africa_middle_east/middle_east_and_north_africa_mena.

Tremblay, Pinar (2014) 'Protesting Erdogan a la Turca', *Al Monitor*, 3 March, www.al-monitor.com/pulse/originals/2014/03/turkish-protesters-get-creative.html#.

Ungerleider, Neal (2010) 'Egyptian cops kill Internet café patron', *True/Slant*, 14 June, trueslant.com/nealungerleider/2010/06/14/egyptian-cops-kill-internet-cafe-patron/.

Vick, Karl (2014) 'Turkey's Erdogan turns off Twitter, turns up nationalism', *Time*, 21 March, time.com/33393/turkey-recep-tayyip-erdogan-twitter/.

Wavell, Stuart (1995) 'Closed societies opened by Internet genie', *The Sunday Times* (London), 3 September, p. 1.

Wharton School of Business (2014) 'Women employees help reshape Saudi Arabia's labor market', 3 February, knowledge.wharton.upenn.edu/article/women-employees-reshape-saudi-arabias-labor-market/.

Wheeler, Deborah (2009) 'Working around the state: Internet use and political identity in the Arab world', in Andrew Chadwich & Phillip Howard (Eds) *Routledge Handbook of Internet Politics* (pp. 305–320). London: Routledge.

Widdershoven, Cyril (2000) 'Mediterranean Development Forum: voices for change, partners for prosperity', *Pharohs*, April, pp. 50–51.

8

RELIGIOUS MINORITIES IN CYBERSPACE

Identity and citizenship among European and British Muslims

Dalia Yousef and Rasha Abdulla

> There was discussion about whether women who wore the headscarf would be advised to remove it for their own safety. I was adamant that this was not something I would consider. I was firm in my belief and I would stand up for it. I refused to change the way I practiced my faith or to let fear stop me from carrying out what I believed in. If I did that, I would have failed in my duty as a citizen.
>
> (Janmohamed, 2010, 143)[1]

The above quote is a good representation of the complexity of issues facing Muslim minorities in the West after the terrorist attacks on 11 September 2001 (9/11). The quote illustrates the multi-layered mesh of feelings and concerns about everyday life that such a religious minority has to face, in this case issues of religious practice, and maintaining identity as it relates to a simple matter of appearance in the face of questioning and confronting discrimination, all while maintaining an active position as a Western citizen, and clarifying your religious beliefs to your society and possibly defending them against charges of terrorism. The mere task of defining a 'minority' is an increasingly difficult challenge. The concept involves different demographic, socio-economic, political, national and international complexities that contribute to its ambiguity. Mahmood (2012, 427) argues that it is difficult to decide whether a 'minority' is 'an objective designation' or a 'subjective psychological process'. Some argue that a more objective definition should refer to ethnic, cultural or linguistic traits distinguishing a (minority) group from the larger circle of the majority, while others underline how only a subjective understanding of a group's distinguishing traits could define their status as a minority. The influences of majority-minority categorization can be found on both the micro (individual) and macro (community) levels, but they should be viewed within their different social, political and historical contexts. Such a categorization does not operate in an isolated vacuum and its impact should not be perceived as a static inevitability. In fact, dramatic changes within the larger context can take place due to possible interaction of diverse voices, actors and power relations. A simplified view, not devoid of truth, tends to suggest that representing people is now the role of the media after it has been largely perceived as the role of literature. However, with the emergence of digital media, some scholars argue that more space has been created for voicing different individual and institutional attitudes.

This study explores the ways in which European Muslims, and particularly British Muslims, utilize the Internet in handling their hybrid identities, and how the different online platforms reveal the diverse perceptions within the same social and religious group. Drawing upon social identity theory, case studies of European and British Muslims' online representations are tackled as major models for analysis, with historical and theoretical propositions recalled and reconsidered throughout. Primary and secondary sources are used in studying offline/online contexts. Certain points in time are also considered while looking into either deconstructing or emphasizing and originating different discourses and narrations. One important instance in this regard is the dramatic incidents of 9/11, which brought to the forefront the question of the relationship between Islam, Muslims and the West.

The question of identity

The study draws on social identity theory, which seeks to explain the different modes of classifying oneself based on attachments to the group(s) to which one belongs. According to Tajfel (1979), one tends to depend on the group one is part of as a source of feelings of belonging, self-esteem and pride. In doing so, one tends to overplay the importance or benefit of one's own group, the in-group or 'us', while also minimizing or belittling the importance of other groups, the out-groups or 'them'. The theory later developed to explore the psychological consequences of a perceived membership of a certain group, and how this group reacts to challenges imposed on it (Turner, 1999). Social identity theory proposes that one's social behaviour will vary from interpersonal behaviour to intergroup behaviour, which is more determined by the norms of the group than of the individual. One will therefore take a position or act in a particular manner according to the position one takes along the extremes of this interpersonal–intergroup continuum. When a certain social group tends to stand closer to the intergroup extreme, its members tend to see the out-group members in a more homogenous uniform manner, which usually serves to amplify the in-group feeling of superiority (Turner, 1999).

With over 2.7 million Muslims in the United Kingdom in 2011, it is important to look at how this growing population constructs its identity online. The Pew Research Religion and Public Life Project expects that Muslims will make up 8% of Europe's population in 2030, up from 4.1% in 1990 and 6% in 2011 (Pew Research, 2011). British Muslims are currently the largest religious minority (not counting those with no religion) in the United Kingdom according to the 2011 census (which is the latest to date), which lists the 2.7 million Muslims as constituting 4.8% of the population (Office for National Statistics, 2011). Figures extrapolated by the Gatestone Institute put the numbers of British Muslims at 3.3 million or 5.2% of the population by the end of 2013, and said Islam was on its way to becoming the largest religion in the UK within the next generation (Kern, 2013). It is expected that the UK will be one of the main countries attracting Muslims in the coming years, with an expected Muslim population of 5.6 million or 8.2% of the population (Pew Research, 2011). Suleiman (2009) had documented that the British Muslim community has grown from 20,000 in 1950 largely due to waves of post-war migration. British Muslims are also the youngest religious group, with nearly half of them under the age of 25, and 88% of them under the age of 50. In comparison, Christians, the majority religious group, have the oldest age profile, with 20% aged 65 and above. While 90% of British Christians are white, British Muslims are the most ethnically diverse (Sedghi, 2013).

Öktem (2014, 4) argued that the numbers of Muslims in Europe constituted a central public concern, especially in Western Europe 'where Islam is still perceived as an immigrant religion'. According to him, the debates on Muslim demographics in Europe can be observed through perspectives of state agencies, Islamophobic actors, Muslim activists and organizations and outside pollsters. The nation-state uses censuses for administrative and security purposes. Both Islamophobic groups and Muslim organizations might inflate the number of Muslims for different causes. While Muslim activists and organizations seek recognition and public visibility through inflating numbers, Islamophobic actors use them to escalate the fear of the 'Muslim demographic bomb'. Islamophobic actors propagate how ageing Europe can be 'colonized' by younger Muslims and their high rate of birth. Far-right political parties invest the Islamophobic fears in electoral policies (Öktem, 2014), but other factors including ideology might contest Islamophobic tendencies. A more recent survey conducted by the Pew Research Center has found a gap between left and right in perceiving Muslims, 'while 47% of Germans on the political right give Muslims an unfavorable rating, just 20% on the left do so'. A similar difference can be found in France, Italy and Greece, with significant differences also found in Spain and the UK (Hackett, 2015).

European Muslims face the question of belonging and loyalty in a bipolar sense. The recurring question is whether they primarily identify themselves as European or Muslim. Hussain (2004, 103) differentiates between the religious philosophical characteristics associated with the level of Muslim identity and the national or territorial characteristics of British identity. He says Muslims are not an exception in this sense: 'Just as one could be Christian and British, or Humanist and British, so one can be Muslim and British, without the need for contradiction, tension or comparison between the two.' He uses the diversity within the UK to stabilize the position of Muslims as British citizens by illustrating that 'Britishness' is not a monolithic or homogenous identity and that travelling through the British Isles could manifest an amazing 'range of different regional customs and habits, norms and subcultures and dialectual [sic] variations' (ibid., 104). British Muslims tend to adopt a blend of primary and sub-identities. Hussain (2004, 86) points out that members of the young Muslim population are blending their multiple local identities to combine the influences of their friends with those of their parents. Eventually, they 'come up with new, hyphenated identities such as British-Pakistani-Muslim'. European Muslims in general are exploring innovative legal and intellectual frameworks to adjust their positions and handle their visibility and unique social code within their larger European societies. These innovative frameworks are dealing not only with the European and British majorities, but also with some members of the Muslim minority itself, who might not be convinced of the need for integration into their majority groups.

The emergence of digital media

The criticism of the discourses and structures of the different models of mainstream media paved the way for the flourishing of 'alternative' media to re-interpret scenes and incidents from different perspectives. As early as 1991, Stone defined communal communication in cyberspace as 'incontrovertibly social spaces in which people still meet face-to-face, but under new definitions of both "meet" and "face"' (Stone, 1991, 83). Seddon (2004) stated that living in any society involves a constant negotiation of our different values and ideas, allegiances and loyalties. Many researchers stressed the negotiable and dynamic nature of the concept of 'identity', a nature that could be expressed and interacted with through cyberspace. Understanding the complications of the virtual individual and collective representations in cyberspace can help in studying minorities and different religious existences online since the Internet seems to be the voice of the voiceless. In cyberspace, one can represent oneself in different ways by highlighting certain aspects of one's experiences and hiding others in a process of selective self-disclosure. Subsequently, cyberspace gives users the opportunity to construct and deconstruct their identities. With that recognition of a heightened sense of individual self-identity in cyberspace, the environment still provides communities with the same opportunity of selective self-disclosure. Fernback (1997, 48) connected our physical and virtual existence and indicated that 'our analogous existence in cyberspace is partially characterized by the tensions that emerge between the individual and the collective in the post-industrial society'.

On another front, Muslims frequently complain that Western media misrepresent Islam or do not cover it adequately, particularly in the wake of 9/11. Nevertheless, sometimes there is a symbiotic relationship between mainstream media and the alternative Muslim media. For example, some British Muslim writers were invited to contribute to the mainstream media, particularly in times of crisis. 'Although events in the US (9/11) were the stimulus and main focus of the media, they also provided an opportunity to consider other matters of significance to Britain's Muslims' (Ahmed, 2005, 118). In this context, the Internet stands to be a source of alternatives to mainstream opinions.

Bunt (2009) detailed how Muslim individuals and groups utilized the web at a time of crisis after the 7 July 2005 (7/7) London bombings, which served to expand their audiences. Different British Muslim organizations promptly published statements condemning the attack on their websites. He described these immediate responses as an effective and significant way to diffuse audiences and reach both Muslims and non-Muslims since 'other media players, such as the mainstream newspapers and broadcasters, placed hyperlinks to them in their reportage' (Bunt, 2009, 9).

Recently, debates over Muslim identity online came to the forefront again with the rise of the Islamic State in Iraq and Syria (ISIS).[2] As violent and extremist as they seem, ISIS caused waves when quite a few European Muslims, including British Muslims, joined their ranks and sometimes flashed it on online videos, which went viral on social media. For example, Aqsa Mahmood is a 20-year-old Scottish Muslim, who left her life and her family to join ISIS in August 2014 and marry a *jihadi* fighter'. Some observers assumed that 'online extremist propaganda' had inspired her to take that decision. Her parents confirmed that she had been brainwashed into 'rejecting her comfortable middle-class Scottish lifestyle through watching online videos and talking to people on social networks' (Leask, 2014).

Claims of radicalization via the Internet are not new. According to Bunt (1999), the Internet has been accused of being a platform for radical groups since its inception. The situation raises questions about the boundaries of free speech online, particularly in light of governments rushing to introduce 'anti-terrorism' laws that eventually cripple free speech and access to information, and allow for mass surveillance of Internet users. On the other hand, some suggested that ISIS will be hindered by the modes of using the Internet itself. Information security analyst Richard Barrett (2014) argued that the successful exploitation of the Internet will work to spread and speed a cycle of internal criticism that will not be tolerated by ISIS. Others argued that the visual brutality of ISIS, for example the beheading of hostages such as British aid worker Alan Henning, as propaganda would backfire, which would deter young Muslims from joining ISIS (White, 2014).

Despite all the challenges and beyond the specifications of the European context, European Muslims, on both the theoretical and practical levels, may serve as a catalyst to re-evaluate important issues and concepts within European societies as well as within the Muslim world. Muslims living in Europe are in a unique position to address complex interactions including different models and requirements of integration, definitions and spaces of religiosity and secularism, attitudes towards people of other faiths, political participation and engagement in civil society. Habermas (2008) viewed the existence of European Muslim communities as a main factor contributing to changes in the public consciousness of Europe as a 'post-secular society', arguing that the European post-secular society has to 'adjust itself to the continued existence of religious communities in an increasingly secularized environment'. Habermas focused on the impact of the Muslim minorities in Europe by addressing how 'the Muslims next door force the Christian citizens to face up to the practice of a rival faith. And they also give the secular citizens a keener consciousness of the phenomenon of the public presence of religion' (ibid., n.p.).

As European Muslims continue to redefine themselves in their communities, discussing choices and decisions on adequate platforms seems of enormous importance. The media play an important role in allowing these platforms to moderate and publicize such discussions. The research study at hand aims to conduct a qualitative analysis of how religious minorities utilize the Internet to re-address their hybrid identities through exploring different online discourses and tools. We analyse the content of some selected websites, and we briefly discuss the utilization of YouTube to reveal different organizational and generational standpoints, especially after the rise of ISIS.

Analysing web content

This study discusses how online expressions vary in addressing the issues of European and British Muslims from two different perspectives: first, the theoretical (macro) perspective, discussing how European Muslims can arrive at intellectual frames of reference, which are clearer and better adapted to Muslims in the European context; and second, the practical (micro) perspective considering the different experiences and views on a daily life basis. The study focuses on how British Muslims encounter questions of affiliation and how they manage their online platforms in reaction. Choosing the Internet as the environment for the analysis facilitates the discussion and re-addresses relevant concepts of marginality, self-image, representation, networking and integration. In this context, the study conducts descriptive and thematic analyses of selected websites of different European and British Muslim entities in order to illustrate how European and British Muslims utilize the Internet to manage their hybrid identities, and the kind of online discourses and tools used to highlight their understandings of citizenship and religious affiliations.

For the purpose of this study, a number of European and British websites and YouTube videos were chosen based on previous literature reviews, and based on a Google search for 'European Muslims' and 'British Muslims'. The massive web content poses different opportunities and challenges for Internet researchers in terms of sample selection. One of the major problems in categorizing and analysing web content is 'inclusiveness' or what to include and what to leave out (Tsatsou, 2014, 170). Inclusiveness might reveal a sense of subjectivity formed by the researcher's experiences and by the actualized contexts. This study focuses on experiences that developed to escape the either/or choices between being Muslim or European/British, and to enhance civic engagement and community building through employing Internet innovations. Therefore, we selected a purposive sample, the parameters of which were established through a process of elimination. We excluded web platforms that reject extremely the European and British affiliations on one hand or the Muslim religious and cultural affiliations on the other. We attempted to disentangle various strands in the European and British Muslim online landscape, but only within the platforms that address the hybrid identities of European and British Muslims. Although there are other useful online platforms (e.g. Euro-Islam[3] or the CLOSER blog[4] by Martijn de Koning), we excluded these websites because they mainly focus on European Muslims as an object of research. Instead, we tackled the web platforms that would allow us to observe the endeavours of European Muslim organizations and individuals regarding representation and social action. To see how the offline world is transferred and reproduced in cyberspace, the study focuses, in most cases, on the web platforms that have existed over a relatively extended period of time (e.g. major organizations, social platforms or blogs). We look at the content, design, composition, services and interactivity of these websites and videos. We chose some websites that represent organizations or networks, as well as websites that represent individuals or individual needs. We also looked at a few YouTube videos that recently proved to be of major significance.

Organizational websites and identity salience: between the network and the circle

Some websites that we chose represented different models and focal points of integration and citizenship. For instance, the European Muslim Network (EMN)[5] website and Facebook page imply that the founders of the network perceive themselves mainly as part of Europe. This perception is emphasized at first glance through the design of the homepage with the colours and the stars of the European Union flag and the logo prominently featuring the word 'European' in much larger font size than 'Muslim Network'. The websites and the Facebook page define the network as a 'think tank that gathers European Muslim intellectuals and activists throughout Europe [with the aim of] fostering communication, views and expert analysis on the key issues related to the Muslim presence in Europe'. The current website is available in English and French, and the content on the Facebook page is mostly in French. EMN echoed the intellectual project of European Muslim thinker Tariq Ramadan,[6] described by Salvatore (2011, 5) as 'the leading speaker for "European Islam"' who is promoting 'the civic engagement and participatory politics of Muslim actors'.

Based on a different concept of identity, the City Circle[7] is a British website seeking 'the development of a distinct British Muslim identity'. The City Circle works more as a community organization, which has its impact on the way the website is designed and functions. Unlike the EMN website, the design of the City Circle homepage does not emphasize the affiliation to Europe. Aiming to indicate the intercultural relations and the common public space between British Muslims and their fellow citizens, the design tends to be modern and simple, and the content is in English. It focuses more on grassroots initiatives, with an updated weekly events section on the homepage. The website emphasizes that '[t]he City Circle offers no doctrinal solutions but instead a space to explore new ideas and a place to ask questions: to challenge and be challenged. That is how we believe creative, confident and dynamic communities develop' (City Circle, 2015).

Shortly before this chapter went to press, in late 2015, the City Circle launched a new version of the website that keeps the old projects and events sections, but widely uses visual attractions through Flash and full-screen images. The new version shows City Circle's social media feeds (from Facebook and Twitter) on the homepage. The 'About us' section leads to an introductory video, set to a Coldplay tune, featuring some members of the management team and volunteers. The video aims to capture the vibes of the activities and ends by presenting bloopers arousing laughs among the team.

The difference between the two approaches of the EMN and the City Circle was pointed out in an in-depth interview with the native British Muslim researcher and activist Yahia Birt, former director of the City Circle. In an interview conducted by the first author, Birt tended to define Europe as an entity that unites different nation-states collaborating on the level of the free market. He therefore criticized Ramadan for rushing to bypass various practical obstacles to reach a 'European' identity. He said Ramadan believed in a more abstract philosophical perception of the European identity, which tended to be 'very French' (Yahia Birt, 2007, personal interview). The online presence of these two organizations (or experiences) illustrates two different levels of integration and empowerment for European and British Muslims.

While the two previous organizations act more as think tanks and are mainly concerned with the question of identity as a concept and with integration as a matter of action, other organizations are more concerned with representing their Muslim communities within the boundaries of European societies. They use the Internet more to publicize their views and promote their agendas on both the European and British levels.

The Federation of Islamic Organizations in Europe (FIOE)[8] is an umbrella organization on the European level. It defines itself as 'a cultural organization, with hundreds of member organizations spread across 28 European States, all subscribing to a common belief in a methodology based on moderation and balance, which represents the tolerance of Islam' (FIOE, 2015). FIOE therefore frames its vision and mission through the concepts of moderation, balance and tolerance of Islam. FIOE was founded in 1989, which is relatively early in the context of organizing European Muslim efforts. The organization claims to be a key contributor in establishing and transforming Muslims from 'mere powerless migrants into positively contributing citizens: enjoying the same rights, and shouldering the same responsibilities as the native population'. The content of the FIOE website is available in English and in Arabic. The FIOE highlights its European affiliation, but it also overemphasizes its Islamic affiliation on both the visual and the content levels. The website issues prompt statements on issues that potentially touch upon the lives of European Muslims. For example, on the day that the *Charlie Hebdo* newspaper was attacked in Paris in January 2015, the website featured a statement that read: 'The Federation of Islamic Organizations in Europe condemns in the strongest terms the barbaric attack perpetrated today.' The statement called the attack 'appalling' and 'bloody', and said it was 'a vile terrorist act, which may not be justified under any circumstances, or attributed to any particular religion, culture, or constituent of society' (FIOE, 2015).

Another example of a European Muslim organization is the Forum of European Muslim Youth and Student Organisations (FEMYSO).[9] Like the EMN, the logo of FEMYSO features the blue stars of the European Union, and the website design is modern and colourful. Established in 1996, FEMYSO, again like EMN, is registered as a nongovernmental organization (NGO) in Brussels, at the heart of Europe. The website states that FEMYSO 'has become the de facto voice of Muslim Youth in Europe and is regularly consulted on issues pertaining to Muslim Youth. It has developed useful links with the European Parliament, the European Commission, the Council of Europe, the Organization for Security and Co-operation in Europe (OSCE), [and] the United Nations' (FEMYSO, 2015).

FEMYSO is concerned with framing the unique position of the younger generation of European Muslims. It emphasizes integrating the Muslim identity with the European through networking among young Muslims all over Europe. It uses emotional language, saying they 'must be in touch, know each other to feel the real Islamic brotherhood', while also young European Muslims have to be 'responsible and constructive members of the European society'. As part of this mission, FEMYSO has set up a wide range of training programmes for students. In terms of citizenship and civic engagement, FEMYSO adopts a human rights approach and attempts to train Muslim youth organizations to tackle Islamophobia in creative ways. For example, the organization ran a campaign to 'Green up my Local Community!' in 2013 in coordination with the MADE in Europe organization. The campaign aimed to bring young Muslims from ten European countries to secure pledges from 20 mosques to become environmentally friendly.

One of the most significant British Muslim organizations is the Muslim Council of Britain (MCB).[10] The MCB defines itself as 'a national representative Muslim umbrella body with over 500 affiliated national, regional, and local organizations, mosques, charities and schools'. The MCB's mission is '[t]o empower the Muslim community to contribute towards achieving a cohesive, just and successful British society' (MCB, 2014). The homepage highlights the news, events and press releases of the MCB and its different committees. There are also highlights of community news and events. The MCB has an obvious interest in business and economics, with regards not only to empowering young Muslim entrepreneurs, but also to showing various Muslim contributions to their society. In this regard, a report titled 'The Muslim Pound' is highlighted on the homepage, with an infographic illustrating the size of the *halal* food and lifestyle industry.

Education is also among the major fields of interest on the MCB website. The section discusses monitoring and contributing to the existing educational systems through the status of Muslim students and children. It also stresses that the so-called 'Trojan Horse plot of a Muslim takeover of schools' is only a myth. The MCB has a Research and Documentation Committee, which aims to create a resource centre for researchers, students and journalists covering issues of Islamophobia, multiculturalism and Muslim integration.

Before this chapter went to press in late 2015, a new version of the MCB website was launched. The new website keeps the same sections of press releases and the community news. Unlike the older version, the new one employs interactive features through 'Get involved' and 'Report an incident' sections highlighted in the header of the website. The users (organizations) can affiliate, participate or donate in 'Get involved', while they can send confidential messages through 'Report an incident' to describe harassment or discrimination for being Muslims. The MCB asks the users (victims) for detailed messages to be used for documentation. The MCB uses Flash files, large images and other visual attractions in the new version of the website. The 'About us' section opens to a video, but, unlike City Circle, the video focuses more on the history and the roots of Muslims in Britain by using black and white photos of early Muslim communities. The video also features the current British Muslim situation and the activities of the MCB. In the 'British Muslims' section, the MCB puts a face to the numbers of Muslims. It might aim to turn the negative connotations of Muslim demographics into positive concepts through using large photos, basic information and catchphrases like 'Rooted in Britain, Connections across the Globe' and 'British Muslims Help Put the "Great" into Great Britain'.

One of the member organizations of the MCB is the Muslim Association of Britain (MAB).[11] Some have argued that the MAB has 'Arab-leaning tendencies' (Abbas, 2011, 150), an assumption that might have been enhanced, since the war against Iraq in 2003, by the MAB's active participation in the Stop the War Coalition. On the ground, the MAB has been concerned with motivating Muslims and sometimes mobilizing them in a political sense. Peace (2013) argued that the success of the MAB in organizing demonstrations for the Palestinian cause helped pave the way for them to co-organize anti-war demonstrations with the Stop the War Coalition. The website of the MAB features sections on news, events, press releases and activities. It states that the MAB's mission is 'serving society by promoting the accepted understanding of Islam with its spiritual teachings, ideals, civil concepts and moral values'. The interest in following the Arab world is clear, and is combined with engaging with incidents in the British and European societies. The focus changes between the Arab world on one hand and British and European Muslims on the other, depending on the actual influential incidents at the time. Different offline and online events in solidarity with Syria and Gaza, and also celebrating Arabic culture, can be found in the online content both in text and video. For example, the MAB issued a press release celebrating International Arabic Language Day (MAB, 2015). On the other hand, and in reaction to anti-Muslim protests in Germany in the wake of the *Charlie Hebdo* attacks in France, an op-ed was featured on the MAB website emphasizing that such protests are 'fanning the flames of racism, intolerance and xenophobia', and pointing to waves of condemnation from counter-protestors. The article celebrated the success of Muslim integration in the UK: 'there are many successful instances where "integration" has taken place and the town of Leicester in the Midlands has been held up [as] an example where diverse communities live in harmony' (Charles, 2015). The MAB also launched a new version of its website in 2015, adding a new section for 'campaigns'. For example, the section had a campaign to introduce Prophet Muhammad to British society through flyers, outdoor advertisements on billboards and buses, and through organizing a conference. In the same context, the campaign page has a two-minute video titled 'Who is Muhammad?' The video features British Muslims of different ages who briefly propose how the legacy of Prophet Muhammad embeds responses to current social and political problems. In the video, a British Muslim woman states that '[Prophet Muhammad] drew up the first constitution in Medina in which the rights of religious minorities were preserved'.

The MAB's 'About us' has a new frequently asked questions (FAQ) sub-section, which includes general information on the MAB as well as information regarding the MAB's ideologies and affiliations. The questions include whether the MAB is an 'Islamist' organization, which it denies, and whether it is a branch of the Muslim Brotherhood, which it neither confirms nor denies. Instead, the website says, the 'MAB shares some of the main principles that the Muslim Brotherhood stands for; like upholding democracy, freedom of the individual, social justice and the creation of a civil society', thus emphasizing that the MAB is an independent organization, although it shares ideology with the Muslim Brotherhood. In doing so, the MAB associates the Muslim Brotherhood with positive values of democracy, social justice and freedom.

The FAQ section also tries to answer accusations that the MAB has faced in recent months. For example, the MAB and FIOE were both included on a terrorist list of 85 organizations endorsed by the United Arab Emirates (UAE) cabinet (Obeid, 2014). The organization denies any links with terrorism, condemns all acts of terrorism, and deems suicide bombings to be anti-Islamic. To put things in perspective, Finn (2014) noted that the UAE list has to be viewed in light of the political confrontation between some Gulf and Arab regimes and the Muslim Brotherhood. Obeid (2014) said that 'human rights and Islamic organizations as well as relief bodies that are legally operating in Western countries have found themselves on the same list as al-Qaeda, the Islamic State and Boko Haram'. The MAB announced that it would be seeking libel charges against the UAE government (Finn, 2014).

The MAB refutes what it describes as a dichotomous category of 'political' and 'non-political' Islam. Despite the political tensions and the involvement in conceptual and actual controversies, the organization continues its work in advocacy and calls for action. For instance, the MAB participated in campaigning against Egyptian President Abdel Fatah El-Sisi's visit to the UK in November 2015. In the 'Events' section, the MAB called for protesting against General El-Sisi and listed reasons for rejecting his visit, including El-Sisi's alleged confiscation of public freedoms and poor human rights record.

Individual tones and needs: *Love in a Headscarf*

While some websites such as those in the previous section represented various European and British Muslim organizations that worked on the collective community level, there are other important online representations that cater for European and British Muslims on the individual level. For example, one popular British Muslim website is SingleMuslim.com, which, in October 2012, celebrated having 1 million registered members. SingleMuslim.com is featured as a safe interactive environment using digital tools to facilitate marriage between Muslims. The popularity of the website is a reflection of the change in the younger generations of British and European Muslims, who cannot adhere to the older model of arranged marriages their parents might prefer them to abide by. Rather than going back to their countries of origin to find a spouse with arguably more traditional values, they prefer to search online within their larger societies, even if that means ending up with a spouse of a different social code.

The organizational characteristics of SingleMuslim.com echo the individual tone in Shelina Zahra Janmohamed's award-winning blog 'Spirit 21',[12] out of which came her book *Love in a Headscarf*. The book and the blog detail the adventures, trials and tribulations of a female British Muslim in her journey to find love while keeping her faith. Written in a creative, humorous style, Janmohamed tells us of the challenges of engaging with her larger society as a Muslim woman. Although Janmohamed's work could be categorized as personal writing, it sheds light upon different complicated details of living as a younger female British Muslim. Her work also touched upon the challenges that faced Muslims in Europe after 9/11, with the rise of Islamophobia and the seasonal rise of radical right-wing groups. The content of Janmohamed's personal experiences on the Internet has been published and translated, indicating an interest in finding and hearing different genuine first-hand Muslim narrations.

To help cater to the psychological needs of British Muslim society, the Muslim Community Helpline[13] was developed in 2007 by the same group of people who had previously run the Muslim Women Helpline in the UK (MWHL) for 19 years.

The Muslim Community Helpline (like the previous MWHL) is an independent organization, which depends on volunteers to provide confidential 'listening and emotional support services' by phone through friendly volunteers who are well versed in British Muslim culture. The organization does not provide online counselling, but instead uses the website to publicize its efforts and its toll-free numbers, to receive help requests and enquiries through email, and to provide information and useful links.

'Happy' British Muslims

Searching for 'British Muslims' on YouTube shows a 'Happy British Muslims' video[14] with over 2.2 million views as of November 2015. The dance video to Pharrell Williams's 2014 BBC Song of the Year, 'Happy', was released in April 2014 by a new type of youth polity. The Honesty Policy[15] introduced itself on its website as a 'moral movement', which believed that 'the real essence of religious character is found outside the traditionally religious spheres'. The organization said it was 'about shifting parameters – movement away from familiar established

FIGURE 8.1 Muslim Community Helpline

structures with the intent of becoming a relevant, contemporary and accessible community'. The members of the Honesty Policy were anonymous, since, as a 'counter-culture group', they sought 'integrity', which, according to them, 'doesn't need a face' (Honesty Policy Group, 2014).

The mere act of defining the organization as a 'counter-culture group' indicates a rejection of the stagnant status quo. The content of the website reflects just that. One blog post titled 'FED UP with Islamic organizations' starts with the shocking statement 'You think the Corporate World is exploitative, judgmental, and egotistical? Try Islamic Organizations'. The post uses the concepts of anti-capitalism and anti-globalization to formulate a blunt, harsh argument of the traditional Muslim organizations (BENI, 2015).

Before this chapter went to press in 2015, the Honesty Policy Group launched a new website and changed its name to BENI.[16] On the homepage, the word BENI is written in both English and Arabic, with the description 'Derived from the Arabic Beni Adam meaning "Children of Adam". A name of an organization dedicated to designing visual imagery that reflects mankind's same origin regardless of race, culture or ethnicity'. Similar to the old website's counter-culture stance, the new website states that 'BENI steers away from narcissism, consumerism and superficiality'. While most new websites of Muslim organizations launched in 2015 aimed to employ new web visual attractions, BENI's website revolves around visual aesthetic meaning. The website combines visual and generational inclinations: 'BENI hopes to join old with the new, giving space to the generation-Y millennial who has an appetite for meaningful aesthetics.' BENI maintains a reference to its older brand name through its Facebook page entitled 'BENI FEED – by The Honesty Policy'.

FIGURE 8.2 BENI

The British Muslim Happy video,[17] which the movement had produced, features a diverse group of Muslim women and men of all ages, clapping, smiling and dancing to the song. The video sparked many controversies that went beyond the likes/dislikes of the video as a piece of entertainment and delved into what exactly comprises Muslim identity and whether it was appropriate for Muslims, who are stereotyped for their conservatism, to sing and dance in the manner featured in the video. On their website, the Honesty Policy bragged that they were able to feature 'scholars, activists, celebrities, students, professionals, bloggers and every-day'ers all in one video'. Defining themselves as British, the post, which had a good amount of almost all positive, sometimes ecstatic, comments, continued, 'We Brits have a bad rep for being a bit stiff, but this video proves otherwise. We are HAPPY. We are eclectic. We are cosmopolitan. Diverse. Creative. Fun. Outgoing. And everything you can think of' (Honesty Policy Group, 2014). An *Economist* article said that the escalating controversy encouraged a member of the Honesty

Policy to describe the video as 'part of a process by which British Muslims workout their identity. That process may be unusually rancorous and painful' (*The Economist*, 2014).

On the conservative side, some worried that the music on the video, as well as the dancing and mixing of men and women, was *haram* (or forbidden in Islam) and diverges from the modesty the religion calls for. In this context, different rival videos were created to pose a *halal* (religiously valid) version of the video or to refute it altogether. Additionally, some cultural critics argued that the video had an artificial reactionary attitude. They said the video aims to break the cycle of stereotyping, but it does so by deepening stereotypes and portraying the good, happy and 'normal' Muslims, who seem to stick to Western code of attitude and dress, versus the traditional angry extreme Muslims. They depicted the video therefore as a way of 'internalizing orientalism and racism'. However, others argued that featuring happiness can in itself be political, as the video 'shows a group of Muslims performing a capacity to stop noticing the negative social imaginaries and miseries of the world while at the same time attempting to tame [the] violence of the racist impositions and the frustrations of feeling powerless against the injustice in the world' (Martijn, 2014).

Indeed, the video shows a new and vibrant way of introducing Muslims to the world, portraying imageries of people in beards and headscarves, who at the end of the day, like everyone else, just want to be happy. The mere controversy caused by the video is a sign of liveliness in a culture long stereotyped as being stagnant and resistant to change.

The rise of ISIS

Ironically, issuing the Happy Muslims video, and its subsequent controversies, has almost coincided with the shocking, violent emergence of ISIS. ISIS has attracted attention through using YouTube and social networks to recruit and target new members, including British and European Muslims, as well as to publicize its violent crimes against humanity. Between the proponents of the Happy Muslims video and the (far fewer) proponents of ISIS, we are represented with two extremely opposed efforts, both of which indicate a thirst for change among British Muslim youth in local and global turbulent contexts, one through dancing and the other through killing to conquer and spread fear.

ISIS seems to have two main purposes for utilizing social networks, especially YouTube. The first is to control through intimidation by capturing its operations, including brutal beheading of hostages, on camera, and counting on the social networks to drive the content viral. The second is to use them as recruitment tools, through propaganda material that argues that joining ISIS helps establish an Islamic Caliphate, and is a path to martyrdom. ISIS videos are usually characterized by high-quality footage and professional editing and sound, including professionally recorded and mixed music-free songs for soundtracks.

It seems unnatural that many Muslim youth would be attracted to the brutality in some ISIS videos. As a matter of fact, White (2014) argued that showing beheadings 'turned the tide' on the inclination to join ISIS. Repeatedly, however, ISIS seems to switch techniques from the violent to the soft and passionate. For instance, and in a continuing attempt to encourage more women to join it, ISIS published a 'feminine manual [of] labour, which teaches different skills women can learn to take part in "jihadi science", including basic first aid, sewing, cooking and editing videos' (Pleasance, 2014). ISIS seems to depend mainly on people sharing their video files on social media, particularly given how shocking most of these videos are. However, at times ISIS members are themselves active, and have hijacked popular Twitter hashtags – for example, during the 2014 World Cup, to reach a wider audience.

On the other hand, European and British Muslims call for avoiding generalizations regarding Islam and Muslims in terms of terrorism. They too are using social networks to get their voices across in this regard. For example, members of the Active Change Foundation[18] started a campaign with the hashtag #notinmyname, aiming to counter ISIS' online propaganda. The campaign used the organization's website, YouTube and Twitter and other social media to let the world know that ISIS does not represent Islam or Muslims. Such campaigns started an interesting debate on whether Muslims should 'apologize' for the terrorist acts ISIS or others commit in their name. Another interesting hashtag, #MuslimApologies, emerged to pay a sarcastic tribute to the idea that Muslims are collectively guilty or responsible for ISIS-style terrorism. Tweets on this hashtag ridiculed the 'apologetic' tendency by tweeting apologies for Islamic civilization achievements, inventions or even general phenomena. The tweets ranged from 'Sorry for Algebra' to 'Sorry for Vanilla Ice' (Izadi, 2014).

Conclusion

European and British Muslims encounter the question of prioritized identities and the different circles of affiliation in forming and framing their representations in everyday life and online. A salient activated identity does not operate only as a cognitive perceptual process but also as a social process in which people may compete or negotiate over category salience. There are different online experiences of European and British Muslims in addressing their concerns and ambitions. From classic organizations to hippy ones to individual tones and needs, these online patterns shed light on the concepts of representation and agency among British Muslims, alongside the internal struggle to settle their positions of being European, British and Muslim, without obscuring their individualism.

Different structural contexts partially determine online representations. For instance, European or British Muslims have no central body of representation. Therefore, websites of different bodies and organizations that seek to represent British Muslims have come into existence. On a different level, British Muslims interact in more scattered and fragmented social circles and groups. Subsequently, and due to the relatively advanced technological infrastructure, British websites for matrimonial services, women and family helplines are among some of the most popular digital platforms.

In terms of using online facilities, European Muslim websites do organize campaigns and activities, whether for the purpose of advocacy or integration. This relative success can be understood in light of the availability of legal and administrative frameworks allowing European Muslims to manage and develop their activities with a reasonable degree of freedom. Most of the European Muslim websites examined in this study clearly state their interest to engage with the larger society, but there is not always enough evidence in terms of content and design that they are actually trying to engage the audiences of these larger societies.

Especially during such moments of crisis, the impact of European and British Muslims' alternative platforms in cyberspace are important, and their effects can be amplified if quoted by the mainstream media. Discussions prevail on the priority of resisting victimization (through self-criticism), as well as on discrimination against groups of Muslims. We are seeing online evidence that most reactionary redundant attitudes are being criticized and rejected, especially by some youth groups, in favour of more creative and authentic integration. Recently, many Muslim organizations started to show a sense of responsiveness by launching new versions of their websites, whether to deal with national and transnational challenges or to benefit from the Web 2.0 applications that enable greater interactivity, networking and enhanced visual representations.

Although young European Muslims are quite diverse, this study shows that the younger generations perceive their positions as citizens through a mixture of resisting stereotypes, sarcasm and searching for a better place. The position of the youth is framed online in different ways, but it is usually coupled with discussing 'radicalization' and 'extremism'. Sometimes, younger groups are introduced in cyberspace as a politicized generation, demonstrated by visualizing Muslim grievances or in a more proactive way by figuring out how faith can work as a vehicle of reform. On other occasions, young Muslims adopt a cultural development approach, whereby they are no longer concerned with the political side of Islam. Rather, they see Islamic identity as a set of cultural expressions, modes of actions, and musical forms on a personal and un-hierarchical level. The rise of ISIS reactivates discussions on chronic problems demanding effective solutions. The continuing challenges problematize the notion of identity and lead to different reactions, both online and offline, including campaigning, mobilization, sarcasm, frustration and sometimes anger. ISIS' effective use of social networks for propaganda makes the Internet look like a disputed territory for influence. Such a position increases the importance of resisting terrorism, but also resisting curtailing civic freedoms in the name of fighting terrorism.

Notes

1 *Love in a Headscarf* by Shelina Zahra Janmohamed. © 2010 by Shelina Zahra Janmohamed. Reprinted by permission of Beacon Press, Boston.
2 Also called ISIL (Islamic State in Iraq and the Levant), or just IS (Islamic State). In Arabic, *Da'esh*.
3 www.euro-islam.info

4 religionresearch.org/closer/
5 euromuslim.net (page inactive since March 2008); www.facebook.com/pages/European-Muslim-Network-EMN/128498273835676; www.euro-muslims.eu
6 tariqramadan.com
7 www.thecitycircle.com
8 www.fioe.org
9 www.femyso.org
10 www.mcb.org.uk
11 www.mabonline.net
12 www.spirit21.co.uk
13 muslimcommunityhelpline.org.uk
14 www.youtube.com/watch?v=gVDIXqILqSM
15 Previously hosted at www.honestypolicy.co.uk
16 www.beni.space/beni/
17 www.youtube.com/watch?v=gVDIXqILqSM
18 www.activechangefoundation.org. A London-based foundation established in 2003 with the aim of facilitating positive change and preventing the spread of violence and extremism.

References

Abbas, T. (2011) *Islamic Radicalism and Multicultural Politics: The British Experience*. London: Routledge.

Ahmed, T.S. (2005) 'Reading between the lines – Muslims and the media', in T. Abbas (Ed.) *Muslims in Britain: Communities under Pressure* (pp. 109–126). London: Zed Books.

Barrett, R. (Ed.) (2014) *The Islamic State* (online). The SOUFAN Group, soufangroup.com/wp-content/uploads/2014/10/TSG-The-Islamic-State-Nov14.pdf.

BENI (2015) 'Fed up with Islamic organisations', *BENI Policy* (online), www.beni.space/blog/2015/5/16/fed-up-of-islamic-organisations.

Bunt, G. (1999) 'islam@britain.net: "British Muslim" identities in cyberspace', *Islam and Christian-Muslim Relations*, 10(3), pp. 353–362.

Bunt, G. (2009) *iMuslims: Rewiring the House of Islam*. Chapel Hill, NC: University of North Carolina Press.

Charles, K. (2015) *Integration and Tolerance – The Effects of Anti-Muslim Protest in Germany*. Muslim Association of Britain, 7 January, www.mabonline.net/integration-and-tolerance-the-effects-of-anti-muslim-protest-in-germany/.

City Circle (2015) www.thecitycircle.com. Video file at: www.thecitycircle.com/about.

The Economist (2014) 'British Muslims: happy or haram? An online video sparks a heated debate', *The Economist*, 3 May, www.economist.com/news/britain/21601544-online-video-sparks-heated-debate-happy-or-haram.

Federation of Islamic Organisations in Europe (FIOE) (2015) 'FIOE condemns the barbaric attack on the offices of a newspaper in Paris', www.fioe.org/ShowNews_en.php?id=157&img=6.

Fernback, J. (1997) 'The individual within the collective: virtual ideology and the realization of collective principles', in S. Jones (Ed.) *Virtual Culture: Identity and Communication in Cyber Society*. London: Sage, pp. 36–54.

Finn, T. (2014) 'UK Muslim groups to pursue legal action against UAE over terrorist list', *Middle East Eye*, November, www.middleeasteye.net/news/uk-muslim-groups-mull-legal-action-against-uae-over-terror-list-547741001.

Forum of European Muslim Youth and Student Organisations (FEMYSO) (2015) www.femyso.org.

Habermas, J. (2008) *Notes on a Post-secular Society*. Address at the Nexus Institute, University of Tilberg, Netherlands, www.signandsight.com/features/1714.html.

Hackett, C. (2015) '5 facts about the Muslim population in Europe', Pew Research Center, www.pewresearch.org/fact-tank/2015/01/15/5-facts-about-the-muslim-population-in-europe/.

Honesty Policy Group (2014) 'Pharrell – Happy – BRITISH MUSLIMS!', www.honestypolicy.co.uk/?p=166.

Hussain, D. (2004) 'British Muslim identity', in H. Dilwar, N. Malik & M.S. Seddon (Eds) *British Muslims Between Assimilation and Segregation – Historical, Legal and Social Realities* (pp. 83–118). Markfield: The Islamic Foundation.

Izadi, E. (2014) 'Why people are tweeting their #Muslim apologies', *Washington Post*, 24 September, www.washingtonpost.com/blogs/worldviews/wp/2014/09/24/why-people-are-tweeting-their-muslimapologies/.

Janmohamed, S. (2010) *Love in a Headscarf*. London: Aurum Press.

Kern, S. (2013) *The Islamization of Britain in 2013*. Gatestone Institute, www.gatestoneinstitute.org/4112/islamization-britain.

Leask, D. (2014) 'Young UK Muslims in protest at Islamic terrorists', *Herald Scotland*, 17 September, www.heraldscotland.com/news/home-news/young-uk-muslims-in-protest-at-islamic-terrorists.25351681.

Mahmood, S. (2012) 'Religious freedom, the minority question, and geopolitics in the Middle East', *Comparative Studies in Society and History*, 54, pp. 418–446.

Martijn, K. (2014) 'The pursuit of happiness – happy Muslims, creativity and political agency', web log comment, Closer, 18 May, religionresearch.org/closer/2014/05/18/pursuit-happiness-happy-muslims-creativity-political-agency/.

Muslim Association of Britain (MAB) (2015) 'Egypt's dictator is coming', Muslim Association of Britain (online), www.mabonline.net/events/.

Muslim Council of Britain (MCB) (2014) 'Infographic: how Muslim pound', in *The Muslim Pound Celebrating the Muslim Contribution to the UK Economy*, www.mcb.org.uk/wp-content/uploads/2014/10/The-Muslim-Pound-FINAL.pdf.

Obeid, H. (2014) 'European Muslim groups angered by inclusion on UAE's terror list', *ALMONITOR*, December, www.al-monitor.com/pulse/originals/2014/12/uae-terrorist-list-european-islamist-groups.html#.

Office for National Statistics (2011) 'Full story: what does the census tell us about religion in 2011?' http://webarchive.nationalarchives.gov.uk/20160105160709/http://www.ons.gov.uk/ons/dcp171776_310454.pdf.

Öktem, K. (2014) 'Counting Muslims: censuses, categories, policies and the construction of Muslims in Europe', in J.S. Nielsen (Ed.) *Yearbook of Muslims in Europe* (pp. 1–16). Leiden: BRILL.

Peace, T. (2013) 'Muslims and the anti-war movement', *Public Spirit*, 18 November, www.publicspirit.org.uk/muslims-and-the-anti-war-movement/.

Pew Research (2011) *Religion and Public Life Project. The Future of the Global Muslim Population*. www.pewforum.org/2011/01/27/future-of-the-global-muslim-population-regional-europe/.

Pleasance, C. (2014) 'Training wives for jihad: ISIS women's group publishes advice on how to be a good companion for the Islamist militant of their dreams', *Mail Online*, 5 November, www.dailymail.co.uk/news/article-2821845/Training-wives-jihad-ISIS-women-s-group-publishes-advice-good-companion-Islamist-militant-dreams.html.

Ramadan, T. (2009) *Radical Reform: Islamic Ethics and Liberation*. New York: Oxford University Press.

Salvatore, A. (2011) 'New media and collective action in the Middle East: can sociological research help avoiding orientalist traps?' *Sociologica*, 1, pp. 1–17.

Seddon, M.S. (2004) 'Muslim communities in Britain: a historiography', in M.S. Seddon, N. Malik & D. Hussain (Eds) *British Muslims between Assimilation and Segregation: Historical, Legal and Social Realities* (pp. 1–42). Leicester: Islamic Foundation.

Sedghi, A. (2013) 'UK Census: religion by age, ethnicity, and country of birth', *The Guardian*, 16 May, www.theguardian.com/news/datablog/2013/may/16/uk-census-religion-age-ethnicity-country-of-birth.

Stone, A.R. (1991) 'Will the real body please stand up? Boundary stories about virtual cultures', in M. Benedikt (Ed.) *Cyberspace: First Steps* (pp. 81–118). Cambridge, MA: MIT Press.

Suleiman, Y. (2009) *Contextualising Islam in Britain: Exploratory Perspectives*. Cambridge: Centre of Islamic Studies, University of Cambridge in association with the Universities of Exeter and Westminster, www.exeter.ac.uk/media/universityofexeter/webteam/shared/pdfs/misc/Contextualising_Islam_in_Britain.pdf.

Tajfel, H. (1979) 'Individuals and groups in social psychology', *British Journal of Social and Clinical Psychology*, 18, pp. 183–190.

Tsatsou, P. (2014) 'Research and the Internet: fast growing Internet research', in *Internet Studies: Past, Present and Future Direction* (pp. 165–215). Farnham: Ashgate.

Turner, J.C. (1999) 'Some current issues in research on social identity and self-categorization theories', in N. Ellemers, R. Spears & B. Doosje (Eds) *Social Identity: Context, Commitment, Content* (pp. 6–34). Oxford: Blackwell.

White, M. (2014) 'Henning murder "turned tide" on IS recruitment', *Sky News*, 4 November, news.sky.com/story/1366257/henning-murder-turned-tide-on-is-recruitment.

YouTube (2014) 'Happy British Muslims! #HAPPYDAY', 15 April, www.youtube.com/watch?v=gVDIXqILqSM.

9

BRITISH ARAB YOUTH

Reconstruction of virtual Islamic identities after the Arab Spring

Khalil Alagha

In the last two decades, there has been growing interest in exploring the possible effect of new media on young people's behaviour, attitudes and identity construction. The possible influence of online media in shaping, reshaping, constructing or reconstructing youth identity has come under extensive investigations in the academic field and gained interest of media and public affairs. Youth of ethnic minorities in the West face a number of challenges – at the top of them their identity construction. Arab and Muslim youth in the West are under even more pressure for various reasons, so that at times of national crisis they are always required to prove their loyalty to their host society. British Arab youth of the second and third generations who are on a 'special journey' of constructing adaptable identities come constantly under fire when an issue of terrorism arises and the media start to propagate their coverage, questioning loyalty and belonging. Arab youth are always submerged with Muslim youth, which may be the source of stereotyping them. Although the Arab community in the UK has been recognized in the latest Census 2011 as an ethnic group, as a community they are still under-researched and unrepresented in mainstream media. There are assumptions in the mainstream media and among the wider British society that British Arab youth are no different to their Muslim peers, mainly because the majority of them share the same religion, Islam. This chapter aims to shed some light on the cultural identity perception of British Arab youth, and in particular the influence of religion on the process of construction and reconstruction of their identities.

Religion is playing a role in one way or another in the construction of Arab people's consciousness. The chapter draws on the results of a combination of quantitative questionnaires amongst 178 British Arabs between the ages of 18 and 25, as well as 40 individual semi-structured interviews of a selected sample of this cohort, carried out during the period 2011 to 2013.

Arab youth (of the second generation) in Britain are part of British multicultural society, but much as this provides opportunities to empower youth of ethnic minorities it also can expose them to means of stereotyping and alienation. The construction of their identity is a complex process that incorporates the effect of various forces interchangeably. The level of effect of these forces, such as family, religion, society and media, may vary depending on the circumstances to which youth are exposed. Most recently, online media are looked at as a major player in the construction of youth's identity (Livingstone, 2002). Youth have the ability, skills and knowledge to select the content of online media to interact/engage with, which in return defines the way they choose to construct their identity, and stands as a theoretical ground to understand how the circumstances that influence youth play a significant role in constructing their identity. That is what motivates youth to turn to online media and select the content that fulfils their needs. This process is reflected back on their identity, which keeps the construction and reconstruction of their identity ongoing.

It is not unusual for people to have multiple identities. People 'could be pulled in different directions by their competing identities, unsure whether their sympathies should be determined by their "race", gender, class or political attitudes' (Pilkington, 2003, 172). If we acknowledge that the 'belief' factor can determine the formation of a certain identity, the 'belief' shaped by inevitable changing forces can provide the ground for another form of identity, and so on.

The 'invisibles': a community in the shadows

After a considerable search, little could be found about the second generation of British Arab youth. The mainstream media are filled with themes of stereotyping, labelling youth of certain ethnic minorities and declaring them a threat to British values. These themes are mainly based on commentators' opinions rather than scientific research or empirical data. If we recognize first that the Arab community belongs to a civilization that dominated the world just a few centuries ago, it deserves to be explored on its own. Considering the potential and risks of this 'invisible community', policymakers and community leaders are required to explore and understand it. The Arab community is heavily under-researched as a consequence of being invisible. As Silverstone and Georgiou (2005, 7) put it: 'Significant ethnic groups (e.g. the Arabs) are left between the white, the black and the others. Non-recognition and non-visibility in official statistics is twofold in its consequences – it increases the sense of symbolic exclusion and it decreases social and cultural service provision towards "invisible" groups.'

Arab youth are a very important segment of the Arab community as they belong to the second generation, which can define the future of the Arab community as a whole in Britain. This study approaches this segment of the Arab community in Britain using qualitative and quantitative research methods in an attempt to provide more accurate and reliable data for analysis. British Arab youth are caught between their portrayal by British society as if their sense of belonging is always questioned, and the assumptions or ambitions of the Arab community. Therefore, their loyalty in turbulent times is scrutinized – that is, when the media play a negative role in putting them under pressure to position themselves, 'us' or 'them'. This position puts British Arab youth on a more complex ground, requiring them first to map their identity and second to identify their sense of belonging culturally and emotionally.

Religion is part of British Arab youth's identity construction that plays a significant role in shaping their mindset and their vision of integration with the rest of society. Online media are gradually providing Arab youth with an alternative source of learning about religion. Previously, the teaching of religious practices was dominated by institutions represented by scholars of a mixed level of post-modernity Islamic knowledge. In Britain, Arab youth have three main sources of learning religious beliefs and practices: parents (family), a Muslim preacher (as an institution) and the Internet. In the last few years, online media seem to have gained more attention, not only amongst researchers and media content producers, but also amongst individuals and groups, who have become both consumers and producers of media content at the same time. Advances in communication technology have allowed easy access to the Internet and a simplified engagement process. Prior to the Arab Spring, young British Arabs tended to turn to the Internet to negotiate their identity by exploring their cultural roots – a shift from traditional institutions of preaching Islam to new sources such as satellite channels (Galal, 2013).

The revival of Muslim identity vs. Arab identity

The emergence of the term 'Muslim identity' in the Arab world as well as in the Western diaspora sparked discussion. The so-called revival of Islamic identity followed, to a great extent, the success of the Islamic revolution in Iran, the war against the Soviets in Afghanistan and the arrival of pro-Islamist rule in Sudan (Barakat, 1993, 101; Esposito, 2003, 4). Since then, Islamic movements have gained in popularity. Prominent names representing 'the notion of restoring Muslim identity started to attract followers' (Badran, 2012). In addition to mosques, online media have witnessed an early presence of Islamic movements, mobilized towards the idea of reviving Muslim identity. Badran (2012) notes that 'in the presence of advanced communication technologies and in the age of globalised materialistic values, Muslims should be aware of these "sneaky values" that could threaten the Muslim identity'. Here it is remarkable how academics and Muslim scholars are engaged with people not only in mosques, the traditional place for Islamic lectures, but also online, where, not surprisingly, they are very active.

The online sphere has been seen as an alternative to traditional media in the Arab world, which are dominated by either the secular or leftists – the traditional opponents of Islamists. Badran continues to argue that Muslims should not close their eyes and let go. They must engage proactively with the media using all available platforms. Online media have provided a powerful tool that, on one hand, can reach almost everyone who has a computer or a mobile, and on the other hand bypass the obstacle of barring them from appearing on traditional satellite channels (Badran, 2012). This discourse is only a drop in the ocean of the ongoing debate around Muslim identity; however, there are dilemmas facing the notion of reviving Islamic identity. First, there seems to be a disagreement amongst Islamists about defining Muslim identity. The dominant movement, the Muslim Brotherhood, adopted a moderate definition, while the emergent Salafists adopted a radical understanding of Muslim identity. Also other non-politicized Islamic streams, such as the *Dawah* group and Sufis, developed a spiritual understanding of how a Muslim must be. Second, the rise of a religious sectarian divide raised concerns within the Muslim community that going that way is too dangerous for the cohesion of their societies, so they would rather stick to a less radical understanding of Islam.

Many forces influence British Arab youth's identity formation process, so it is worthwhile looking at the background of these forces. Along with the effect of the export of Western values through globalization, particularly of the mass media, one can conclude that Arab culture is undergoing profound changes at the present time. Commentators argue that this has led to an Arab 'identity crisis', focused around the paradox created by a desire on the part of many in the Arab world to study and work in the West, and the threat to traditional Arab and Islamic values which many conservatives view Western culture as representing.

Religion and Arab identity

Islam is the predominant religion among Arabs, and is practised by around 210 million people in the Arab world, 90% of its population. The proportions of Muslims in different countries range from around 60% in Sudan to almost 100% in Oman and Qatar. Many countries have significant Christian minorities, particularly Sudan, Egypt, Syria, Palestine, Jordan, Lebanon and Iraq. Prior to 1948, Morocco, Egypt, Yemen and Iraq also had significant Arabic-speaking Jewish populations. Islam permeates almost every aspect of life in the Arab world. For religious Muslims, it is considered a way of life, whereas, for the non-religious, it is a cultural guardian.

For the purpose of this study, a questionnaire designed specially to explore young British Arabs indicates that religion has an important position in their lives, and in one way or another a certain influence on the construction of their identity. The questionnaire answers came with no surprises and confirmed this fact. Some 75.2% of all respondents confirmed the importance of religion in their lives. Less stress on the importance of religion was found in 16% of all respondents. There were significant differences among those of Christian and Muslim parents. Figure 9.1 classifies respondents into three groups: 1 those who consider religion an *important* factor in their lives; 2 those who consider it *less important*; and 3 those who consider it of *no importance* in their lives.

The average for respondents with one or both parents Christian is 18.5%. The number of respondents with both parents Muslim is 68.3%. The rest are either of mixed Muslim and Christian parents or with one parent Muslim or Christian.

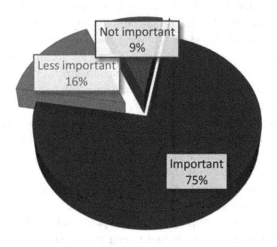

FIGURE 9.1 Level of importance of religion amongst Arab youth in Britain

Among Muslim families, religion has higher importance than in Christian families, although the majority of both noted 'it is important'.

In an interview with a Palestinian family of mixed-religion parents (Muslim father, Christian mother), in London, the parents stressed the importance of teaching their children about their religion (the father and mother agreed to raise the children as Muslims). The mother, Nadin (48), said: 'Religion helps our children to maintain our culture and our language. But this means also to encourage them to respect others' beliefs and be open-minded to debate with anyone regardless of their religion or faith.' The father, Isam (51), added: 'In Palestine we were brought up without any prejudice against anyone's religion. My wife's family, who are Christian, were our neighbours. This is how actually I met Nadin. Both our families were happy and they are still friends up until today. This is how we want our children and their children to be. This is our culture. We are proud of it.' It is worth mentioning here that in Palestine both Muslims and Christians live in mixed neighbourhoods and have a long tradition of mixed marriage. It is unlike any other Arab country where Christians live mainly in separate neighbourhoods and there is less of a tradition of mixed marriage.

Recent studies in the Arab world show a growing interest in religion among youth. Arab youth in the UK show similar results. In an interview with Touba (female, 23), from London, who was born in Tunisia, she said, 'I do respect our religion. Although I don't wear hijab, neither does my mother, but we grew up respecting the values of our religion [Islam]. However, I must say that I think we in North Africa have an open-minded understanding of Islam. You can say we are moderate.' Although the word 'moderate' could be interpreted in many ways and

TABLE 9.1 Importance of religion among Arab Muslims and Christians

Importance of religion among Arab Muslims and Christians	Religion of parents			
	Muslim		Christian	
	Both parents	One parent	Both parents	One parent
Very important	90.2%	–	66.7%	–
Somewhat important	8.1%	–	23.8%	–
Not important	1%	–	5%	–
Missing	9% (either left it blank or answered 'don't know')			

according to different standards, in most places in this chapter, where the word is mentioned, it is the counter meaning of 'extremist'.

Hamza (male, 21), from London, emphasizes the role of religion by saying:

> Unlike many youths' views in the West about religion, Islam has a meaningful aspect in our lives. It is simply a source of inner peace and guidance through this rough life. Islam for me is a guard for morals, and behaviour. Islam is not some rituals performed in the mosque and that's it. It's much more beyond that. Whether some people accepted or not, it is part of "ourselves" and an important part. Islam is mixed with our culture, our identities. It's defining who we are. I always believe religion has a positive influence on our attitudes and beliefs. The true Islam is not what some people claim that is Islam!

However, Yara (female, 18), from Guildford, thinks that the behaviour and attitudes of some Muslim boys and girls distort the image of Islam. 'I feel sometimes ashamed of their behaviour, especially when they reflect their attitudes upon Islam. I think the real essence of Islam is to reflect that every human is respected. All humans have equal rights, no one is above anyone else.'

Some youth went further to distinguish between religious and non-religious people, regardless of their ethnicity. One of the very few examples was Osama (male, 21), from Glasgow, who disagrees with the notion that religion should be in the mosque or in the church only. He says: 'I feel more comfortable with religious people, no matter which religion they believe in. Two of my close friends are Christian. It seems we can easily go with each other and have many things in common. My parents like them as well. We visit each other as a family regularly. This is why I think those who believe have the manner and discipline more than non-believers.' There was no similar point of view and therefore this cannot be considered as mainstream among Muslim believers.

These views reflect recognition and acceptance of the role of religion in British youths' lives. They also reflect respect for religion in general. According to my personal observations, collected from informal interviews, the majority of British Arab youth has a fair understanding of religion and its role in preserving their cultural identity, bearing in mind that many members of British society have negative attitudes towards Islam in particular. Having said that, there are some Arab youth who are influenced by extreme religious views, but I see this in the context of a 'self-defence mechanism' against isolation, lack of recognition, and alienation by society and the community. It is also an effect of society's behaviour against some members, who lean towards extremism, regardless of religion, faith or race.

Influence of religious views in interaction with media content

The questionnaire supports the results that the highest proportion of those who tend to think that religion plays an important role in their lives are among the *heavy online users* (those who use online media five hours a day or more are considered heavy users). They present a majority of 62.7% of the highest daily consumers of the Internet.

Based on empirical data collected from interviews, youth were extremely divided about the role of religion in their lives. Arab youth generally show respect for religion (Islam and Christianity), regardless of their commitment to practise it. They revealed that their understanding of religion might differ from that of their parents. This could be attributed to being heavily exposed to new media in its two main forms: satellite channels and online media. Here are some views from a few British Arab youth.

Hussain (male, 21), from Bristol, mentions that he learnt how to recite the Quran while he was in primary school. His father was keen to teach him Arabic in order to be able to recite and understand the Quran. He says:

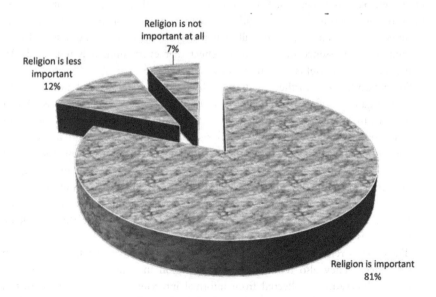

FIGURE 9.2 Level of importance of religion amongst heavy online media users

> After I moved to Bristol to study at university, I am still praying, but I do skip sometimes because of classes and commuting. My dad knows [...] he gets upset, but he understands that I don't do it deliberately. You know, I think I have to pray on time [...] I do my best.

When I asked Hussain if he drinks alcohol or has a girlfriend, he said he is committed to the rules of Islam in this regard.

Yumna (female, 19) asserted that she respects what her parents taught her about respecting the rules of religion. She explains further:

> I also do not accept extreme views or allow anyone to monitor my behaviour. I think Islam has great rules and ethics for every human being, not only for Muslims. Of what I learnt about Islam, God is the only one who has the right to penalize me if I do something wrong, not humans.

Karim (male, 25), from London, says about practising Islam in the UK:

> I feel absolutely free to practise Islam in the UK, more than I do in Egypt. No one judges you because of how you dress or look like. My behaviour is part of my identity, so no one has the right to argue it with me as long I behave responsibly and respect others' rights. Some Muslim mates, easily judge you because of your behaviour [...] I think this is very absurd. I am sorry to say that but I think many Muslims have no clue what Islam is all about.

Ezzeddin (male, 23), from Birmingham, says that 'religion is one of the important regulatory factors in our lives, as I believe. I consider it as a guard or as a sign on our life journey. It should not be of total control of my life but rather a guidance when I need a guidance'.

Hussam (male, 19), from London, suggests that religion plays a role in his life but as much as everything else does. He says his parents have 'moderate views' of religion and he and his two sisters and brother think alike about religion. He argues that 'the practice of religion is up to the individual to decide what is best for him/herself'. He describes religion as 'part of a cultural tradition'. He does not consider himself 'religious' but at the same time he is not against religious people if this is their own choice. Here we can see a different understanding of religion, where young people put freedom before religion.

Samira (female, 20), from London, is against the idea of religion controlling someone's life. She suggests that 'everyone should make his choice and not be influenced by anyone'. She says:

> Even parents should not make the choice on behalf of their children. Children should be given the choice to make their way in life. Religion can sometimes be an obstacle if it is taught to children mixed with extreme views or wrong practices. I am not against religions but I am against the way it is brought to us

by people who do not even understand it. Look at those extremists who harm Islam with their scary views about non-religious or non-Muslim people. If this is religion, I don't accept it.

Khubaib (male, 18), from London, says:

> Religion is the most important thing in my life, it is shaping my identity and tells me who I am. I admit my parents brought it to me but after I became eighteen, when I have the right to make my own choices, I continued to consider religion as the most important thing in my life. I also like to learn about other religions and respect them as well.

It is clear that religion plays an important role in youths' lives, in particular within the younger age group. Although there are differences among Arab youth in terms of how important a role religion should play in their lives, there is a sense of admittance that religion is an important player in Arab youths' lives. It is also a reflection of differences of perception of the role of religion among the parents' generation, who came from various parts of the Arab world where understanding and practices of religion are not the same. British Arab youth of the second generation have experienced utterly different circumstances in terms of technological advances in the field of online media and in terms of the expansion of religious knowledge, which is probably no longer limited to scholars and religious preachers. Moreover, the deep disagreement and controversy amongst religious schools in the Arab and Muslim world have given many youth in the diaspora a reason to turn to online resources in an attempt to find 'convincing evidence' that is more related to their lives in the West.

Religion shapes identities and influences attitudes

Responses to questions about the role of religion in British youth's life did not show a significant change in terms of leaning towards radicalization, for instance, or any extreme views against non-Muslims. This may be explained in the light of the increasing influence of researchers with strong secular views who, for one reason or another, ignore the role of religion in general in the construction of youth identity, more specifically that of youth of Arab origin. I have discussed the role of religion in the lives of the Arab and Muslim communities in the Arab world. In this study, I have explored the importance of Islam in British Arab youths' opinions. The ignorance of the role of religion is in accordance with Peek's view, when he says: 'While there has been much social scientific exploration of identity over the past decade, major reviews of identity theory and research have largely over-looked the role of religion in forging identities for individuals and groups' (Peek, 2005, 216).

The clash between science and religion remains a complicated and multifaceted issue as it is claimed to provide different understandings of the world (MacKenzie & Wajcman, 1999; Dunwoody et al., 2009). Through its influence on the values that construct cultural identity, religion has an impact on various consumption patterns in society (Rice & Al-Mossawi, 2002; Essoo & Dibb, 2004). Young people nowadays increasingly rely on online media to expand their knowledge and fulfil their needs. Sanaktekin et al. (2013) attempted to discover the extent to which religion has an influence on the level of Internet consumption in Turkey. The study found that: 'There are still a considerable number of high believers using the Internet. Furthermore, it is interesting to see that high believers, compared to moderate or non-believer groups, use the Internet more for the purpose of searching for information' (ibid., 1559). Not far from this finding, Dawson (2000, 31) also notes that the 'technological services that the Internet presents provide useful grounds for religious communities and encourage individuals to engage in dialogue free from limitations of time, space and mobility'.

It is important to indicate that religion is not only an effective part of Arab culture, but is also interrelated with all aspects of people's lives. It may vary from one country to another, but is evident in tradition, customs, dress code, celebrations, art and history, and even in politics. There is a reason for talking about Islam as synonymous with religion, which is that Islam is in fact the dominant religion among all Arabs and it is very influential on Arab culture. However, Christians, whose religion dominated at an earlier stage in the Middle East, evidently contributed massively to modern Arab culture too. Boháč (2010) investigated the history and the existence of a group of Christians in the Middle East, noting: 'In spite of the wide-spread geographical imaginations of the Middle East as an Arabic and Islamic monolith, supported by Western mass media and some Middle Eastern states' high politicians, the Middle East is quite a heterogeneous region. This region comprises numerous ethnic, national, religious, linguistic or ethno-religious groups' (ibid., 69). In theory, this is a fact; however, the Arab world, especially in the Middle East and North Africa, has experienced a number of phenomenal Christian figures who have left their footprints everywhere – in art, music, publishing, poetry, politics and the military. In fact, Arab culture is a product of the co-existence of Muslims and Christians. For instance, the first book-printing press in the Arab world was introduced by the Church in Lebanon in 1734, and the first newspapers printed in the Arab world (Syria, Lebanon and Egypt) were mainly established by Arab Christians, or by both Christians and Muslims, according to Essoulami (2006, cited by Mellor et al., 2013). The reason for this historical timeline is to assert two facts: first, the signs of religion are in all aspects of Arab culture; and second, Arab culture is a product of the interrelated co-existence of the Islamic and Christian faiths.

Religion in the social context has gained ground through the influence of the Islamic movements in the Arab world. From the 1960s onwards, the rise of Islamic movements has been seen as a reaction to the increasing influence of leftist movements and later on as a form of resistance to the 'Westernization' wave. Many people looked upon them as guardians of religion and culture against leftist and the Western influences. Religion (mainly Islam) is looked at with respect in the Arab culture and in the average Arab citizen's consciousness. The affiliation of Islamic movements with Islam is what gave them the power of influence. They proved successful in providing clean and down-to-earth public services such as charity, educational institutes and health. In the 1980s they took a step farther by unlocking the public political arena. That is when they were confronted by authoritarian regimes, which always brutally confronted any challenge to their absolute dominance of the political practice. Since then, Islamic movements have been regarded as victims to be prohibited, persecuted and crushed by Arab governments. The consequence is more empathy with them. Their followers were mainly of the youth section of society. Youth, who represent the majority of any Arab society, were politically marginalized, economically ousted and socially overlooked, gained recognition through those movements. This may explain to some extent the popularity of the movements among youth. Islamic movements then constituted the largest and most organized opposition in most Arab countries. Mellor et al. (2013, 86) give us an example of the political atmosphere in Egypt before the Arab Spring by stating that 'since the 1952 military coup, Egyptian liberal and leftist movements have been constrained by Islamic movements to publicly challenge the Islamic foundation of the Egyptian constitutions'. The Arab Spring has given the Islamic movements, as well as other political opposition parties, a golden opportunity and probably a once-in-a-lifetime chance to prove that they are capable of presenting themselves as an alternative to the corrupt regimes and fragmented opposition. Mellor et al. put it: 'Undoubtedly, the 2011 revolution provided a unique opportunity for all these groups – Islamists, liberal and socialist groups – to consolidate their position on the political scene' (Mellor et al., 2013, 87).

The Arab Spring: Islamic movements, religion and politics

The online sphere attracted Arab youth from all over the world to engage with the Arab Spring day-to-day events, most specifically in the first half of 2011. British Arab youth supported the Arab Spring in various ways. Online forms of activity, however, dominated their participation. As online media increasingly make it easier to engage, empirical data collected during the early stages of the Arab Spring show that British Arab youth were motivated to engage with the Arab Spring using online media. That motivation increased their willingness to engage as they experienced instant outcomes in the form of ousting heads of regimes in a few months. Organizing free elections in the aftermath of toppling regimes has sparked this participation as it was seen as a democratic evolution that had not been experienced before in the Arab world.

Islamic movements, led by the Muslim Brotherhood, had the opportunity to present themselves as 'saviours of the nation' by reminding the population of their 'white hands' in providing services for society for decades. Although Islamic movements joined the revolutions at a later stage, and regardless of the circumstances, they were part of these political changes and proved to be active in terms of mobilization and public political engagement. They relied both on their own well-organized structures, and on the weak and badly organized liberal and leftist opposition parties.

The promises then made by leaders of the parties affiliated with Islam to establish a 'cleaner model' of ruling nations on backing themselves with an ideological background, succeeded to attract young and middle-class people to support them, entwined with their wide popularity amongst Arab youth in general. That has been demonstrated by allowing them to win parliamentary and presidential elections in Tunis and Egypt. Supporters of Islamic movements, and ordinary people who thought 'religiously politicized' parties could provide a new model of rule, pushed towards that win. British Arab youth who supported them were also very optimistic that the Islamic movements were capable of success. Even those who were not in favour of what they call 'political Islamists' ruling their governments have at some point compromised their doubts in accepting the win as *de facto*. They might have voted for them, not in favour of them but after admitting that Islamic parties were well organized and had the ability to stand for elections against the resistance of the old regime forces who were trying to restore the pre-revolution powers. However, after Islamic parties made it into government, they were unable to satisfy public demands. Their practice of politics has been labelled by many activists as 'the same old ways'. Public demands were so high that most probably no party alone could have achieved them. Regardless of many facts that led the 'Brotherhood' in Egypt to fail to meet public demands in a short time, they were considered by many activists to have failed.

That failure was transnational in terms of its effects. As a matter of fact, the challenge for the Brotherhood to rule one of the most politically influential Arab countries was huge and put a great deal of pressure on them, as it was seen by many pro-Islamic ideology supporters as the model that had to prove that an 'Islamic system can be an alternative to corrupted secular regimes'. The inability to stand against the 'shadow powers of old regimes' has caused deep disappointment and raised doubts about the capability of Islamic parties to rule based on their vision of the role of ideology in accordance with existing political rules.

This disappointment went beyond geographical boundaries and affected British Arab youth who were divided into three groups in terms of their expectations. The first group believed Islamic parties could provide a new model. These were mainly supporters of Islamic movements. Another group were less optimistic but looked at it as a stage that could be built on. A further small group were pessimistic about the ability of any opposition group to bring about change. In a question directed to one participant in my interviews regarding whether she was (or is still) supporting young Arab revolutionaries, Maha said: 'Every one of us should do. They demand democracy, social equality, and better economy. What I mostly liked is that the protesters were mostly young people. What I later found it upsetting is that political parties were trying to benefit from what those young people died for. I truly think they were opportunistic.' Maha is only one example of those who expressed their anger at a later stage of the Arab Spring. A few of them also blamed the parties that associated themselves with Islam for raising the ceiling of expectations by 'promising ordinary people to achieve more than they can actually achieve' (Ahamed, male, 23).

Interviews conducted with British Arab youth for this purpose took place over the course of almost two years. The shift in their views is evident, after witnessing the rise and fall of political expectations in the Arab Spring countries, with civil war taking place in other countries – Syria, Libya and Yemen. Consequently, three main groups emerged. They are to some extent representative of Arab youth in the diaspora. The first are convinced that Islamic parties have a long way to go in terms of their ability to adapt to public politics and to be able to 'share' and cooperate with non-Islam affiliated parties. The second are the pro-Islamic parties, who believe Islamic parties are victims of a global conspiracy that has prevented them from having 'enough time' to prove their ability to present a new model of ruling a nation on the basis of Islamic ideology. The third group, which is also the smallest, believes that it is still too early to imagine that the Arab world is ready for democracy. In their opinion, democracy needs to be educated and practised on all levels before reaching the top. They also believe that parties of all backgrounds, including Islamic, are rather 'opportunistic'. Amal (female, 20), from London, backs that opinion by stating that 'political parties of all backgrounds have miserably failed to prove they can constitute an alternative to the previous corrupted regimes. They show no differences. They are fragmented and have almost no experience'.

Emad (male, 23), also from London, who has pro-Islamic views, disagrees with Amal by arguing that 'Islamic parties were alone against a global conspiracy. The so-called liberals and leftists have stood aside or even in some cases supported the deep state [which represents the old regime supporters] against their revolutionary partners. I don't accept the idea that they have failed. They were failed by other forces, who wanted to see them failing, because they reject the concept of Islam ruling'.

In a comment on both opinions, Sara (female, 21), from London, states that:

> Islamic parties have sold us a lot of promises that they knew from the beginning they can't fulfil. I'm against squeezing religion into politics. When Islamists won the elections in Egypt, I cautiously agreed that they can do better. They only relied on the notion of representing Islam, a concept believed to be very influential on ordinary people. I respect Islam and Christianity but with all respect, no one is able to represent religion and consider for instance criticizing their political practices as criticism of Islam. This is utterly misleading. That is why I believe, and I think many others do, political parties should compete on their achievements not ideology. Arab people are capable of implementing democracy if they follow the right rules.

We can notice from the three opinions discussed above that British Arab youth are divided in terms of their opinion towards religion and politics. The recent experience of the Brotherhood in Egypt, and not excluding Islamist political performances in other countries, has enhanced the belief amongst young British Arabs that religion and politics should be separated. Of 17 youths questioned, nine believe that religion should not be mixed with politics, although they noted that religion should be respected no matter what. Only five opposed that opinion and insisted that Islam must be represented and those who represent it are capable of proving Islam can rule. The other three could not form a definitive opinion.

This ongoing debate is a direct implication of youth using online media to negotiate their political and also religious beliefs. The overall engagement with online media could be seen as part of negotiating identity. In a sense, it allows them to argue and counter-argue with their peers. Those with inherited beliefs, who used to take culture on its face value, are confronted with new realities that force them to rethink and reshape the way they tend to perceive their culture of origin. Entwined with the influence of learned experiences of the host society (British), young British Arabs can to a greater extent critically assess cultural content and filter concepts.

According to an instrumentalist/circumstantialist approach to construction of identities, 'people choose who they want to be' (Pilkington, 2003, 18). Other factors, such as the influence of family, friends and communities, should not be ruled out as main factors influencing the process of identity construction and reconstruction. In our case, British Arab youth, who engaged heavily with online media, mainly social media, experienced new circumstances and political outcomes that in one way or another influenced their understanding of religion and its relationship to politics. That will probably be reflected in their future engagement with politics in the UK, and also in the entire understanding of the relationship between politics and religion.

Conclusion

British Arab youth are living in a special era that witnesses a radical change in communication technologies, political and social changes. These changes come with a great deal of risk as well as opportunities, assuming they incorporate new and social media into their daily lives, such as in using them to challenge inherited cultural beliefs. The main challenge, however, is related to their sense of belonging in a native home country versus their sense of belonging in Britain.

British Arab youth may seem to lean towards more secular views in regards to political practices while at the same time they revere the role of religion in their daily lives. They may differ from the older generation who adopted secular political views and distanced themselves from religion. One thing we can ascertain from the fieldwork summarized here is that young British Arabs are now more responsive to the changes sweeping their countries of origin as well as their communities in Britain.

References

Badran, A. (2012) 'Islamic identity conflict', www.alwaei.com/site/index.php?cID=1085.
Barakat, H.I. (1993) *The Arab World: Society, Culture and State.* University of California Press.

Boháč, A. (2010) 'Assyrian ethnic identity in a globalizing world', *Beyond Globalisation: Exploring the Limits of Globalisation in the Regional Context*, pp. 66–72.
Cerulo, K.A. (1997) 'Identity construction: new issues, new directions', *Annual Review of Sociology*, 23, pp. 385–409.
Choudhury, T. (2007) *Role of Muslim Identity Politics in Radicalisation*. Department for Communities and Local Government.
Dawson, L.L. (2000) 'Researching religion in cyberspace: issues and strategies', *Religion on the Internet*, 8, pp. 25–54.
Dunwoody, S., Brossard, D. & Dudo, A. (2009) 'Socialization or rewards? Predicting US scientist-media interactions', *Journalism & Mass Communication Quarterly*, 86(2), pp. 299–314.
Esposito, John L. (2003) *The Oxford Dictionary of Islam*. New York: Oxford University Press.
Essoo, N. & Dibb, S. (2004) 'Religious influences on shopping behavior: an exploratory study', *Journal of Marketing Management*, 20, pp. 683–712.
Galal, E. (2013) 'The influence of religious media in the eyes of the audience', Paper presented at Sigtuna, Sweden, 29/10/13–31/10/13.
Georgiou, M. (2003) *Mapping Diasporic Media Across the EU: Addressing Cultural Exclusion*.
Livingstone, S. (2002) *Young People and New Media: Childhood and the Changing Media Environment*. London: SAGE.
MacKenzie, D.A. & Wajcman, J. (eds) (1999) *The Social Shaping of Technology*. Second edition. Buckingham and Philadelphia, PA: Open University Press.
Mellor, N., Rinnawi, K., Dajani, N. & Ayish, M.I. (2013) *Arab Media: Globalization and Emerging Media Industries*. John Wiley & Sons.
Peek, L. (2005) 'Becoming Muslim: the development of a religious identity', *Sociology of Religion*, 66, pp. 215–242.
Pilkington, A. (2003) *Racial Disadvantage and Ethnic Diversity in Britain*. Houndsmill, Basingstoke: Palgrave Macmillan.
Rice, G. & Al-Mossawi, M. (2002) 'The implications of Islam for advertising messages: the Middle Eastern context', *Journal of Euromarketing*, 11(3), pp. 71–96.
Sanaktekin, O., Aslanbay, Y. & Gorgulu, V. (2013) 'The effects of religiosity on Internet consumption', *Information, Communication & Society*, 16, pp. 1553–1573.
Silverstone, R. & Georgiou, M. (2005) 'Editorial Introduction: Media and Minorities in Multicultural Europe', *Journal of Ethnic and Migration Studies*, 31, pp. 433–441.
UK Government (2007) *The Arab World: An Introduction to Cultural Appreciation*. www.gov.uk/government/uploads/system/uploads/attachment_data/file/16871/arab_world_introduction_cultural_appreciation_booklet.pdf.

10
TRANSNATIONAL MEDIA AMONG THE MUSLIM COMMUNITY IN EUROPE

Khalil Rinnawi

Introduction

There are undoubtedly new modes of media consumption among Muslim minorities in Europe and this new use can be contextualized within the framework of media globalization. According to this approach, the globalization process, which has become an integral part of our lives (Appadurai, 1996), is inevitable. A central claim of this approach is that globalization is actually extending the very basis of communication and cultural exchange (Fiske, 1987; Ang, 1990; Robins & Aksoy, 2000). This implication of the globalization phenomenon is evident among Muslim Arabs in Europe (Miladi, 2006; Harb & Bessaiso, 2006; Matar, 2006). It is, for instance, evident among Muslim minorities living in Germany (see e.g. Stolcke, 1995; Goldberg, 1995; White, 1997; Robins & Aksoy, 2000). This chapter focuses on recent fieldwork that explores the impact of consumption of pan-Arab media, such as satellite TV and the Internet, on these community members with their unique characteristics and history.

The Muslim Arab community in Berlin may be considered a 'new' community, especially in comparison to the Turks who have been in Germany since the 1950s and 1960s. The majority of Muslim Arabs are of Palestinian or Lebanese origin. The majority of them came to Germany as refugees. A further distinguishing feature of this community, particularly since the 1990s, is its high degree of politicization relating directly to cultural and ideological divisions and struggles within the Arab Middle East and North Africa (AMENA). The power of these cultural and ideological dynamics has been reinforced by the consumption of transnational Arab media in this community. Images of daily events in the AMENA, such as the so-called 'Arab Spring', have served to strengthen the importance of the AMENA as a cultural, religious and political reference point. There is no exact number of Muslim Arabs in Germany. Unlike the Muslim Arab communities in other parts of

Europe, there is no real Muslim Arab community in terms of local support structures dealing with culture and welfare.

Theoretical consideration

The theoretical framework of this study comes from sociological research (Lockwood, 1964; Pfetsch, 1999), which has paid much attention to the strategies of individuals belonging to minority and immigrant groups in their daily life in host societies. It also draws on the cross-cultural psychological approach, which examines the links between cultural context and the behaviour of individual members of minorities, in particular immigrant communities (Berry, 1997; Olshatain & Horenczyk, 2000). According to this approach, an immigrant minority group faces two problems: first, contact with and participation in the host society; and second, the maintenance of original identity and cultural heritage. In this context, Berry (1997) offered a model based on dichotomous attitudes to two issues: the value of maintaining one's distinct identity, and the value of maintaining relationships with the host society. As a result of such a potential dichotomous attitude, minority group members may develop acculturation strategies that have two ends and four options: assimilation, separation, marginalization and integration (ibid.).

In this context, Grillo (2001) classifies two kinds of multiculturalism: weak and strong. Weak multiculturalism refers to the ideal – that ethnic minorities share the same fundamental values and norms, employment patterns, health care, welfare and education systems with the mainstream population. Cultural differences, distinct beliefs and practices, religious traditions, language, etc. are permitted in the private sphere. Strong multiculturalism, on the other hand, recognizes cultural differences in the public sphere, providing, for example, separate schools or hospitals. Whereas the weak version of multiculturalism is widely held as the Western ideal and informs, for example, French policies, Britain has tended more towards strong multiculturalism.

Transnational media have had a crucial role in the process of connecting these minorities to their native cultural heritage. The main outcome of these tendencies is threatening and challenging to the nation-state formula by strengthening sectarian tendencies among the different communities that make up the nation-state. In contrast, many participatory democracies work to promote policies that enhance the social integration of different national-cultural minorities into the mainstream culture of the nation-state.

Transnational media and cultural order

This brings us to the implications of media and cultural organizations and practices in the transformation of cultural spaces and identities. Studying the media can provide rich insights into what is happening to the above practices in their various contemporary manifestations.

First, wider transformations occurring in contemporary media industries and markets, associated with the development of new 'space-transcending' technologies (satellite TV, the Internet), must be examined. An important consequence has been the construction of new transnational communicational and cultural spaces in and across continents. In this new media order, audiences that were once marginalized as 'minority interests' within the national broadcasting regimes may now be reconstituted as significant elements in transnational services that embrace diasporic interests and identities.

It is in this broader context that we may situate the particular developments associated with Arab media and transnational Arab audiences. Perhaps the most crucial development has been in Arab television, where the historical monopoly of state broadcasting organizations was undermined in the early 1990s as a consequence of both pirate broadcasting and new liberal economic policies (Sakr, 2000; Rinnawi, 2006). As a consequence, there was a proliferation of commercial channels in the AMENA region. Additionally, there was the inauguration of the pan-Arab TV channels, such as Al Jazeera and Al Arabiya, and new religious channels such as Iqraa, of which there are well over 50 today. All these stations provide innovative coverage of Arab society and represent the multiple dimensions of Arab society (Rinnawi, 2010). Moreover, these channels have also actively sought to make their programmes available to the Arab communities all over the world, not only through satellite links, but also by means of deals with Internet links and social media. Programming to Arab Islamic diasporas has now become an integral part of their scheduling practices. Arab state broadcasters have also gone transnational, with new channels. This new logic of transnational marketing has also become apparent in other forms of production: Arabic newspapers are now published online, reaching Arabs in every corner of the world; Arabic music and other kinds of the arts are aimed at the European and American markets.

Significantly, pan-Arab media allow audiences, whether local or in the diaspora, to engage with familiar cultural, religious and nationalistic issues. This engagement is particularly important to the Arab diaspora, usually living in non-Muslim, non-Arab, Western environments (Kraidy, 2002). Through Arab transnational media, these people become members of an invisible, imagined, virtual community (Rinnawi, 2006). As indicated in field research, via TV, members of this virtual community feel they are no longer a downtrodden minority, but rather members of the majority (Sedgwick, 1998; Miladi, 2006; Harb & Bessaiso, 2006; Matar, 2006; Rinnawi, 2010). Mark Sedgwick (1998), for example, argues that the web makes Western Muslims less of a *minority*, increasing the frequency of their contact, the range of their contacts (which might previously have been limited to their local mosque, but may now extend across continents), and the speed with which information is disseminated and – sometimes – acted upon. In making Arabs and Muslims in the West less of a minority, the web increases not only their sense of identity as Arabs and Muslims, but also their self-confidence (ibid.). Several field studies on the Arab diaspora in Europe reach the same conclusion concerning the crucial implications of Arab transnational media on the Arab diaspora in the West since the 1990s (Miladi, 2006; Harb & Bessaiso, 2006; Matar, 2006; Rinnawi, 2010).

Consequently, I argue that through transnational information communications technologies (ICTs) the widespread displacement of people and re-creation of communities with shared ethnicity or language have blurred social and national identities. They have opened up possibilities for 'multiple affiliations and associations' outside and beyond the nation-state and the state where they live, giving rise to 'diasporic allegiance' – a proliferation of 'transnational identities that cannot easily be contained in the nation-state system' (Cohen, 1997, 174–175). Arjun Appadurai (1996, 301–302) uses the same terminology to describe, among other things, the displacement of people and the creation of 'invented homelands'.

In this context, Pintak (2009) argues that the media play a fundamental role in the formation of national identity, most famously detailed in Benedict Anderson's theory of the imagined community. In the AMENA region, a media revolution is contributing to the emergence of a reawakened national Arab consciousness. A comparison of data from the first major regional survey of Arab journalists and the results of various public opinion polls in the region indicate that Arab journalists stand on the borderlands of Arab identity, shaping an emerging 'imagined' *watan* (nation), which, in some ways, transcends the traditional lines in the sand that define the nation-state.

The globalization effect produced by the emergence of transnational media on the Muslim Arab community in Germany can be traced to the concept of 'imagined community' as suggested by Benedict Anderson (1993). This instant nationalism, or McArabism (see Rinnawi, 2006), is a form of imagined community, principally composed of Arabs inside the AMENA, but also Muslim Arabs in the diaspora. According to Anderson, the emergence of new nationalism results from a process of 're-imagination' conditioned by drastic transformations in the conscience and media within a modern framework. The ancient (imagined) nations, themselves a process of re-imagining positioned in the rise of contemporary nationalism based upon the concept of ethnic solidarity, are a process of imagination framed by radical social changes that have taken place during the 20th century. In the case of the Muslim Arab minority in Germany, the entrance of the Arab transnational ICTs is a strong factor impacting upon the process of re-imagination, built upon their nostalgic past in their homeland. Finally, it is imagined as a community, because the nation is always conceived as a deep, horizontal comradeship. The conditions Anderson describes here are relevant to the Muslim Arabs in the diaspora, as we will see later.

In light of the above discussion, this chapter explores the implications of Arab transnational media on the specific Muslim Arab refugee community in Berlin in order to underline the contours of this community vis-à-vis others. The main focus of this study is the impact of exposure to pan-Arab transnational media in terms of their relationships to their homeland and with their host society. The aim is to show the ways this community of Muslim Arabs in Berlin consumes media, and an analysis of media use and cultural practices across generations. The study of media is one means to gain insight into the interweaving triad of culture, identity and community in the diaspora. The study is based on face-to-face interviews conducted in Berlin with 50 families during a three-month period in the summer of

2013. Participants were randomly chosen and they were all Muslim Palestinian and Lebanese refugees. The study was an update of previous fieldwork carried out in 2008.

General modes of media consumption

The data gathered in 2013 show that the mass media are an integral part of this cohort's daily life, and that new media have a crucial role in filling their time, while connecting them to their homeland. All interviewed families mentioned that new media such as satellite TV and social networks, not the traditional written media, were their sole source of information. This is for several reasons, such as the absence of local Arabic-language media in Berlin. Even if some Arabic newspapers were available, the younger generations were usually not fluent in reading Arabic so they could not access such print media.

The second general finding is the dual modes of media consumption: they consume German media, through local cable channels, in order to keep up with the events in their daily life in Germany, and they consume media in Arabic, through satellite dishes (Nilesat and/or Arabsat). Fatima (46 years old), who is originally Palestinian from Lebanon, says: 'In terms of media consumption, we, the Muslim community in Berlin, are dividing our time of media consumption between the Arab satellite TV channels and the Internet deeply surfing through the social networks such as the Facebook connecting ourselves to our people and relatives in Lebanon and Palestine.'

Moreover, participants reported that they were heavy television viewers, especially the parents, who viewed a minimum of a couple of hours of satellite TV per day, typically during the afternoon and evening, when they had nothing else to do. At the same time, the young generation consumes media via the Internet, especially social network sites. Zahra (57 years old), a Lebanese, says:

> MBC is our media platform for entertainment, waiting for 'the Arab Idol' and 'the Voice' deeply involved with the episode results and at the same time al-mayyadeen satellite TV channel is our main news channel to follow up and to be updated on the news of our region ... As to Internet is very far from my world except sometimes talking through the Skype to my relatives in Lebanon.

Due to the fact that most parents belong to the first generation, who are normally unemployed refugees, they live on benefits from the state and thus they have a lot of time at their disposal. Therefore, they spend a lot of time, especially in the evening and at night, watching Arabic television. This is particularly true for women viewers, who tend to spend longer hours (than men) watching Arabic TV. Khaldeyeh (51 years old) says, 'watching moving from one to another TV channel, from one Arabic drama to another Turkish one, besides the other reality TV such as the "Arab Got Talent" become our daily sport here in this place'. As for the younger generation, the picture is similar, but in terms of consuming new media such as via the Internet. Arab children in Berlin spend a lot of hours on their smartphones or on computers, especially after school.

Generational-cultural cleavages

The findings indicate an important generational gap: although the first generation has access to social media, television is still their preferred medium. On the other hand, the Internet and social media are the most important media for the young generation. This tendency can be justified by the different educational levels between the first and second generations as most parents had a modest education in their homeland, while the young generation had higher educational levels in Germany. The difference can also be attributed to the fact that the younger generation is 'computer oriented' like its counterparts in Germany. Hassan (21 years old), originally from Lebanon, says:

> Unlike our parents we as most of the other young Arab Muslim people in my age and even the younger are addicted to social networks consuming most of our news about the Arab world through different Internet platforms. We use social media through our smartphones to contact our relatives and friends in our homeland and know almost everything what is happen[ing] there on [a] daily basis.

These differences indicate deeper generational-cultural cleavages, which have various implications for both generation groups.

There is also a kind of 'collective viewership', where parents tended to watch TV in groups while their children reported that they normally view television alone in their bedrooms – normally connected to German TV channels. The interviews reveal that parents viewed pan-Arab television channels and little German TV because they did not understand German well, and did not feel the same cultural affiliation to Germany, compared with their children. The older generation also regarded pan-Arab television channels as more credible when it comes to news about Arab issues, compared with German channels. Miladi (2006), and Harb and Bessaiso (2006) have noted similar findings among the Arab diaspora in Britain. For the young Arabs in Britain, viewing Arabic channels is also difficult, particularly news and current affairs, because it is usually in formal Arabic, which is rather difficult for younger generations to understand.

Contrary to the first generation, the children were quicker to adapt to the German culture through schooling, they quickly learned German, and most of them could not read or write Arabic. Many could not speak Arabic well, particularly those of 4–18 years old. When they did watch Arab TV, it was mostly for entertainment – particularly reality TV programmes coming from the Arab world. For instance, Nisreen (16 years old) says: 'Normally I only watch Arab television to follow up the reality TV programme especially "the Voice" or "Star Academy" … Other political and news programmes are not relevant to me.' The generational differences are also noticed in the way the concept of 'homeland' is interpreted across generations. For the first generation, it means the Arab world, where they were born and grew up, while for the second generation it referred to a virtual world called the Arab world, while feeling a sense of belonging to their host society (Germany).

Children and youth were rather interested in Arabic TV news about the recent Arab uprisings but depended on their parents for translation and clarification. The majority of the second-generation viewers said that those events helped them understand the political as well as social and cultural aspects of their homelands. Siraj (17 years old), for instance, says: 'Along with watching German media, I feel like watching Arabic in order to understand what is happening in the Egypt and the other Arab Spring countries which put me closer to my homeland besides improving my Arabic-language skills while viewing a bit of my heritage.'

Many children claimed that, besides watching Arabic programmes with their parents, as well as some news about the Arab Spring, they mainly connected to social media such as Facebook, which has become their main media platform. Asmaa (14 years old) says: 'Almost all of the young generation are addicted to Facebook which is becomes our media channel to our people in the homeland ... we use Facebook to contact our family members in Lebanon as well as many Muslim Arab young in the Arab world building [a] personal relationship.' The consumption of social media among this generation has also increased their exposure to sites about Islamic practices.

Segregational modes of media consumption

Nonetheless, this young generation is rather isolated from the rest of German society through their modes of media consumption. Our findings indicate a clear tendency among the new generation within the Arab Islamic community in Berlin, which can be referred to as 'segregational modes of media consumption'. It is especially the cohort between 14 and 25 years old who use the Internet and social media to follow modern Islamic preachers such as Amr Khalid. In so doing, they share a sense of alienation from their host society while creating a virtual community based on ethnic and religious identities. For instance, Hassan (19 years old) says:

> We the new Arab Islamic youth are online almost all the time through the smartphone with Islamic leaders be influencing by their lessons about Islam exposing us to our religion and Islamic heritage that make us proud about ... from the other side through the social media such as the Whats[App], Viber and Tw[it]ter we are all the connected to other youth from Arab and Islamic origin exchange experience especially no pleasant one as a minority members ... but not less important is our daily connection with our relatives and families in the Lebanon and Palestine which sometimes make us feel that we are living with them in the same place.

In terms of gender, our findings indicate almost no difference between men and women in media consumption. In terms of news consumption, there is no doubt that the events of the so-called 'Arab Spring', starting from the end of 2010, were the main reason for following pan-Arab TV channels by both men and women. Reality TV shows such as 'Arabs Got Talent', 'The Voice' or 'Arab Idol' attract all family members or, as Ali (34 years old) put it, 'the Arab Spring events in the one hand and the Voice in the other hand were the most important factors which forced us as a family despite the gender differences to be stacked in the front of the TV'.

A large number of the men and women interviewed stated that they heavily used social networks such as Facebook and Twitter in order to remain in touch with their friends and more importantly to remain connected with their relatives in their homeland.

In general, entertainment was dominant among female viewers (see also Bihagen & Katz-Gerro, 2000; Robinson & Killen, 1995), or, as one female participant put it, 'I like to watch these channels, the Syrian and Lebanese ones and of course MBC, because they have many shows to entertain, such as Arab movies, telenovelas, both Egyptian and Syrian, as well as music clips and parties, that let me feel like I am still living in the Arab society. It makes me nostalgic for the Arab culture that I lived in before coming to Berlin.' In terms of the consumption of Internet and social media, both men and women use the same platforms for the same purposes, or, as Mohamad (32 years old), from Lebanon, says: 'Almost each one here are connected to Facebook and to WhatsApp application which is the most important and cheap tool making our life as Muslim Arabs very easy in terms of connecting us to our families in the Arab region.'

Implications of the new modes of media consumption

Recent political upheavals, including the Palestinian Intifada, the war in Iraq in 2003, the war in Lebanon in 2005, the war in Gaza in 2009 as well as the Arab Spring, have all contributed to the centrality of pan-Arab media amongst Arab communities in Berlin. Meanwhile, these communities have to confront increasing antagonism in Europe towards Arab and Islamic minorities, and biased representation of them in the European media. On the other hand, the emergence of transnational pan-Arab channels such as Al Jazeera, as well as social media, has facilitated these communities' link with their homelands.

Living in a non-Muslim environment, those interviewees do not have the opportunity to adopt an Islamic lifestyle such as observing Islamic holidays and feasts and other specific social-religious ceremonies, which they used to do when living in the Arab world. Transnational pan-Arab media (and social media) have helped bring these traditions back to their daily lives, or, as one participant put it, '[o]ne of the reasons I connected to the Arab satellite [channels] is so that my children would get a sense of their Islam religion, especially during the holidays and Ramadan'. Pan-Arab television channels invest in intensive programming during Ramadan, for instance. Social media have added a new dimension to connection with one's homeland, or, as Nader (20 years old), from Lebanon, says: 'The Facebook made our Islamic experience, in normal time as well as during special dates, more attachable in [a] non-Islamic environment using its advantage to make online Islamic life strengthened by the more easily personal connection with our families and relatives in Lebanon and Palestine through the Whats[App] and the FaceTime connections.' Such media have also made it easy for the old and young generations alike to note prayer times, for instance during Ramadan, as one participant says: 'I have been able to create a festive environment for my children during the holidays and especially Ramadan. I can also teach them the habits and prayers of Ramadan and how to enjoy it. Also, I can now know more punctually and specifically when the prayer times and fasting times are and thus respect them.' Another participant (Ameneh, 33 years old) adds: 'With Facebook, Skype and the other smartphone applications, we feel all the time connected to our families ... Actually we feel that we live among them in Palestine and the refugee camps in Syria from where we came here.'

Such media have also helped provide Arab Muslims with a sense of better understanding of Islam, or as Ahmad (24 years old) says:

> [T]he exposure of the new generation to the social media bring them directly to Islam without any mediation from local Imams ... most of them who never prayed before are now religious and even very religious. They use social media to better understand Islam ... the intensive adoption of the Facebook and the Islamic websites make the young people here returned to Islam.

It can be argued that the constant exposure of these Muslim communities to transnational pan-Arab media may reduce their chances of integration into their host society (Meyrowitz, 1985), while enforcing a sense of belonging to the Muslim and Arab world, albeit virtually.

Concluding remarks

Muslim Arabs in Berlin consume German and Arabic transnational media, but while the first generation of immigrants relies on transnational pan-Arab media, the young generation depends mainly on new and social media. Nevertheless, the young generation shows a very strong identification with their Arab-ness. This could be due to the recent upheavals in the region, coupled with the antagonistic attitude towards such minorities in Europe, particularly post-9/11. This strengthening of Arab identity may reduce their chances of assimilating or integrating into their host society, and one direction for future research is to examine closely these generations' media habits and their implications, particularly with regard to their religious views and solidarity.

References

Anderson, B. (1993 [1991]) *Imagined Communities: Reflections on the Origin and Spread of Nationalism*. London: Verso.

Ang, I. (1990) 'Culture and communication: towards an ethnographic critique of media consumption in the transnational media system', *European Journal of Communication*, 5(2), pp. 239–260.

Appadurai, A. (1996) *Modernity at Large: Cultural Dimensions of Globalization*. Minneapolis, MN: Minnesota University Press.

Berry, J.W. (1997) 'Immigration, acculturation and adaptation', *Applied Psychology: An International Review*, 46(1), pp. 5–68.

Bihagen, E. & Katz-Gerro, T. (2000) 'Culture consumption in Sweden: the stability of gender difference', *Poetics*, 27(5–6), June 2000, pp. 327–349.

Canclini, N.C. (1995) *Hybrid Cultures: Strategies for Entering and Leaving Modernity*. Minneapolis, MN: University of Minnesota Press.

Cohen, R. (1997) *Global Diasporas: An Introduction*. London: UCL Press.

Fiske, J. (1987) 'The cultural economy of fandom', in Lisa A. Lewis. (Ed.) *The Adoring Audience: Fan Culture and Popular Media* (pp. 30–47). London: Routledge.

Goldberg, D.T. (1995) 'Introduction: multicultural conditions', in D.T. Goldberg (Ed.) *Multiculturalism: A Critical Reader* (pp. 1–45). Oxford: Blackwell.

Grillo, R. (2001) *Transnational Migration and Multiculturalism in Europe*. Oxford: Economic and Social Research Council.

Harb, Z. & Bessaiso, E. (2006) 'British Arab Muslim audiences and television after September 11', *Journal of Ethnic and Migration Studies*, 32(6), pp. 1063–1076.

Kraidy, M. (2002) 'Arab satellite television between regionalization and globalization', *Global Media Journal*, 1(1), Fall.

Lockwood, D. (1964) 'Social integration and system integration', in G.K. Zollachan & W. Hirsch (Eds) *Social Change: Explorations, Diagnoses and Conjectures* (pp. 370–383). New York: Halsted Press.

Matar, D. (2006) 'Diverse diasporas, one meta-narrative: Palestinians in the UK talking about 11 September 2001', *Journal of Ethnic and Migration Studies*, 32(6), pp. 1027–1040.

Meyrowitz, J. (1985) *No Sense of Place: The Impact of Electronic Media on Social Behavior*. Oxford: Oxford University Press.

Miladi, N. (2006) 'Satellite TV news and the Arab diaspora in Britain: comparing Al Jazeera, the BBC and CNN', *Journal of Ethnic and Migration Studies*, 32(6), pp. 947–960.

Olshatain, E. & Horenczyk, G. (Eds) (2000) *Language, Identity and Immigration*. Jerusalem: Hebrew University, Magnes Press.

Pfetsch, B. (1999) *In Russia We Are Germans and Now We Are Russians: Dilemmas of Identity Formation and Communication Among German-Russians Aussidler* (pp. 1–48). Berlin: Wissenschaftszentrum Berlin fur Sozialforschung (in German).

Pintak, L. (2009) 'Border guards of the "imagined" watan: Arab journalists and the new Arab consciousness', *The Middle East Journal*, 63(2), pp. 191–212.

Rinnawi, Kh. (2006) *Instant Nationalism: McArabism and Al Jazeera: Transnational Media in the Arab World*. Lanham, MD: University Press of America.

Rinnawi, Kh. (2010) 'Cybernauts of diaspora: electronic mediation through satellite TV: the case of Arab diaspora in Europe', in A. Andoni & P.J. Oiarzabal (Eds) *Digital Diasporas*. Reno, NV: The University of Nevada Press.

Robins, K. & Aksoy, A. (2000) *Banal Transnationalism: The Difference that Television Makes*. WPTC-02-08.

Robinson, Thomas N. & Killen, Joel D. (1995) 'Ethnic and gender differences in the relationships between television viewing and obesity, physical activity, and dietary fat intake', *Journal of Health Education*, 26(2).

Sakr, N. (2000) *Satellite Realms: Transnational Television, Globalization and the Middle East*. London: I.B. Tauris.

Sedgwick, M. (1998) 'Muslim diaspora in the West and the new media', *Middle East Journal*, 54(1), pp. 15172.
Stolcke, V. (1995) 'Talking culture: new boundaries, new rhetoric of exclusion in Europe', *Current Anthropology*, 36, pp. 1–13.
White, J. (1997) 'Turks in the new Germany', *American Anthropologist*, 99(4), pp. 754–769.

PART III
Mediated Islamic practices

11

THE NEW SAUDI NATIONALISM OF THE NEW SAUDI MEDIA

Gilbert Ramsay and Sumayah Fatani

Introduction

Saudi Arabia has been a late starter as far as the Internet is concerned. In keeping with the cautious approach it has historically taken to all new media, from photography to satellite television (Kraidy, 2006), public Internet access was made available to Saudi citizens only in 1999, after some years of weighing the costs and benefits of the new technology. Since then, however, the country has made up for lost time. Between 1999 and the present, the percentage of Saudis with an Internet connection has grown from less than 1% to over 60%, giving it the largest population of Internet users in the Arab world (InternetWorldStats, 2014; Ddarabia. com, 2014a). Still more remarkable has been the extent to which Saudis have taken to social media. Today, Saudi Arabia is per capita the world's biggest user of the video-sharing site YouTube and micro-blogging site Twitter (Ayed, 2014).

Something remarkable is happening – but what, precisely? What are the implications for how Saudis understand themselves and their society? Serious discussions of the Internet in Saudi Arabia tend either to be narrow, dry and technical – focused primarily on a professional audience of technologists, marketers or investors – or to be rather cursory and superficial. Within the academic literature, two general trends can be discerned. Those coming from the starting point of Saudi Arabia's internal politics have tended to see the Internet as having empowered Saudi citizens. Stephan Lacroix (2012, 2967) argues that Internet forums constituted a 'veritable Saudi parliament', in which members would 'freely discuss the country's political, religious and economic affairs'. For Caryle Murphy (2012, 294), the Internet means that 'Saudi Arabia is no longer a closed society. Its ramparts were breached first by satellite television ... Now the Internet has reduced those ramparts to rubble'. Marwan Kraidy (2006) has gone perhaps even further, arguing that hypermedia have created a space that is fundamentally antithetical to core principles of Saudi social organization, such as free mixing of sexes.

Interestingly, this view contrasts sharply with that taken by specialists in the politics of the Internet, for whom Saudi Arabia has become a textbook case of the effective governmental control of national cyberspace (Kalathil & Boas, 2003; Deibert, 2008; Morozov, 2011). These authors point to the sophisticated technological controls built into the Saudi version of the Internet, which is directed through a single gateway managed by the King Abdul Aziz City for Science and Technology, and filtered using state-of-the-art software for content deemed incompatible with Islamic values or national security. They also suggest, however, that the government has become increasingly adept at deploying a subtler range of sticks and carrots in order to guide discussion in national cyberspace in a manner perhaps not altogether dissimilar to governance of Saudi Arabia in the 'real world'.

In this chapter, we examine these contrasting claims by looking at the rise of new forms of Saudi video content on YouTube, a phenomenon that we refer to as the 'new Saudi media'. Our argument will be, broadly speaking, that the idea of Saudi YouTube shows as a 'dissident' and politicized phenomenon has been overstated. New Saudi media on YouTube were, from the outset, less interested in political critiques of the establishment than they have been presented as being, and over time they have become still less so. In retrospect, the significance of the new Saudi media has reflected not so much the rise of a Saudi public sphere, as its ability to articulate popularly a particular vision of Saudi identity which is often in line with the broad policies of the present Saudi government, but is in marked contrast to more reactionary, and perhaps more centrifugal tendencies within Saudi society and the religious establishment.

The emergence of the new Saudi media

The growth of the Internet and, in particular, social media use by Saudis is, of course, intimately and inherently connected to the emergence of new types of online content that Saudis have created in going online, and that have been created in order to satisfy the demands of this new media audience. With regard to YouTube in particular, Saudis have not merely discovered a new way to access and share familiar and pre-existing forms of material. On the contrary, entire new categories of content have emerged and with them a whole new industry.

If we consider what are, at the time of writing, the 20 most popular Saudi channels on YouTube, three trends become immediately apparent. First, Saudi YouTube content production in Saudi Arabia is relatively professionalized. Of the 20 most popular Saudi Arabian YouTube channels by number of subscribers, (Vidstatsx.com, 2014), ten are the product of small but professional Saudi start-up firms specializing in making video entertainment for YouTube, of which the most significant are Uturn Entertainment in Jeddah and Telfaz11 in Riyadh. Sa7i Online Entertainment, another Jeddah-based company, appears less prominent by this metric, since it consolidates all its regular programming into a single YouTube channel. However, based on the very large numbers of views received by its most popular shows, such as the *Broadcast Show* or *Nuṣṣ al-Jabha*, it is probably comparable to the previous two. Also important are two independent producers of cartoons, Lumink, and the Jordanian import Kharabeesh. Independent 'vlog'-style material (with the partial exception of computer game commentary), while still perceptible in the format of many popular shows, has generally been elaborated and commercialized (see Table 11.1).

A second observation relates to the nature of the content. Overwhelmingly the most popular material on Saudi YouTube channels is either comedy (in various forms), or computer games, represented by a large number of channels that appear largely to be the personal businesses of semi-professional computer game players and reviewers. By contrast, religious content is markedly absent. Only two Saudi channels with a religious focus make the top 20, both of them by relatively moderate clerics: Ghuram al-Bishi and Dr Muhammad al-'Arifi.

Finally, it is significant to note that Saudi YouTube content has produced its own stars. With the arguable exception of the religious clerics just mentioned, only one of Saudi Arabia's top YouTube channels is the personal channel of a celebrity

TABLE 11.1 Popular Saudi channels on YouTube

Name of channel	Subscribers	Producer	Material
EyshElly	2,206730	Uturn Entertainment	Comedy
Sa7i	1,782,586	Sa7i Online Entertainment	Mixed/comedy
Al-Temsa7	1,669,535	Telfaz11	Comedy
d7oomy_999	1,117,781	Uturn Entertainment	Computer games
AhmadAlShugairi	1,072,598	Ahmad al-Shugairi/MBC	Documentary
Lumink	993,660	Lumink	Cartoons
Khambalah	949,801	Telfaz11	Comedy drama
3al6ayer	848,434	Uturn Entertainment	Political comedy
La Yekthar Show	834,611	Telfaz11	Comedy
Documentary Film Site	792,252	Al Jazeera/ National Geographic	Documentary
Ghuram al-Bishi	716,252	Ghuram al-Bishi	Religion
Kharabeesh	666,167	Telfaz11	Cartoons
KhaledDQ84EveR	577,613	Khaled Kuwayti	Computer games
Fir4sGamer	559,355	Firas al-Juhni	Computer games
TakkiSeries	490,392	Uturn Entertainment	Drama
N2OComedy	480,131	Kharabeesh	Live stand-up
AlarefeTV	470,876	Dr Muhammad al-'Arifi	Religion
DvLZStation	468,658	DVLZStation/Vgstations	Computer games
Ayoub6669	465,259	Ayyub al-Harbi	Computer games

who acquired fame through the mainstream media: the MBC presenter and documentary maker Ahmad al-Shugairi. Indeed, the most popular Saudi YouTube shows are comparable in numbers of subscribers even to the YouTube channels of such pan-Arab media giants. MBC's YouTube channel, for example, presently has 2,811,553 subscribers – presumably drawn from all over the Arabic-speaking world. This is more, but not overwhelmingly more, than the most popular Saudi YouTube channel EyshElly, just one of the productions of Jeddah's Uturn Entertainment. The official channel of Rotana, another Middle Eastern media giant (and also, like MBC, under Saudi ownership), has 953,944 subscribers – which would place it seventh in the list of most popular Saudi YouTube channels.

In this chapter, we will be exploring the products of these small, professional new media production companies that dominate the new Saudi media space. We shall refer to them, and their products, as the 'new Saudi media' (sometimes shortened to NSM). The use of what might seem an inherently ambiguous term is intended to reflect a similar ambiguity in the way in which it is talked about by Saudis themselves. In discussing what they do, creators of NSM content seem to refer simply to 'new media' (*al-i'lām al-jadīd*), or 'social media' (*al-i'lām al-ijtimā'ī*), as if their own specific forms of content were simply natural outgrowths of the medium, or as if it were simply obvious that the Internet is the only appropriate outlet for the 'new' content they are creating – in other words, that the medium is the message.

This notion, of course, elides a more complex and specific history. The first productions that would fall into our NSM category as defined above began to appear in 2010, starting with the news satire *Al-Tasi'a Illa Rub'* (A Quarter to Nine), followed shortly after by *3al6ayer*,[1] another news satire, and by *La Yekthar*, a one-man comedy show that frequently addressed key social and political issues. However, these regular, slickly produced products did not come from nowhere. Organizationally and logistically, they can be located in an increasingly vibrant 'start-up' culture among Saudi Arabia's young elite. According to Abdullah Mando, co-founder of the Jeddah-based production company Uturn Entertainment, *3al6ayer* was the result of a rigorously business-minded selection process. In an interview with Saudi business website Wamda (Wamda tv, 2014), Mando recalled how:

> The initial idea was that each project should have a completely separate group of people working on it. The group of people don't have to be professionals – they can be amateurs. And we were willing to finance each project by allocating a fund for everybody, let's say 5,000 riyals, 10,000 riyals – it didn't matter. It's just the cap was 20K for each project. We would design the team, and then help them, guide them to create the show. After we had a final product we would actually put it on YouTube, without a brand name, then test the waters – see how it works. Would people like it? Would they want to watch it? What is the feedback? We did this for three months. We interviewed I think 200 people, some of whom were still at school and didn't even work before. And out of these projects, *3al6ayer*.

The success of *3al6ayer* in this process was, in turn, no mere fluke. Its creator and host, Omar Hussein, by this time had well over a year of experience as a comedian. The Saudi stand-up scene had largely emerged in 2008 as a consequence of the arrival in Bahrain of the 'Axis of Evil Comedy Tour', a troupe of American-Arab and American-Muslim comedians. The search for local talent to open the show led to slots being given to Fahd al-Butayri, a Saudi national who had previously performed as a stand-up while studying in the United States, and to Rehman Akhtar, a British expatriate and Aramco employee who had, some years previously, had an active comedy career culminating in a televised performance for the BBC.

The Bahrain experience led to Akhtar organizing a series of stand-up nights held under the auspices of Aramco, which in turn prompted the recruitment of more Saudi talent, including Omar Hussein, at that time a chemical engineering student at King Fahd University of Petroleum and Minerals. These early performances, carried out in a private space, but one that, crucially, included Saudis as well as expatriates, served as a stepping stone that enabled comedy to move into relatively mainstream (albeit sometimes remote) Saudi social space, facilitating the emergence of yet more home-grown talent, and a shift in the language of comedy from English to Arabic.

New media in Saudi society

Recounting the origins of the new Saudi media is helpful in placing it within the context of Saudi society. While some commentators (Kraidy, 2006, 2010) have argued that 'hypermedia' (including the Internet, mobile telephony and satellite television) constitute a space that is inherently antithetical to core Saudi principles regarding the organization of social life (for example, prohibitions on the free mixing of sexes), such analyses seem to misread the extent to which Saudi Arabia's social organization is in practice premised not on a monolithic society, organized exclusively according to the strictest tenets of Wahhabism, but rather in terms of a number of distinct sectors or 'fields' (Niblock, 2006; Le Renard, 2008; Hertog, 2010; Lacroix, 2012; Stenslie, 2012), which vary considerably in terms of the types of practices that are acceptable within them. Hence, while obviously 'public' spaces (including the state school system) may indeed be organized strictly along these lines, much of everyday life is in fact conducted not within these spaces, but rather in a complex system of private, semi-private and privatized spaces in which different rules may apply.

In addition to 'cyberspace' itself, the new Saudi media can be seen as arising from a number of spaces that represent crucial meeting points between distinct spheres of the otherwise quite rigidly sectoralized Saudi society. First, experience of entrepreneurs such as Abdullah Mando is suggestive of the importance of the Saudi government's generous scholarship programme for funding foreign study in helping to import norms relating to commercial entrepreneurialism and individualistic self-reliance into Saudi youth culture (Saudi Ministry of Higher Education, 2014). Second, the emergence of the Saudi stand-up scene points to the role of often closeted spaces of exception within Saudi Arabia itself. While the parallel world created by firms such as Saudi Aramco has been identified by scholars such as Robert Vitalis as complicit in the creation of a stratified 'Jim Crow' system in the country, it has also seemingly served at least in more recent years as a limited conduit for experimentation and innovation within native Saudi society.

Finally, the NSM owes a clear debt to the distinct 'realm' (Sakr, 2001) created by satellite television, which from the early 1990s will have shaped the experiences of precisely those young people who have gone on to create media material of their own, allowing access, via the television screen, to a world in which, whether in its Western or Lebanese variants, almost every norm of Saudi society was turned upside down. In the same Wamda interview, Abdullah Mando describes how:

> I never related to the content I loved the most. I never related to the American film where the hero is always American and the bad guy is always Russian, German or maybe an Arab. So after watching … I think it was *Gladiator*, I realised how powerful media can be … One man with his influence on entertainment … you can actually decide the opinion of a nation. We decided we want to make films, and these type of films would be different. It will be as amazing and as mesmerising as popular Western films, but as local and cultural as possible.
>
> *(Wamda tv, 2014)*

In these few lines, we can see much of the ambiguity that, this chapter will argue, has characterized the new Saudi media project. Despite not having 'related to' Western content, which is ostensibly seen as pure 'entertainment', it has clearly been in some ways a formative influence. Despite aspiring to make content that is 'local and cultural', there is also the ambition to 'decide the opinion of a nation'. Culturally, new Saudi media are creatively torn between cosmopolitanism and localism; in terms of their mission they are torn between producing commercial entertainment for Saudi society as it is, and actively promoting change. It is this tension that we now propose to explore.

NSM as political commentary

Appreciating the roots of the new Saudi media in the commercial and entertainment spheres is important to any evaluation of how far it has succeeded in the unasked-for task of serving on the front line of a new Saudi public sphere. The first two years or so of the NSM's emergence, from late 2010 onwards, were indeed dominated by shows that dealt with serious news topics, and quite frequently criticized the political establishment. Conversely, from mid-2013 onwards, these shows by and large disappeared, with more recent trends emphasizing lighter material. In both cases, however, it must be remembered that the original stated purpose of the NSM was not to reshape society or to hold power to account, but to make money by entertaining people, and to have fun in the process.

Uturn's show *3al6ayer* offers a particularly striking example of this. Despite being frequently compared to Jon Stewart's *Daily Show*, the original model for this production was a 'Late Show format' along the lines of the talk show hosted by David Letterman (Wamda tv, 2014). Even when the show was first launched it was, according to one source, 'just a normal social show'. The movement of the programme into more risky political topics, in this account, was driven by audience demand, rather than the other way round, and was initially very cautious. Before running an early section critical of the minister of labour, the show's writers obtained the minister's explicit permission, on condition that the criticism was constructive, rather than being merely insulting. Even the firmly pro-revolutionary stance that *3al6ayer* took after the revolutions in Tunisia and Egypt was not initially perceived by the show's writers to be contrary to Saudi state policy. According to one insider:

> Now one thing you've got to recognize is that with the Arab Spring we gave an opinion that was not in line with the opinion of the Saudi government which was very weird [...] We didn't recognize it. We figured it out afterwards [...] The government were with Hosni Mubarak. In our episode we actually bashed on Hosni Mubarak.

A new media producer working for Riyadh-based Telfaz11 – the parent company of hit show *La Yekthar* – makes a similar, if broader point:

> [The] Arab Spring was just a coincidence, because it coincided with the technology serving us here. The cameras that we have, the technology that we have, how easy it is to make videos happened to be around 2009, 2010, and 2011. OK the peak was in 2011, because we've been doing this for since 2010, but 2011 we were ready, seasoned, but not because what happened in Egypt what happened in here. We became braver, we became more [...] OK our Telfaz11, the 11 is an homage for the year of the revolution, and we launched at 11.11.11. Everyone had a personal revolution basically. I think it's a coincidence [...] we never discussed the Arab Spring in our shows.

Presumably more intentionally controversial was when, in mid-2012, Uturn launched *WsmAl3odah*, a series of spiritual reflections featuring the famous dissident Sheikh Salman al-'Awda. Al-'Awda's material varied from personal reflections to coruscating attacks on the political corruption and injustice of Arab leaders, which, through the accompanying visuals, were obviously levelled at Saudi officials. For a religious figure once known for his firebrand social conservatism to partner with a production company dominated by committed liberals made for an unlikely pairing on both sides, and a major theme of the episodes was Al-'Awda's reflections on how his personal attitudes had changed. However, it is not implausible to see the decision as commercially savvy, as well as consonant with an overarching social reformist agenda. The meditative use of background music, and visual vocabulary of haunting landscapes, archive footage and arty portraits of human suffering and dignity represented a clear foray into the large market for sentimental and uplifting *Islamiyyat*.

If *3al6ayer*'s beginnings as a political satire show were hesitant and somewhat haphazard, so too would seem to have been the show's ultimate end. Like all Saudis, the show's writers were acutely aware of living in a society in which unfettered freedom of expression exists neither in practice nor in principle. Indeed, the limits on what can be said in Saudi Arabia were humorously explored by the show in various ways. Following a banned episode in the first season, for example, *3al6ayer baa'* opens with the creators brainstorming possible topics for their next episode. After considering which topics can be appropriately satirized, and which ones have not already been discussed by other shows, they suddenly look up, to reveal that the glass wall upon which they are scribbling their ideas rises up many storeys above their heads. The message is clear, but its meaning would seem to be double: on the one hand, even with some restrictions, there is plenty left for Saudis to talk about. On the other hand, there is a pressing need to talk about it, because up to the present time, many have still not had the courage to do so.

Over time, *3al6ayer* became bolder in what it was prepared to say, and began to take a more obviously liberal editorial line. According to one of those involved:

> All channels have an opinion – they all have an agenda, you see it's not wrong. Either you hide it, or you lie for your agenda. You have to be truthful, but maybe you emphasise one thing or you emphasise another. And because of this he [a friend who had studied media] said to me *3al6ayer* has to have an agenda [...] In the end you have to have an agenda, whether it's reform whether it's change whether it's liberal whether it's conservative. So this is why, at the end of season two we go OK, in our agenda we will give our opinion in [certain] circumstances.

By the end of season three, it is obvious to anyone watching that *3al6ayer* was coming under pressure to tone down these expressions of opinion or stop altogether. This much is made clear in the final episode of the show. This opens with a succession of characters warning the host to abandon his satirical ways and stay out of trouble 'before you get hurt', and closes with the show's anchor, comedian Omar Hussein, observing candidly:

> After monitoring the types of problem in the news, a person may have certain questions, but he avoids tackling them for his own personal safety. But maybe out of excitement he tackles a certain issue and he ends up suffering the repercussions. There's a saying that says: 'the power of the media is frail. Without the support of the people it can be shut off with the ease of turning off a light switch.' The question here is: how effective is our media, really? Or is it just a set of tools for letting off steam and doping people. If it is like that, I can't be a tool to let off steam, or to dope people.

These words eloquently convey the limitations that NSM producers were discovering to their online freedom of expression. Yet it seems likely that the circumstances that brought about the end of the show were not quite as straightforward as might be imagined. At the outset, *3al6ayer*'s writing team had been surprised to discover that they could get away with broaching subjects they had previously imagined to be off-limits. Now, they appeared to have discovered the opposite lesson: that even seemingly acceptable subjects may, depending on specific circumstances, suddenly become problematic. As a Telfaz11 employee put it:

> The thing is, what is frustrating – there is no written rule for anything. We don't have written rules. For example – women driving? Everyone has been talking that there is no written law against women driving. There is no written law against a guy singing in the street. There is no written law against – whatever. The understanding regarding mixing between sexes is not clear. The understanding regarding sacred matters is not clear [...] It's frustrating, because sometimes we think that 'that's not a red line – no one will say anything'. But it's not [the case].

In the case of *Mal3ob 3alayna*, for example, another early show with a firmly critical stance, those associated with the programme seem to have been shocked when they were arrested for two weeks for an episode dealing with the problem of poverty – something they had presumed to be a relatively safe topic. Their surprise might have been compounded by the fact that the programme – with its relatively harsh and direct tone – had been running for five months before the arrests occurred. In fact, it appears that the arrests were precipitated not by the unacceptability of the content itself, but by the fact that it had been repeated by *Islah*, a dissident Saudi satellite channel based in London.

It is rumoured that not entirely dissimilar circumstances conspired to push *3al6ayer* over the lines of acceptability. Seemingly, the offending content appeared not in anything immediately preceding the end of the show's third season, but rather in *3al6ayer 310* – an episode uploaded three months and four episodes before the series ended, which tackled the subject of the commercialization of Mecca. According to this account, the problem arose not from the nature of the content as such, but rather from the embarrassment resulting from the fact that its release coincided with a meeting of the Gulf Cooperation Council, meaning that it cast aspersions on Saudi Arabia's stewardship of the sacred sites on an especially sensitive occasion.

In the end, notwithstanding what seems eventually to have amounted to a collision with authority, the critical content of shows such as *3al6ayer* is unquestionably 'constructive' and reformist in its nature. In its attempts to highlight the shortcomings of government officials and highlight a familiar catalogue of mostly concrete grievances such as unemployment, poor standards of hygiene in hospitals, uninspiring teachers and decaying infrastructure, and official corruption, nepotism and incompetence, *3al6ayer*, and shows like it, still retained at least as much of the

Islamic notion of *shura* as the robust public contention presumed by the norms of liberal democracy.

NSM as social commentary

In short, it is important not to over-stress the idea that the flourishing of Saudi media on YouTube must be understood in terms of the emergence of an autonomous public sphere in the conventional Western sense. Indeed, in their capacity as 'social activists' or engaging in 'social criticism', NSM producers can more typically be seen as working hand in hand with certain strands of state policy than operating as informal opposition to it. At times, of course, material that claims to be directing itself to the reformation and education of 'society' can be seen as inescapably taking stances on what are in reality also political questions in Saudi Arabia, of which probably the most obvious are women's issues.

BanaTube, for example, is described by its production company blurb (BanaTube, 2014) as 'shedding light on the situation of women and their affairs and all those things that are relevant to them'. This remit seems to place the show firmly within the safe bounds of the 'women's sector' in Saudi society. Yet *BanaTube* is unflinchingly opinionated on issues such as women driving or workplace discrimination. The show, in other words, clearly states what effectively political opinions are, but it does not develop these into clearly articulated political claims or demands directed at any authority in particular.

Yet in other cases, material with a clear 'social' agenda appears to function more in the role of offering a public information service than advancing any kind of partisan agenda, well concealed or otherwise. In such material, the aim instead is to encourage and empower citizens to solve problems for themselves, without recourse to making claims on the state.

3almezan, for example, created by young Saudi doctors Obai Albashir and Rayyan Karkadan, aims to educate Saudis on fitness and healthy eating, with the aim of combating the kingdom's growing epidemics of obesity and type-2 diabetes. More recently, *Men Elaa* sets out to tackle the problem of unemployment by educating Saudis on how to apply for jobs. While not addressed quite so obviously at a social problem, *Fallimha* arguably fits into the same category, helping Saudis to improve their English through extracts from Hollywood films.

It is tempting to view shows of this kind either as one-offs, without any shared agenda, or as tactical attempts to tackle divisive issues by drawing them away even from the relatively safe social sphere and into the realms of scientific competence. In reality, however, it would seem that shows of this kind actually reflect a 'solutionist' tendency within the NSM that is both more thoroughly worked out, and more sincerely held, than one might imagine. For example, as *3almezan* co-creator Obai Albashir argues (interview conducted 2014):

> I don't believe in criticising government. I believe in speaking about a problem, offering a solution [...] This is just destructive, there is no benefit to it

in general. Generally speaking it produces excuses and sleepiness and passiveness among the people, which we don't support.

This perspective is perhaps even more clearly stated in another Uturn production, *Here is Silicon Valley* (Uturn Entertainment, 2014), when, early on, its presenter says:

> In our region, many people suffer from unemployment. Not only that, we also suffer from other problems like poverty, life expenses, potholes and many others. The bigger issue is that when we face a problem we blame others, we blame the officials, or anyone else. But we never give thought to how as individuals we can solve the problem, or at least become part of the solution ... pick up any problem, come up with an innovative solution that will make people happy and you will make money, and by doing so, you will think like an entrepreneur.

Even so, like all similar approaches, it is one thing to want sincerely to avoid having to take a stand on controversial issues, and another actually to succeed in doing so. In *3almezan*'s case, for example, the seemingly neutral goal of promoting health and fitness has also had to take a position in favour of women taking part in sport, but this is of course a divisive social issue in Saudi Arabia. Nor is it merely divisive at the 'social' level. For one of the major obstacles to the introduction of sport for Saudi girls is also the control exerted over education in the kingdom by the religious establishment.

This being so, the question of whether shows like *3almezan* or *Men Elaa* can be taken at face value, as manifestations of a wide solutionist approach or as tactical devices for promoting an otherwise controversial agenda, is arguably moot. Even if all they do is 'what they say on the tin', they will, on occasion, find themselves dragged into controversy.

A third type of social activism to be found in some NSM content does not merely stumble into controversy, but seems actively to thrive on it. In these cases, 'taboo subjects' are actively, even shockingly broached, but always in such a way as to avoid flagrantly breaching core Saudi values. A particularly well-known example of this is the Telfaz11 video 'No Woman, No Drive', in which comedian Hisham al-Faqih, assisted by musician and producer 'Alaa' Wardi, produces a parodic a cappella rendering of the Bob Marley classic. As the above-mentioned media producer describes it:

> We know that this is a culture that's conservative. They don't like music, they don't like to see women, and they don't support women driving. So we made a cover that is a cappella, without musical instruments, by Saudis with *shemaghs* singing 'no woman, no drive'. They're singing against women driving, but it is very satirical. There is anti-comment. It can go both ways and that is exactly what happened. People loved it, when they knew what it means. And some other extremists liked it because they said 'look at this guy, he is preaching about women not driving, and he doesn't have music, it's amazing'.

For this interviewee, this is part of a clear, but cautious strategy of boundary testing. As he continues:

> We need to adapt. We need to adapt all our ideas. We have an episode where we show three guys drinking alcohol and having tattoos and flirting with girls. But we got it away with them because we made them Mexicans in the [United] States, I mean, we gave them a mask that is the Mexican. They didn't do it as Saudis, they did it as Mexicans, although you know that those are actually Saudis who represent the kingdom in America. But we always work around it. We work around it. After that episode we got away with drinking so we did another episode in [the] UK where there are two guys who want to go [to] a bar, afterwards there was a drunk Saudi, and no one said anything.

Another interviewee, associated with Jeddah's Uturn Entertainment, makes a similar point:

> there is no accurate way to measure the red lines. We're learning this by pushing the bar slowly, episode by episode. Sometimes we want to say something, we have to learn how to package it right sometimes. If you package it in another way it could cause some problems.

An important point about such material is that, at one level, it appears to work simply by being different things to different people. Cosmopolitan, Anglophone Saudis watching 'No Woman, No Drive' can read the video as a witty joke, not only at the expense of Saudi policies with regard to driving, but also at the expense of their less sophisticated co-nationals, who read the video in a different way. Significantly, Hisham al-Fagih himself has refused to state publicly what his own stance on the driving issue actually is (BBC News, 2013).

Something similar may be true for the two episodes of the sketch comedy *Khambalah* featuring alcohol. In both cases there is, of course, no question that the sinful practices engaged in by the characters are unacceptable, but there is a subtle modulation in the level of condemnation from one episode to the next. In the first, a group of Saudis in America, fearing Islamophobic persecution, decide to disguise themselves as Mexicans, under which guise they engage in numerous forbidden activities. Eventually they are interrogated by a mysterious official, and crack when they are unable to resist a meal of traditional Saudi *kabsa*. In this way, they are restored to their true Saudi identity.

In the second episode, things are more complex. A diabetic Saudi in London experiences a dangerous sugar crash and enters the first place available – a pub – to order a sugary drink. Once in the pub, he catches sight of another man whom he recognizes as a fellow Saudi. Fearing for his reputation should he be identified by this other Saudi as a person who frequents sinful establishments, he pretends to be a native Londoner and a doctor. In order to maintain this fiction he is obliged to pretend to drink several alcoholic beverages bought for him by a friendly local, and to perform the Heimlich manoeuvre on the local's choking girlfriend. At this moment he is spotted by a third, conspicuously drunk Saudi who has suddenly staggered into the doorway of the establishment.

This episode represents a rather elegant pushing of boundaries relative to its predecessor. In the first, the Saudi protagonists are unquestionably wrong and cowardly to deny their Saudi identity. However, they do so in a generally hostile environment, the hostility of which would seem to be merely reflected in its myriad forms of degeneracy. In the second, things are complicated in at least three ways. First, the protagonist's motivation for getting himself in a difficult situation is more justifiable. Second, the regulars at the pub, mired as they are in the sins of alcohol and debauchery, are conspicuously friendly and welcoming. Finally, the real fault in the episode – the title of which is 'A Victim of Reputation' – is not a personal shortcoming so much as something presented as a distinctively Saudi cultural value: the notion of saving one's reputation even, if necessary, at the cost of strict honesty.

The agenda of the new Saudi media

Broadly considered, the new Saudi media can be identified as representing a fairly clear set of stances and values. In many cases, these stances do indeed place it in opposition to entrenched conservative beliefs in Saudi Arabia, and therefore within the kingdom's existing tradition of reformist or 'liberal' politics. However, while there have been forays by NSM productions into mild criticism of political authorities, the idea that Saudi Arabia's love affair with YouTube has heralded a radical departure from pre-existing possibilities for political debate in Saudi Arabia, or that the agenda of Saudi Arabia's new class of media entrepreneurs prevents them from forging partnerships with government, now seems naïve. Indeed, it is a matter of record that at least some members of the Saudi political establishment have conspicuously given their blessing to production companies such as Uturn, as for example when the offices of Uturn Entertainment were visited in 2013 by prince Mit'ab bin 'Abdullah (Murphy, 2014), who, according to one Uturn employee, said on this occasion that 'five or six of you are going [in future] to be the decision makers in this country'. According to the creator-presenter of one successful show, on another occasion a provincial governor specifically tried to recruit two Uturners as his social media advisers.

Indeed, at the cultural level, a key project of much NSM material would appear to be a kind of modernist nationalism, which actually fits rather well with the modernizing policies of the Saudi government itself (Lacroix, 2012; Otterbeck, 2012). As media entertainment made 'by Saudis for Saudis', NSM content trades heavily on localness, drawing its humour from its intimate familiarity with the everyday experience of Saudi Arabia – while at the same time trying to transcend traditional rivalries between different parts of the kingdom, especially between Hijaz and Najd. In this sense, NSM, for all its DIY aesthetic and reliance on cutting-edge technology, has at least something in common with the 'dramas of nationhood' which Lila Abu-Lughod (2005) saw in the great Egyptian drama series.

NSM content, in its multifarious formats and idioms, repeatedly emphasizes the values of education (over hearsay), individual enterprise (over reliance on social connections), the nuclear family (over the extended family or the tribe), private, spiritualistic religiosity (over political Islam), consumer choice (over tradition), and the preservation of folkloric heritage (over the actual relevance of traditional forms of social organization). At the same time, it also challenges a number of foreign influences. For example, it prioritizes Arabic over English, local Saudi products over imports and, of course, Saudi media over foreign entertainment – whether in its Western or pan-Arab versions.

Conclusion

Caryle Murphy (2012, 2652) predicts that Saudi Arabia's governing authorities will 'pragmatically and slowly adapt to the demands of young people, but also will try to co-opt many of them'. Given the development to date of new Saudi media, this has already begun to happen in the media sphere. However, to present 'young people' as straightforwardly demanding and government as simply reacting is to oversimplify the relationship between innovative young Saudis and the state. Despite the apparently much greater freedom of expression offered by the Internet, Saudi production companies have a surprisingly unified agenda, which amounts to a technocratic and to some extent individualist, but also very much a nationalist vision for the future of their country. Far more modernist than postmodernist, the underlying worldview they seem to champion is of a strong, bureaucratic and essentially benign state envisaged as in opposition to the power of tribalism, religious extremism and certain versions of tradition. Paradoxically, however, the way in which this message is presented continues to conform with the traditional 'Islamic' channels for public discourse within Saudi society. Criticism of political authorities, where it exists, tends to correspond to a concept of constructive criticism, which bears some resemblance to the Islamic notion of *shura*. Similarly, interventions at the level of society are often as much about urging individuals to reform their behaviour within already accepted norms as trying to re-shape fundamental beliefs and values – an approach that might be compared to the Islamic practice of *islah* of 'reform' at the level of personal behaviour. While the new Saudi media continue to flourish and innovate, and while they, and the sweeping sociological changes in Saudi Arabia of which they are emblematic, no doubt herald important changes for the kingdom in future, their Saudi identity remains every bit as important as their novelty.

Note

1 In transliterating the names of shows our practice has been as follows: where a show already uses a particular transliteration as its official name in English, we reproduce this. Where the show names itself only in Arabic on its official YouTube site, we follow the transliteration conventions of the *International Journal of Middle East Studies*. Often, the transliterations used by the shows for rendering colloquial Arabic in English follow that

'Arabish' formula of substituting numbers for letters unavailable in English. For our purposes, the relevant examples of this are: 3 = Arabic *'ayn*, 7 = Arabic ḥā', 6 = Arabic ṭā'. Hence the name '3al6ayer' renders Arabic *'alā al-ṭāyyir*, or colloquially *'āṭṭayyir*. In transliterating names of people, we have used some discretion. For example, we have chosen to write Salman al-'Awda (the more or less formal transliteration adopted in academic writing on this scholar), even though he spells his own name (rendering the Saudi pronunciation more accurately) as Salman Alodah, Salman al-Oadah or Salman al-Ouda on social media. On the other hand, we have preferred to write Omar Hussein (as his name is routinely spelled in English-language media) rather than, for example 'Umar Husayn, or even *'Umar Ḥusayn*.

References

Abu-Lughod, L. (2005) *Dramas of Nationhood*. Chicago, IL: University of Chicago Press.

Ayed, N. (2014) 'Why Saudi Arabia is the world's top YouTube nation', www.cbc.ca/news/world/nahlah-ayed-why-saudi-arabia-is-the-world-s-top-youtube-nation-1.1359187.

BanaTube (2014) www.youtube.com/watch?v=JaBg4TIHHM8&list=PLJar-Z9ethyqYtaBJ0DfVvK9l1GVZgntz (accessed 7 July 2014).

BBC News (2013) 'Trending: the story behind no woman, no drive', www.bbc.co.uk/news/magazine-24711649.

Ddarabia.com (2014a) 'Statistics', ddarabia.com.statstool.com.

Ddarabia.com (2014b) 'Saudi new media 2.0', www.ddarabia.com.

Deibert, R. (2008) *Access Denied*. Cambridge, MA: MIT Press.

Hertog, S. (2010) *Princes, Brokers, and Bureaucrats*. Ithaca, NY: Cornell University Press.

InternetWorldStats (2014) 'Saudi Arabia', www.internetworldstats.com/me/sa.htm (accessed 11 July 2014).

Kalathil, S. & Boas, T.C. (2003) *Open Networks, Closed Regimes*. Washington, DC: Carnegie Endowment for International Peace.

Kraidy, M. (2006) 'Hypermedia and governance in Saudi Arabia', *First Monday*, 7, firstmonday.org/ojs/index.php/fm/article/view/1610/1525.

Kraidy, M. (2010) *Reality Television and Arab Politics*. Cambridge: Cambridge University Press.

Lacroix, S. (2012) *Awakening Islam*. Cambridge, MA: Harvard University Press.

Le Renard, A. (2008) '"Only for women": women, the state and reform in Saudi Arabia', *The Middle East Journal*, 62, pp. 610–629.

Morozov, E. (2011) *The Net Delusion*. London: Allen Lane.

Murphy, C. (2012) *A Kingdom's Future: Saudi Arabia Through the Eyes of its Twentysomethings*. Washington, DC: Wilson Center.

Murphy, C. (2014) 'Young Saudis embrace Internet satire, rejecting ultraconservative Islam', *GlobalPost*, www.globalpost.com/dispatches/globalpost-blogs/belief/young-saudis-embrace-internet-satire-Islam.

Niblock, T. (2006) *Saudi Arabia*. First edn. London: Routledge.

Otterbeck, J. (2012) 'Wahhabi ideology of social control versus a new publicness in Saudi Arabia', *Contemporary Islam*, 6, pp. 341–353.

Sakr, N. (2001) *Satellite Realms*. First edn. London: I.B. Tauris.

Saudi Ministry of Higher Education (2014) 'King Abdullah Foreign Scholarship Program', mohe.gov.sa/en/aboutus/Institutions/Pages/Emission-of-the-outer.aspx (accessed 7 July 2014).

The Social Clinic Editorial Team (2013) *The State of Social Media in Saudi Arabia 2013*. The Social Clinic. www.thesocialclinic.com/the-state-of-social-media-in-saudi-arabia-2013/.

Stenslie, S. (2012) *Regime Stability in Saudi Arabia*. First edn. Milton Park, Abingdon, Oxon: Routledge.
Uturn Entertainment (2014) *Here is Silicon Valley*. Video.
Vidstatsx.com (2014) 'YouTube top 100 most subscribed Saudi Arabia channels list – top by subscribers', videostatsx.com.
Wamda tv (2014) *Entrepreneur of the Week: Abdullah Mando of UTURN Entertainment in Saudi Arabia*. Video. www.youtube.com/watch?v=jK8ilYc9eoE.
YouTube (2014) *Qawarir Channel*. www.youtube.com/user/Gawareer.

12
THE DYNAMICS OF THE SAUDI TWITTERVERSE

Mohammed Ibahrine

Introduction

Islam is the fastest-growing religion in the world. It is especially popular among young people who are connected to social media platforms. What is strikingly common about Islam and social media is the *sociological* relationship, or the human sociality. Just as everywhere around the world, the Muslim majority countries have witnessed a rapid diffusion and adoption of social media platforms such as Facebook, Twitter and YouTube in recent times. In the Arab world, Facebook is still the leading social networking website, with more than 81 million users. Twitter follows with nearly 6 million users (Arab Social Media Report, 2014). The Arab region is second to the USA when it comes to the number of YouTube daily views. With 90 million video views per day, Saudi Arabia has the world's highest number of YouTube views per Internet user (Arab News, 2012).

The popularity of social media platforms in the Arab world will likely have an impact on the way Muslims understand and practise their religion (Ibahrine, 2014). Of course, Twitter was not initially considered a religious tool. However, religious leaders have quickly realized the potential of this platform. Some scholars have sought to track discernible structural impacts of the new media on patterns of religious behaviour (Bunt, 2000). While the common argument is that social media have the potential to change people's religiosity and practices of piety, some scholars believe that digital platforms are, in fact, shaping Muslims' religious identities (Echchaibi, 2009).

One of the most recent debates in contemporary study of Islam from a communication perspective concerns the extent to which traditional patterns of religious life can be sustained in the face of the power of digital media, particularly the Internet. The central claim is that new media, 1 abrades the existing religious hierarchy of the religious establishment; 2 challenges the most glaring monolithic structures and values within traditionally opaque societies; and 3 perhaps thus strengthens other religious groups that have been deprived for many decades of obtaining attention to articulate their interpretation and to reach the youth.

This chapter will focus on how Twitter has markedly impacted the religious life of many Saudis, including their religiosity, religious practices, issuing *fatwas* and building virtual communities. Among the questions this chapter explores are the following. To what extent, and in what ways have religious leaders used Twitter to disseminate religious content among social media users in Saudi Arabia? Have digital platforms undermined the authority of religious leaders and alternatively empowered the new interpreters of the sacred texts? To what extent have digital platforms contributed to the rise of personalized *fatwas* and the fragmentation of religious authorities?

A particularly useful method of data collection in Arab societies where oral transmission of culture is the norm and word-of-mouth exchange of messages is key to communication is qualitative interview (Hofstede & Hofstede, 2005). A total of seven in-depth interviews were conducted over a three-month period (July–October 2014). Unstructured, face-to-face interviews were conducted in London, Dubai and Sharjah. The respondents came from different walks of life. All of them use Twitter and other digital platforms such as YouTube. Furthermore, the respondents have different educational levels, ranging from holders of university diploma, to those holding PhDs. Subsequent interviews were conducted with two key social media activists in Saudi Arabia. Most of the questions revolved around the key themes that dominated the Saudi Twitterverse.

The first section of this chapter offers a brief review of the literature on Islam, media and the Internet as an introduction to explore the new politics of religious discourses and identity formation. The second section traces the diffusion of Twitter and the formation of the Twitterverse in Saudi Arabia. The third section discusses the implications and consequences of Twitter, emphasizing questions about its key role in effecting new forms of religious discourse and conflict.

Islam and media research

In the 1980s, there was no systematic study that brought together media and Islam. This situation was understandable given the highly restrictive media policies applied to media systems in the Arab and Islamic world. The 'missing' link between media, politics and Islam was established during the 1980s. During this period Islamic groups seemed to acquire progressive influence among the youth partly due to the Iranian Revolution of 1979.

Since the early 1990s, there have been signs of interest in studying the role of media and religion in the Arab countries. This interest sparked off quite a variety of studies in connection with this issue. The French Islam expert Gilles Kepel demonstrated in his study the extent to which Islamic religious preachers used new tools for disseminating their message. Kepel showed how Sheikh Abdal-Hamid Kishk used cassette to circulate the message of Islam (Kepel, 1984).

With the publication of *Small Media, Big Revolution* in 1994 by Sreberny-Mohammadi and Ali Mohammadi, audio cassettes became accredited as a serious agent not only of political change, but also of a revolution with global ramifications. The authors argue that, by distributing religious sermons of Ayatollah Khomeini in the late 1970s, the audio cassettes' range of distribution contributed to the fragmentation of political as well as cultural authority of the shah's regime.

In centralized, hierarchized and closed information environments, these informal networks of small media have undermined the formal efforts to control the flow of information. Situated outside the strict regime's control, the small media have provided the much-needed means of political communication for political opponents, particularly Islamic movements, activists and preachers, who have been blocked by rigid media restrictive policies. Using alternative small media tools, Islamic movements have created for themselves a place to construct an Islamized public opinion and have thus triggered political change and even a revolution in the Iranian case.

Islam and Internet research

In the early 1990s, scanned translations of the Quran and *Hadith* were uploaded on websites created and run by Muslim students and professionals in North America, Europe and Japan (Anderson, 2003). By digitizing Islamic content, they paved the way for widespread access and later use. In the first generation of the Internet, there were some traditional websites like Islam Online that acted as one-stop shops for religious information and comprehensive services to Islamic communities, including *fatwas* (Gräf, 2008). The 'ask the imam' websites provided believers with concise information to specific questions. Believers sought religious guidance and orientation through questions and answers that were available online. Some Muslims showed their religious affiliation by browsing specific websites. These new types of websites highlighted the conflict between established sources of traditional religious knowledge and the new resources.

Research on Islam and the Internet emerged in the late 1990s as scholars began to examine the different ways in which religious actors and groups used the Internet to disseminate religious content and messages (Eickelman & Anderson, 2003). This early research arguably suggested that a new class of 'interpreters of Islam' had emerged due to information and communications technologies (ICTs).

The Internet gained momentum in the Arab world in 2000, when a number of Islamic leaders and preachers posted religious information material on their websites (Bunt, 2000; Ibahrine, 2005). That paved the way for these preachers and religious leaders to orient more imagination, time and energy towards the Internet. The publication of religious materials would have been unthinkable in the early 1990s, when the communication sphere was blocked to Islamic preachers.

Some scholars suggest that the advent of digital media in the Arab and Islamic world would be in the service of religious leaders to advance their monolithic strict and orthodox interpretations (Šisler, 2006b). Others argue that these accounts sound rather unconvincing and simplistic, since digital media would have a very limited effect on culture in the Arab and Islamic world (El-Nawawy & Khamis, 2009).

In the early 2000s, Gary R. Bunt examined how religious authority has been executed and how religious communities (*ummah*) have been formed in virtual environments. Recent research suggests that the nature of religious authority might be altered (Bunt, 2000). As Bunt argued, millions of Muslims rely on the Internet, including websites and email. The argument is that the Internet has a profound effect on Islamic culture in the Arab and Islamic world, and that it is not only the educated minority who are behind the emergence and dynamism of the public sphere. Shirley and her team found that religiosity affects Muslim surfers' level of religious activities online and that religiosity is a positive factor when it comes to digital religious activities (Shirley et al., 2008, 108). Other scholars argue that the digitization of Islam represents a challenge to the conventional understanding of Muslim identity (Ibahrine, 2014).

Despite the popularity of social media, empirical research on Islam and social media has been surprisingly sparse. This research lacuna may be due to the fact that much of the academic research focused mainly on the so-called Arab Spring, focusing mainly on the role of social media and political transformation (Howard, 2011). To fill the existing gap in research on the relationship between Islam and social media, this chapter attempts to provide an overview of the religious activities of Muslim social media users. There is space for more studies of religious values, symbols and rituals on digital platforms, including Facebook, Twitter and YouTube, and the relationship between offline and online environments.

Twitter has become a field where different configurations of religious power and interpretation struggle to manifest themselves. This chapter is an attempt to trace, describe and explain the different uses and the eventual impact of Twitter on religious power in Saudi society.

Mapping the Twitterverse in Saudi Arabia

Some Arab countries have witnessed a rapid diffusion of social media platforms such as Facebook, YouTube and Twitter. The rise of social media has been made possible by the huge growth of the Internet infrastructure and low barriers to entry. As of 2013, there were 125 million Internet users in the Arab world (total population 300 million), with more than 53 million users regularly posting entries, sharing viral videos, establishing social networking sites (blog.bayt, 2013). The social media have gradually developed into a mass medium; ordinary people as well as many public figures, opinion leaders, religious leaders and intellectuals use social media to inform, to communicate and to network with their audiences, followers and communities. The low barriers to Twitter, empowered by mobile phones, will substantially help the massive proliferation of social media among large segments of Arab demographics.

Over the last five years, Twitter has become one of the most preferable and popular social media platforms. As of 2014, the total number of active Twitter users in the Arab region hit more than 6 million. With about 2.4 million users, Saudi Arabia accounts for over 40% of all active Twitter users in the Arab region, 32% of the online Saudi population, and about 11% of the 28 million Saudi population (Arab Social Media Report, 2005). The Twitter.com website is currently the seventh most visited in Saudi Arabia (www.alexa.com).

Before 2009, the first wave of Twitter users in Saudi Arabia was initially limited to influential people and bloggers who knew about the platform. In 2010, the number of Saudi Twitter users was only several hundred thousand. After Al-Waleed bin Talal, a Saudi business magnate, invested US$300 million in the company in December 2011, Twitter became more popular (Rahal, 2013), and tweets originating from Saudi Arabia increased by more than 3,000% from 2011 to 2012, and currently amount to 50 million tweets monthly (Social Clinic, 2013).[1]

Compared to other social media platforms, Twitter is such a simple medium. The fact that a tweet must be no longer than 140 characters appealed to many Saudis, and it was easy for non-English speakers to use it. The availability of Twitter's interface in Arabic (translated by a group of volunteers) has contributed to the wide adoption of Twitter among the Saudis. Now, about 90% of Twitter users in Saudi Arabia tweet in Arabic (Rahal, 2013)[2] and Arabic has become the sixth most popular language on Twitter, used in 2.8% of all public tweets (Leetaru et al., 2013). According to a recent study, over 4% of the entire Twitter user population is deemed to be based in Saudi Arabia (PeerReach, by Boghardt, 2013). Riyadh, the capital of the kingdom, is one of the world's most active cities on Twitter.

The largest age group of Saudi Twitter users are the 25–34-year-olds. The second largest group are those aged between 18 and 24 (Jiffry, 2013), and Twitter activity rises noticeably on Friday (the beginning of the Saudi weekend) (Rahal, 2013).

What makes Twitter so useful in the Saudi context is the synchronicity of messaging (Puschmann & Gaffney, 2014, 429). According to a recent study, about 73% of Saudi Twitter users access their accounts through their mobile phones (Social Clinic, 2013). This suggests that Twitter activity has become an integral part of everyday lives of Saudi youth.

Trending topics in the Saudi Twitterverse

Retweeting is an indication of enhancing the followership as well as offering strong support. For instance, some of the most retweeted messages in Saudi Arabia's Twitter history were those using the hashtag #VisitIbrahim, which circulated through social media circles and within just 24 hours had been retweeted over 200,000 times (Simpson, 2014).[3] The community of contributors to hashtag #VisitIbrahim is wide-ranging, including individuals, media organizations and religious leaders. What is striking about this hashtag is its rapid popularity and its impact to enhance human sociability. The use of Twitter in Saudi Arabia is intertwined with the use of other social media platforms such as Facebook and Tumblr.

TABLE 12.1 Twitter in selected Arab countries

Name of country	Population	Internet users	Penetration (% of population)	Twitter users March 2014	Female	Male	Tweets in March 2014	Number of tweets	Languages
Algeria	38,700,000	6,404,264	16.5%	37,500	45%	55%	4,030,000	524,449	French
Egypt	86,000,000	43,065,211	49.6%	1,090,000	35%	65%	93,000,000	3,525,031	Arabic
Kuwait	2,889,000	2,069,650	75.5%	344,000	36%	64%	55,800,000	5,762,894	Arabic
Morocco	32,666,179	18,472,835	56.0%	76,700	48%	52%	4,340,000	654,931	Arabic
Saudi Arabia	28,660,000	16,544,322	60.5%	2,400,000	36%	64%	213,900,000	10,398,970	Arabic
Tunisia	10,982,800	4,790,634	43.8%	37,100	44%	56%	3,100,000	1,489,239	Arabic
United Arab Emirates	8,089,000	8,101,280	88.0%	502,000	43%	57%	46,500,000	6,179,415	Arabic

The very compact nature of a tweet of 140 characters, designed especially for easy use and memorability, is a perfect tool for memorizing the Quran and the Prophet's sayings. It is almost as if Twitter were designed specifically for the Quran and *Hadith*. Tweeting Quranic verses and sayings from the Prophet has become a part of Ramadan religious rituals and habits such as *Adhkar* (remembrances of Allah), which are short individual prayers. Early research has found that Twitter is used for a number of intentions, which vary considerably. For instance, Akshay Java and his colleagues presented a brief taxonomy of user intention on Twitter, by analysing the aggregate behaviour across communities of users. They identified four main categories of users of Twitter, namely daily chatter, conversations, sharing information and reporting news (Java et al., 2007, 2). Religious leaders in Saudi Arabia are no exception.[4] The *ulama*, scholars of religion, have a special relationship with ICTs. They originally denounced and objected to television in the 1960s, satellite television in the 1990s and the Internet in the 2000s, but later adopted these technologies and became active users (Al-Rasheed, 2007, 56).

The Twitterverse and religious orthodoxies and heterodoxies

This chapter focuses on Saudi religious leaders on Twitter, given their high popularity in the Twitterverse and that the *ulama* fare well in the social sphere (Al-Rasheed, 2007, 57). They exercise their sway in subtle, silent ways (Obaid, 1999, 52). The power of religious leaders resides in their symbolic and cultural capital. Traditionally, Saudi *ulama* refrain from interfering in the political field. The king, the centre of political power in Saudi Arabia, takes the religious leaders' views into account when it comes to key social and religious decisions, but their influence is limited to the religious and social affairs of Saudis. On Twitter, religious leaders have the most attention and the most followers (Rahal, 2013). They have managed to build a loyal follower base on Twitter. Initially, some religious leaders advised believers not to use Twitter, because it was regarded as a source of lies. For instance, Abdul Aziz Al Shaikh, Grand Mufti in Saudi Arabia, advanced a critical stance towards social media platforms such as Facebook and Twitter because, according to him, these media disseminate lies and may destroy established relationships within Muslim families (BBC, 2014). Abdul Aziz Al Shaikh warned millions of Muslims that Twitter was a threat to the unity of the *ummah*. The significance of his sermon stemmed from the fact that he delivered it on the *Eid al-Adha* feast in 2014.[5] The sermons were broadcast on satellite TV and were watched by millions of Muslims. Moreover, in August 2014, Abdul Moneim al-Mushawwah, head of the al-Sakina campaign, said that Twitter was the primary contact point in recruiting the youth to go to Syria (Al-Arabiya, 2014). For instance, Abdulaziz Al-Mulhem, the spokesperson for the Saudi Ministry of Information and Culture, said that it was challenging to win the struggle of interpretations of religious meaning on digital platforms, implying the impossibility of monitoring and controlling social media (Batrawy, 2014).

Other religious leaders are using Twitter to engage directly with the community of believers and enhance their religious loyalty. The religious leaders have started to tweet what they call 'wisdom of Prophet Muhammad' and summaries of allegories, stories and wisdom of life as well as religious information. Their tweets are all written in formal written Arabic. Other religious leaders have set up Facebook pages and YouTube channels. Religious preachers and leaders are able to produce content for their blogs and their YouTube channels, since the production of content requires only small production units consisting of one volunteer.[6] Unlike many Twitter users who do not display their full name and instead use pseudonyms as user names, religious leaders use their real names and even post their portrait photos to add a personalized and human face to their digital profiles. Mohammad Al-Arefe topped the list of such clerics with 10 million followers on Twitter, followed by Aid al-Qarni with 7 million followers, and Ahmad al-Shugairi with 8 million followers (see Table 12.2). Like other social actors, they use Twitter to enhance their fame, visibility and leadership. Haewoon Kwak and colleagues conclude that the number of followers alone does not reflect the user's influence (Kwak et al., 2010, 5). Thus, popularity offline may not translate into online popularity (Lomborg, 2014, 104).

In the Saudi Twitterverse, religious issues get the most attention (Rahal, 2013), generating high traffic, because religious leaders prove very prolific. The relationship on Twitter is based on two poles: users (to follow) and followers. This relationship model allows followers to identify with their followees and generate a collective emotion and connection that transcends the digital network. Moreover, religious leaders possess a great deal of cultural capital illustrated by the use of classical (written) Arabic as a symbol of religious 'distinction' in Bourdieusian terms. To sum up, Saudi religious leaders have significant influence on Twitter and they have recognized the potential of digital media in creating a large network of supporters.

Mohammad Al-Arefe

In the Saudi context, religious leaders use their traditional knowledge of the Quran and *Hadith* as a way to assert their cultural capital and religious legitimacy. Some of them developed solid, smart social media strategies and tactics in order to attract and maintain the undivided attention and the most faithful followers. For instance, Mohammad Al-Arefe (a famous Saudi cleric) topped the list of the most influential on Twitter, with 10 million followers, joining the list of the top 120 Twitter accounts worldwide (Nada & Faris, 2013).[7] Some prominent journalists claimed that Saudi religious leaders and celebrities bought their followers on Twitter via social media agencies. According to *Al-Eqtisadiah*, a Saudi daily newspaper, about 25% of Mohammad Al-Arefe's 10 million Twitter followers are 'imaginary' and almost 50% more are 'inactive'. Following such sceptical media reports, some religious leaders denounced the fake followers and considered such a practice as a lie (De Muth, 2012). Those who are sceptical about the numbers of the religious

The dynamics of the Saudi Twitterverse 211

TABLE 12.2 Network and Twitter activity

Participant	Following	Followers	Total number of tweets	Total number of photos and videos
Mohammad Al-Arefe	4	10 million	24,000	3,728
Ahmad al-Shugairi	125	8 million	6,809	46
Aid al-Qarni	0	7 million	21,777	2,274

leaders' followers said that the Grand Mufti was right when he described Twitter as a source of lies and deception (De Muth, 2012).

Al-Arefe has managed to build a strong relationship with his followers, who are very engaged with his Twitter accounts and his tweets. In one of his tweets, he denied reports made by an Egyptian TV channel about his illness; his tweet generated a total number of 17,382 comments, which were posted on his account (socialeyez.blog, 2013). The number of followers and the number of comments on his Twitter stream determines the high connectivity he enjoys. For instance, on 27 September 2014, which coincided with the Friday before *Eid al-Adha*, he posted more than nine tweets. Aware of his popularity, Al-Arefe used Twitter for proselytizing. For instance, in one of his tweets, he urged Ahlam [a famous Emirati singer] to turn into a preacher: 'You are a believer and you love God. Why don't you make today a turning point in your life so when Ramadan is here, you are Ahlam the preacher, and not Ahlam the singer.' Ahlam responded to Al-Arefe in a very polite and diplomatic manner by retweeting his tweet and asking him to pray for her. Al-Arefe's and Ahlam's followers forwarded the tweet. As a result, an exchange of tweets surfaced in the Twitterverse, since both the religious leader and the singer have a high number of fans (Gulf News, 2013).

According to some media accounts, Mohammad Al-Arefe is a very controversial religious leader (Al-Arabiya, 2012). He recently made headlines for his derogatory MBC3 Children tweet.[8] In his tweet, he announced his boycott of MBC3 Children; he asked parents to prohibit their children from watching the channel because, as stated in his tweet, 'MBC3 Children has scenes that are full of ideas of atheism and corruption'. His tweet called his followers to action.

Heterodoxies

The use of Twitter for disseminating religious content is not limited to religious leaders but is also used by ordinary Muslims who started tweeting Quranic verses and *Hadith*. Twitter is an increasingly important source of religious information for many Saudis. For some of them, Twitter has become the primary source of religious content. When asked about the importance of Twitter as a means of information, most of my informants confirmed that Twitter has become a source of information beyond what mainstream media provides. The majority of them said they would use many types of mainstream media to get informed but that Twitter had become their primary source of information, especially when it came to news that was not covered by the mainstream media. As one of the interviewees explained:

> Twitter has been useful, but with limited impact. Twitter made some peripheral events that previously would not have attracted the attention of the mainstream media, to be covered appear in the Twitterverse. In the offline space, journalists waited for permission to publish their news, now in the online sphere, Twitter is blurring the boundaries. For him, if it is happening in the kingdom, it is happening on Twitter.
>
> *(Personal interview, 31 July 2014)*

As Bunt noted, what is new about digital networks is the emergence of a new type of provider of *fatwa* services, who have no formal and traditional religious education and thus ordinary believers contribute to the development of a new understanding and practice of Islam (Bunt, 2003). As a result, it can be argued that a new religious culture is emerging, which has a significant impact on the Saudi consciousness. Pierre Bourdieu argued that television bears dangers for reflexively intellectual thinking. For him, television rewards fast thinkers, who offer predigested and pre-thought culture (Bourdieu, 1996). Likewise, Twitter has elicited new forms of imams who offer easy-to-understand and friendly-to-practise *fatwas*.

This makes their digital presence strongly felt and a constant source of fear by religious leaders. In most Islamic countries, where *fatwas* are strictly monopolized, platforms like Twitter permit individuals and laymen to bypass official religious leaders and contribute directly to the free flow of *fatwas*. The massive availability of *fatwas* on digital platforms has triggered a trend of personalized *fatwas*, meaning that a believer has the opportunity to access different religious scholastic interpretations, thereby controlling his or her religious practices (Šisler, 2007).

This personalized interpretation is a direct affront to the dominant doxa typically inscribed as the right interpretation in a sacrosanct religious filed. Digital platforms then may have contributed to democratizing religious knowledge and interpretation. Only those religious leaders with the highest symbolic capital are able to generate *fatwas* and replicate traditional hierarchies of preachers. Their orthodox Islam can be considered as doxa, and rules to be taken for granted by their followers, given those leaders' long and laborious religious training. One of the people I talked to, for instance, stressed the importance of Twitter as a technology of networking:

> Twitter is an individual channel of communication, but it is useful for creating communities and highlighting the value of the community in the lives of Saudis who share a common element such as a place, culture, history.
>
> *(Personal interview, 18 August 2014)*

Clearly, there were concerns about the simplification of *fatwas* as well as the commodification and commercialization of *fatwas*. Unlike conventional media, designed to mass broadcast the orthodoxy, Twitter is intended for particular and personalized messaging. As a result, Twitter might be understood as a multi-layered mesh of digital platforms without boundaries and limits. The Twitterverse has intensified the fragmentation of communities of believers and *corpora* of religious and sacred interpretations. Some believers like interpretations that present a new perspective on the *Hadith* and argue in favour of a particular *fatwa*. The new imams capitalize on Twitter to tailor their *fatwas* according to the needs of different believers. Such imams tend to create hybrid interpretation, combining the 'remix' of different interpretations from other religious schools and sources (Eickelman & Anderson, 2003). When asked about the importance of Twitter as a means of information, most interviewees confirmed that Twitter has become a source of information beyond the mainstream media. The majority said they would inform themselves using a variety of mainstream media, but that Twitter was their primary source for news not being covered elsewhere. An insightful comment by one informant confirms that Twitter may have an effect on the freedom of thought and expression:

> Twitter is widening the scope of our horizon, especially when it comes [to] freedoms of interpreting the sacred text. If you read some of the statistics about the use of Twitter, YouTube and smartphones by the Saudi youth and the amount of time they spend on these virtual spaces, you will conclude that they are looking for a change at least on the digital world. For them, it is a change; it is a kind of a virtual migration to places and spaces of unlimited freedom. Twitter is the land of freedom.
>
> *(Personal interview, 4 September 2014)*

Thus, the prominence of new religious experts has created a new kind of contestation, as the religious leaders are competing not only between themselves, but also with a new group of interpreters or the so-called free imams. Twitter has made it possible for users to create content regardless of their religious capital, expertise and symbolic authority (Anderson, 2003; Bunt, 2000). In this sense, digital platforms provide incentive to provide bespoke messages to targeted audiences, and in turn the numerous communication channels contribute to fragmenting Muslim audiences. The outcome is a fragmented *ummah*. F-*fatwas* (or *fatwas* produced on Facebook and Twitter) have introduced a new paradigm to the practice of religious instruction and education in the way they were formulated, issued, disseminated, received and acted upon. For many, Twitter has become an ideal platform, the new mosque or *madrasa*, for the dissemination of the Islamic faith. Currently, there is a great deal of public debate over the nature and value of *fatwas* circulated via Twitter and other digital platforms. F-*fatwas* spark commentary and feedback among many sectors of Muslim society, including religious authorities, Islamist intellectuals and young urban or secularized Muslims. However, Yusuf al-Qaradawi, a famous religious authority in the Islamic world, does not consider this kind of production of religious knowledge by laymen as a danger for the interpretation of the sacred text. For him, this is a kind of *ijtihad* (Gräf, 2008, 11).

The societal role of religious leaders is no longer to defend political power, but rather to struggle against any new form of power that transcends their centrality for the religious *ummah*. Christian Fuchs claims that religious leaders exist only because they enter into religiously constructed social relationships. They exchange symbols of capital in these relationships (Fuchs, 2014). For centuries, interpretations of the Quran were kept as a reserved domain for a tiny minority of *ulama*. Religious leaders demonstrated their expertise and knowledge so that Muslim laymen accepted and even expected their symbolic authority. Symbolic power is an important dimension and a powerful resource of the religious institution.

In the context of the free flow of data on digital platforms, the Saudi religious leaders recently found themselves on the defensive. For instance, Khaled El-Dakheel, a Saudi intellectual, argues that the official religious establishment is under serious attack. In one of his tweets, El-Dakheel said that many social and political actors, including the king, are publicly criticizing religious leaders. This marked a shift in their relationship.

To sum up, the strategy of religious leaders aims at achieving two goals – namely, to confront and compete with laymen Muslims, thereby dominating the Twitterverse, and to create and enforce traditional definitions of Islam. Their different tactics aim at consecrating a certain interpretation of Islam as legitimate.

Conclusion

Exploring how Islam is practised on digital platforms may help us understand the cultural shifts at work within traditional societies such as Saudi Arabia. Twitter has made visible the contradictions within religious discourses and interpretations of the sacred text. The interpretation battles have illustrated how religious orthodoxies perceive the emerging heterodoxy as a threat and an aberrant deviation from the right path. Social networking websites, microblogging platforms and mobile social apps have become new avenues for disseminating competing interpretations. The blossoming of digital *fatwas* is an indication of the splintering of orthodoxies and the emergence of heterodoxies, undermining the traditional concept of religious authority. On the other hand, religious leaders are attempting to propagate their traditional understanding of Islam into the Twitterverse, thereby enforcing their particular interpretation.

For centuries, interpretations of the Quran were kept a reserved domain for a tiny minority of *ulama*, but the new type of Facebook *fatwa* is likely to shift the balance of power in shaping religious interpretation. Consequently, religious authority has become a contested domain, rather than an accepted reality. Twitter permits individuals to change the dynamics of a collectivist society and it has the potential to change people's religiosity and practices of piety, making its impact visible even in a conservative and traditional environment like that in Saudi Arabia.

Notes

1 In an interview, Twitter CEO Dick Costolo said that Saudi Arabia was the fastest-growing country, 'with a 3,000 percent growth last month' (Al-Arabiya, 2012).
2 Taghreedat (Letstweetinarabic), a group of 400 volunteers, translated the microblogging site.
3 Ibrahim, the recent social media star in Saudi Arabia, was paralysed and alone; he tweeted asking for a visit in the hospital. His tweet generated massive hospital visitors as well as generous donors, who contributed financially to fund his $130,000 surgery in Germany (Simpson, 2014).
4 I use the term religious leaders to describe the most influential Muslim figures who have reached a digital fame and popularity in terms of numbers of followers. The selection is also based on tweeted messages and retweets.
5 *Eid al-Adha* means the feast of the sacrifice.
6 Ironically, some leading religious leaders have social media accounts even though they have already passed away, because their followers aim to reach the younger generations by creating Facebook pages and Twitter streams as well as YouTube channels.
7 twitter.com/MohamadAlarefe/ is the official Twitter account of Mohammad Al-Arefe, and it is the one linked to his official website. However, there are more than 150 Twitter accounts carrying his name, such as twitter.com/MohammadAlarefe and twitter.com/ma refeeng.
8 MBC3 is a children's entertainment channel.

References

Ahmed, Q. (2013) 'Saudi Arabia's struggles with social media: Twitter clowns and Facebook fatwas', www.theblaze.com/contributions/saudi-arabias-struggles-with-social-media-twitter-clowns-and-facebook-fatwas/.
Al-Arabiya (2012) 'Controversial Saudi preacher needs psychiatric help, MBC statement suggests', english.alarabiya.net/articles/2012/12/25/257033.html (accessed 25 July 2014).
Al-Arabiya (2014) 'Facebook and Twitter gain more users in Saudi Arabia', english.alarabiya.net/en/media/digital/2014/01/09/Use-of-mobiles-in-social-media-on-the-rise-in-Saudi-Arabia.html.
Al-Rasheed, M. (2007) *Contesting the Saudi State: Islamic Voices from a New Generation*. Cambridge: Cambridge University Press.
Anderson, J. (2003) *The Internet and Islam's New Interpreters*, ed. D. Eickelman & J. Anderson. Bloomington, IN: Indiana University Press.
Arab News (2012) '90 million videos viewed daily on YouTube in KSA', www.arabnews.com/news/536196 (accessed 7 July 2014).
Arab Social Media Report (2014) *Arab Social Media Report*, www.arabsocialmediareport.com/home/index.aspx (accessed 4 November 2014).
Batrawy, A. (2014) 'Arab states lag in media war against extremists', *AP The Big Story*, 21 September, bigstory.ap.org/article/8a48f8875bf94e3893effb8d5709d6b9/arab-states-lag-media-war-against-extremists.
BBC (2014) '#BBCtrending: why Twitter is so big in Saudi Arabia', www.bbc.com/news/blogs-trending-25864558.
blog.bayt (2013) 'How the internet is transforming the Arab region', blog.bayt.com/2013/04/how-the-internet-is-transforming-the-arab-region/ (accessed 13 July 2014).
Boghardt, L. (2013) *Saudi Arabia's War on Twitter*, www.washingtoninstitute.org/policy-analysis/view/saudi-arabias-war-on-twitter (accessed 11 July 2014).

Bourdieu, P. (1996) 'On television. The new press', www.nytimes.com/books/first/b/bour dieu-television.html.
Boyd, D., Golder, S. & Lotan, G. (2010) 'Tweet, tweet, retweet: conversational aspects of retweeting on Twitter', www.danah.org/papers/TweetTweetRetweet.pdf.
Bruns, A. & Hallvard, M. (2013) 'Structural layers of communication on Twitter', in K. Weller, A. Bruns, J. Burgess, M. Mahrt & C. Puschmann (Eds) *Twitter and Society* (pp. 15–28). New York: Peter Lang.
Bunt, G.R. (2000) *Virtually Islamic*. Cardiff: University of Wales Press.
Bunt, G.R. (2003) *Islam in the Digital Age*. London: Pluto Press.
Bunt, G.R. (2006) 'Towards an Islamic information revolution?', in E. Poole, J.E. Richardson (Eds) *Muslims and the News Media*. London: I.B. Tauris.
De Muth, S. (2012) 'Twitter fake followers and a fatwa', *The Middle East*, www.biyokulule.com/view_content.php?articleid=5833 (accessed 8 October 2014).
Echchaibi, N. (2009) 'Hyper-Islamism? Mediating Islam from the halal website to the Islamic talk show', *Journal of Arab and Muslim Media Research*, 1(3), pp. 199–214.
Eickelman, D.F. & Anderson, J.W. (2003) *New Media in the Muslim World: The Emerging Public Sphere*. Bloomington, IN: Indiana University Press.
El-Nawawy, M. & Khamis, S. (2009) *Islam Dot Com: Contemporary Islamic Discourses in Cyberspace*. New York: Palgrave Macmillan.
Etling, B., Kelly, J., Faris, R. & Palfrey, J. (2009) 'Mapping the Arabic blogosphere: politics, culture, and dissent', *Berkman Center Research Publication*, pp. 1–62, cyber.law.harvard.edu/sites/cyber.law.harvard.edu/files/Mapping_the_Arabic_Blogosphere.pdf.
Ford, M. (2011) 'Reconceptualizing the public/private distinction in the age of information technology', *Information, Communication & Society*, 14(4), pp. 550–567.
Fuchs, C. (2014) *Social Media: A Critical Introduction*. London: Sage.
Ghafour, A. (2013) 'Women use Twitter to raise issues', *Arab News*, www.arabnews.com/news/461751.
Gräf, B. (2008) 'IslamOnline.net: independent, interactive, popular', www.arabmediasociety.com/articles/downloads/20080115032719_AMS4_Bettina_Graf.pdf.
Gulf News (2013) 'Saudi cleric Mohammad Al Arifi urges singer Ahlam to turn into preacher', gulfnews.com/news/gulf/saudi-arabia/saudi-cleric-mohammad-al-arifi-urges-singer-ahlam-to-turn-into-preacher-1.1195053 (accessed 15 July 2014).
Hirschkind, C. (2006) *The Ethical Soundscape Cassette Sermons and Islamic Counterpublics*. New York: Columbia University Press.
Ho, S., Lee, W. & Hameed, S. (2008) 'Muslim surfers on the Internet: using the theory of planned behaviour to examine the factors influencing engagement in online religious activities', *New Media & Society*, 10(1), pp. 93–113, nms.sagepub.com/content/10/1/93.full.pdf+html.
Hoetjes, G. (2013) 'Unemployment in Saudi Arabia: a ticking time bomb?', muftah.org/unemployment-in-saudi-arabia-a-ticking-time-bomb/#.U7VhuI2SxVs.
Hofstede, G. & Hofstede, G.J. (2005) *Cultures and Organizations: Software of the Mind*. New York: McGraw-Hill.
Howard, P. (2011) *The Digital Origins of Dictatorship and Democracy Information Technology and Political Islam*. Oxford: Oxford University Press.
Ibahrine, M. (2005) 'Morocco: Internet making censorship obsolete', *Arab Reform Bulletin*, 3(7).
Ibahrine, M. (2007) *New Media and Neo-Islamism: New Media's Impact on the Political Culture in the Islamic World*. Germany: Akademiker Verlag.
Ibahrine, M. (ed.) (2014) 'Islam and social media', in Kerric Harvey (Ed.) *Encyclopedia of Social Media and Politics*. England: Sage Publications.

Java, A. et al. (2007) *Why We Twitter: Understanding Microblogging Usage and Communities.* Paper presented at the International Conference on Knowledge Discovery and Data Mining, San Jose, CA.

Jiffry, F. (2013) '#Saudi Arabia world's 2nd most Twitter-happy nation', *Arab News,* www.arabnews.com/news/452204.

Kepel, G. (1984) *Le Prophète et Pharaon: les mouvements islamistes dans l'Égypte.* Paris.

Kwak, H., Lee, C., Park, H. & Moon, S. (2010) 'What is Twitter, a social network or a news media?' pp. 591–600, www.eecs.wsu.edu/~assefaw/CptS580-06/papers/2010-www-twitter.pdf (accessed 6 July 2014).

Leetaru, K. et al. (2013) 'Mapping the global Twitter heartbeat', *First Monday,* 18, firstmonday.org/article/view/4366/3654 (accessed 6 July 2014).

Lomborg, S. (2014) *Social Media, Social Genres: Making Sense of the Ordinary.* London: Routledge.

Nada, G. & Faris, S. (2013) 'Twitter sheikhs of Saudi Arabia', www.al-monitor.com/pulse/originals/2013/12/twitter-sheikhs-saudi-arabia.html# (accessed 15 August 2014).

Obaid, N. (1999) 'The power of Saudi Arabia's Islamic leaders', *Middle East Quarterly,* September, pp. 51–58, www.meforum.org/482/the-power-of-saudi-arabias-islamic-leaders (accessed 22 July 2014).

Puschmann, C. & Gaffney, D. (2014) *Twitter and Society.* New York: Peter Lang.

Rahal, M. (2013) 'How do Saudis use social media?', infographic, www.wamda.com/2013/12/how-do-saudis-saudi-arabia-social-media.

Saudi Gazette (2013) '"Prostitutes": Saudi cleric insults recently-appointed female Shura members', *Saudi Gazette,* 25 February, www.saudigazette.com.sa/index.cfm?method=home.regcon&contentid=20130225154564.

Schmidt, J. (2014) 'Twitter and the rise of personal publics', in K. Weller, A. Bruns, J. Burgess, M. Mahrt & C. Puschmann (Eds) *Twitter and Society* (pp. 3–15). New York: Peter Lang.

Shirley, S., Lee, W. & Hameed, S.S. (2008) 'Muslim surfers on the Internet: Using the theory of planned behaviour to examine the factors influencing engagement in online religious activities', *New Media and Society,* 10(1), pp. 93–113.

Simpson, J. (2014) 'Paralysed Saudi Arabian man's tweet asking for someone to visit him in hospital becomes most retweeted message in Saudi Arabian Twitter history', *The Independent,* 16 May, www.independent.co.uk/news/world/asia/paralysed-saudi-arabian-mans-tweet-asking-for-someone-to-visit-him-in-hospital-becomes-most-retweeted-message-in-saudi-arabian-twitter-history-9385715.html.

Šisler, V. (2006a) 'Islamic jurisprudence in cyberspace: construction of interpretative authority in Muslim diaspora', in R. Polčák, M. Škop & P. Šmahel (Eds) *Cyberspace 2005.* Brno: Masaryk University.

Šisler, V. (2006b) 'Representation and self-representation: Arabs and Muslims in digital games', in M. Santorineos & M. Dimitriadi (Eds) *Gaming Realities: A Challenge for Digital Culture.* Fournos: Athens.

Šisler, V. (2007) 'The Internet and the construction of Islamic knowledge in Europe', *Masaryk University Journal of Law and Technology,* 1(2).

Smith, L. & Ayish, S. (2013) 'Saudi prince: blocking social media platforms is a "losing war"', edition.cnn.com/2013/05/07/world/meast/saudi-arabia-social-media.

Social Clinic (2013) 'The state of social media in Saudi Arabia 2013', www.thesocialclinic.com/the-state-of-social-media-in-saudi-arabia-2013/ (accessed 11 July 2014).

socialeyez.blog (2013) 'Buzz Report: Weekly Top 5', blog.socialeyez.ae/2013/06/02/buzz-report-weekly-top-5-may-26-30-2013/ (accessed 7 July 2014).

Sreberny, A. (2002) 'Media, Muslims, and the Middle East: a critical review essay media', *Political Communication,* 19(2), pp. 273–280.

Sreberny-Mohammadi, A. & Mohammadi, A. (1994) *Small Media, Big Revolution: Communication, Culture, and the Iranian Revolution.* Minneapolis, MN: University of Minnesota Press.

Worth, R. (2012) 'Twitter gives Saudi Arabia a revolution of its own', *The New York Times,* www.nytimes.com/2012/10/21/world/middleeast/twitter-gives-saudi-arabia-a-revolution-of-its-own.html?pagewanted=all&_r=1&.

13

THE NEO-LIBERAL ISLAMIC PREACHERS

'It is not enough to believe, but you must act on your faith'

Nermeen Alazrak and Alamira Samah Saleh

> I'm a reformer. My role is of a reformer using faith, using and talking about hope. My role is to give hope and big dreams. Talk to young people about their dreams in the future. Send me your dreams. Hopes and dreams. I want to believe in them and give hope. I have a message for the Arab youth, especially now in Egypt, Tunisia, Algeria, Yemen, and Libya. All of us have to respect your dreams: you are a treasure. You're the treasure – not the oil or the gas. You have to dream and think. You will change your country and make a better future. And at the same time, you have to accept others. My message to Arab youth is this: you need each other. You need coexistence. Extend your hands.
> *(Amr Khaled, cited in* The Cairo Review, 2011*)*

Introduction

Dawah (or Call for Islam) has always been a major concern for Muslims, beginning with the Prophet Muhammad who was not only the preacher of a new religion and the head of a new community, but also an effective teacher and an enthusiastic promoter of learning. The second half of the 20th century has been marked by the increasing pace of Muslim missionary activities, ranging from publications, tapes and public seminars, to *dawah* in mosques and on street corners. Until the late 1980s, interpersonal communication was an inevitable part of the *dawah* missions. Those seeking deeper knowledge of Islam or thinking of converting to Islam needed a preacher or *da'eyah*. Likewise, the *da'eyah* needed audiences with whom they could engage in meaningful discussions about faith. However, the last two decades have witnessed a radical change in *dawah* as people no longer need to leave their homes or offices in order to contact a Muslim *da'eyah*, as they can now receive an instant response to their queries about Islam while staying in permanent live contact. Internet technology has facilitated this change, allowing people to obtain an enormous amount of information with a simple click of a button. Online conferences and discussions on Islam and Islamic teachings have become common and abound with information about *dawah*. Thus, offline contact has been increasingly supplemented with virtual contact. In the face of these developments, Muzammil Siddiqi argues that:

> *Dawah* in this kind of global exchange medium takes on a whole new flavor. It is no longer sufficient to meet on a one-on-one basis. We are talking about mass appeal and an approach to mass communication. Despite this aspect, *dawah* remains a communication between hearts, and thus the global information technology is only a door for individuals to introduce themselves to other individuals.
>
> *(Siddiqi, 1998)*

There have been various studies done on *dawah* by Western and Arab Muslim scholars alike. In contrast to the Western studies about preachers, the Arab media studies focused mainly on three elements of *dawah* – namely, the discourse of Islamic religious speech, the content and style of religious media channels, and the audiences' uses and gratifications. However, many of these studies did not focus on the preachers as the main communicators in this communication process and this chapter attempts to shed new light on the role of preachers – particularly young ones – taking Egypt as a topical case study. The aim is to identify these young preachers' new role in the public space compared to traditional preachers who depended on terrestrial television as well as audio cassettes to disseminate their *dawah*.

The following discussion also aims to illustrate this role as perceived by a sample of young audiences. For this, we have conducted a survey amongst a sample of 400 students in Egypt chosen through a probability sample distributed within four universities: Cairo University, Ain Shams University, the Arab Academy for Science, Technology and Maritime Transport (AASTMT), and the American University in Cairo (AUC). The four universities represent different kinds of higher education institutions in Egypt. Thus, the AUC represents the first foreign higher education institution in Egypt, while the AASTMT represents one of the modern private institutions, and Cairo University and Ain Shams University are two of the oldest state universities in Egypt. Moreover, the students in these four universities come from different governorates of Egypt, so they can be claimed to constitute a representative sample of Egyptian youth. The majority of the sampled students were female (63%), while male students accounted for 37% of the sample. The number of students in the sample is distributed equally amongst the four institutions, or 100 students per university.

The study aimed to reveal the attitudes of those university students towards the new preachers' messages, and how students assess these messages. The study also aimed to identify the channels used to access the new preachers' messages, e.g. new media and the students' perception of these messages.

The study was divided into two stages: the first stage was devoted to a pilot study amongst 40 university students and the results were used to further refine and adjust the questionnaire and interview questions. During the second stage, a questionnaire of four parts was distributed amongst the sample of 400 students. The first part of the questionnaire asked the respondents about their perceptions and attitudes towards the new preachers, the second part of the questionnaire includes questions about the students' rationale for following the preachers' programmes, the third part asks about students' interaction with the preachers, and the last part of the questionnaire was about demographical information. The researchers also carried out two focus groups in order to gather in-depth responses about the students' perception of the new preachers.

In the following sections, we report a summary of the main findings of the questionnaire and focus groups, but first we elaborate on the role of the new preacher as *da'eyah*.

The Muslim preacher (*da'eyah*)

Elaborating on the moral character of *da'eyah*, the Saudi preacher Salman al-Oudah rhetorically asks, 'If embellishing oneself with moral excellence is obligatory for all Muslims, what about the *da'eyah* (preacher) who carries the banner of *dawah* calling people to join it?' (cited in Racius, 2004, 81). Al-Oudah proposes this answer: 'His *dawah* has to be a reflection of who he is. That is why possessing moral integrity is obligatory and essential, for carrying out properly that which Allah burdened him with' (ibid.) *Dawah* actions are no less important than knowledge and faith, and Muslims are urged to set an example and a model of the Islamic way of living, for non-Muslims to follow. Thus, *Dawah* should manifest itself in everyday life and all activities of Muslims from daily interactions to acts of worship. A good deed is thought to be as convincing as good words. All *dawah* advocates are in agreement that the best *dawah* encompasses both the word and the living example (conduct and action): 'Witnessing by word, *Shahadah bilqaul*, and reinforcing it by action, *Shahadah bilamal*, are two sides of the same coin – both are complementary and necessary to the other' (Ahsan, 1989, 14). *Dawah*, then, 'is presented primarily through conveying the message, preaching you may call it, and by practicing it and as such presenting practically the living example' (Khurshid, 1982, 44).

Moreover, it is argued that 'social service is one of the foremost duties of every Muslim in general and of every missionary Muslim in particular. He will preach and teach, and these untiring efforts will be his practical efforts to help and support those in need' (Racius, 2004, 86). The Arab Islamic world has various models of successful preachers, of whom the most prominent, especially in Egypt, are Mustafa Hosny, Ahmad Alshokairy, Moez Masoud, Amr Khaled, Khaled Elgendy, Tarek Suwaidan and Amr Mahran.

One of the most prominent preachers in the region is Amr Khaled, who explains the role of preachers to be integrated in civil society, or as he put it, referring to his *Life Makers* project:

They stopped all my activities. They feared that civil society would be active or achieve something – the basics of democracy. They got that. They knew I didn't talk about political issues. But what I was doing was the root of democracy and politics. They tried to ban anything like it. We tried, but they stopped us. So we went to other countries with our Egyptian youth, to do it in other countries, in Jordan, Algeria, Sudan, and Yemen. We succeeded with one thousand families. And we felt so sorry we had to [do] this outside of Egypt and not [in] our country. But now they have all come back to establish this project with a huge number of families and youth; to work in Egypt.

(Amr Khaled, cited in The Cairo Review, *2011, 70–71)*

The preachers then, to use the words of one of our informants, 'illustrate how Islam can be a way of life and how it can be used as a way to reach one's goals' (male, Arab Academy, 19 years old). Also, the new preachers depend on upbeat rhetoric to attract audiences and they sometimes host celebrities such as models, artists and media professionals to talk about their own experiences as born-again Muslims and how their lives changed for the better when they adopted Islamic values and acted according to the Sharia. Also, the new preachers refrain from issuing *fatwa* or a pronouncement for their followers, and they admit that as preachers they are not qualified to issue *fatwa*, which, according to them, must be limited to Al Azhar.

In the next section, we discuss the way these preachers adapt to an ever-changing political and cultural situation in Egypt and how they utilize new tactics to face such challenges. We then elaborate on the way young audiences receive this preaching and its influence on their daily lives.

New ways of *dawah* as part of Egyptian popular culture

Some Muslim youth are caught between two extremes as they are sometimes forced to live in virtually two different worlds, or between culturally Muslim homes and an outside world that may seem Islamophobic at times. The main concern therefore for such youth is the issue of identity and particularly their religious identity. The issue of identity is vitally important for self-esteem and for mental, emotional and personal development. At the same time, mosques have lost their monopoly in disseminating religious messages, particularly with the explosion of Islamic satellite channels as well as online Islamic forums. One consequence of this media liberalization is a renewed sense of moral panic among certain Islamic organizations, which view media liberalization as an immoral process that could spread chaos and threatens traditional Islamic values (Widodo, 2008). Since the mid-1990s, there has been a dramatic rise in the number of Islamic satellite channels and an equal increase in the number of young Muslim preachers who feature on such channels promoting what they term a moderate vision of Islam in a new modern preaching style. Their preaching programmes (or *waaz*) depart from the old-style preacher who cites the holy Quran and preaches in perfect classical Arabic.

On the other hand, ritualized practices such as Friday preaching or *khutba* have developed into new rhetorical and performative preaching delivered by a new generation of preachers or the so-called 'new preachers' such as the Egyptian Amr Khaled. Thus, face-to-face sermons and *fatwas* have become increasingly mediated, and Islamic discourse has become more embedded in traditional as well as new media forms. Scholars such as Salvatore and Eickelman (2006), and Eickelman (1999) argue that we are witnessing a new Islamic public sphere characterized by open debate through the use of new media. For instance, Salvatore and Eickelman (2006) regard the Islamic public sphere as the space for Muslim scholars and intellectuals to engage in open debate and discussion about issues of common interest. Likewise, Gary Bunt (2002, 17) argues that the term for this public sphere can be coined as a digital *umma*, referring in particular to the online Islamic forums. Clearly, this does not necessarily mean the egalitarian status of participating interlocutors given the vast diversity of Muslim populations spread across several continents around the world (see also El-Nawawy & Khamis, 2010, 233).

Budiman (2002, cited in Hariyadi, 2010) points out two key factors that have influenced the spread of Muslim popular culture, and these are the globalization of world economies as well as the globalization of media and communication technologies. Traditionally, preachers used to give lessons in mosques, while nowadays such lessons are offered online or even via email and chat rooms, blogs, satellite channels and DVDs. The creators of *virtual dawah* make use of all available communication tools, and Internet users can now easily download an audio recitation of the whole Quran, listen to their preferred preachers, and follow their favourite Islamic talk shows.

In pointing out the tremendous effects of new media on the new Islamic culture, Charles Hirschkind refers to the typically short video clips circulated on the Internet, that a 'phenomenological feature of the media's architecture' is that it does not support 'the thread of an unfolding discourse, but the sudden surprise of an effect [...] shifts too quick for the unfolding of an argument, but enough to allow for the triggering of a fleeting sensation [...] a burst of excitement, terror, fear, silliness, sadness, sentimentality, and so on' (cited in Shehata et al., 2012, 134). In the particular case of Hirschkind's study, the videos in circulation were one- to ten-minute excerpts of hour-long Islamic sermons, and generally consist of the more poignant and emotionally intense segments of the performance (Shehata et al., 2012, 134). The Internet adds a new communication dimension, and cyber time and space frames often do not support the unfolding of a long argument. It is useful, therefore, to look at the development of online practices, and to see the developments in Islamic discourses and practices as part of a larger phenomenon of the commodification of Islam. At the same time, attention must be paid to a concurrent phenomenon of sanctification, which occurs when new religious experiences emerge from audiences' responses to Islamic messages online or on-air (Shehata et al., 2012, 135).

In this chapter, we argue that the new preachers' religious speech is related to the construction of the national identity, especially among the youth who are actively seeking role models and new sources of authority. This is illustrated in one comment by an informant from Ain Shams University: 'With the preachers' advice I became more religious, more open-minded and a practising Muslim' (male, 23 years old).

Two of these new preachers who have secured a vast audience base inside Egypt and across the whole Arab region are Amr Khaled and Moez Masoud. Amr Khaled, 47 years old, was dubbed by *Time* magazine one of the 100 most influential people in the world. Khaled emerged as a middle-class preacher who appealed mainly to middle- and upper-middle-class Muslims. Likewise, Moez Masoud, 35 years old, who came from an affluent family and was educated in Western colleges, has appealed to the same social groups, who have been attracted to Masoud's messages of compassion and tolerance towards all other groups in society, including homosexuals and non-Muslims (Sullivan, 2007).

One of our interviewees explains the enthusiasm to follow such new preachers as follows:

> They meet our interests. Their discourse is very appropriate to us, in terms of their age. They present the entertainment in addition to the religious information and they help us to make something different in our relationship with Allah. It has become a habit especially in Ramadan to follow their programmes. They are so enthusiastic about our problems and conduct. In general, their religious discourse is so attractive.
>
> *(male, 21, Ain Shams University)*

On the other hand, preachers such as Amr Khaled, who was interviewed in the wake of the 2011 revolution, stress their role in empowering civil society in Egypt.

> [I]nitiatives like Life Makers, work for the development of this country and for empowering the youth. I believe the straight line to solve a lot of the problems in our country is by empowering the youth in civil society, who should do something to build Egypt. That's my role now. And I will build it. A lot of youth organizations, Muslim and Christian, are working with me. Ten million people are illiterate in Egypt. That can't be the case.
>
> *(The Cairo Review, 2011)*

Thanks to the new technologies of mass communications and social media, such preachers have been provided with unprecedented opportunity to appeal to a large number of audiences, thereby creating a sense of solidarity among Sunni Muslim Arabs from diverse backgrounds. The new preachers' *waaz* shares something in common not with the traditional preachers but rather with authors of self-help books. Yasmin Moll has pointed out that the 'virtuous viewing' of religious TV programmes, specifically those of the more charismatic new preachers, constituted a form of televised devotional experience, which she calls 'pious entertainment' (Moll, 2010a). There is no doubt that such new preachers are very capable of reaching out to vast audiences (Hassan, 2009), and their communication skills enable them to deliver religious edu-tainment, or religious education in an entertaining style (Millie, 2009). The rise of Islamic television ratings has already attracted many advertisers, thereby making Islamic televangelism a new commodity. Islamic tele-preachers have become celebrities, and some of the famous tele-preachers have set up their own trade brand and businesses (Hariyadi, 2010). One of the reasons behind these preachers' appeal is that they do not ask young audiences to denounce their worldly interests such as music, film or sport, as long as these interests do not conflict with Islamic values.

The preachers' seeming tolerance coupled with their modern attire, and the fact that their programmes are recorded in modern television studios or on yachts in the Red Sea, help viewers reconcile Islamic preaching with a comfortable lifestyle rather than seeing a contradiction between seeking wealth and piety at the same time. For instance, one preacher, Khaled el Gendy, who turned from a petty merchant into a savvy businessman with an impressive monthly income of US$50,000, sees no contradiction in seeking worldly pleasures:

> I have three cars. A Mercedes is not yet one of them, but I will have one by the end of the year, God willing. The saying of the Prophet Muhammad goes: 'God's blessing has its enemies.' It was said, 'Who are they, messenger of God?' He said: 'Those who are envious of people for what God has given them of His blessings.' There is another thing that we should be frank in discussing: Is wealth legitimate or illegitimate? Is wealth or the love of money legitimate or illegitimate? Have you forgotten that there was a prophet like Solomon, who said 'My Lord, forgive me, and grant me a kingdom never attained by anyone else. You are the Grantor'? The important thing is not wealth in and of itself, but rather how this money or this wealth was obtained. If it was through legitimate means, then there's nothing wrong with that. If it was through swindling and deceiving, then it is undoubtedly unacceptable, according to divine laws, reason and morality.
>
> *(cited in Zaied, 2008, 24)*

Such preachers then have become celebrities in their own right, hailed by their believing 'fans' in much the same way as secular celebrities are. They have social networking accounts and fan pages, and their fans organize events on Facebook. Their importance is illustrated in a comment by one of our female interviewees from Cairo University: 'Society now drift[s] toward what individuals want instead of what Allah wants or asked them to do, and those preachers' simple way of communication urges us youth to follow Islamic rules and to do what Allah wants us to do' (female, 19 years old).

Mustafa Hosny: the new face of Islamic preachers

A quick glance recently at the top ten religious websites reveals the overwhelming popularity of the Egyptian preacher Mustafa Hosny who presented many famous programmes and has large audiences and followers especially amongst youth. Our study revealed that the majority of our informants followed Hosny as their preferred preacher with around 36% of the respondents preferring to watch him, while 24% preferred to watch Ahmed Elshokary, 23% follow Moez Masoud and only 17% follow Amr Khaled.

Mustafa Hosny presented various noted programmes such as 'Alkanz Almafqoud/The lost treasure', 'Nedaa Alrahman/The call of the most gracious', 'Amma Ba'd/And then (next)', 'Ahla Hayat/The most beautiful life', 'Lao Kanoo Ya3lamoon/If they knew', 'Ala Bab Aljannah/On the doors of Heaven', 'Khadaouka FaKaloo/Deceiving myths', 'Madrasato Alhoob/School of love', 'Ohiboka Rabi/I love you God', 'Ommar Al Ard/Land builders', 'AlaTarik Allah/On the way to God', 'Sihr Addounia/Charm of life', 'Ahl Eljannah/The people of paradise' and '3eesh Ellahza/Live the moment'.

The core message of Hosny's shows is to urge youth to discover the real meanings of Islam, their own individual capabilities and how to utilize these to be a productive Muslim. In general, Hosny always depends on specific rhetorical tactics such as using upbeat messages. Moreover, he uses the vernacular in his talk, and not the heavy classical Arabic used by traditional preachers, and this secures him a wider reach, particularly among young audiences. He also often draws on real stories and cases of people who have changed their lifestyle to be more in line with Islamic principles, and Hosny emphasizes the success and happiness enjoyed by those individuals as born-again Muslims.

Hosny uses multiple models of successful projects and activities that can be considered an extended call for Islam in a practical way and at the same time are the perfect proof of the success of his programmes and his speech.

Hosny's focus is on identity and individual piety, which can be argued to be deeply rooted in neo-liberal popular culture. For instance, Hosny's programmes are always accompanied by pleasant songs with good lyrics and popular singers, which contributes to embellishing the programme and imparting the desired meanings of these programmes. Such songs are part of Hosny's communication and rhetorical strategy to attract young audiences. His shows can be watched across multiple platforms ranging from television to his website and YouTube, as well as on social media accounts. It is notable that Hosny leads diverse religious and social initiatives, being the board director of Ommar Al Ard or the Institution of Land Builders, which he founded in 2012 as a charity, and one of this institution's projects is 'River of good' or Nahr Alkheir, aiming to supply the poorest villages in Upper Egypt with water. Hosny is also a founding board member of the Life without Smoking charity, and a member of an Egyptian charity for blood donation dedicated for children.

Hosny's website includes several links to his shows accessible on different platforms, links to true stories of people who converted to Islam and a poll to follow the users' views about various issues such as how they spend their leisure time and whether they do their daily prayers. Hosny also has a link called 'I love you God', in which he focuses on the love between humans (God's slaves) and God, and how God loves humans and how they can show their love in all their deeds. Finally,

Hosny often posts a poll on his website entitled 'How To', where he asks users' input on how to perform certain acts, such as how to study well, how to manage time, how to succeed in a job interview, or how to think positively.

Popularity of televised *dawah*

Our study amongst Egyptian university students shows that the majority of them follow televised preaching programmes and only a minority rarely watch these shows. Some of the respondents said that they would also follow traditional preachers' programmes such as Sheikh Metwalli al-Shaarawi (d. 1998), who enjoyed widespread popularity among audiences across the Arab world for his talent for explaining the Quran in a very informal style using the Egyptian vernacular in his preaching, instead of the written variety of Arabic used by traditional clerics. Al-Shaarawi was named Preacher of the Century for his television series explaining the meaning of the Quran.

The majority of students in our sample (82.3%) strongly agree on society's need for preaching (*dawah*), and provided a range of reasons behind this need. Below is a selection of these reasons:

1. 'We need these preachers, because the role of mosque[s] in our society has been confined to weekly sermons and Quran recitation' (male, Cairo University, 21 years old).
2. 'Our parents are always in a hurry, so we need a reliable source for our religious knowledge' (female, Cairo University, 20 years old).
3. 'Nowadays we have many temptations in our life especially that we live in a global society, so we truly need someone who can help us maintain a good contact with Allah' (female, AUC, 22 years old).
4. 'Many Islamic [political] parties distort Islam, and many young people need help and support to find the true essence of Islam, and this is exactly what we found in the new preachers' religious discourse' (female, AASTMT, 19 years old).
5. 'This kind of preaching can challenge extremist discourses' (male, AUC, 21 years old).
6. 'The new preachers talk about very significant concepts, such as justice, peace, charity, kindness, generosity, and mercy, and these are significant values acutely needed in our society' (female, AASTMT, 20 years old).
7. 'New preachers discuss real problems and touch on urgent issues in our society, presenting some practical solutions, so we are in a real need of such programmes' (male, Ain Shams University, 21 years old).
8. 'Teens and middle-aged people are drifting away from religious practice and values, which can harm our society, so the new preachers help these groups reconsider their actions and behaviour' (female, AASTMT, 23 years old).
9. 'These preachers encourage young people to participate in different charities to improve our society, so it is not just talk but action too' (female, AUC, 24 years old).

We asked our respondents about the channels of communications that they use to access the preachers' talks. Only 32.3% of the sampled students said that they attend the new preachers' talks in clubs, universities, mosques and public gatherings, stressing their preference of this face-to-face communication to establish rapport with the preachers, which helps them adopt the preachers' advice and change their lifestyle. On the other hand, nearly 72% of the sampled students follow the preachers on television as their preferred medium because of its convenience. The majority, however, or around 73% of the sampled students, follow the new preachers via social media sites such as Facebook, Twitter and the official websites of the preachers. They stress the role of new media as an inevitable medium for knowledge and information, which they often access in addition to traditional media such as television, radio and newspapers. Another advantage of using new media is that they enable them to share messages amongst themselves and add comments or join online discussions. Thus, they feel active participants of the online communication process.

As Table 13.1 shows, the most important rationale for following the new preachers is to realize their teachings as a step towards serving Islam, including responding to the preachers' call for action to serve society.

The most important contribution of these new preachers is that they have reinvigorated the public sphere in Egypt calling on the new generation to engage in community activities such as projects to eradicate illiteracy, to collect used clothes, or to collect donations for the poor. In fact, many middle-class young people have participated in charity organizations such as *Resala*, which means 'message' in Arabic. *Resala* was launched in 1999 by a group of student activists from the College of Engineering at Cairo University, doing community service ranging from painting the walls of buildings to preparing Ramadan food bags for the service workers on campus (Atia, 2008, 241–244).

Around 48% of our sample confirmed that they participated in various projects as a result of following their favourite preacher's programmes and some of these projects were founded by the same preacher, such as Life Makers (launched by Amr Khaled) or Ommar Al Ard (launched by Mostafa Hosny). Some students have also joined other projects founded by young people independently of those

TABLE 13.1 Reasons for following the new preachers

Reason	Frequency
To take actual steps to serve Islam	23%
To realize the real essence of Islam	21%
To learn about the prophet's life	17%
To enforce our Islamic identity	12%
To learn about values and principles of Islam	10%
To form our outlook on life	9%
To organize our priorities in life according to the teachings of Islam	8%

preachers. On the other hand, more than half of the respondents (around 52%) have not been involved in any charity or community work.

In total, around 72% of the respondents were touched one way or another by the new preachers' messages, which helped them find new meanings in their lives by participating in charities and community activities, and rediscovering their Islamic identity. Some of the female respondents said that they wore the veil after listening to the new preachers' programmes about the veil. On the other hand, only 28% of the respondents said that they were not affected by the preachers' messages because they viewed their lifestyle as being moderate and responsible, and their engagement in the community to be adequate.

Conclusion

While previous Arabic studies focused on the religious discourse in Arab societies including the role of *fatwa* on Muslims' lives (Esani, 2008; Zaid, 2005; Alfarouk, 2009; Saleh, 2007), the above study focused on the perception of university students of the new preachers such as Amr Khaled, Mostafa Hosny and Moez Masoud, who heavily rely on the new media including satellite television and social media to reach out to their audiences, mostly of young people. These new preachers disseminate messages that promote hard work, self-awareness and ambition in life. They also stress the role of faith in maintaining ethical values.

A quick glance on the social media accounts of such preachers shows the vast number of followers of these accounts whose comments are usually positive. We conclude with this comment by one of our respondents who emphasizes the country's need for these preachers: 'The society needs such preachers because some people view Islam as being rigid prohibiting them from leading enjoyable lives. The new preachers present a new way to embrace Islamic teaching while working on reaching our goals in life.'

References

Ahsan, M. Manazir (1989) 'Dawa and its significance for the future', in Merryl Wyn Davies & Adnan Khalil Pasha (Eds) *Beyond Frontiers: Islam and Contemporary Needs* (pp. 13–21). London: Mansell.

Alfarouk, Nihal (2009) *Islamic Religious Discourse as Presented by the Islamic Programs in English at the Arab Satellite Channels* (Arabic). MA, Faculty of Mass Communication, Cairo University.

Allam, Rabha (2012) *Engaging with Traditional and Modern Islamic NGOs in Egypt*. Al-Ahram Center for Political and Strategic Studies ACPSS. media.leidenuniv.nl/legacy/policy-brief—islamic-ngos-in-egypt.pdf.

Atia, Mona (2008) *Building a House in Heaven: Islamic Charity in Neoliberal Egypt*. Unpublished PhD dissertation, University of Washington.

Bunt, Gary R. (2002) *Virtually Islamic: Computer-mediated Communication and Cyber Islamic Environment*. Cardiff: University of Wales.

The Cairo Review (2011) 'Inside Egypt's uprising: *The Cairo Review* interviews, Vol. 1', www.aucegypt.edu/GAPP/CairoReview/Pages/articleDetails.aspx?aid=50.

Dorpmueller, Sabine (2012) 'New Egypt – new media scape? Policy brief on the shifts in the Egyptian media scape after the revolution with a focus on Islamic actors and the new media', media.leidenuniv.nl/legacy/policy-brief—new-egypt-new-mediascape.pdf.

Eickelman, Dale (1999) 'The coming transformation of the Muslim world', *Middle East Review of International Affairs*, 3(3), www.biu.ac.il/SOC/besa/meria/journal/1999/issue3/jb3n3a8.html.

El-Nawawy, Mohammed & Khamis, Sahar (2010) 'Collective identity in the virtual Islamic public sphere: contemporary discourses in two Islamic websites', *International Communication Gazette*, 72(3), pp. 229–250.

Esani, Rahima (2008) 'Algerian's youth attitudes toward the Islamic satellite channels and its role in their awareness against extremism & terrorism' (Arabic), www.philadelphia.edu.jo/arts/13th/papers/rahemah_3ysani.do.

Hariyadi (2010) 'Islamic popular culture and the new identity of Indonesian Muslim youths', http://www.academia.edu/5321255/Islamic_Popular_Culture_and_the_New_Identity_of_Indonesian_Muslim_Youths.

Hassan, Ammar Ali (2009) *Al-Tanshe'aAlseyyassialel-TuruqElsufiyya fi Masr* (Arabic: The political socialization of the Sufi orders in Egypt). Cairo.

Khurshid, Ahmad (1982) *Christian Mission and Islamic Da'wa. Proceedings of the Chambesy Dialogue Consultation*. Leicester: The Islamic Foundation.

Millie, Julian (2009) 'Preachers, politics and piety: Dakwah oratory in a changing Indonesia', *Asian Currents: The Asian Studies Association of Australia's e-bulletin*, August, asaa.asn.au/publications/ac/asian-currents-09-08.html (accessed 1 October 2014).

Moll, Yasmin (2010a) 'Islamic televangelism: religion, media and visuality in contemporary Egypt', *Arab Media & Society*, 10.

Moll, Yasmin (2010b) 'Islamic satellite channels and the ethics of entertainment in Egypt', *Arab Reform Bulletin*, Carnegie Endowment for international peace.

Racius, Egdunas (2004) *The Multiple Nature of the Islamic da'wa*. Dissertation. ethesis.helsinki.fi/julkaisut/hum/aasia/vk/racius/themulti.pdf.

Saleh, Sohair (2007) 'Role of Islamic television channels in supplying its audience with the religious knowledge', paper presented to the 13th Conference of Faculty of Mass Communication, Cairo University, on mass media and the social and cultural benefit of the Arab citizen (Arabic).

Salvatore, Armando & Eickelman, Dale (2006) 'Preface', in A. Salvatore and D. Eickelman (Eds) *Public Islam and the Common Good* (pp. xi–xxv). Boston, MA: Brill Publishers.

Shehata, Dina et al. (2012) *Mapping Islamic Actors in Egypt*. Netherlands: Flemish Institute in Cairo, Al-Ahram Center for Political and Strategic Studies. A report commissioned by the Project Office Islam Research Program, webcache.googleusercontent.com/search?q=cache:imKoFCz6AmQJ:https://www.idmarch.org/document/Al-g.

Siddiqi, Muzammil (1998) 'Da'wah in a global exchange medium', in *Abstract of Papers. Muslims and Information Superhighway International Conference (MISIC'98)*, 10 April. www.kol.org/abstracts.html.

Sullivan, Keith (2007) 'Younger Muslims tune in to upbeat religious message', *The Washington Post*, 2 December.

Widodo, Amrih (2008) 'Writing for God: piety and consumption in popular Islam. Inside Indonesia 93', August–October, www.insideindonesia.org/weekly-articles/writing-for-god.

Wise, Lindsay (2003) *Words from the Heart: New Forms of Islamic Preaching in Egypt*. Unpublished MA thesis, St Antony's College, University of Oxford.

Zaid, Ahmed (2005) 'Islamic discourse's map in Egypt', paper presented to the research project Renewing the Islamic discourse in Egypt, Center for Research & Political Studies, Faculty of Political & Economic Studies.

Zaied, Al-Sayed (2008) 'Da'wa for dollars: a new wave of Muslim televangelists', *Emerging Social and Religious Trends – Arab Insight*, 2(1), pp. 21–27.

14

FATWA ONLINE

Novel patterns of production and consumption

Roxanne D. Marcotte

Online religious authority remains a broad and still rather undefined concept. Yet, it remains an important characteristic of quite a few religious practices online (Campbell, 2012). Needless to say, it has to contend with both the challenges the Internet poses, as an empowerment tool, to traditional authoritative religious figures or hierarchies, and the possibilities it paradoxically offers for the reinforcement or consolidation of control mechanisms and structures of religious authority (ibid.). For some, the Internet fosters greater individualization, even leads to greater neglect of religious obligations, or worse, to a loss of religious belief (Crul & Heering, 2008; Jacobi & Yavuz, 2008), through what some view as a process of de-legitimation of religious authority (Peter, 2006). For others, however, new media open up possibilities for the increased visibility of 'new reformation' discourses proposed by a number of contemporary Muslim intellectuals (Mazrui & Mazrui, 2001). For others, new communication technologies, local, national and transnational networks (Helland, 2007, 2008), globalization and transnationalism (Mandaville, 2001, 2007) accentuate ongoing processes of pluralization of religious authority, and the enduring politics of religious knowledge. Only a few studies have looked into the shifts or displacement of religious authority that occur in these novel digital environments (Campbell, 2007, 2010b; Cheong, 2011; Cheong et al., 2011; Golan, 2011).

In the Islamic tradition, religious authority is embodied in the Muslim scholar's mastery of Islamic knowledge, religious scholars and the circles of their peers being called upon to provide 'legal opinions', or *fatwas*, congruent with the sacred texts and the principles of well-established Islamic legal traditions (Masud et al., 1996). Mosques, religious circles, seminaries and Islamic courts remained for centuries the traditional sites of production of Islamic knowledge. With globalization, the advent of digital technology and the ever-increasing democratization of religious knowledge, Muslims now have direct and unmediated access online to sacred texts, as well as to the works of medieval and contemporary Muslim scholars (in original languages or translations). They listen online to recordings of an increasing number of celebrity preachers' TV programmes, or the sermons of their local sheikh (religious scholar) and those of Muslim scholars from all over the world. They participate in live online sessions with cyber-muftis, religious scholars who issue *fatwas*, or with Muslim counsellors (Kutcher, 2009; Šisler, 2011).

Each of those digital platforms contributes and embodies discrete aspects of intellectual, moral, spiritual, inspirational or legal religious authority on these novel virtual 'Muslim public spheres' (Mishra & Semaan, 2010; Marcotte, 2010a), and enables the emergence and cohabitation of a very wide range of 'authoritative' Islamic voices: Muslim scholars like al-Qaradawi (Gräf, 2007, 2008, 2010; Gräf & Skovgaar-Petersen, 2009), popular preachers like Amr Khaled (amrkhaled.net) (Echchaibi, 2011; Gauthier & Uhl, 2012), mosque imams and their sermons (Fink, 2010), Muslim intellectuals like Tariq Ramadan (tariqramadan.com), Salafi scholars like Shaikh Mohammed Alothaimeen (d. 2001) (www.ibnothaimeen.com), Islamists like the Muslim Brotherhood (ikhwanweb.com), and so on. The Internet continuously offers increasingly diversified 'imagined, mediated, and performed' forms of Islam (Sunier, 2011, 152–153; Helland, 2007, 2008; Reimer, 2008).

Some, like Bunt (2000, 2003, 2009a), have written much on cyber Islamic environments (a term he coined). Others, like Larsson (2011, 145–166), have studied a number of well-known religious scholars' legal opinions regarding the advent of the Internet and its usage. Nowadays, though, not only are individuals putting up opinions and *fatwas* on their websites, but so are local, national and transnational Muslim organizations – some putting up online *fatwa* collections, databases or *fatwa* banks, which Muslims from all over the world can browse. Many websites enable petitioners to email their questions and queries to religious scholars and to receive, online or offline, a scholarly reply (Bunt, 2009b: 293–294). The Internet enables European cyber-muftis to deal with elements of Islamic law and European legal systems that may conflict, and to propose, quite often, 'harmonizing' interpretations (Šisler, 2009). The Internet not only enables greater visibility for new religious interpreters (Mariani, 2011), but also functions as a 'cyber-mufti' for younger Muslims who live in the diaspora by bringing 'Islamic values and customs' to Europe (Rinnawi, 2012), as well as facilitating identity consumption in Muslim America (Zaman, 2008).

Located at the junction of legal theory and social practice (Caeiro, 2004, 2006, 2011a, 2011b), the *fatwa* may be said to epitomize the embodiment of Islamic religious authority. It occupies a place of choice among all those elements that, taken together, partake of online Islamic religious authority. Some have noted how Islamic knowledge, in the form of Islamic law and *fatwas*, has become both an idealized concept and a point of contestation, often related to authority in Western Muslim minority contexts (Peter, 2006; Saint-Blancart, 2004; Caeiro, 2003, 2004, 2006, 2010, 2011a, 2011b); others have noted that the Internet provides undeniably new safe anonymous spaces for Muslims to exchange views (Piela, 2011b; Marcotte, 2010a, 2015), to learn about Islam or to find guidance (Brouwer, 2004, 2006; Piela, 2010, 2011a), often in the form of *fatwas* or religious advice.

Online production and consumption of *fatwas*

With every day that goes by, the virtual '*fatwa* universe' (Caeiro, 2011a, 2011b) expands with the migration of *fatwas* online. This may well represent the litmus test for specific 'territorialized' religious interpretations grounded in particular historical, geographical, intellectual and cultural contexts, in an age when many Muslims no longer follow uncritically religious authorities, or those who pose as such. In some instances, traditional sources of knowledge and authority become secondary, as more and more Muslims strive to read, for themselves, the religious texts, interpret them, and evaluate the status of the Islamic legal and scriptural texts (Karim, 2009). This is particularly true of many Muslims (converts and non-converts) who live in the West and for whom online forums have become novel agorae, where anyone can question or reassert authoritative claims. Some of today's young Muslims no longer follow blindly any *fatwa* they find online or, for that matter, those posted by someone else. This is particularly true with *fatwas* that are unsubstantiated by evidence or make preposterous claims based on medieval reasoning and legitimizing processes. The dissonance (Ali, 2006, 151) that then occurs between a medieval episteme and a modern one, grounded in contemporary scientific knowledge (Moosa, 2002), may lead to a re-evaluation of religious knowledge and religious authority (Marcotte, 2010b).

The Internet and social media have thus become empowering tools for the development of individual autonomous abilities to seek out religious knowledge, to interpret tradition and to apply it to one's own life. This is what Mishra and Semaan (2010) have labelled an interpretative 'religious agency' – one that was once only beheld by traditional religious scholars, but which is now gradually being put forwards by ordinary lay Muslims who have increased access to various sources of knowledge, the diversity of legal and religious opinions and views, and the anonymity and confidentiality that online forums afford.

Since the particular contexts of *fatwa* production, circulation and consumption remain part and parcel of the process of generating, recirculating and using 'authoritative' interpretations, this chapter seeks to answer the following questions: What happens when the *fatwa* migrates into these novel cyber Islamic environments, where it is now at the mercy of the novel communicational logic of digital environments and the practices that emerge from them? More generally, could the Internet foster some changes, even subtle, in the dynamics of production, distribution and consumption of *fatwas*? What follows seeks to provide some insight into the ways the Internet may, first, enable the cohabitation of various global voices in *fatwas* found on one Middle Eastern Muslim website that discuss Jews and, second, enable the cohabitation of global Middle Eastern voices with local voices in Australian Muslim minority context online forums. A general socio-anthropological perspective (Granjon & Denouël, 2011; Campbell, 2010a) may shed some light, together with the content analysis of selected *fatwas* and forum threads by examining the ways contexts and perspectives presented may be framed, concepts or issues be foregrounded (or backgrounded), assumptions, attitudes or points of view be expressed online, issues be 'topicalized', the presence of agent/patient relations, location of authority (or power), presence of connotations, and so on — all issues that are at the heart of critical discourse analysis (Paltridge, 2006, 185). These will assist in the description and interpretation of 'discourse in context', i.e. social and political issues, relations and ideologies, and power relations that are negotiated, constructed, performed and reflected through discourse (Paltridge, 2006, 179–84).

Islam Online and the production of *fatwas*

Let us turn to *fatwas* that discuss issues related to Jews, what may be labelled the 'Jewish' *fatwas*. Though their production may be grounded in a long exegetical (*tafsir*) and jurisprudential (*fiqh*) tradition, their construction of 'situated' gazes at the Jewish 'Other' remains inseparable from the contemporary contexts of their production (Nathan, 2010a, 2010b). Contemporary political conflicts, like the current ones in the Middle East, remain fertile ground for the mediation of the Jewish 'Other' (Parfitt & Egorova, 2004, 109–248), which, nowadays, has migrated online (Krutikov & Krutikov, 2004). The inherent digital forces at work in the dissemination of information online foster a renewal of the social constructions of religious interpretations (cf. Johansen, 1999; Masud, 2002; Caeiro, 2004), shaped by established or unsettled power relations and reflecting socially negotiated and constructed interpretations of this Jewish 'Other' (Hall, 1973). Online 'Jewish' *fatwas* thus partake in resolutely contemporary, transnational and quite often ideological discourses, their content frequently dependent on the 'situatedness' (time and space) of their production, producers and consumers. One cannot fail to notice the 'social situatedness' of the jurisprudential interpretations of religious authorities whose interpretative horizons are inextricably grounded in, and interconnected with, recent social, economic, political or cultural developments of the Middle East and of the global Muslim *Ummah*.

The ways in which the Internet enables the cohabitation of various modulations of global voices in the production of 'Jewish' *fatwas* may be illustrated with two examples found on IslamOnline.net, a very popular Middle Eastern Muslim website (English and Arabic), which was created in 1999. While the site was closed down in 2010, it resumed its activities the same year with the creation of OnIslam. net (OnIslam Staff, 2010). In addition, Islam Online migrated most of its content, including its *fatwa* bank, to its new website. Like a number of specialized Islamic sites, it has an English section called 'Ask the Scholar',[1] where one could find over 100 'Jewish' *fatwas* (as of March 2010), published between 2000 and the beginning of 2010 (with nine reissued at least once) (Nathan, 2010b). One cannot fail to notice that a number of the 'Jewish' *fatwas* were penned by Muslim scholars living in the West. This suggests the existence of diversified global and transnational responses to the question of the Jewish 'Other'.

The following two examples, while not providing in any way a comprehensive picture of the content of all the 'Jewish' *fatwas* available on Islam Online (as of

March 2010) (see Nathan, 2010b), nonetheless provide statements that prove enlightening in terms of the subtle shifts enabled by the migration of *fatwas* online. In their 'Ask the Scholar' *fatwa* response to a first query on 'Dealing with Jewish Neighbors' (Islam Online, 2002), the editorial team appealed to Dr Muzammil Siddiqi to pen its reply to a Muslim (from India) who wanted to know how to live with Jews settled in his neighbourhood and how to deal with their 'Zionist pro-Israeli posters'. Siddiqi notes that Muslims must be respectful and courteous towards their Jewish friends, in spite of their political and ideological stances. He advises Muslims to find occasion to talk to their Jewish neighbours and to explain to them the disastrous consequences of their Zionist ideology on the lives of millions of Palestinians.

In their 'Ask the Scholar' *fatwa* response to a second query by Martin (identified as such on OnIslam) on 'Working for a Jewish Company' (Islam Online, 2004), the editorial team called upon Zeinab Mostafa, a woman, and Sheikh Faysal Mawlawi (d. 2011) to craft their reply. At the outset of the *fatwa*, the editorial team identified these consultants as a 'Group of Mufti' and combined their 'authoritative' statements to craft its answer to a petitioner who wanted to know whether it was 'wrong' to work for a Jew and to receive earnings from him, the petitioner also noting how understanding his Jewish boss was and how he made allowances for him to take a few minutes off work to pray and to leave earlier during Ramadan (to prepare for the break of the fast).

The editorial team appeals, first, to the authority of Zeinab Mostafa, who explains that it is possible to work for a Jew, 'because Islam allows a peaceful Jew to coexist with Muslims as long as he does not attack Islam […], especially if he is understanding and accommodating', concluding that earnings from 'that company is definitely *halal* [lawful]'. What is interesting in the excerpts included by the editorial team is the other statement of Zeinab Mostafa advising to '[…] make sure that this company or employer does not support the illegal Zionist state in Palestine. We believe that our struggle is against Zionism as a political theory and not with Judaism as a religion. We respect everyone's religion and we believe that all human beings can live peacefully on this planet if they have mutual understanding and respect'. The editorial team then adds the 'authoritative' statements of Faysal Mawlawi that '[a] Muslim is not permitted to work for any Jewish company within the Palestinian territories. Surely, those companies assist the occupation forces' and that working for a Jewish company that is located outside Palestine would be permissible '*as long as* [emphasis in original text] that Jewish company does not provide any form of support to the Zionists in Palestine'.

Nowhere does the editorial team provide any reference to the statements attributed to Siddiqi, Mostafa and Mawlawi it quotes in the two *fatwas*. The reader is neither told whether what is quoted comes from personal exchanges (email or other) with those 'authorities', nor provided with any references to titles of works from which the quotes might have been taken. Nevertheless, the editorial team mentions the scholarly credentials of its 'authorities': Muzammil Siddiqi is identified as a 'former president of the Islamic Society of North America (ISNA)',[2]

Zeinab Mostafa is described as a 'London-based scholar and *da'eyah*',[3] or preacher, and Faysal Mawlawi is mentioned as having been the 'deputy chairman of the European Council for Fatwa and Research'.[4]

For all of its *fatwas* posted on the 'Ask the Scholar' section of its website, the editorial team of Islam Online almost always appeals to sources deemed 'authoritative', some better known than others. For its 'Jewish' *fatwas*, the editorial team quoted statements from 44 different muftis, religious scholars or preachers, either as sole named authority, or as members of a 'Group of Muftis', among whom six individuals figure predominantly: Yusuf al-Qaradawi (22 mentions),[5] Mawlawi (18 mentions), Siddiqi (nine mentions), Sheikh Muhammad Saleh al-Munajjid (five mentions),[6] Sheikh Ahmad Kutty (five mentions)[7] and Sheikh 'Atiyyah Saqr (five mentions) (Nathan, 2010b, 37–40).[8] Although most of the 44 scholarly 'authorities' were trained in the Middle East, including Siddiqi, Mostafa and Mawlawi, at least eight of them are or were associated with organizations, universities or religious institutions located outside the Arab world – namely Ireland, Canada, the United States, United Kingdom and Malaysia. One should not forget that a substantial amount of material selected to craft Islam Online's replies includes translations of legal opinions originally written in Arabic. This is significant if one takes into consideration the fact that 22 of the 44 religious authorities called upon to pen the 'Jewish' *fatwas* came from the Arab world, namely Egypt, Bahrain, Gaza, Jordan, Kuwait and Saudi Arabia. These scholars' interpretative horizons would undoubtedly be quite different from those of Siddiqi, Mostafa and Mawlawi.

We need to keep in mind that the editorial team is mostly staffed with Egyptians whose commitment to the Islamic cause is of paramount importance (Gräf, 2007, 2008, 2010; Gräf & Skovgaar-Petersen, 2009; Abdel-Fadil, 2011, 2013). Working from Cairo, they live in close proximity to the more than 60-year-old conflict zone whose regional socio-political repercussions remain the backdrop of Islam Online's production of 'Jewish' *fatwas*. The second *fatwa* illustrates perhaps best their editorial choices, with the additional passages that 'foreground' the regional Israeli–Palestinian conflict. The editorial team reproduces, crafts, even at times recasts, and then disseminates to the English-speaking world their particular representations of the Jewish 'Other'.

We also need to keep in mind that the editorial choices, at times, shape and nuance (whether consciously or not) the scope of the religious opinions (*fatwas*) with their appeal to quite a variety of religious scholars and individuals, some living in the West, and statements that do more than merely foreground the regional conflict. Greater awareness of the non-Muslim contexts in which Muslim minorities live and the targeted audiences of their English website may account for this. For example, Siddiqi, who was born in India, where he received his religious education from traditional institutions such as the Darul Uloom Nadwatul Ulama (Lucknow) and then from the Islamic University of Medina (Saudi Arabia), has also earned an MA in Theology from Birmingham University in England and a PhD in Comparative Religion from Harvard University. In addition to his professional affiliations in the Middle East, he has been active in the United States where he is also the current president of the Academy of Judaic-Christian and Islamic Studies at the University of California in Los Angeles.[9] Mostafa was born in Egypt where she was trained and worked as a lawyer before engaging in the *da'wah*, i.e. Call to Islam. She then settled in London where she became director of a British Muslim magazine, was in charge of The Muslim Women Organization in Britain, between 1999 and 2000, and worked as a *da'eyah*, i.e. a preacher, in the London area. Faysal Mawlawi, who studied not only in Lebanon but also in Paris (Sorbonne), lived and worked in the field of Islamic law in Lebanon, one of the most pluralist societies in the Middle East, and also became deputy chairman of the European Council for Fatwa and Research. The statements of all these three 'authorities' included in Islam Online's replies concur with and uphold the conceptual normative framework of Islamic jurisprudence, even addressing regional Middle Eastern sociopolitical issues, while some of their statements, nonetheless, present more neutral, less polemical or bellicose views towards this Jewish 'Other'. Let us now turn to the online recirculation and consumption of *fatwas*.

Muslim Village and the consumption of *fatwas*

Not only does a thriving online *fatwa* market, with innumerable digital platforms, ensure the global distribution and circulation of various religious opinions (Hosen, 2008; Zaman, 2008; Šisler, 2011), but so do online forums, virtual Islamic public spaces (El-Nawawy & Khamis, 2012), or virtual 'e-third spaces' (Marcotte, 2010a, 133–135) where views can be shared regarding issues relevant to Muslims and the online communities in which they participate. Participants can add links to, post and often zealously discuss *fatwas* that 'Google Shaykh' puts at their disposal. They can use *fatwas* either to support or to disclaim views put forwards by others regarding any number of social, political, religious, ethical or moral views or issues. Obviously, online Muslim forums participate in the redistribution and the recirculation of countless *fatwas*.

To explore the online consumption of *fatwas* and their usage in those virtual public spaces, one may turn to any well-attended online Muslim forum. If one takes into account the nature and the volume of interaction generated by Muslim Village's online forums,[10] with their claimed 27,285 members (not all active) and 944,807 posts (as of 30 September 2014), they undoubtedly constitute Australia's largest 'online community' (Wellman & Gulia, 1999; Smith, 1999) and provide us with a window onto contemporary (mostly young) Muslims' online *fatwa* consumption.[11] On its thousands of publicly available forums, Muslims living in a Muslim minority context, many born in Australia, engage online, not only with one another, but also with the online *fatwas* to which they, or others, appeal when dealing with the 'heterogeneous set of cultural systems' (Morey & Yaqin, 2010, 146) prevailing in Australia and with which they are confronted. In their daily Australian lives, many of them need to negotiate a number of issues relating to gender and sexual norms that may not conform to more traditional normative views, especially for those who are more religious (Marranci, 2008, 49–50). It is thus not uncommon for online participants to seek 'religious rulings' and to provide hyperlinks to, or to copy on the forums *fatwas* they find online or media reports of *fatwas* issued by well-known Middle Eastern religious scholars, relevant to the issues they are discussing.

The example of online forum discussions surrounding hymenoplasty, the hymen reconstructive surgery some women undergo to restore (physical) virginity, while only exemplifying one type of online consumption of 'authoritative' religious opinion, nonetheless offers us a glimpse into the ways Muslims can appeal to and make use of online *fatwas*. Muslim Village's online participants discussed the surgery, the motives that could lead to resorting to the surgery, its social and religious consequences, as well as its religio-legal status (Rispler-Chaim, 2007). While discussions of participants revolved around a number of real-life incidents, they quickly sought *fatwas*, jurisprudential (legal) opinions penned by religious 'authorities', to find out whether the practice was permissible or forbidden. A female participant posted a link to a *fatwa* issued by Muhammad Saleh Al-Munajjid, found on the Saudi Salafi cleric's website, which ruled that virginity restoration was religiously forbidden (*haram*).[12] However, the same participant later posted a link to an article that mentioned that the Grand Mufti, i.e. the highest religious authority, of Egypt, Ali Gomaa, had ruled that the surgical procedure was religiously permissible (*halal*): women were not to disclose personal matters to their future spouses and the non-disclosure of the procedure was not an issue of honesty. While this Muslim woman's post did not give any reason to believe that she endorsed the Grand Mufti's view, she was the one who circulated this second and less common, and for some controversial, religious ruling. More interesting is the fact that she incorporated it into her own deliberations, as she was working out an interpretation of the practice that could be congruent with her own understanding of the Islamic tradition.

With the posting of those two religious opinions, all participants were reminded that eminent religious scholars can hold divergent and, at times, opposite views, an occasion for some to note and to highlight the flexibility that Islam affords Muslims. Moreover, another female participant wrote that her own local sheikh held the view that it was permissible to keep certain things secret from one's partner. This led another female participant to provide links to two *fatwas* she had found on the American SunniPath website, which put forward similar views: one was penned by Shaykh Faraz Rabbani[13] and the other by Ustadha Zaynab Ansari.[14] Mistakes (or sins) one had committed in the past were to remain between Allah/God and the repentant sinner; even one of the male moderators of the forum was in agreement with this position (Marcotte, 2015, 71–72).

Originally sought out for the 'authoritativeness' they embody, *fatwas* and the divergent religious opinions they put forward may be viewed under a different light when juxtaposed on online forums, examined, questioned and even re-evaluated by participants who, along with administrators and moderators, are often not religious scholars (Mishra & Semaan, 2010). While Muslim Village's participants may not be scholarly arbitrators of divergent religious claims (Illar, 2010), their usage of *fatwas*, nonetheless, signals their engagement with, and involvement in, a diffuse-like type of religious authority in their quest for 'real' Islam, with their respective cultural (Mishra & Semaan, 2010), or essentialized and deculturized understandings (Saint-Blancart, 2004). While, at times, some participants, administrators and moderators do remind participants of 'legitimate' or more 'generally accepted' religious opinions, no single authority 'strategically arbitrates' between the various and, at times, conflicting *fatwas* participants post on the forums (cf. Cheong et al., 2011). Online interaction and discussion that take place on these less structured and less hierarchical online forums may generate individual and/or collective diffuse-like exploration and 'arbitration' processes for defining the forums' 'e-normativity' (Marcotte, 2010a; Stowasser & Abul-Magd, 2008).

Globalization, delocalization and deterritorialization

Nowadays, online production, circulation and consumption of *fatwas* occur in the context of ever-increasing globalization. Digital technology has paved the way for unprecedented transnational 'cyber public spaces' (Bowen, 2004). Some have heralded the advent of unparalleled 'deterritorialization' (Roy, 2000) of religious authority. Others have proposed its 'delocalization' (Echchaibi, 2011), far from its traditional institutional Middle Eastern milieux (e.g. Egypt or Saudi Arabia for Sunni Islam). The novel dynamics of 'translocalities' that cyber Islamic environments (Mandaville, 2001, 2007) and the new loci of *fatwa* production, circulation and consumption facilitate both impact on religious authority online and, in some instances, open up new interpretative possibilities, even kindle buds of reconfiguration.

The first two examples of 'Jewish' *fatwas* from Islam Online, on the one hand, illustrate the subtle shift globalization imparts on the production and distribution of *fatwas*, with the novel digital dissemination and circulation loops of religious interpretations generated by Muslim scholars living all over the world. With Islam Online's migration of *fatwas* online, one witnesses a diversification of collaborators-producers of its 'Jewish' *fatwas*, which, in turn, brings about a subtle change in the interpretative horizons of the Muslim gaze at the Jewish 'Other'. New sensitivities emerge that voice tolerance, as opposed to merely agonistic responses, and thus new possibilities, although too faint for some, do peek over the horizon to reconfigure subtly the Muslim gaze at the Jewish 'Other'. This 'deterritorialization' or 'delocalization' of religious authority may be a response to a number of Muslim states' authoritarian rule or, in other instances, to the institutional control of religious organizations that, in the past, embodied traditional religious authority (Echchaibi, 2011, 28). The consequences of such changes can, on the one hand, potentially introduce 'relativism' into religious authority, even threatening it, as is the case with some Hindu traditions' encounter with new media (Scheifinger, 2010). On the other hand, it may also herald the advent of a novel 'transnational Islam' (Mandaville, 2001, 2007), one that re-evaluates and rethinks its relation to traditional religious authorities.

The last two examples of *fatwa* usage from Muslim Village's forums, on the other hand, illustrate another subtle shift, as online *fatwa* consumption and recirculation take place in novel 'glocally' contextualized and socially constructed discourses (Geelhoed, 2011; Khan, 1998; Marret, 2008; Wellman, 2004), often quite different from the original context of the *fatwa*'s production. One should thus neither be blind to the original social, political and cultural contexts of those who pen, distribute and circulate *fatwas*, nor ignore the social, political and cultural contexts of those who make use of them (Caeiro, 2006, 2011a; cf. Koningsveld, 2006) – location and context of their production, distribution and consumption do indeed matter (Agrama, 2010).

Any analysis of *fatwa* consumption by Muslims living in a minority context should take into consideration processes by which young Muslims re-inscribe themselves into 'believing pathways' (Hervieu-Léger, 1993) and 'revitalize a memory capital that individual auto-realization requirements revisit and invigorate' (Saint-Blancart, 2004). Online patterns of *fatwa* consumption may, in fact, indicate interpretative 'religious agency' (Mishra & Semaan, 2010), individuals tapping into online religious 'authoritative' knowledge to incorporate counter-hegemonic discourses in their own religious discourses (ibid.).

Muslims living thousands of kilometres away from *fatwa* production sites tap into the online *fatwa* market, and redistribute and recirculate selected ones into new loops of dissemination of selected religious interpretations on Muslim forums. They are working out, for themselves, understandings of what is normatively acceptable in their environment by tapping into globally produced knowledge that serves as material for their construction of novel glocal understandings. Saeed (2003, 212) has noted, for instance, that Islam is 'now being shaped by the prevailing values, norms and practices of Australian society [...] now being accommodated into what is considered to be Islam [...] an Islam that is comfortable with these values which will remain meaningful and relevant to their life in Australia'.

Participants who appeal to the views of scholars and *fatwas* selected from thousands readily available online may well generate what Bucar labels 'creative conformity' (Bucar, 2010, 2011; cf. Mahmood, 2006). Here, online usage of *fatwas* is inscribed into the new contextualized and socially constructed representations many online participants share. The double constraints of this 'dianomic' process (Bucar, 2010, 2011) shape the discursive performativity of their 'religious agency': online participants remain bound by their interaction with the religious normative discursive tradition of habituation and by their quest for some form of autonomy, as they deal with the unanticipated elements of the new social contexts in which they find themselves and the tensions these generate. In some instances, Muslim Village participants engage in highly polemical 'strategic actions' (Habermas) to try to change other participants' positions or beliefs (El-Nawawy & Khamis, 2012, 44–45), with, amongst others, repeated appeal to 'authoritative' views and *fatwas* of scholars, as was the case when they tackled, for example, issues such as polygyny (polygamy) and homosexuality (Marcotte, 2010a, 124–133).

In short, examples discussed above may illustrate what happens when vectors of religious authority, which the *fatwa* embodies, are no longer bound by physical and geographical spaces, and decoupled online from the contexts of its production, dissemination and consumption – changes whose 'many complexities and challenges to religious beliefs' inevitably affect not only religiosity (Hesapci-Sanaktekin et al., 2013, 1567), but also other contemporary usages of *fatwas*, such as their use in '*takfiri*' circles or in relation to terrorism (Weimann, 2011). This is but the tip of the iceberg of the 'emergent' and 'infinite field' of Muslims and new information and communication technologies (Hoffmann & Larsson, 2013).

Acknowledgement

Research for this chapter was made possible with a small grant awarded by the Faculteé des sciences humaines de l'Université du Québec à Montréal.

Notes

1 www.onislam.net/english/ask-the-scholar.html.
2 onislam.net/english/politics/259-Advisers/168994.html.
3 onislam.net/english/culture-and-entertainment/259-Advisers/169117.html.
4 onislam.net/english/politics/259-Advisers/179226.html; cf. European Council for Fatwa and Research, see www.e-cfr.org.
5 onislam.net/english/politics/259-Advisers/168999.html,
6 www.onislam.net/english/politics/18-autho/423332-Muhammad%20Saleh%20Al-Munajjid.html.
7 onislam.net/english/politics/259-Advisers/179125.html.
8 www.onislam.net/english/politics/18-autho/418927-Sheikh%20%60Atiyyah%20Saqr.html.
9 isocmasjid.weebly.com/dr-muzammil-siddiqi.html.
10 Muslim Village is a Sydney-based Muslim community organization website established in 2001, see muslimvillage.com/about-muslimvillage.
11 For forum statistics, see muslimvillage.com/forums.
12 He founded the Salafi website IslamQA.info where his *fatwas* are available in 13 languages. The website was eventually banned in Saudi Arabia.
13 He was associated with SunniPath, before he founded in 2008 SeekersGuidance: see kersguidance.org/home/teachers/faraz-rabbani.
14 She was associated with SunniPath (2004–09), before joining SeekersGuidance: see kersguidance.org/home/teachers/zaynab-ansari.

References

Abdel-Fadil, M. (2011) 'The Islam-Online crisis: a battle of wasatiyya vs. salafi ideologies?' *CyberOrient*, 5(1), www.cyberorient.net/article.do?articleId=6239.

Abdel-Fadil, M. (2013) 'Islam Online guides spouses towards marital bliss: Arabic vs. English counselling perspectives on marital communication', in T. Hoffmann and G. Larsson (Eds) *Muslims and the New Information and Communication Technologies* (pp. 49–71). Dordrecht: Springer.

Agrama, H. (2010) 'Ethics, tradition, authority: toward an anthropology of the fatwa', *American Ethnologist*, 37(1), pp. 2–18.

Ali, K. (2006) *Sexual Ethics and Islam: Feminist Reflections on Qur'an, Hadith, and Jurisprudence*. Oxford: Oneworld.

Bowen, J. (2004) 'Beyond migration: Islam as a transnational public space', *Journal of Ethnic and Migration Studies*, 30(5), pp. 879–894.

Brouwer, L. (2004) 'Dutch-Muslims on the Internet: a new discussion platform', *Journal of Muslim Minority Affairs*, 24(1), pp. 47–55.

Brouwer, L. (2006) 'Giving voice to Dutch Moroccan girls on the Internet', *Global Media Journal*, 5(9), pp. 1–10 (art. 3), dare.ubvu.vu.nl/bitstream/handle/1871/25786/194682.pdf?sequence=2.

Bucar, E.M. (2010) 'Dianomy: understanding religious women's moral agency as creative conformity', *Journal of the American Academy of Religion*, 78(3), pp. 662–686.

Bucar, E.M. (2011) *Creative Conformity: The Feminist Politics of U.S. Catholic and Iranian Shi'i Women*. Washington, DC: Georgetown University Press.

Bunt, G.R. (2000) *Virtually Islamic: Computer-Mediated Communication and Cyber Islamic Environments*. Cardiff: University of Wales Press.

Bunt, G.R. (2003) *Islam in the Digital Age: e-Jihad, Online Fatwas and Cyber Islamic Environments*. London: Pluto Press.

Bunt, G.R. (2009a) *iMuslims: Rewiring the House of Islam*. Chapel Hill, NC: University of North Carolina Press.

Bunt, G.R. (2009b) 'The digital umma', in A.B. Sajoo (Ed.) *A Companion to the Muslim World* (pp. 391–310). London: I.B. Tauris.

Caeiro, A. (2003) 'Debating fatwas in the cyberspace: the construction of Islamic authority in four Francophone Muslims Internet forums', in *Sacred Media – Transforming Traditions in the Interplay of Religion and the Media (Conference Proceedings)*. www.sacredmedia.jyu.fi/mainpage.php#caeiro.

Caeiro, A. (2004) 'The social construction of Shari'a: bank interest, home purchase, and Islamic norms in the West', *Die Welt des Islams*, 44(3), pp. 351–375.

Caeiro, A. (2006) 'The shifting moral universe of the Islamic tradition of Ifta': a diachronic study of four adab al-fatwa manuals', *The Muslim World*, 96(4), pp. 661–685.

Caeiro, A. (2010) 'The power of European fatwas: the minority fiqh project and the making of an Islamic counterpublic', *International Journal of Middle Eastern Studies*, 42, pp. 435–449.

Caeiro, A. (2011a) 'Transnational ulama, European fatwas, and Islamic identity: a case study of the European Council for Fatwa and Research', in M. van Bruinessen & S. Allievi (Eds) *Producing Islamic Knowledge: Transmission and Dissemination in Western Europe* (pp. 121–140). Abingdon: Routledge.

Caeiro, A. (2011b) 'The making of the fatwa: the production of Islamic legal expertise in Europe', *Archives des Sciences Sociales des Religions*, 155(3), pp. 81–100.

Campbell, H.A. (2007) 'Who's got the power? Religious authority and the Internet', *Journal of Computer-Mediated Communication*, 12(3), pp. 1043–1062.

Campbell, H.A. (2010a) *When Religion Meets New Media*. London: Routledge.

Campbell, H.A. (2010b) 'Religious authority and the blogosphere', *Journal of Computer-Mediated Communication*, 15(2), pp. 251–276.

Campbell, H.A. (2012) 'Religion and the Internet: a microcosm for studying Internet trends and implications', *New Media Society*, 15(5), pp. 680–694.

Cheong, P.H. (2011) 'Religious leaders, mediated authority, and social change', *Journal of Applied Communication Research*, 39(4), pp. 452–454.

Cheong, P.H., Huang, S. & Poon, J.P.H. (2011) 'Religious communication and epistemic authority of leaders in wired faith organizations', *Journal of Communication*, 61(5), pp. 938–958.

Crul, M. & Heering, L. (eds) (2008) *The Position of Turkish and Moroccan Second Generation in Amsterdam and Rotterdam*. Amsterdam: Amsterdam University Press.

Echchaibi, N. (2011) 'From audio tapes to video blogs: the delocalisation of authority in Islam', *Nations and Nationalism*, 17(1), pp. 25–44.

El-Nawawy, M. & Khamis, S. (2012) 'Divergent identities in the virtual Islamic public sphere: a case study of the English discussion forum "IslamOnline"', *Journal of Arab and Muslim Media Research*, 5(1), pp. 31–48.

Fink, S. (2010) 'A new domain for co-workers of God: accessing Khutbas on the Internet', *Australian Religion Studies Review* (new title is *Journal for the Academic Study of Religion*), 23 (3), pp. 301–324.

Gauthier, F. & Uhl, M. (2012) 'Digital shapings of religion in a globalised world: the Vatican online and Amr Khaled's TV-preaching', *Australian Journal of Communication*, 39(1), pp. 53–70.

Geelhoed, F. (2011) *Purification and Resistance: Glocal Meanings of Islamic Fundamentalism in the Netherlands*. Rotterdam: Erasmus University Rotterdam. hdl.handle.net/1765/31685.

Golan, O. (2011) 'Reconstruire les frontières religieuses en ligne: l'émergence d'un internet juif confessionnel', *Le Temps des médias*, 17(2), pp. 1–14.

Gräf, B. (2007) 'Sheikh Yūsuf al-Qaraḍāwī in Cyberspace', *Die Welt des Islams*, 47(3/4), pp. 403–421.

Gräf, B. (2008) 'IslamOnline.net: independent, interactive, popular', *Arab Media and Society*, 4 (winter), www.arabmediasociety.com/?article=576.

Gräf, B. (2010) 'Media fatwas, Yusuf al-Qaradawi and media-mediated authority in Islam', *Orient*, 51(1), pp. 6–15.

Gräf, B. & Skovgaar-Petersen, J. (eds) (2009) *Global Mufti: The Phenomenon of Yūsuf al-Qaraḍāwī*. London: Hurst & Co.

Granjon, F. & Denouël, J. (2011) 'Penser les usages sociaux des technologies numériques d'information et de communication', in J. Denouël & F. Granjon (Eds) *Communiquer à l'ère numérique: Regards croisés sur la sociologie des usages* (pp. 7–43). Paris: Presses de Mines.

Hall, S. (1973) *Encoding and Decoding in the Television Discourse*. Birmingham: Centre for Cultural Studies, University of Birmingham.

Helland, C. (2007) 'Diaspora on the electronic frontier: developing virtual connections with sacred homelands', *Journal of Computer-Mediated Communication*, 12, pp. 956–976.

Helland, C. (2008) 'Canadian religious diversity online: a network of possibilities', in P. Beyer & L. Beaman (Eds) *Religion and Diversity in Canada* (pp. 127–148). Boston, MA: Brill.

Hervieu-Léger, D. (1993) *La religion pour mémoire*. Paris: Le Cerf.

Hesapci-Sanaktekin, O., Aslanbay, Y. & Gorgulu, V. (2013) 'The effects of religiosity on Internet consumption: a study on a Muslim country', *Information, Communication and Society*, 16(10), pp. 1553–1573.

Hoffmann, T. & Larsson, G. (2013) 'Muslims and the new information and communication technologies: notes from an emerging and infinite field – an introduction', in T. Hoffmann & G. Larsson (Eds) *Muslims and the New Information and Communication Technologies: Notes from an Emerging and Infinite Field* (pp. 2–11). Dordrecht: Springer.

Hosen, N. (2008) 'Online fatwa in Indonesia: from fatwa shopping to Googling a Kiai', in G. Fealy & S. White (Eds) *Expressing Islam: Religious Life and Politics in Indonesia* (pp. 159–173). Singapore: Institute of Southeast Asian Studies (ISEAS).

Illar, D.J. (2010) 'Cyber fatwās and classical Islamic jurisprudence', *Journal of Computer and Information Law*, 27(4), pp. 577–592.

IslamOnline (2002) 'Dealing with Jewish neighbors', *IslamOnline.net*, 25 June (reposted on OnIslam.net), www.onislam.net/english/ask-the-scholar/international-relations-and-jihad/relations-during-war/175441-dealing-with-jewish-neighbors.html.

IslamOnline (2004) 'Working for a Jewish company', *IslamOnline.net*, 16 May (reposted on OnIslam.net), www.onislam.net/english/ask-the-scholar/financial-issues/earning-livelihood/170228.html.

Jacobi, W. & Yavuz, H. (2008) 'Modernization, identity and integration: an introduction to the special issue on Islam in Europe', *Journal of Muslim Minority Affairs*, 28(1), pp. 1–6.

Johansen, B. (1999) *Contingency in a Sacred Law. Legal and Ethical Norms in the Muslim Fiqh*. Leiden: Brill.

Karim, K.H. (2009) *Changing Perceptions of Islamic Authority among Muslims in Canada, the United States and the United Kingdom*. Montreal: Institute for Research on Public Policy.

Khan, M. (1998) 'Constructing identity in "glocal" politics', *American Journal of Islamic Social Sciences*, 15(3), pp. 81–106, works.bepress.com/muqtedar_khan/16.

Krutikov, M. & Krutikov, A. (2004) 'Arab.ru: the virtual other on the Israeli-Russian web', in T. Parfitt & Y. Egorova (Eds) *Jews, Muslims and Mass Media: Mediating the 'Other'* (pp. 144–156). London: RoutledgeCurzon.

Kutcher, J. (2009) 'The politics of virtual fatwa counseling in the 21st century', *Masaryk University Journal of Law and Technology*, 3(1), pp. 33–49.

Larsson, G. (2011) *Muslims and the New Media: Historical and Contemporary Debates*. Farnham: Ashgate.

Mahmood, S. (2006) 'Secularism, hermeneutics and empire: the politics of Islamic reformation', *Public Culture*, 18(2), pp. 323–347.

Mandaville, P. (2001) *Transnational Muslim Politics: Reimagining the Umma*. London and New York: Routledge.

Mandaville, P. (2007) 'Globalization and the politics of religious knowledge: pluralizing authority in the Muslim world', *Theory, Culture and Society*, 24(2), pp. 101–115.

Marcotte, R.D. (2010a) 'Gender and sexuality online on Australian Muslim forums', *Contemporary Islam*, 4(1), pp. 117–138.

Marcotte, R.D. (2010b) 'The "religionated" body: fatwas and body parts', in E. Burns Coleman & K. White (Eds) *Medicine, Religion, and the Body* (pp. 27–49). Leiden: Brill.

Marcotte, R.D. (2015) 'Let's talk about sex: Australian Muslim online discussions', *Contemporary Islam*, 9(1), pp. 65–84.

Mariani, E. (2011) 'Cyber-fatwas, sermons, and media campaigns: Amr Khaled and Omar Bakri Muhammad in search of new audiences', in M. van Bruinessen & S. Allievi (Eds) *Producing Islamic Knowledge: Transmission and Dissemination in Western Europe* (pp. 157–168). Abingdon: Routledge.

Marranci, G. (2008) *The Anthropology of Islam*. Oxford: Berg.

Marret, J.-L. (2008) 'Al-Qaeda in Islamic Maghreb: a "glocal" organization', *Studies in Conflict and Terrorism*, 31(6), pp. 541–552.

Masud, M.K. (2002) 'Islamic law and Muslim minorities', *ISIM Newsletter*, 11(1), pp. 17.

Masud, M.K., Messick, B. & Powers, D. (eds) (1996) 'Muftis, fatwas, and Islamic legal interpretation', in *Islamic Legal Interpretation. Muftis and their Fatwas* (pp. 3–32). Cambridge, MA: Harvard University Press.

Mazrui, A. & Mazrui, A. (2001) 'The digital revolution and the new reformation', *Harvard International Review*, 23(1), pp. 52–55.

Mishra, S. & Semaan, G. (2010) 'Islam in cyberspace: South Asian Muslims in America log in', *Journal of Broadcasting and Electronic Media*, 54(1), pp. 87–101.

Moosa, E. (2002) 'Interface of science and jurisprudence: dissonant gazes at the body in modern Muslim ethics', in T. Peters, M. Iqbal & S.N. Haq (Eds) *God, Life, and the Cosmos: Christian and Islamic Perspectives* (pp. 329–356). Aldershot: Ashgate.

Morey, P. & Yaqin, A. (2010) 'Introduction: Muslims in the frame', *Interventions: International Journal of Postcolonial Studies*, 12(2), pp. 145–156.

Nathan, J. (2010a) 'IslamOnline's portrayal of Jews', in J. Cesari (Ed.) *Islamopedia Online: Translation, News and Analysis of Contemporary Islamic Thought*, 21 December, www.islamopediaonline.org/editorials-and-analysis/julie-nathan-analyzes-islamonline%E2%80%99s-portrayal-jews-and-judaism.

Nathan, J. (2010b) *The Portrayal of Jews on IslamOnline*. Honours thesis. Brisbane: The University of Queensland.

OnIslam Staff (2010) 'IslamOnline founders launch OnIslam', *OnIslam*, 9 October, www.onislam.net/english/news/global/449313-islamonline-founders-launch-onislam.html.

Paltridge, B. (2006) *Discourse Analysis*. London: Continuum.

Parfitt, T. & Egorova, Y. (eds) (2004) *Jews, Muslims and Mass Media: Mediating the 'Other'*. London: RoutledgeCurzon.

Peter, F. (2006) 'Individualization and religious authority in Western European Islam', *Islam and Christian-Muslim Relations*, 17(1), pp. 105–118.

Piela, A. (2010) 'Muslim women's online discussions of gender relations in Islam', *Journal of Muslim Minority Affairs*, 30(3), pp. 425–435.

Piela, A. (2011a) 'Beyond the traditional-modern binary: faith and identity in Muslim women's online matchmaking profiles', *CyberOrient*, 5(1), www.cyberorient.net/article.do?articleId=6219.

Piela, A. (2011b) 'Piety as a concept underpinning Muslim women's online discussions of marriage and professional career', *Contemporary Islam*, 5(3), pp. 249–269.

Reimer, S. (2008) 'Does religion matter? Canadian religious traditions and attitudes towards diversity', in L.G. Beaman & P. Beyer (Eds) *Religion and Diversity in Canada* (pp. 105–126). Leiden: Brill.

Rinnawi, K. (2012) '"Instant nationalism" and the "cyber mufti": the Arab diaspora in Europe and the transnational media', *Journal of Ethnic and Migration Studies*, 38(9), pp. 1451–1467.

Rispler-Chaim, V. (2007) 'The Muslim surgeon and contemporary ethical dilemmas surrounding the restoration of virginity', *Hawwa*, 5(2/3), pp. 324–349.

Roy, O. (2000) 'La communauté virtuelle. L'internet et la déterritorialisation de l'islam', *Réseaux*, 18(99), pp. 219–237.

Saeed, A. (2003) *Islam in Australia*. Crows Nest: Allen and Unwin.

Saint-Blancart, C. (2004) 'La transmission de l'islam auprès des nouvelles générations de la diaspora', *Social Compass*, 51(2), pp. 235–247.

Scheifinger, H. (2010) 'Threats to Hindu authority: Puja-ordering websites and the Kalighat', *Asian Journal of Social Science*, 3(4), pp. 636–656.

Šisler, V. (2009) 'European Courts' authority contested? The case of marriage and divorce fatwas on-line', *Masaryk University Journal of Law and Technology*, 3(1), pp. 51–78.

Šisler, V. (2011) 'Cyber counselors: online fatwas, arbitration tribunals and the construction of Muslim identity in the UK', *Information, Communication and Society*, 14(8), pp. 1136–1159.

Smith, M.A. (1999) 'Invisible crowds in cyberspace: mapping the social structure of the usenet', in M.A. Smith & P. Kollock (Eds) *Communities in Cyberspace* (pp. 195–221). New York: Routledge.

Stowasser, B.F. & Abul-Magd, Z. (2008) 'Legal codes and contemporary fatawa: Muslim women and contesting paradigms', *Journal of Women of the Middle East and the Islamic World*, 6, pp. 32–51.

Sunier, T. (2011) 'The making of Muslim youth cultures in Europe', in M. Bailey & G. Redden (Eds) *Mediating Faiths: Religion and Socio-Cultural Change in the Twenty-First Century* (pp. 147–158). Farnham: Ashgate.

Van Koningsveld, P.S. (2006) 'The significance of fatwas for Muslims in Europe: some suggestions for future research', *Nederlandsch theologisch tijdschrift*, 60(3), pp. 208–221.

Weimann, G. (2011) 'Cyber-fatwas and terrorism', *Studies in Conflict and Terrorism*, 34(10), pp. 765–781.

Wellman, B. (2004) 'The glocal village: Internet and community', *Ideas*, 1(1), pp. 26–29.

Wellman, B. & Gulia, M. (1999) 'Virtual communities as communities: net surfers don't ride alone', in M.A. Smith & P. Kollock (Eds) *Communities in Cyberspace* (pp. 167–194). New York: Routledge.

Zaman, S. (2008) 'From imam to cyber-mufti: consuming identity in Muslim America', *The Muslim World*, 98(4), pp. 465–474.

15

HOW ISLAMIC IS ISLAM ONLINE COUNSELLING?

Mona Abdel-Fadil

Introduction

>Title: I am thinking of divorce and my husband is very religiously committed [*mūltazim*]
>
>Female questioner:
>
>My husband is very religiously committed [...] and is very kind to me, and in short is a man of good manners and morals [...] My problem is that my husband does not love me, and he has confessed this to me [...] this life is harming my psyche [...] so what are your opinions? [...]
>
>Second counsellor response:
>
>[...] I cannot get past your 'religiously committed' husband's actions [...] religious commitment [*al-iltizām*], my sister, is following the path of the Prophet [...] and he was the gentlest of people [...] No, my sister [...] the religiously committed as I know him does not tell his wife that he does not love her [...] this is at best 'rude' as Egyptians say, or at worst, psychological abuse and harsh.
>
>*(Excerpt from counselling exchange, IslamOnline.net, 2004, 95–100)*[1]

Islam Online (IOL), founded in 1997, has been characterized as one of the most prominent and influential religious portals in the world (Bunt, 2003; Gräf, 2008; Hofheinz, 2007). IOL's main offices were in Cairo and the website offered a wide range of interactive services, such as *fatwas* and counselling. According to Gräf (2008), the founders of IOL envisioned a website encompassing all aspects of life, and welcomed the integration of secular sciences with Islamic perspectives. This is due to the view that muftis cannot always answer questions beyond Islamic jurisprudence and theology (Gräf, 2008, 1).

In the words of Selim,[2] IOL and the pioneering Arabic-language online counselling service *mashākil ū ḥulūl* (Problems and Solutions) was founded on an ideological aspiration: 'Islamist ideology is not enough, we need a wider perspective to deal with relations with humans' – Selim (personal communication, 21 June 2010).[3] At the heart of the creation of Islam Online lay a vision, a contemporary formulation of Islam, and articulation of Islam that sought out other sources and influences than religious scripture, and was intent on dealing with 'real life',[4] or, as one counsellor put it, 'Islam Online forged a link between the religious, the social and the psychological' (Safwat, personal communication, 23 June 2010).[5]

Problems and Solutions can be considered the emblem of IOL's efforts to unite secular and Islamic perspectives and relate to contemporary Muslims' real lives and problems. Unparalleled by any other Islamic website, Problems and Solutions was serviced by counselling professionals with a background in secular fields such as psychology and psychiatry. Problems and Solutions was launched on IOL in the late 1990s, and later migrated to www.OnIslam.net in the autumn of 2010, following the IOL crisis.[6] IOL and Problems and Solutions counselling was founded on 'the message' (al-risāla),[7] which connotes a middle-way approach (wasatiyya) to Islam, is contemporary and centred on real life, tackles controversial topics, and aims to empower and create self- and social awareness amongst its users. At times, IOL – and particularly Problems and Solutions – harboured harsh critique for being too 'open' or even 'un-Islamic' in their views and dealings with sensitive topics (Abdel-Fadil, 2011), and, according to Rana (personal communication, 23 June 2009), some critics maliciously retorted that IOL ought to have been called 'Secularism Online'. For adherents of this latter view, being 'secularist' is evidently a serious offence and not compatible with being 'Islamic'.

In a refreshing article called 'Second thoughts about the anthropology of Islam, or how to make sense of grand schemes in everyday life', Samuli Schielke (2010) argues that there is 'too much Islam in the anthropology of Islam'. He maintains that Asad's (1986) seminal deliberation of 'the anthropology of Islam' has become dogmatic and given rise to a volume of literature on Islamic piety, ethics and tradition that over-focuses on the *theorizing* of Islam on the basis of pious, conservative and moralist activists.[8] In consequence, anthropologists run the risk of juxtaposing Islam and secular liberal thought, as if secular and religious ideas cannot be fused within a Muslim person's lifeworld. This skewed and reductionist dichotomy is blind to the complexities and ambiguities of everyday life and the lifeworlds of individual Muslims, argues Schielke. In my view, this is a very valid inference. The case of Islam Online and Problems and Solutions counselling is particularly interesting to examine against this backdrop. First, the negotiations and configurations of religious-secular boundaries of Islamic identity that underpin Problems and Solutions counselling are of a different calibre to those of conservative moralist activists. Second, Problems and Solutions is a platform from which Muslim counselees delve into the struggles and complexities of their everyday lives. Third, Problems and Solutions serves as an intellectual hub where counselling professionals produce 'Islamic' solutions to real-life problems.

Previous studies of religious websites tend to argue that the Internet is a space for negotiation and contestation of traditional religious authority. Still, as Campbell (2007, 2) points out, such claims are rarely sufficiently substantiated. Taking

Problems and Solutions as a case study, this chapter examines the way Problems and Solutions carves out space for negotiation and contestation of traditional Islamic authority and identity, by tapping into what Krüger (2005, 11–12) calls 'invisible aspects' of online religious communities. Drawing on, first, a longitudinal (offline) ethnographic study of the work environment in Cairo where Problems and Solutions was produced[9] and, second, online research of counselling content,[10] this chapter aims to provide a layered, contextualized understanding of online Islamic counselling by highlighting and analysing the 'invisible', 'behind the screens', meaning-making activities and ideological stances that inform the online output of Problems and Solutions counselling. As will be demonstrated in subsequent sections, Islam Online's counselling services inherently entail a negotiation of the boundaries of religious authority and what is to be considered 'Islamic'.

Counselling as defined by Hough (2006, 1) consists of a 'helping relationship', 'is based on the principle of "empowerment" and "seeks to help people identify their own resources"'. In my analysis, Problems and Solutions counselling draws on a person-centred or humanistic counselling approach. This (secular) counselling approach, according to Hough (2006, 119–121), rests on the assumption that all counselees hold the potential to solve the problems in their lives, if given guidance.[11] The goal is to help clients identify their own resources, and counsel clients on how to use their inner resources to improve their situation (Hough, 2006, 129–135). In the following, I will substantiate this claim by giving centre stage to the Problems and Solutions counsellors' own descriptions of their counselling approach.

Not giving a solution

> We founded the IOL paradigm … the IOL tone. It is about teaching a way of thinking […] My goal is always if you get another problem like this later, you will know how to deal with it […] It is a way of thinking, teaching people how to fish rather than giving them the fish […] We want to strengthen their ability of thinking and choosing the path that is less damaging to them.
>
> *(Selim)*

Selim describes how, despite the name 'Problems and Solutions', serving a 'direct solution' goes against the shared and professed counselling ideals of the Problems and Solutions counsellors. When Selim speaks of clients 'choosing the path that is less damaging to them', he is thinking of securing their well-being. More importantly, Selim is indicating that 'learning to fish' is not only about learning how to make a choice, but actually learning how to make a *good* choice. In this particular answer, Selim does not address religion explicitly, although 'choosing the path that is less damaging to them' may have a religious undertone. Other counsellors address religion more explicitly when they respond to my question about Problems and Solutions' counselling philosophy. For instance, Omar (personal communication, 30 May 2010)[12] says:

> The philosophy is that it is not Islam in the scripture sense, it is Islam *with* life: communication with my wife, watching TV, my leisure time ... all is related to Islam. The basis of Islam – is in all of social life. There is a red line we do not cross with regards to values and principles [...] The first rule is that it is not our responsibility to make a decision. *She* has to make this decision. I cannot tell her to get a divorce, even if this is what I think is best. You give a person enough information for them to be able to make a good decision [...] Part of 'the message' is that we want to teach people how to choose. We do not want to teach dependency, we want you to learn how to choose.[13]

Omar's emphasis on 'Islam *with* life' and Islam being in all social life is reminiscent of Islamist slogans such as 'Islam is the solution'. Moreover, he discusses 'a red line that cannot be crossed', signalling that there are Islamic rules that must be taken into account. I will return to this later. At the same time, Omar underlines that the counselee must be the one to choose her own path. Indeed, Omar is remarkably clear on this point. He says, 'We do not want to teach dependency, we want you to learn how to choose'. This stance entails that counsellors prefer to avoid giving directive advice. Instead, the goal is to teach 'empowering tools'. In a similar vein, Safwat talks of teaching 'life skills' and 'problem-solving skills'. This seems to be a core value of Problems and Solutions counselling.[14] The goals of teaching independence and focusing on the client's own resources for conducting a choice is consistent with the humanistic counselling model.

Opening up paths and widening the vision

> I do a type of contextualizing, I [re-]formulate the words, repeat the complaints and problems of the questioner in a scientific manner. I contextualize, I show that [the problem] has these sides, I start to point out choices, and I start to expand, I expand the apprehension of the problem and the solutions. I light up different paths for him, so he does not feel trapped in a tunnel.
>
> *(Safwat)*

Safwat talks of 'lighting up paths' and 'expanding the apprehension of the problem' by pointing out different sides to the problem, and various choices of action. In a similar vein, Khadiga (personal communication, 13 June 2010) speaks of 'pinpointing problems', 'showing paths' and 'opening up paths'. An interrelated concern is sketching out the possible consequences of paths.[15] For instance, Khadiga talks of how she breaks down the choices to the client by explaining how each path 'will have 1, 2, 3 consequences'. In a similar manner, Dina (personal communication, 13 April 2010) describes 'possible solutions and what consequences each solution will have'.[16] Moreover, Dina relates that she tends to 'take the perspective of the other, and analyse the problem from this perspective'. 'The other' refers to a significant other mentioned by the client as being involved in the problem discussed. Another important point raised by Safwat's response is ensuring that the client 'does not feel trapped in a tunnel'. This is much in line with Nadya's (personal communication, 9 June 2010) assertion that the objective of counselling is 'learning how to deal with a problem when you are stuck in the desert' and 'keeping the door of hope open'.[17] Both Safwat and Nadya construe metaphors of the client being 'stuck' or 'trapped' with no way out, as the antithesis of what they wish to accomplish. One of the primary goals of Problems and Solutions counselling thus appears to be restoring a client's sense of hope.

A number of counsellors talk about the significance of seeing the problem in context. For instance, Omar says, 'I try to see the problem in a wider context [...] from a wider perspective, political, cultural, or economic'. Similarly, Dina declares that the target is 'develop their [client's] brain so that they see things from a wider perspective'. Widening the vision of counselees and assisting them to see a problem from several angles is related to the goal of restoring a client's belief in hope, and improving skills of self-reflexivity. Indeed, several counsellors consider it important to cultivate social awareness and self-awareness in counselees.

Cultivating self- and social awareness

The following dialogue with Safwat contextualizes Problems and Solutions counselling goals:

M: Is there is a particular message you are trying to send [out] to society?
SAFWAT: Yes, it is an awakening of society, philosophical, educational, social, ambitions, expanding the rationality of people, improv[ing] their life skills. Very often we say that 'we do not give a finished answer, but rather the skills to solve, how to think, the way to think, the way to think in order to find a solution' [...] We start with the context [of the problem], then open up. We then try this perspective, etc. [...] like a tree, from the trunk, to the branch, branching out, branching out [...] We do not stop at a closed passage.

Safwat once again underlines the importance of not being 'stuck' in 'a closed passage' and the importance of teaching skills. Interestingly, Safwat uses the term *nahda*, a word often used by Islamists to describe a religious awakening. Here, the term is used with a slightly different emphasis, to describe Problems and Solutions' counselling as part of an intellectual and social awakening of Arab societies. In other words, the goal of cultivating social awareness in individual counselees is interlinked with a greater goal of awakening a people. This ties into my previous analysis of the importance of 'the message' amongst the producers of Problems and Solutions (Abdel-Fadil, 2011). In response to the same question, 'Is there a particular message you are trying to send out to society?' Khadiga discusses developing awareness at the micro-level:

> The message, *my* message is to solve people's problems and make them happy. But, I think that IOL was trying to spread social awareness. Instead of people each time they are in trouble saying 'rescue me', the idea was to spread awareness [for them to be able to] look at the problem, find a solution, know how to avoid problems, and if in a problem, realize where it came from, and how to get out of it ... developing awareness.

Several of the Problems and Solutions counsellors underline the importance of self-reflexivity and thus the technique of reflection, in that the client sees both her good and negative points. According to Manar (personal communication, 2 June 2010), self-reflexivity is an essential prerequisite for improving the situation:

> He needs to move, not create apathy or depression. You must make him believe he can change his situation. He is part of the problem, but he is also the only one who can solve it.

Indeed, Manar's emphasis on avoiding apathy or depression is in line with previous responses from the Problems and Solutions counsellors, who wish to avoid clients being 'stuck', employing metaphors such as 'in a tunnel' or 'in the desert', and more fundamentally 'keeping the door of hope open', and the future orientation of humanistic counselling. Actually, Dalia (personal communication, 27 June 2010) describes shared values amongst Problems and Solutions counsellors in the following manner:[18]

> We have things in common. For example we do not give people solutions. This is common. And we clarify choices and the positives and negatives of each choice, and we leave the choosing up to them [clients]. This is common for us all. We also take him [the user] out of the narrow problem. I mean, he is buried in a narrow problem ... We get him out of there, so he can see the picture from a wider angle. And we try, as much as we can, to give a skill or two, or open up a path for him.

Dalia's response may perhaps be considered a synopsis of the Problems and Solutions' 'teaching to fish' approach to counselling. It demonstrates how Problems and Solutions counselling is skills-focused, entails widening the vision of the counselee, and leaving the selection of a solution up to the counselee. In Problems and Solutions counselling, there is a strong emphasis on skills: life skills, problem-solving skills, self-reflexivity, and learning a way of thinking and self-dependency. It can be argued that the Problems and Solutions counselling model is an appropriation of Western counselling models such as the humanistic model.[19] Nevertheless, the adaptation to local Arab contexts appears to result in a link between developing self-awareness and social awareness, and a stronger emphasis on social responsibility than in Western counselling models. This, I maintain, is related to greater goals of creating an intellectual awakening, not only at the individual level but also in society at large ('the message'). In the next section I discuss in what ways Problems and Solutions is influenced by an 'Islamic framework'.

Counselling within an Islamic framework

> I'll never forget ... once a woman wrote [to IOL]: 'God gave us everything, the best of which is that He exempted us from the need to think!' [laughs]. She wrote [laughs]: 'The grace of God is that we do not need to think!' Can you believe it?! [Laughs.]
>
> *(Dina)*

In an animated, humorous and exasperated manner, Dina tells me of how a Problems and Solutions counselee expressed gratitude that God had generously relieved humans of the necessity to employ brainpower for all eternity. Unbeknownst to this Problems and Solutions user, she succeeded in articulating the very antithesis of the brand of Islam that IOL employees strove to promote. Rather than promote blind obedience of 'religious verdicts', the Problems and Solutions counsellors encourage and practise critical engagement with traditional religious interpretations and cultural practices that they perceive as detrimental. As I will demonstrate in subsequent sections, just as the Problems and Solutions counsellors encourage counselees to reflect on various angles of a difficult situation and its possible solutions, they also encourage counselees to evaluate Islamic positions and ethical stances critically.

Before proceeding to discuss how Islamic values and ethics are integrated into Problems and Solutions counselling, it is important to note that the differentiation between 'teaching the art of fishing' and an 'Islamic framework' is an analytical construction. For most counsellors both of these frames of reference inform their practice simultaneously,[20] as is well illustrated in Khadiga's comment:

> I do not give him a solution. I show him the picture, I create awareness, I try to open up all paths, and to see where each path will lead, within the positives, within the religious boundaries. [They are] not religious answers, but are within the boundaries. We cannot accept the unlawful or not take our society into account, but without it being talk stuffed with Quran verses and *ahadith*.[21]

Khadiga's remark that their counselling is not meant to be packed with religious references is a common sentiment amongst the Problems and Solutions counsellors.[22] Not all counsellors would subscribe wholeheartedly to her statement that 'we cannot accept the unlawful'. Still, several of the counsellors speak of counselling '*within* the boundaries of religion/Islam',[23] and of 'not crossing the red line'. What do they mean by this? More importantly, do they necessarily mean the same thing?

Fluctuating Islamic boundaries

The counselling psychology focus, or therapeutic focus, of IOL and Problems and Solutions counselling goes hand in hand with a more explicitly religious focus. In this section I shall discuss how counsellors describe and operationalize the 'Islamic framework' in their counselling approach.

As quoted above, Omar underlines the relevance to real life and the counselling values of autonomy and empowerment, typical of solution-focused brief therapy and American counselling including the skills focus, or teaching people how to choose. At the same time, he indicates that Islamic values and principles have a role to play in IOL counsellors' responses and that there is a red line that ought not to be crossed. What this response indicates is how all of these influences are integrated into one whole – i.e. the Problems and Solutions counselling model. The responses of Problems and Solutions counsellors indicate that there are more than two interlinked counselling influences, but I employ here two analytical categories in an attempt to demonstrate the multiple influences of the Problems and Solutions counselling model. This is not to say that Problems and Solutions counsellors do not make explicit claims about the religious framework of their counselling praxis and orientation. For instance, Khadiga says: 'All [Problems and Solutions] counsellors have religious ideas, I mean we are all religious, otherwise we would not have chosen IOL, you know.'

At first glance, Problems and Solutions counsellors' references to 'Islamic boundaries' and 'red lines' pose as clear-cut and indisputable admonishments of what is '*halal*' vs. '*ḥarām*'. Observe, for instance, how Dina explains how the concept of religious boundaries may be practised:

> It is important that we do not contradict religion. Someone wishing for more sexual desire will not be told to go watch porn movies [...] We will not contradict religion, the intentions [*maqāsid*] of Shari'a.

The concept *maqāsid* is often translated as 'intentions' (Nielsen & Christoffersen, 2010, 5). Furthermore, *maqāsid* is associated with reform-oriented Islamic thinkers, and may often refer to non-literal interpretations of religious sources with an emphasis on religious values and ethical principles, and adaptation to contemporary society (March, 2010, 10). Another example of staying within 'Islamic boundaries'[24] is provided by Safwat, who states that 'IOL cannot for instance accept "open marriages"'.[25] On a similar note, Omar says:

> For example, if a woman commits illicit sexual acts or adultery [*zina*] with her neighbour, I cannot tell her to continue this relationship. It is outside the religious boundaries [...] So I must advise her to drop that relationship or legalize it [marry him] [...] *Not doing so would be akin to deception.* [26] There are religious boundaries ... there is a red line we do not cross.

A key point raised by Omar is that not mentioning religious boundaries 'would be akin to deception'. This pertains to the assumption that clients seeking counselling on IOL want and expect the counselling answers to be within the religious boundaries. Still, it is important to note that several counsellors remark that considering adultery undesirable is not only Islamic, but 'that this is universal in human relations'. Substantiating this stance, Dina adds: 'What is prohibited in religion is limited [...] it is prohibited because it harms.'

According to Safwat, the Problems and Solutions counsellors' engagement with Islamic boundaries coincides with the expectations of the Problems and Solutions users:

> The one who enters IOL is doing so on the basis of the answer being within the boundaries of Islam. It [IOL counselling] has parts that are social, psychological, educational, etc., but the user wants it Islamic. If he just wanted counselling, he would have gone elsewhere. You do not close in on his choices. Within Islam there [are] many choices [...] but there are the boundaries ... He cares about the boundaries. He entered IOL because he wants to care about the boundaries.

It holds true that both Problems and Solutions clients and counsellors may be concerned with 'Islamic boundaries'. More importantly, how Problems and Solutions counsellors construe what constitutes Islamic boundaries and how transgressions ought to be managed suggest fluctuating boundaries and subjective interpretations. Evidence of fluidity can be found in the following depictions:

> If an Islamic rule is not applicable to a situation, then there is no need to tighten the rope, or make the opening too narrow.
>
> *(Omar)*

> When I have a room that I do not open, I am not *wasati*.
>
> *(Selim)*

These statements illustrate that the *wasatiyya* branding of Problems and Solutions demands that the counsellors do not get too stringent in their interpretations of Islamic boundaries, thereby closing in on too many alternatives for the counselee. In sum, fluidity and flexibility is considered key. In their excellent discussion of religious counselling in the USA, Worthington et al. (2008, 28) contend that how well clashes of value are managed depends on whether or not the counsellor tolerates values outside their own religious beliefs:

> A few therapists have a zone of toleration that is narrowly centered on their own values. They tolerate few differences with others. Most therapists – by selection and by training – have a wide zone of toleration [...] Most therapists

have some limits to their tolerance. Often these limitations arise from religious beliefs and values.

Indeed, my empirical data from IOL support this argument. As discussed in detail elsewhere (Abdel-Fadil, forthcoming), on the question of what is to be considered *ḥarām* vs. *halal*, Problems and Solutions counsellors take varying positions on a continuum ranging from lenient to strict renderings. This is aptly summed up by Khadiga, who not only considers herself 'religiously strict', but also admits to being considered 'a little strict with regards to *halal* and *ḥarām*' by other Problems and Solutions counsellors. In addition, the default counselling styles of Problems and Solutions counsellors range from gentle and compassionate to brutally honest shock therapy. In the following intriguing depiction by Safwat, he not only captures apparent differences between the individual counsellors, but also suggests that there may be an interrelation between a counsellor's zone of tolerance and their preferred counselling style:

> Yes. For example, a certain counsellor may be very strict or firm … For example, if a woman is having extra-marital relations [*zina*], some counsellors say, 'You must end this immediately, and do not make excuses for yourself!' … After this … then they will start to help, but first they will take a firm stand. Another counsellor, will say, 'what are the problems between you [and your husband] that made you have a relationship outside marriage? Is there no satisfaction or saturation of emotional or sexual needs? Or is it because he [the husband] is looking for an extra-marital affair or that he tried to marry a second wife previously?' The counsellor walks with her [client] with gentleness or compassion, a few steps at a time, until she herself is able to make the decision to stop [the extramarital affair].

Safwat implicitly points to the fact that at times there may be a correlation between having a wide zone of tolerance and a gentle counselling approach. Upon closer examination, then, what exactly constitutes 'Islamic boundaries' is fluctuating, situational, subject to individual interpretation, and contingent upon an individual counsellor's zones of tolerance and personal counselling style. Still, it is important to note that for Problems and Solutions counsellors this variation in stance is not considered a flaw that undermines the 'Islamic-ness' of the service, but rather a strength that demonstrates that there may be a spectrum of 'Islamic perspectives' on any given topic, and that it is up to the counselee to select what speaks to her heart or mind.

The Problems and Solutions counselling model fuses secular counselling influences and Islamic ethics into an integrated whole. In line with the analytical distinction between secular and Islamic counselling influences, I maintain that there are two main Problems and Solutions counselling goals within an Islamic framework: 1 cultivating the ethical self; and 2 correcting erroneous religious interpretations, which I will outline in the following.

Cultivating the ethical self

> We are not floggers! It is not our job to judge you [...] We help you so that you can judge yourself, leading to you accepting or not accepting your actions.
>
> *(Dalia)*

Ideally, then, according to Dalia, IOL users ought to rely less on being told what is right and wrong by Problems and Solutions counsellors, and instead learn how to cultivate an ethical self.[27] The statement 'we are not floggers' can be construed as an implicit critique of the 'fear pedagogies' of other Islamic movements.[28] For Problems and Solutions counsellors it is important that ethical acts stem from *conviction* rather than fear of God's wrath. This entails cultivating and acquiring the knowledge and skills to assess whether or not one's actions are ethical.

According to Ziad (personal communication, 15 June 2010),[29] conducting oneself in an ethical manner is also a question of social responsibility and empathy towards other human beings. Ziad recalls how a Problems and Solutions counselee wrote in to IOL stating that he had allegedly turned over a new 'religious' leaf and subsequently abandoned the woman with whom he had engaged in extramarital sexual relations – due to her 'impropriety and immorality' (for engaging in such illicit acts with him). With obvious agitation in his voice, Ziad exclaims that this man may have some serious flaws in his understanding of 'religious', but more importantly, the man's reasoning and conduct are devoid of social responsibility. Ziad conveys that his counselling response to the Problems and Solutions user was not exactly subtle, and then, with an air of theatrical performance, he proceeds to roar out the following admonishment:

> I mean, were you doing it alone?! [...] Your freedom of choice is absolute. I do not judge you 'morally'. I judge you socially. I judge responsibility. It is *your* responsibility for getting into a[n] [extramarital] sexual relationship with this girl.

While some Problems and Solutions counsellors may have centred their response around the immorality of *zina*, and the extramarital affair being beyond the religious boundaries, Ziad is preoccupied with the man in question taking social responsibility for his own acts, and ensuring a basic level of compassion for other humans. At a deeper level, the Problems and Solutions counsellors' preoccupation with self- and social awareness may be said also to reflect an existential stance: that no human is ever truly autonomous or free from all forms of responsibilities to humankind.

Another interesting reflection on the freedom of choice is provided by Dalia, who recollects the following Problems and Solutions online counselling exchange:

I remember this one problem we had, from a young man who wrote that it is a pity that his youth had passed without him being able to live, without him being able to play around or sleep with any girls! [Laughs] [...] [I told him:] 'If you are upset that your time is gone, that your friends were happy and you are not – I tell you that the time has not passed. I am sure you will enjoy these pursuits. But, you sit and think about whether you can accept yourself. If you think you will accept yourself ... I say do it!' [Laughs] [...] Everybody is free to do what they want! But, they must know if it is accepted by religion or not.

Dalia underlines the importance of freedom of choice and self-acceptance for the counselee, while simultaneously making transgressions of 'Islamic boundaries' clear. Agrama (2010, 6), based on anthropological fieldwork at Al-Azhar's Fatwa Council in Cairo, argues: 'Because fatwas are responses to questions about how to live rightly, they are very clearly necessarily part of an ethical practice.' Moreover, Agrama suggests that it is fruitful to consider *fatwas* 'as a form of care of the self, and its authority linked to how it connects selves to broader practices, virtues and aims of contemporary Islamic tradition' (Agrama, 2010, 6). In a similar vein, he argues: 'the fatwa is the practice that puts the questioner on a journey of ethical cultivation', and can be seen as a quest for the 'ideal self' (Agrama, 2010, 12–13). These descriptions I believe are highly suitable for the Problems and Solutions counselling service, even if it cannot be considered a *fatwa* service. In fact, I would argue that cultivation of an ethical self may be even more pronounced in the case of Problems and Solutions counselling.

A recurring concern for Problems and Solutions counsellors is that many Problems and Solutions users appear to have a hollow or superficial understanding of being religious or devout (*multazim*). For Problems and Solutions counsellors, cultivating an ethical self goes hand in hand with harbouring deeper reflections on what *al-iltizām* actually means and how that translates in everyday interactions. It can be useful to think of Problems and Solutions counselling output along a continuum with the analytical constructs 'thinking Islam' and 'living Islam' at either end. I will briefly define them.

'Thinking Islam' entails boiling Islam down to particular ethical principles that the counsellor believes ought to influence contemporary Muslims' way of thought – for instance, 'peaceful', egalitarian, just, responsible, etc. The user is stimulated to think through his or her understanding of Islam both at a general, abstract level, and also to apply these ethics to the specific theme or problem at hand. The other end of the continuum is 'living Islam' and focuses more on the concrete ways to solve the problem at hand at the practical level. Although the abstract ethical principles may not always be explicitly conveyed, they nonetheless influence the repertoire of solutions. Whereas 'thinking Islam' focuses on abstract ideas such as being honourable or ethical, 'living Islam' focuses on 'how to be ethical' in practice. In this sense, the living Islam approach is the translation of thinking Islam into practical life.

In short, in Problems and Solutions counselling, cultivating the ethical self is far more complex than a clear-cut dichotomy of *halal* vs. *ḥarām*.

Correcting erroneous religious interpretations

> It is a problem that men consider women second-rate creatures – some of this is from erroneous interpretations of religion ... Some of it is inherited from customs and traditions.
>
> *(Dalia)*

If they say it is religious, then we have to use religious arguments to break these ideas. For example, [if they say] 'women cannot talk about this', then you must hand it to them as 'Sayyida Aisha did ...' [...] or 'Omar changed his army for women ...' [...] or 'the Prophet's nature as an individual ...'

(Dina)

One professed Problems and Solutions counselling goal is correcting erroneous religious interpretations, and this is particularly evident when counsellors discuss gender relations. Part and parcel of Problems and Solutions counselling is thus contributing to correcting religious misunderstandings that lead to undesired behaviour. Moreover, Problems and Solutions counsellors express a pragmatic attitude with regard to employing religious references because they 'work' or 'have an impact'. Invoking the Prophet Mohammed is the most salient of possible religious connotations, and this fact is not lost on the counsellors. In the words of Nader (personal communication, 13 December 2009):

> If a problem's solution will become clearer by incorporating religious references like *aḥādīth*, we will do this. For example, using the Prophet as an example and role model for fathers could add extra strength to an argument, that fathers should spend more time and play with their children [...] [T]o add extra vigour to an argument, the use of religious sources is very helpful.

The example of the Prophet and *aḥādīth* are thus used in order to strengthen the call to Arab men for a transformation of their 'masculinity' along these suggested lines. A similar plea is made by Selim in the excerpt from Problems and Solutions quoted at the beginning of this chapter. The Prophet Mohammed is depicted as the ideal role model for contemporary husbands to emulate. These are examples of how counsellors may attempt to correct erroneous religious interpretations by citing the exemplary role of the Prophet, a professed goal of Problems and Solutions counselling (Abdel-Fadil, 2011).

While employing the example of the Prophet in this way to motivate men to take a more active role in romance and family life is one with which I am familiar from previous fieldwork in Egypt (Abdel-Fadil, 2002), what was new to me when I studied the case of IOL counselling was how this 'gentle Islamic masculinity construct' – the ideal of a man who shows his emotions and is involved in his family, etc. – is also reminiscent of the construction of 'the new man' in American counselling psychology. Illouz's argument is that the American popular psychology trend has produced a new, 'softer' ideal of masculinity. Illouz (2008) terms this ideal 'the new man' – a man who is both more in touch with his feelings and able to express his emotions. The call for 'the new man' in the Problems and Solutions context looks for inspiration in the past, from the ideal character of the Prophet Mohammed. The Prophet is frequently described in Problems and Solutions counselling exchanges as being a gentle, playful, loving and romantic husband. This is a call for a gentle form of Muslim masculinity, and is consistent with Samuel's (2011, 309) argument that constructs of Muslim masculinity, drawing on the example of the Prophet Mohammed, are being reconfigured towards a 'gentler more feminised male'.[30]

Problems and Solutions counsellors engage in what Woodhead and Heelas (2000) classify as 'detraditionalizing', i.e. critiquing out-dated or conservative religious interpretations, and thereby renewing religious tradition 'from within'. This is most evident in what the counsellors deem 'correcting erroneous religious interpretations', particularly with regard to gender relations. Intriguingly, the Problems and Solutions counsellors explicitly speak of the power and persuasiveness of religious arguments, or what Starrett (1998) has called 'putting Islam to work'. Most importantly, Problems and Solutions counsellors wish to encourage Problems and Solutions counselees to cultivate critical thinking, also in the realm of religious interpretations and authority.

Concluding reflections

The counselling philosophy of Problems and Solutions is founded on the ideal of cultivating self- and social awareness amongst the users of the service. Awareness in this context goes hand in hand with reflecting on ethical principles in Islam, and is fused with therapeutic knowledge. Problems and Solutions counsellors strive to open up the scope of possible Islamic perspectives, and draw on a range of secular sciences and influences, such as psychology, in their enterprise.

The case of IOL and Problems and Solutions demonstrates how 'Islamic' traditions, boundaries and identities are constantly negotiated behind the scenes. Rather than echoing critics of Islam Online in deeming Problems and Solutions 'un-Islamic', I would argue that the Problems and Solutions counsellors' understanding of Islam is an example of what Woodhead and Heelas (2000) label 'religions of humanity'. Indeed, 'religions of humanity' are held to have 'characteristic confidence in the powers of human reason', and tend to be critical of religious tradition:

> Religions of humanity are generally willing to subject what they see as the unquestioned dogmas of previous ages to historical scrutiny. Likewise, they

tend to be respectful of modern science, more generally, and to argue that religious truth can never be allowed to contradict scientific truth. The humane, human experience, and human reason become the measure of truth. Since individuals must be free to choose, decide, believe, and make up their own minds where matters of religion are concerned, both *tolerance* and *freedom*[31] are key values [...] Often they are characterized by a strong sense of the importance of the collective dimension of human existence and by active ethical and political concern [...] They argue that doctrine and dogma are secondary to action. What counts are good deeds, not fine words; compassionate actions, not doctrinal correctness; active love, not empty rituals [...] The best deeds are those which aid one's fellow human beings, respect their rights, and exemplify kindness and compassion [...] Their appropriation of many insights of the modern science – historical, biological, psychological and social-scientific – is another example [of the 'turn to the human'].

(Woodhead & Heelas, 2000, 71–72)

In my view, this description is a very close match to the manner in which Problems and Solutions counsellors construe Islam. It even encompasses the link that the Problems and Solutions counsellors have forged between the religious, the social, the political[32] and the psychological. Deeds, reason, human existence, and active ethical and political concerns are all important features of the ideas and the working practices of the counsellors. Classifying my research participants' approach to religion as a 'religion of humanity' captures the fact that, for Problems and Solutions counsellors, the diversity of sources and influences is intended, crucial and integral to their articulation of Islam.[33] Problems and Solutions and IOL may not satisfy the criteria set by conservative moralists or the counsellors of other Islamic websites for what constitutes 'Islamic', but in my analysis the project is deeply 'Islamic'. By classifying IOL and Problems and Solutions as 'deeply Islamic' I am well aware of the risk of 'putting too much Islam in the anthropology of Islam' (Schielke, 2010). Yet, by categorizing Problems and Solutions counsellors' rendition of Islam as a 'religion of humanity', I hope to have balanced that out and contributed to a more nuanced understanding of how contemporary religious-secular boundaries of Islamic identity may manifest themselves online.

Notes

1 This is a counselling exchange that featured on Islam Online's Arabic website, and in IOL's printed collections of counselling exchanges. The reference is to the printed version. The translation from Arabic into English is my own.
2 I conducted in-depth interviews with a selection of Problems and Solutions counsellors. All interviews were audio-recorded, transcribed and thematically coded in NVIVO. Initially I had planned to use the counsellor's real names in this text, in line with Tilley and Woodthorpe's (2011) discussion of how anonymity may not necessarily always be the ideal for contemporary qualitative research, especially when conducted in urban settings with educated informants who are well aware of what research actually entails. One of the aspects they discuss is that certain research participants *want* to be identified.

Tilley and Woodthorpe argue that at times it might be *un*ethical to deny research participants ownership of their conceptualizations. The recent arrest of one of the key figures of former IOL Arabic, while I prepared this manuscript for publication (October 2015), prompted me to revisit my original intent. In light of political tensions in Egypt, I have taken the extra precaution of anonymizing the citations in this chapter, so as to minimize any potential harm that may be bestowed upon my research participants as a result of this publication.

3 All subsequent quotes from Selim are from this interview.
4 The creation of IOL and the formative years are discussed in detail in Abdel-Fadil (2013).
5 All subsequent quotes from Safwat are from this interview.
6 Following a major dispute between employees in Cairo and funders in Qatar, the Cairo offices of IOL were shut down in March 2010. In August 2010, the Problems and Solutions service migrated to a new website called On Islam, created by previous employees of IOL. At the time of writing (October 2015) new exchanges on Problems and Solutions have been temporarily suspended following lack of funding for the Arabic-language website of On Islam. However, previous counselling Problems and Solutions exchanges are still available online.
7 This is an emic concept, and the main trope of what I have analysed as IOL's 'institutional narrative', building on Linde's work. For more details on 'the message' and IOL's institutional narrative, see Abdel-Fadil (2011, 2013).
8 The two most prominent studies in this genre are those of Charles Hirschkind (2006) and Saba Mahmood (2005).
9 I conducted fieldwork in IOL's main offices in Cairo, from the beginning of December 2009 until the end of June 2010. My research participants include the team that produced Problems and Solutions and counsellors. Dialogues referred to in this article took place in colloquial Egyptian Arabic. Translations into English are my own. By virtue of being of partial Egyptian desent, in the field, I am neither fully an 'insider' nor an 'outsider' but fluctuate somewhere in between. I understand most cultural codes, but am nonetheless not entirely immersed in them. In addition, my research participants and I have overlapping modes of professional knowledge, since I have previously worked as a counsellor. In my view, my counselling background has been important with regards both to facilitating my fieldwork, and the subsequent analysis. In this sense my study can be considered a case of what Hannerz (2004) calls 'studying sideways'.
10 This article draws extensively on semi-structured, in-depth, qualitative interviews, conducted with ten Problems and Solutions counsellors (March–June 2010). I analysed online data that span from 1999 to March 2010. Online monitoring and analysis was carried out from January 2009 to March 2010. I logged tendencies and coded the following online material: counselling essays (protocols) about marital communication; and Problems and Solutions exchanges about pre-marital and marital problems.
11 See Abdel-Fadil (2013) for a more detailed analysis.
12 All subsequent quotes from Omar are from this interview.
13 Emphasis in original speech.
14 It is also interesting that Omar uses the example of his considering divorce the best option for a client. This signals that Problems and Solutions counsellors do not necessarily preach a conservative religious stance on divorce.
15 All subsequent quotes from Khadiga are from this interview.
16 All subsequent quotes from Dina are from this interview.
17 All subsequent quotes from Nadya are from this interview.
18 All subsequent quotes from Dalia are from this interview.
19 For a more in-depth discussion of the influence of secular counselling models, see Abdel-Fadil (2015).
20 Adaptation of secular counselling models to religious ethics (of various religions) appears to be commonplace in the USA, resulting in multiple ad hoc counselling models (Onedera & Greenwalt, 2008; Worthington et al., 2008; Zinnbauer & Pargament, 2000).

21 Traditions about the Prophet Mohammed's utterances and deeds.
22 See Abdel-Fadil (2015) for a more thorough discussion of contrasts between ideals and praxis.
23 *Ḥudūd* is an Arabic word in circulation in everyday language, and means 'limits' or 'boundaries'.
24 Being a practising homosexual is likewise considered unlawful (*ḥarām*), and beyond the boundaries of Islam, although the counsellors' terminology and judgement differ. A discussion of homosexuality is beyond the scope of this article.
25 'Open marriages' is said in English. Open marriage refers to marriage arrangements in which spouses agree that they may pursue sexual relations with partners other than their spouse.
26 My emphasis.
27 For the Problems and Solutions counsellors, it is the 'ethical self' that takes centre stage, in contrast to the empirical data from other studies of Islamists in Egypt, where the 'moral self' is the focal point (Ismail, 2007; Mahmood, 2005).
28 Among the people Mahmood studies, religious symbols (such as the hijab) and the focus on the correct execution of religious rituals are the primary measures of 'morality'. For her research participants in the women's mosque movement in Cairo, the acts of worship are goals in themselves, and serve as both important outward markers of religiosity and a vehicle for the embodiment of faith. Furthermore, Mahmood highlights how the 'fear pedagogies' of the movement's sermons serve to enforce pious acts and 'right praxis'. What is particularly interesting about Mahmood's (2005, 144) research is that her informants are *positive* towards this fear inducement, and consider fear of God 'something that must be learned'. In a similar vein, Rudnyckyj's (2009) analysis of the Emotional and Spiritual Quotient in Indonesia suggests that his informants have a positive evaluation of the fear-inducing elements of the courses. Both ethnographic studies highlight how (albeit in different ways) the emotive elements of fear, through ritualized weeping sessions centred on repenting for past sins, are part and parcel of acts of worship in these two contexts.
29 All subsequent quotes from Ziad are from this interview.
30 Some Problems and Solutions counsellors jokingly refer to Turkish soap operas shaking many marriages in the Arab world. Particularly the lead character Muhanad in the series *Noor* is said to have led to unrealistic expectations of the gentle, compassionate and romantic nature of a future husband, and to have contributed to marital conflicts. According to the Problems and Solutions counsellors, references to Turkish soaps and heightened expectations of romantic partners pop up in counselling exchanges. Indeed, this topic has received both journalistic and scholarly attention. See for instance Gubash (2008), Buccianti (2010) and Salamandra (2012) for more on how Arab audiences are entranced by Turkish soap operas. Still, it can be argued that Muslim ideals of masculinity framed as mirroring the gentle nature of the Prophet Mohammed share a number of the very same traits as the iconic character Muhanad, such as being compassionate and romantic.
31 Emphasis in original.
32 For more on the political goals of IOL and Problems and Solutions, see Abdel-Fadil (2011, 2013, forthcoming).
33 This, however, does not mean that their tolerance is without boundaries. As I have illustrated, the 'zones of tolerance' vary from counsellor to counsellor.

References

Abdel-Fadil, M. (2002) *Whose Right to Divorce in Contemporary Egypt? Competing Interpretations of Islamic Sources*. MPhil thesis, University College of Oslo.
Abdel-Fadil, M. (2011) 'The Islam-Online crisis: a battle of wasatiyya vs. Salafi ideologies?' *CyberOrient*, www.cyberorient.net/article.do?articleId=6239.

Abdel-Fadil, M. (2013) 'Islam offline – living "the message" behind the screens', *Contemporary Islam*, 7(3), pp. 283–309.

Abdel-Fadil, M. (2015) 'Counselling Muslim selves on Islamic websites: walking a tightrope between secular and religious counselling ideals?' *Journal of Religion, Media and Digital Culture*, www.jrmdc.com/journal.

Agrama, H.A. (2010) 'Ethics, tradition, authority: toward an anthropology of the fatwa', *American Ethnologist*, 37(1), p. 16.

Asad, T. (1986) *The Idea of an Anthropology of Islam*. Center for Contemporary Arab Studies, Georgetown University. Occasional Papers Series.

Buccianti, A. (2010) 'Dubbed Turkish soap operas conquering the Arab world: social liberation or cultural alienation?' *Arab Media and Society*, 10.

Bunt, G.R. (2003) *Islam in the Digital Age: e-Jihad, Online Fatwas and Cyber Islamic Environments*. London: Pluto Press.

Campbell, H. (2007) 'Who's got the power? Religious authority and the Internet', *Journal of Computer-Mediated Communication*, 12(3), jcmc.indiana.edu/vol12/issue3/campbell.html.

Gräf, B. (2008) 'IslamOnline.net: independent, interactive, popular', *Arab Media and Society*, www.arabmediasociety.com/?article=576.

Gubash, C. (2008) 'Soap opera upends traditional Arab gender roles', *World Blog NBC News*, worldblog.nbcnews.com/_news/2008/07/31/4376465soap-opera-upends-traditional-arab-gender-roles.

Hannerz, U. (2004) 'Introduction', in *Foreign News: Exploring the World of Correspondents*. Chicago, IL: The University of Chicago Press.

Hirschkind, C. (2006) *The Ethical Soundscape: Cassette Sermons and Islamic Counterpublics*. New York: Columbia University Press.

Hofheinz, A. (2007) 'Arab Internet use: popular trends and public impact', in N. Sakr (Ed.) *Arab Media and Political Renewal: Community, Legitimacy and Public Life*. New York: I.B. Tauris.

Hough, M. (2006) *Counselling Skills and Theory*. London: Hodder Education.

Illouz, Eva (2008) *Saving the Modern Soul: Therapy, Emotions, and the Culture of Self Help*. Berkeley, CA: University of California Press.

IslamOnline.net (2004) *Min Ḥawaā L-Ādam: Shakāwiyy Al-Zawjāt* (From Eve to Adam: The Complaints of Wives). Beirut: Arab Scientific Publishers.

Ismail, S. (2007) 'Islamism, re-Islamization and the fashioning of Muslim selves: refiguring the public sphere', *Muslim World Journal of Human Rights*, 4(1).

Krüger, Oliver (2005) 'Discovering the invisible Internet: methodological aspects of searching religion on the Internet', *Online – Heidelberg Journal of Religions on the Internet*, 1(1), archiv.ub.uniheidelberg.de/ojs/index.php/religions/article/viewFile/385/360.

Linde, C. (2001) 'Narrative and social tacit knowledge', *Journal of Knowledge Management*, 5(2), p. 11.

Mahmood, S. (2005) *Politics of Piety: The Islamic Revival and the Feminist Project*. Princeton, NJ: Princeton University Press.

March, A. (2010) *Shari'a (Islamic Law)*. Oxford: Oxford University Press.

Nielsen, J.S. & Christoffersen, L. (2010) *Shari'a as Discourse: Legal Traditions and the Encounter with Europe*. Farnham: Ashgate.

Onedera, J. & Greenwalt, B. (2008) 'Introduction to religion and marriage and family counseling', in J. Onedera (Ed.) *The Role of Religion in Marriage and Family Counseling*. New York: Routledge.

Rudnyckyj, D. (2009) 'Spiritual economies: Islam and neoliberalism in contemporary Indonesia', *Cultural Anthropology*, 24(1), pp. 104–141.

Salamandra, Christa (2012) 'The Muhannad effect: media panic, melodrama, and the Arab female gaze', *Anthropological Quarterly*, 85(1).
Samuel, G. (2011) 'Islamic piety and masculinity', *Contemporary Islam*, 5(13).
Schielke, S. (2010) 'Second thoughts about the anthropology of Islam, or how to make sense of grand schemes in everyday life', *Zentrum Moderner Orient*, Working Papers, p. 2.
Starrett, G. (1998) *Putting Islam to Work: Education, Politics, and Religious Transformation in Egypt*. London: University of California Press.
Tilley, L. & Woodthorpe, K. (2011) 'Is it the end for anonymity as we know it? A critical examination of the ethical principle of anonymity in the context of 21st century demands on the qualitative researcher', *Qualitative Research*, 11(2).
Woodhead, L. & Heelas, P. (2000) *Religion in Modern Times: An Interpretive Anthology*. Oxford: Blackwell Publishers.
Worthington, E.L. et al. (2008) 'The effects of a therapist's religion on the marriage therapist and marriage counseling', in J. Onedera (Ed.) *The Role of Religion in Marriage and Family Counseling*. New York: Routledge.
Zinnbauer, B.J. & Pargament, K. (2000) 'Working with the sacred: four approaches to religious and spiritual issues in counseling', *Journal of Counseling & Development*, 78(2).

16
ISLAM IN THE NEWS
The case of Al Jazeera Arabic and the Muslim Brotherhood

Mohammed-Ali Abunajela and Noha Mellor

Introduction

In 2006, the Mohammed cartoon controversy triggered a hot debate amongst European journalists regarding the distinction between freedom of speech versus respect for religion (Phillips & Lee, 2007). Several Arab media were very critical of the cartoons, thereby showing solidarity with the audiences who found the cartoons offensive and unethical (Mohamad, 2006). The controversy provided a vivid example of the intersection between news media and religion, which lies at the heart of this chapter. Stolow (2005, 120) argues that '[t]he conjunction "religion and media" encloses a vast array of objects, practices, discourses, modes of knowledge and techniques of representation – a multiplicity which is just as much the product of a flourishing arena of activity as it is of the enhanced'. Perhaps the central concern in the study of media and religion, particularly Islam, is how individuals and groups use media to construct religious meaning in life (White, 2007), given that Islam regulates all aspects of human life.

This chapter sheds new light on the link between the media and Islam, focusing on the coverage of the Muslim Brotherhood (MB) by Al Jazeera Arabic as one topical and recent example. In July 2013, a military coup, with apparent popular support, overthrew the MB's Mohammed Morsi, who, together with other MB leaders, were put in jail and prosecuted. Egyptian media outlets linked to Islamists were shut down, as were all Al Jazeera's offices, and its journalists were banned entry into Egypt. According to the BBC News (2014), about 20 reporters from Al Jazeera Mubashir Masr (Egypt Live) and Al Jazeera English were arrested and charged with joining or aiding a terrorist organization – the MB. *Gulf News* reported that some 22 members of Al Jazeera Mubashir Masr resigned over 'biased' coverage (Sharaf, 2013). This chapter zooms in on Al Jazeera Arabic journalists' perception of their professional mission and how distinct this can be from their identity as Muslims.

We argue that journalists from Al Jazeera Arabic and Al Jazeera Mubashir Masr have managed to reconcile religious ethics with their professional code of detachment and objectivity, which has been influenced by Anglo-American values. Ethics here is understood as the process of 'pursuing an understanding of morality, which provides understandings of ourselves as bearers of responsibilities in the service of values' (Walker, 2000, 89). We situate this discussion within the overall emerging discipline of media and religion, illustrating how some gestures by professional journalists, e.g. wearing the veil or defending a religious group, could serve as a counter-hegemonic act against authoritarian rule while asserting a new professional identity balancing journalistic codes with Islamic ethics.

The intricate relationship between media and religion

The study of media and religion, according to Paul Soukup (2002), can help us comprehend how and why religion appears in the media as it does, and to understand why and how a social force like religion interacts with the other primary social forces. By and large, religion has overwhelmed the fields of mass communication research and media studies (Hoover, 2002). There are studies that enforce the role of the media as the primary source of religious ideas, drawing on a discourse that shapes religious imagination in accordance with the genres of popular culture (Hjarvard, 2006, 2). The media, therefore, are significant social agents, with the potential to influence community perceptions (Akbarzadeh & Smith, 2005), including religious perception and ideology. Media, then, play an important social role in our community and its ability to influence people means that journalists too are shaped by various social forces, which contribute to their understanding of religion such as Islam. Also, editorial practices and writing styles can significantly shape the type of language and images that will form portrayals of Muslims and Islam, and the type of information provided (ibid.). Although the media often play a decisive role in shaping public perceptions of religions and cultural diversity, they may well also be disruptive when focusing on negative aspects of a certain faith, particularly those related to fundamentalist views (Lefebvre & Guyver, 2009).

As Stewart Hoover (2002) argues, the study of media and religion must take into account the question of lived culture and actual practice. It must be methodologically daring, inventive and creative. It is a study that explains how and where this construction is articulated and made meaningful. Stig Hjarvard (2006, 1) also contends that a theory of the interface between media and religion must consider the media and religion in the proper cultural and historical contexts, and the mediatization of religion is not assumed to be a universal phenomenon, historically, culturally or geographically. The media as a cultural environment have taken over many of the social functions of the institutionalized religions, providing both moral and spiritual guidance and a sense of community.

As far as the news media are concerned, the key question is whether journalists let their religious beliefs guide their reporting (Biernatzki, 1995). In the USA, for instance, journalism is regarded as a secular profession, with journalists serving as watchdogs defending the right of people against the power of state (Steele, 2011, 535), and thus '[t]he journalistic impulse to detach, to be an observer, to watch the world from the safety of the outsider's stance is endemic to the profession, and the challenge to this position by those who claim that religious experience should be trusted can be a deeply disturbing proposition for the journalistic personality' (Underwood, 2008, 27). The role exerted by Islam as a religious influence in an Arab newsroom is a case in point. In fact, Islam is argued to exert a great influence on Muslim journalistic practices such as in the case in the Arab region, as we discuss in the next section.

The media and Islam

Lawrence Pintak (2008) sees that Islam for many Muslims is a complete way of life. According to Pintak, the Islamic approach calls for the media actively to 'form' or shape 'a correct opinion' in the minds of the news consumers, hence a proactive stance built on a specific agenda, and in this case *dawa*, the Muslim call to follow the straight path to God. Pintak (2014) further argues that journalists in Muslim countries aspire to Western-style journalistic values such as seeking the truth and being impartial, but they do so within their own social, political and cultural constraints. In contrast to a Western orientation to news, the Islamic conceptualization of communication embraces 'the entire gamut of socio-cultural structure and function', with the 'imperative for stimulating any social change' (Elliott & Greer, 2010, 417).

What defines Muslim communication is a topic of great debate. Siddiqi (2013, 19) noted that 'no firm definition of the Muslim media exists, but the determining elements of content, media ethics and commitment to Islam are often used as a rough guide'. Islamic conferences have striven to define a Muslim approach to communication by developing a Muslim code of journalism that emphasizes Islamic rules of conduct for the journalist and consolidation of the faith in the individuals as the goal of the communication message (ibid., 20).

Lawrence Pintak (2008) argues that modern media technologies including satellite television and the avalanche of new media have transformed communication, redefined Muslim identity politics and put control of science into the hands of anyone with a computer. It was known that the primary mission of Arab journalism is that of fostering political and social change in the Arab world, with a secondary role of defending the Arab/Muslim people and values against outside interference. Pintak (2008), however, debates the idea that Arab journalists are significantly less overtly religious than their respective publics. Muslim Arab journalists, in contrast to journalists in other Muslim countries such as Pakistan and Indonesia, tend to appear more secular-oriented in that they are less likely to define themselves as religious Muslims and they accept state laws that may contradict Islamic Sharia (Pintak, 2014). In fact, Pintak (2014) argues that Muslim clergies were seldom cited in Arab newspapers, despite the central role of the Islamic religion in Arab countries. Because these news accounts were in English and aimed at a world audience, the emphasis may primarily aim to bridge between groups rather than promote divisions. This aligns with Mowlana's (2008) definition of *tabligh*, being a way to reach out to others and show a way of life rather than using communication merely for religious propaganda. The influence of Islam needs to be considered an influence on the concept of newsworthiness, and those previous ideas of government–press relationships or development journalism may be affected by the religious values of this faith, such as the influence Islam may have on the choice of topic, actors in the news, orientation of the news and use of sources (Elliott & Greer, 2010, 426–427).

Indeed, one key question in this intricate dynamism between religion and news reporting is the influence of Islamic values on Arab journalistic ethics. Clearly, journalists mediate a sense of reality to their audiences, and in so doing they entrench one main signifier of their professional identity as the public's confidant. At the heart of this role is the task of transmitting facts, exalting objectivity as the dominant norm, at least in the Anglo-American journalistic model. The news, then, has become the manifestation of the 'culture of factuality' (McNair, 2005, 27), where the real acquires a privileged status. Like their American counterparts, Arab journalists desire to embrace objectivity while keeping a safe distance from subjectivity or indulging in emotion, thus parting company with an old stereotype of the Arab journalist as a mouthpiece and mere stenographer for political forces. However, there are also other antagonistic identities as counter-hegemonic points of identification for journalists. Carpentier (2005) places objectivity at one level on a continuum, stressing factuality and impartiality, and linking it to the autonomous identity of the journalist as watchdog, juxtaposed at the other level of the continuum to subjective identifications of the journalist as ideologist. Thus, journalists can assume a position at any of these points without totally abandoning the hegemonic articulation of the professional identity. The identity of a journalist is then based on a set of roles and identification points of objectivity (a natural and impartial account of events) and subjectivity (the interpretation and investigation of truth).

For Arab journalists, social responsibility is one of the most important ethical values in their profession. This was mentioned in the Arab Journalists Union's charter in 1964, stating that Arab journalists should be honest in expressing their own editorial opinion, bearing in mind the general consequences of that opinion on the general public. They should also be careful in gathering news and should verify the information they have before publishing it. Another obligation is to avoid distorting facts, and not to seek personal interest. Social responsibility is not only confined to the task of reporting and commenting on the news, but journalists are also obligated to reveal other journalists' violation of these codes (Al Jammal, 2001, 66f). For scholars propagating the development of Islamic journalistic ethical code (such as Siddiqi, 2013), the value of social responsibility should not be interpreted from the secular or Western media perspective, which roots this value in pluralistic individualism. The Islamic principle of social responsibility, however, is based on 'commanding right and prohibiting wrong', or preparing individuals and the community to accept Islamic principles and apply them in their daily lives in order to serve society (Siddiqi, 2013). Community here can refer to the *Ummah*, or the larger Muslim community across the world, and the role of journalists here is to create cohesion and unity while eliminating tension and conflict within the community (ibid.). Thus, social responsibility as a major journalistic task in Arab newsrooms echoes the concept of communitarianism, seeing the individual as interdependent with the group, acting for the benefit of the whole community and not just for themselves. In light of this, responsibility, objectivity and detachment, valued in liberal Anglo-American journalistic ethics, may come second to the value of fairness and justice for the community (Coleman, 2000, 51–52).

Moreover, Muslim journalists may be motivated by the goal of justice rather than freedom, argues Steele (2011, 543), and they are likely to show obedience to their ruler except when the ruler exerts unjust powers, which could motivate rebellion against the ruler. Such rebellion, argues the Egyptian Islamic thinker Muhammad I'mara (1988, 11), can trigger angry revolution, which he equates with 'victory', implying a radical change and also the victory of the weak and oppressed. As a religion, argues I'mara, Islam is in itself an embodiment of an ideological, social and political revolution in the history of mankind (ibid., 18), for it rebelled against many of the social customs and traditions at that time.

One vivid example illustrating the conflicting values of subjectivity and objectivity is the case of the pan-Arab channel Al Jazeera, which was claimed to have an Islamic stance (Fandy, 2000). It is notable that Al Jazeera has profiled itself in the Arab world not only by its distinctive news coverage but also by a very few religious programmes. For instance, Barkho (2009, 85) asserts that Al Jazeera relies on its religious programmes to garner and sustain wide viewership, and it has propelled Sheikh Yousef Qaradawi to star status in the Arab and Muslim world for his weekly phone-in programme, *Al-Sharia wal-Hayat* (Islamic Law and Life). Qaradawi gained popularity and legitimacy throughout the Arab world by questioning the authority of the state, reaching a broad audience through his regular appearances on Al Jazeera (Malka, 2003).

Indeed, since its establishment, Al Jazeera has thoroughly covered key historical moments in the Arab world, including the wars in Iraq 2003, Lebanon 2006, Gaza 2008/09, and most recently the so-called Arab Spring. Largely, the channel has been claimed to revive the sense of pan-Arab identity and to have revolutionized the Arab media scene.

Al Jazeera: a secular or Islamic voice?

Khaled Hroub (2011) noted that, for 15 years, Al Jazeera created a new venue for political freedom, which has culminated in its unreserved support for Arab revolutions. Al Jazeera's scope of influence on the public represents a turning point in the history of the Arab mass media (Al-Theidi, 2003). Many of Al Jazeera's correspondents were drawn to work for the station because they believe that it provides an alternative perspective, particularly from the American and British news media

(Sharp, 2003; El-Nawawy & Iskandar, 2003). Several scholars (e.g. Miladi, 2003; Seib, 2005; Quinn & Walters, 2010; Ghosh, 2003) assert that Al Jazeera has inspired other Arab channels to improve their broadcasting quality and open up to opposing views. The station stands as an example of pushing the boundaries of what is politically possible on Arab television. It gives more than the official view, and deliberately offers opinions from different viewpoints, creating ripples in the stagnant pool of Arabic broadcasting. Al Jazeera's reputation for controversy, while operating in Qatar rather than a European capital, represents a breakthrough in media-related development in the Middle East (Sakr, 1999). Philip Seib (2008) argues that Al Jazeera may not be a stalking horse for the United States, Israel, Islam, or even Qatar's ruling family, but it is the latest in a line of media ventures that have sought to use mass media to help establish a pan-Arab identity.

The channel's funding revenue has been under scholars' scrutiny. This factor represents an ongoing temptation for researchers to define the thin-line boundaries between the channel and its major financial sponsor, Qatar. Tatham (2006) claims that the failure of Al Jazeera to approach financial independence is due to limited advertising revenue, thus obliging the station to maintain its relationship with the Qatari royal family in order to survive. However, Khalil Rinnawi (2006, 92) retains his enthusiasm for Al Jazeera's future plans to approach independence, while Zayani (2005) critically points out that, due to the financial support from Qatar, the channel rarely criticizes the country's domestic and foreign policy.

Although a substantial topic, the extent to which Al Jazeera helps promote Islamic values has been under-represented in Arab and Western scholarship, with the exception of a few studies on Al Jazeera's promotion of the Islamic veil. For instance, Sam Cherribi (2006) notes that Al Jazeera is equivalent to the Christian Broadcasting Network (CBN) and not to the Central News Agency (CNN). He argues that Al Jazeera devotes significant time to the views of Islamic leaders, and its religious message is mono-denominational. Moreover, Dima Dabbous-Sensenig (2006) provides an analysis of selected episodes from the *Al-Sharia wal-Hayat* television programme, and argues that the show promotes 'the opinion and the same opinion', contrary to Al Jazeera's motto, *Opinion and Another Opinion*. According to Dabbous-Sensenig, the diversity that is celebrated in Al Jazeera news and current affairs is abandoned in its religious programmes, which promote 'Orthodox Islamic discourse' (ibid., 64). This, argues Abeer Al-Najjar (2009), poses one of the main challenges facing Al Jazeera English in the West to maintain its brand, given the reputation of its sister Al Jazeera Arabic, with the latter channel being accused by many US officials of being representative of 'terrorists and Jihadists', 'Jihad TV', 'Killers with Cameras' or 'the most powerful ally of terror in the world' (ibid., 4).

Likewise, Haim Malka (2003) argues that the Islamic debate over suicide attacks is described by Al Jazeera as 'martyrdom operations' against Israel. He argues that some Muslim clerics and other commentators justify such attacks on political, moral and religious grounds. Moreover, Oren Kessler (2012) explains that the channel is perceived as favouring freedom and democracy against dictatorships, but clearly appears to be supporting Islamic parties. Kessler demonstrates how the channel promoted the Taliban in Afghanistan and similarly in Iraq: 'words like terror and insurgency are rarely mentioned with a straight face, usually replaced with "resistance" or "struggle".' It also shows the US viewpoint on Al Jazeera coverage of Arab upheavals. Kessler projects other opposing views like those of Judea Pearl, who warned that 'unconditional support of Hamas's terror in Gaza, the Hezbollah takeover in Lebanon and the Syrian and Iranian regimes betray any illusion that democracy and human rights are on al-Jazeera's agenda'. Judea Pearl further argues that the channel's agenda is being 'the most powerful voice of the MB' (quoted in Kessler, 2012, 49).

More recently, Sultan Al-Qassemi (2012) criticized Al Jazeera Arabic and its relationship with the MB, and argued that Al Jazeera's love affair with the MB was evident from the very beginning. He further claimed that such a relationship is mutually beneficial due to its blatant bias towards the MB. Ahmed Mansour, Al Jazeera Arabic's star presenter and an MB member, was rewarded with several interviews not only with Khairet El-Shater, but also with General Guide Mohammed Badie and Mohammed Morsi, argues Al-Qassemi: 'The Brotherhood also appreciates this relationship and even bizarrely extends official congratulations and "support" to al-Jazeera on significant occasions. When Morsi's office wanted to kill the story of what seemed to be a fabricated Iran news-agency interview with the president, it knew exactly who to call' (ibid.).

In his article on the Middle East Online, Ahmad Azem (2012) argues that the alliance between the MB and Qatar is becoming a noticeable factor in the reshaping of the Middle East. Also, the Israeli former ambassador in Egypt, Zvi Mazel (2009), notes that this relationship has existed since the second half of the 20th century. 'The first wave came from Egypt in 1954, after Nasser had destroyed their organisation. The next wave came from Syria in 1982 after Hafez el-Assad bombed their stronghold in Hama. The last group arrived after September 11, 2001 – from Saudi Arabia.' This should be seen in light of recent developments: for instance, in February 2012 the political leadership of Palestinian Islamist group Hamas moved from Syria to Qatar (Cafiero, 2012). In 2013 Afghanistan's Taliban movement opened its first official overseas office in Qatar (BBC News, 2013). Notable is the paradox in Qatar's foreign policies: it not only accommodates Islamists but also hosts one of the biggest US military bases, Al-Udeid. Rinnawi (2006) suggests that Qatar possibly has a desire to occupy a leading role in the region and therefore requires a solid PR tool such as Al Jazeera. According to WikiLeaks documents, Qatar may be using Al Jazeera as a bargaining card in its foreign policy towards Iran, Hezbollah and Syria, and also to enhance Qatar's relationship with other nations, particularly Saudi Arabia. Thus, the transnational channel has proven an influential source of power for Qatar (Tamimi, 2012, 84–85).

In an attempt to explore further this link between Al Jazeera and the Muslim Brotherhood, the next section draws on the views of a selected sample of Al Jazeera Arabic's main anchors and presenters, situating these views in the context of Islamic ethics, which, for these professionals, are reconcilable with the Anglo-American values of objectivity and impartiality, which for them justifies the stance they take in covering the MB. The journalists were asked specifically about their channel's relationship with the MB and their evaluation of their coverage of the MB since the toppling of Morsi's rule in July 2013.

Al Jazeera journalists: a voice for voiceless Muslims

One way of examining journalistic practices, argues Zelizer (2004, 176), is to apply the cultural inquiry of journalism, which sees journalism 'through journalists' own eyes'. The cultural analysis of journalism helps shed light on the way journalists act as 'producers of culture, who impart preference statements about what is good and bad, moral and amoral, and appropriate and inappropriate in the world' (Zelizer, 2004, 177). Incorporating this methodological consideration into our study of Al Jazeera's journalists, we relied on interviews with seven main anchors and presenters, of whom one left Al Jazeera in 2013, following the closure of their offices in Egypt. The interviewees also include the former head of Al Jazeera Arabic, Wadah Khanfar. The interviews were supplemented by discourse analysis of several episodes of two flagship programmes on Al Jazeera Arabic but, due to the limited scope of this chapter, we focus only on a selected sample of the interviews. The interviews were conducted between January and March 2014, suggesting some responses to the criticism facing Al Jazeera Arabic that the channel supports Islamists, particularly the Muslim Brotherhood, and that support has been intensified since the toppling of Morsi's rule in Egypt in July 2013. The selected sample of anchors were also asked to situate this harsh criticism within the overall ethical standards of objectivity and impartiality.

The most important theme emerging from these interviews was the need to incorporate the value of communitarianism and social responsibility into journalistic practices in Arab journalism. One way of highlighting this responsibility is through giving a voice to voiceless Muslims and politically marginalized groups in Arab societies. For instance, Mohammed Krishan, presenter of the flagship programme *Revolution Talk*, launched early 2011, said that people should acknowledge the fact that the most powerful opposition movements in the Arab world are Islamists. When Al Jazeera covers their news all the time, it may appear to support Islamists: 'If the strongest opposition movements were Marxists, Al Jazeera might appear to support Marxism.' He admitted that some presenters occasionally show empathy towards Islamists. He also said that Al Jazeera always provides the MB with a media platform that has been denied them in their own country: 'Some movements in Egypt wish to close their eyes and then open them to find the MB [has] disappeared. The MB is an existing political power and if people consider al-Jazeera as giving them the platform is empathy, then it's up to them.'

Khadija Ben Gannah, one of the main anchors, who also created headlines around the world following her adoption of the veil (Cherribi, 2006), explained that Al Jazeera Arabic supports human beings and the will of nations, therefore, as revolutions belong to nations rebelling against standing regimes, Al Jazeera Arabic supports such revolutions:

> If we put countries of Arab revolutions under the microscope, we'll see that the MB, and Islamists in general, were the most prominent element in the electoral scene. How can any media service ignore their existence? [...] If we take the case of Egypt, should al Jazeera take the side of Morsi's supporters against Sisi's supporters or the side of those who support democratic rule via voting ballots? I think al Jazeera remained faithful to its mission which is to stand by the right [...] if people elected president, government and regime, then al Jazeera takes the sides of those voters who insisted on reclaiming legitimacy [shariyaa]. Even if al Jazeera has lost a number of viewers in Egypt, although I don't have statistics to know, it still won ethically. Because if it loses by taking sides, then it wins by being faithful to its ethical mission.

When Ben Gannah was asked about the reasons for closing all Al Jazeera network offices and arresting its journalists in Egypt, she argued that such action against Al Jazeera was because the channel constitutes a concern for the authorities and because the regime that overthrew the legitimate president is itself illegitimate. According to Ben Gannah, however, Al Jazeera has not abandoned its liberalistic ethics of objectivity, by providing a platform to the military council and to liberal and secular voices as much as it has given to the MB.

The former head of Al Jazeera Network, Wadah Khanfar, shares this view that sees journalism as centring on compassion:

> In journalism, there is compassion towards victims, not because they are Brotherhood, secularists or nationalists. You show compassion towards victims of injustice [...] if we do not do this, we would not be fair or neutral. Impartiality does not mean standing in the middle between what is right and what is clearly an assault on freedoms [without saying anything]. Al Jazeera's code of ethics tell[s] us that we are here to defend Arabs' right to knowledge, freedom and democracy.

Waddah Khanfar, who resigned almost a year after the breakout of the revolutions, said that media services sometimes sympathize with oppressed human beings: 'al-Jazeera's code of conduct clearly states in its opening that the institution stands for the Arab citizens' rights to knowledge, freedom, democracy and choosing their own government. This isn't a secret. In my view, standing beside the Arab Spring is in line with our values adopted by the channel.' When asked about the Al Jazeera motto, he agreed that it should be revisited, as people no longer have the opinion of opposition versus the opinion of government: 'now we have different views and colours, I hope to find a motto that is more comprehensive to address this era.'

For Ahmed Mansour, the presenter of *Without Border*, the Western notion of media impartiality is a lie: 'Journalists should always stand on the side of the weak and the oppressed. Journalists are witnesses of truth not lies – this is what I've learned from international media teachers.' Although Mansour is known for his empathy towards the MB, he denied such accusations and noted that his role as a presenter is to challenge all views, including those of Islamists. It is worth noting that Mansour's social media posts have been followed closely by a number of Egyptian media outlets who accuse Mansour of using social media to incite public opinion against the Egyptian Army and President Abdelfattah el-Sisi. One example was a Facebook post published in February 2014, claimed to belong to Mansour, in which there was explicit incitement to kill Egyptian security officers. Mansour immediately denied that he owned a Facebook account and said that the post was fabricated in order to tarnish his name. The post was circulated via Ikhwan Online, the Muslim Brotherhood Internet portal, but the site later announced that the Facebook post attributed to Mansour was not verified by official sources, and condemned the attack on Mansour. Several mainstream media such as the newspaper *Youm el-Sabei* (or Youm7) launched an offensive against Mansour, casting doubt on his motives for writing such a post, and two television anchors on Tahrir TV, Rania Badawi and Jihan Mansour, demanded the revocation of Mansour's Egyptian citizenship as a penalty for his alleged Facebook post. The post has also prompted the Egyptian Journalists Syndicate to threaten to dismiss Mansour from the Syndicate, but Mansour warned that he would take all legal measures against the Syndicate if it went ahead with this dismissal (Al Jazeera, 2014). Mansour tweeted that he never wrote the Facebook post and that the Egyptian authorities had misled the media, including Ikhwan Online, to publish this post under his name. Nonetheless, Mansour does not hesitate to express his personal view on Twitter, and never concealed his rejection of the rule of el-Sisi and the overthrow of the Brotherhood. In one tweet, for instance, posted on 8 August 2014, Mansour wrote that the current President 'Abdel Fattah el-Sisi, who stole the nation, army and Egyptians' will and wealth and hope, has stolen the Suez Canal project from President Mohamed Morsi'. In October 2014, Mansour was sentenced in absentia to 15 years' prison on charges of torturing and assaulting a lawyer in 2011 during the uprisings against Mubarak (Nader, 2014).

Zein al Abeeden Tawfik, the former BBC Arabic presenter and one of the main anchors on Al Jazeera Mubashir Masr, sees his audience as subscribing to the Islamic *nahda* [revival] project:

> Al Jazeera embraced the issue of Palestine which is the closest to Arab viewers and adopted other issues of importance to our identity and the Islamic nation. Talking as a viewer and not on the name of the channel, I think no one follows al Jazeera unless they have a national, Islamic or *nahda* project, because this kind of media informs citizens about their rights and what matters to them … The time is ripe for such revolutions, after suffering social, political and economic blockage. These are reforming revolutions and they can take place anywhere in the world … Political Islam movements are the most popular in the Arab world and they reconcile with the [Islamic] nation's heritage and tradition. They represent an ideology that is the most spread amongst Arab populations. Are they substitute for dictators? I do not know, but only

voting ballots can shows us. But what is the best alternative for dictators? I think it is the democratic rule where citizens practice their freedoms, regardless of whether Islamists or secularists rule the region.

Surely these presenters can understand the accusations against Al Jazeera as being a tool in Qatar's foreign policy. For instance, Mohammed Krishan notes that Qatar's increasing role in the Arab world has made it considerably difficult to convince audiences that Qatar's policies have no influence on Al Jazeera:

> I do not blame those who see matching between the editorial line of al-Jazeera and Qatar policy, because it is difficult, for example, to see a separating line between France and Channel 24, Russia and Russia Today Channel, and between the US and al-Hurra TV, and so on. However, we need to be fair in saying that the impact of Qatar's policy on al-Jazeera is not in all aspects. Qatar's role in the Arab Spring countries might be seen more predominant than in other countries, but it is not possible for us to cover everything, according to Qatar's foreign policies.

Mahmoud Mourad, one of Al Jazeera presenters, confirms the same view: 'I don't think states set up satellite channels as a form of charity [with no gain]. [T]ake the BBC for instance, it somehow works to fulfil the aims of the British foreign policy [...] I personally do not think there is a contradiction between al Jazeera's editorial line and the Qatari foreign policy.'

Thus, through the rhetoric of justice and helping the weak groups in society, these journalists establish an implicit link between their religious ethics and journalistic practice. In so doing, they implicitly apply the Islamic principle based on the belief of media freedom conditioned by the individual's accountability before God and one's duty towards society and other citizens (Hegab, 2002, 80).

On the other hand, those who left Al Jazeera (or Al Jazeera Mubashir Masr) following the toppling of Morsi in July 2013 prefer to justify their exit by their belief in the Western value of objectivity, which Al Jazeera, they argue, failed to embrace during that period. For instance, the former BBC journalist Karem Mahmoud, a presenter who resigned from Al Jazeera Mubashir Masr due to what he described as editorial partiality towards the MB, says that 'audiences in Egypt have seen bias in al-Jazeera's telling of what is happening in Egypt. When al-Jazeera has chosen to stand by the MB's side, they've lost the trust of Egyptian people [...] It has opened its doors widely to the provocative speeches delivered by the MB leaders from Rabia'a Square, from where they protested'. Mahmoud also argues that Qatar, a tiny emirate, has gained a global brand by being 'the country that hosts al-Jazeera', and that 'no one would think that there's a split-up between Qatar and al-Jazeera's editorial policies'.

Through its coverage of the so-called Arab Spring, it has been argued that Al Jazeera's self-references reflect the station's position in the ongoing conflicts. For instance, Nasr (2014, 410) contends that the analysis of Al Jazeera's visual discourse shows how the station 'embeds its journalists among the freedom fighters on the ground, evoking a fusion of news anchors, reporters, and camera operators with citizen rebels and victims of state oppression. Rather than focusing exclusively on reporting news of the rebellion, al-Jazeera identifies its central role as democratizing the world both in how it documents the world as well as in how it reaches that world through its broadcasts'. Moreover, Mehdi (2011) highlights the losses of Al Jazeera correspondents and producers, of whom some were arrested and harmed, such as the cameraman Ali Hassan al-Jaber, who was killed by pro-Gaddafi fighters in Libya.

Conclusion

The above case study illustrates how Al Jazeera Arabic's anchors justify the station's stance, especially in their coverage of the toppling of the Brotherhood's rule in Egypt since 2013. In particular, the justification seems to rest on the influence of value of communitarianism where journalism aligns with the Islamic ethics of aiding victims while combating injustice. In fact, several Arab media scholars advocating the incorporation of Islamic ethics into journalistic practices (such as Al-Demeiry, 1988, 64) argue that news in Islam has different functions, such as advancing the culture in Islamic societies through good deeds, exalting good Muslims, revealing the corrupt and discouraging bad deeds. Seen in light of these functions, news is defined as: 'a truthful account or substantiated report about an event and its value is conditioned by its usefulness to people's lives' (ibid.).

For the majority of Al Jazeera journalists, the MB are the victims, and therefore it is the channel's moral duty to defend the MB's rights against injustice as they are the 'voiceless', the 'oppressed' and the 'weak'. Such an issue is widely contested and Al Jazeera Arabic has chosen to stand on one side against the other, which lost the channel at least those viewers who are supporting the military role rather than the MB. Moreover, the journalists' use of social media was a good example of how much the channel was actively participating by showing its opinions and expressing views during unfolding events in the Arab Spring countries such as Egypt. Some presenters such as Mansour regularly criticize the military coup against the MB, therefore positioning themselves and, arguably, the channel in favour of the Islamic movement, the MB, while angering supporters of the military coup and the so-called *Floul* (remnants) or supporters of Mubarak.

Indeed, Al Jazeera journalists may appeal to the ethical, moral and cultural values of Islam as a driver to give voice to the voiceless, or those whom they regard as the weak groups in society, although it is fair to say that the station has not provided a similar opportunity when covering other minorities or groups such as Bahaais or Shiite. On the other hand, other journalists, such as those who resigned from Al Jazeera in protest at its ideological stance, may hold on to the Western concept of objectivity in an attempt to detach themselves from Al Jazeera coverage.

The aim of the above discussion was to revive the debate about the impact of religious values on journalists' professional identity and practices. Indeed, journalists' professional identity is not fixed, 'but fluid and unstable', argue Zandberg and Neiger (2005, 141), inasmuch as journalists may move back and forth between a professional community that propagates libertarian ethics like objectivity and detachment, and a national hegemonic community (ibid.). In addition, pan-Islamic identity represents another value in addition to the national (territorial) patriotism that is part of the professional identity of Arab journalists. This is especially true in pan-Arab newsrooms such as Al Jazeera, where journalists represent a range of Arab nationalities but may feel united by their religious values.

References

Akbarzadeh, Shahram & Smith, Bianca (2005) 'The Representation of Islam and Muslims in the Media', *School of Political and Social Inquiry*.
Al-Demeiry, Moustafa (1988) *The Press in Islam*. Mecca: University Student Publishing.
Al Jammal, Rasem M. (2001) *Communication and Media in the Arab World* (in Arabic). Second edition. Beirut: Center for Arab Unity Studies.
Al Jazeera (2014) 'Ahmed Mansour disown an article inciting to violence', *Al Jazeera.net*, 25 February, www.aljazeera.net/news/arabic/2014/2/25/أحمد-منصور-يتبرأ-من-مقال-يحرّض-على-القتل.
Al-Najjar, A. (2009) 'How Arab is Al Jazeera English? Comparative study of Al Jazeera Arabic and Al Jazeera English news channels', *Global Media Journal*, 8(14).
Al-Qassemi, S. (2012) 'Morsi's win is Al Jazeera's loss', *Al Monitor*, www.al-monitor.com/pulse/originals/2012/al-monitor/morsys-win-is-al-jazeeras-loss.html (accessed 15 June 2013).
Al-Theidi, A. (2003) Al-Jazeera Satellite Channel: From Regional to Global – A Question of Objectivity and News Flow. Brighton: University of Sussex.
Azem, A. (2012) 'Qatar's ties with the Muslim Brotherhood affect entire region', Middle East Online, www.middle-east-online.com/english/?id=52341 (accessed 2 March 2014).
Barkho, Leon (2009) 'Fundamentalism in Arab and Muslim media', in Stewart M. Hoover & Nadia Kaneva (Eds) *Fundamentalisms and the Media*. London: Continuum International Publishing Group.
BBC News (2013) 'Q&A: Afghan Taliban open Doha office', www.bbc.co.uk/news/world-asia-22957827 (accessed 3 March 2014).
BBC News (2014) 'Al Jazeera journalists deny charges at Egypt trial', www.bbc.co.uk/news/world-middle-east-26268692 (accessed 2 March 2014).
Biernatzki, W.E. (1995) 'Religion in the mass media', *Communication Research Trends*, 15(2), 1, pp. 3–37.
Cafiero, G. (2012) 'Foreign policy in focus: "Hamas in the new Middle East"', fpif.org/hamas_in_the_new_middle_east/ (accessed 2 March 2014).
Carpentier, Nico (2005) 'Identity, contingency and rigidity. The (counter-)hegemonic constructions of the identity of the media professional', *Journalism*, 6(2), pp. 199–219.
Cherribi, S. (2006) 'From Baghdad to Paris: Al Jazeera and the veil', *The Harvard International Journal of Press/Politics Online*, gaz.sagepub.com/cgi/content/abstract/69/2/115 (accessed 23 April 2012).
Coleman, Renita (2000) 'The ethical context for public journalism: as an ethical foundation for public journalism, communitarian philosophy provides principles for practitioners to apply to real-world problems', *Journal of Communication Inquiry*, 24(1), pp. 41–66.
Dabbous-Sensenig, D. (2006) 'To veil or not to veil: gender and religion on Al Jazeera's Islamic law and life', *Westminster Papers in Communication and Culture*, www.westminster.

ac.uk/__data/assets/pdf_file/0013/20137/4WPCC-Vol3-No2-D_Dabbous_Sensenig.pdf (accessed 11 June 2012).

Elliott, Charles W. & Greer, Clark F. (2010) 'Newsworthiness and Islam: an analysis of values in the Muslim online press', *Communication Quarterly*, 58(4), pp. 414–430.

El-Nawawy, Mohammed & Iskandar, Adel (2003) *Al-Jazeera: The Story of the Network that is Rattling Governments and Redefining Modern Journalism*. Cambridge, MA: Westview.

Fandy, Mamoun (2000) 'Information technology, trust, and social change in the Arab world', *The Middle East Journal*, 54(3).

Ghosh, A. (2003) 'Iraq: media challenge', *Economic and Political Weekly*, 38(20), pp. 1933–1934.

Hegab, Mohamed Munir (2002) *Islamic Media: Principles, Theory and Practice*. Cairo: Dar el-Fagr (in Arabic).

Hijjawi, A. (2011) 'The role of Al Jazeera (Arabic) in the Arab revolts of 2011', Heinrich Böll Stiftung, lb.boell.org/downloads/Perspectives_02-10_Aref_Hijjawi.pdf (accessed 14 February 2012).

Hjarvard, Stig (2006) *The Mediatization of Religion/A Theory of the Media as an Agent of Religious Change*. A paper presented to the Fifth International Conference on Media, Religion and Culture: Mediating Religion in the Context of Multicultural Tension, The Sigtuna Foundation. Sigtuna, Sweden, 6–9 July.

Hoover, Stewart (2002) 'The culturalist turn in scholarship on media and religion', *Journal of Media and Religion*, 1(1), pp. 25–36.

Hroub, K. (2011) 'Al Jazeera: the source of Arab Springs', www.abc.net.au/religion/articles/2011/10/20/3344402.htm (accessed 4 March 2013).

I'mara, Mohamed (1988) *Islam and Revolution*. Cairo: Dar al Shorouk (in Arabic).

Kessler, O. (2012) 'The two faces of Al Jazeera', *Middle East Quarterly*, winter, www.meforum.org/meq/pdfs/3147.pdf (accessed 25 June 2012).

Lefebvre, Solange & Guyver, Jennifer (2009) 'Media and religion in Quebec's recent debates', *The Proceedings of the Cultural Dialogue, Religion and Communication – Ottawa University*, 22 October, pp. 127–145.

Malka, H. (2003) 'Must innocents die? The Islamic debate over suicide attacks', *Middle East Quarterly*, Spring, pp. 19–28, www.meforum.org/530/must-innocents-die-the-islamic-debate-over (accessed 25 June 2012).

Mazel, Z. (2009) 'Al Jazeera and Qatar: the Muslim brothers' dark empire?', *Jerusalem Centre for Public Affairs*, 8(29), 14 May, jcpa.org/article/al-jazeera-and-qatar-the-muslim-brothers%E2%80%99-dark-empire/ (accessed 1 March 2014).

McNair, Brian (2005) 'What is journalism?', in Hugo De Burgh (Ed.) *Making Journalists*. London: Routledge.

Mehdi, H. (2011) 'Voice of the Arab Spring', www.newstatesman.com/broadcast/2011/12/arab-channel-jazeera-qatar (accessed 25 June 2012).

Miladi, N. (2003) 'Mapping the Al Jazeera phenomenon', site.iugaza.edu.ps/mamer/files/War-and-the-Media1.pdf#page=164 (accessed 23 April 2012).

Mohamad, Ibrahim (2006) 'Arab protests are calculated political response', *Deutsche Welle*, 9 February, en.qantara.de/content/analysis-mohammed-cartoon-conflict-arab-protests-are-calculated-political-response.

Mowlana, Hamid (2008) 'Theoretical Perspectives on Islam and Communication', *China Media Research*, 3(4), pp. 23–33.

Nader, Aya (2014) 'Sentencing of journalist Ahmed Mansour "politicised" and "absurd": Al Jazeera', *Daily News Egypt*, 15 October, www.dailynewsegypt.com/2014/10/15/sentencing-journalist-ahmed-mansour-politicised-absurd-al-jazeera/.

Nasr, Assem (2014) 'Al Jazeera and the Arab uprisings: the language of images and a medium's stancetaking', *Communication, Culture & Critique*, 7, pp. 397–414.

Phillips, Angela & Lee, David (2007) 'The UK, a very British response', in Risto Kunelius, Elisabeth Eide et al. (Eds) *Reading the Mohammed Cartoon Controversy*, Working Papers in International Journalism 1, p. 68.

Pintak, Lawrence (2008) *Media in the Twenty-first Century. Islam, Nationalism and the Mission of Arab Journalism*. Unpublished PhD thesis, University of Wales.

Pintak, Lawrence (2014) 'Islam, identity and professional values: a study of journalists in three Muslim-majority regions', *Journalism*, 15(4), pp. 482–503.

Quinn, S. & Walters, T. (2010) 'Al Jazeera: a broadcaster creating ripples in a stagnant pool', 3(1–4), pp. 57–73.

Rinnawi, K. (2006) *Instant Nationalism: McArabism, Al Jazeera, and Transnational Media in the Arab World*. Lanham, MD and Oxford: University Press of America.

Sakr, N. (1999) 'Satellite television and development in the Middle East', *Middle East Research and Information* project, www.merip.org/mer/mer210/satellite-television-development-middle-east (accessed 11 March 2013).

Seib, P. (2005) 'Hegemonic no more: Western media, the rise of Al Jazeera, and the influence of diverse voices', *International Studies Review*, 7(4), pp. 601–615.

Seib, P. (2008) *The Al-Jazeera Effect: How the New Global Media are Reshaping World Politics*. Washington, DC: Potomac Books, Inc.

Sharaf, A. (2013) 'Al Jazeera staff resign after "biased" Egypt coverage', *Gulf News*, gulfnews.com/news/region/egypt/al-jazeera-staff-resign-after-biased-egypt-coverage-1.1206924 (accessed 1 March 2014).

Sharp (2003) 'The Al-Jazeera News Network: opportunity or challenge for US foreign policy in the Middle East?', fpc.state.gov/documents/organization/23002.pdf (accessed 11 March 2014).

Siddiqi, Mohammad A. (2013) 'Islamic journalism destroys myths', *The Brunei Times*, 17 May, p. B5.

Soukup, P.A. (2002) 'Media and religion', 21(2), Centre for the Study of Communication and Culture, cscc.scu.edu/trends/v21/v21_2.pdf (accessed 11 June 2013).

Steele, Janet (2011) 'Justice and journalism: Islam and journalistic values in Indonesia and Malaysia', *Journalism*, 12(5), pp. 533–549.

Stolow, J. (2005) 'Religion and/as media', *Theory Culture Society*, 22(119), www.irtvu.com/files/119.pdf (accessed 24 November 2014).

Tamimi, Nawwaf (2012) *Public Diplomacy and Nation Branding*. Doha: Al Jazeera Center for Studies (in Arabic).

Tatham, S. (2006) *Losing Arab Hearts and Minds: The Coalition, Al-Jazeera, and Muslim Public Opinion*. London: Hurst and Co.

Underwood, Doug (2008) *From Yahweh to Yahoo! The Religious Roots of the Secular Press*. University of Illinois Press.

Walker, M.U. (2000) 'Naturalizing, normativity, and using what we know in ethics', *Canadian Journal of Philosophy* (supp. vol.), 26, pp. 75–101.

White, Robert A. (2007) 'The media, culture, and religion perspective', *Communication Research Trends*, 26(1).

Zandberg, Eyal & Neiger, Motti (2005) 'Between the nation and the profession: journalists as members of contradicting communities', *Media, Culture & Society*, 27(1), pp. 131–141.

Zayani, Mohamed (2005) *The Al-Jazeera Phenomenon: Critical Perspectives on New Arab Media*. London: Pluto Press.

Zelizer, Barbie (2004) *Taking Journalism Seriously*. London: Sage.

INDEX

3al6ayer 190–1, 193–5
3almezan 196–7

'Abduh, Muhammad 69
Abdulla, Rasha 111, 132–3
Abu Dhabi 93
Abu-Lughod, Lila 88, 199
accountable government 125
Active Change Foundation 153
Agrama, H. A. 257
Al Akrawi, Ali Faisal 56
al Barak, Musallam 126–7
Al Jazeera: Arab Spring coverage 275–6; bias in 275; journalists 272–6; Muslim Brotherhood 271–2; Qatar and 271; secular v. Islamic voice 269–72
Al Jazeera Arabic 270–3
al Khorafi, Jassim 127
al Sada, Naseema 131
Al Shaikh, Abdul Aziz 209
al-Afghani, Jamal al-Din 69
al-Albani, Nasir al-Din 71
Al-Arefe, Mohammad 210–11
al-'Awda, Salman 193–4
al-Baghdadi, Abu Bakr 67, 72–3
Albashir, Obai 196–7
al-Butairi, Fahad 130
al-Duri, Izzat Ibrahim 67
al-Fagih, Hisham 197, 198
Al-Fuzai, Muna 127–8
Algerian *khutba* 95–6, 97
al-Ghaddami, Abdullah 78
al-Huzaymi, Nasir 71

Ali, Muhammad 72
'Alim, universalizing the Muslim *ummah* 92–4
al-Jama'a al-Salafiyya al-Muhtasiba (JSM) 71, 77
al-Janabi, Abu Bakr 82n3
Al-Khalifa, Hamad 8
al-khawarij 93–4
al-Maqdisi, Abu Muhammad 68, 71–2, 74
al-Mushawwah, Abdul Moneim 209
Al-Oudah, Salman 10
al-Oudah, Salman 221
al-Qa'ida 80, 82n16, 117
Al-Qa'ida texts 72
Al-Qaradawi, Yousef 74, 213–14
Al-Qassemi, S. 271
al-Qayrawan Media Foundation 40
Al-Rawi, A. 108
al-Shaarawi, Metwalli 227
al-Sharia, Ansar 40–1
al-Shaykh, Abd al-Aziz Al 74
al-Shinqiti, Abu'l-Mundhir 73–4
al-Shugairi, Ahmad 189–90, 210
al-Sudis, Abd al-Rahman 93–4
Al-Udeid 271
al-Utaybi, Juhayman 68, 71
al-Wahhab, Muhammad ibn 69
Alyami, Tamador 131
al-Zarqawi, Abu Mus'ab 67
al-Zawahiri, Ayman 72–3, 117
Al-Zaytouna Mosque 35, 46n4
Amar 404 21–2
Amina Femen 27

Anderson, John 107
Angel Hackers 117
anonymity of social media 39–40, 116, 130, 233, 260n2
anonymity online 38–9
Appadurai, Arjun 176
Arab Christians 118
Arab identity: Muslim identity v. 160–1; religion and 161–4; *see also* identity
Arab journalists 268–9, 272–6
Arab media, development of 175
Arab Middle East and North Africa (AMENA), importance of 173–4
Arab satellite television: compartmentalization on 88; Friday *khutba* on 87–90; objective of 89
Arab Spring: Al Jazeera coverage of 275–6; British Arab youth support for 168–70; defined 129; Islamic movements 168–71; social media and 8, 50–2; in Tunisia 17
Arab states: private stations 87; reaction to 9/11 attacks 111; satellite television 87–90
Arab television 175, 177–8
Arab youth. *See* British Arab youth
Arabi, Ibn 68–9
Arabic language, as source of Tunisianess 29–30
Asad, T. 247
Assakina Campaign for Dialogue 116
Association for the Safeguarding of the Quran 18
Ataturk, Kemal 68
Azem, Ahmad 271

Baathist figures 67
bad governance 125, 126–8
Badran, A. 160
Bagram Air Base 106, 113
Bahrain: collective memory 49–50; martyrs' commemoration online 51–4; opposition movement 50–1, 54; social media in 51
Bahraini opposition movement 50–1
BanaTube 196
Barkho, Leon 269
Barthes, R. 51–2
Barthes's classification of connotative procedures 52
Bawer, Bruce 2
Bayat, Asef 123–4
BBC News 265
Ben Ali regime 19
BENI 149–51
Benkler, Y. 107
Berger, L. P. 44

Berry, J. W. 174
Bessaiso, E. 178
bin Baz, Abd al-Aziz 77
bin Laden, Osama 72
binationality v. revolutionary authenticity 27–9
Birt, Yahia 145
Boháč, A. 167
Bourdieu, Pierre 41, 212
Bourguiba, Habib 35–6, 46n6
Boyle, K. 37
British Arab youth: challenges of 158; freedom before religion 165–6; as invisible community 159–60; Islamic movements 169; Muslim youth v. 158; national loyalties of 159–60; religion, importance of 161–3; religion, influence of 164–6; religion, understanding of 164; religion's role in consciousness 158; stereotyping 159
British Muslims: central body of representation 153; identity and 140–1; online expressions 143–4; population of 139–40
Bunt, Gary R. 1, 106, 141–2, 206, 212, 223, 232
Burgess, J. 109

Cameua, Michel 18
Campbell, H. 3, 247
Carpentier, Nico 268
Castells, Manuel 133
Cherribi, Sam 270
Chouikha, Larbi 21
citizenship websites 144
citizen-to-citizen social media 129
City Circle (website) 144–5
Clash of Civilizations theory 2
Clinton, Hillary 105
collective identity 6
collective memory 49–50
colonialism 79–80, 96
Colonna, Fanny 81
Committee for Propagating Virtue and Preventing Vice 10
communication technologies, to resist bad government 122
communitarianism: concept of 269; value of 276
compartmentalization 88
computer-mediated framing 108
consciousness, global trend of 40
Conway, M. 111
Cook, D. 59
Cooper, S. 107–8

Coptic CPR Government in Exile 118
Costolo, Dick 215n1
counselling within an Islamic framework 252; *see also* Problems and Solutions counselling
counter-framing 107–8
creative conformity 240
culture of factuality 268
cyber graveyards 59
cyber Islamic environments 1, 232
cyber-mufti 232
cyberspace: communal communication in 141; concept of 141; effective governmental control of 188; virtual community 40, 108

Dabbous-Sensenig, Dima 270
Dahmen, Zouha 21
dawah: actions 221; described 219–20; elements of 220; need for 227; as part of Egyptian popular culture 222–5; televised 227–9
Dawson, L. L. 167
death: commemoration of 48; in the media 49–50; purpose of remembrance 51–4
Destourian Socialist Party (PSI) 18–19
diaspora identity 6
digital *fatwas* 212–13, 214
digital media: advent of, in Arab and Islamic world 205–6; as avenue of resistance 123; to create network of supporters 210; diversity and 99; emergence of 141–3; power of 203–4
digital memorials 48
digital *ummah* 223
disinhibition effect 109–10
dissociative anonymity 110
Douai, A. 109, 111
Ducrot, Oswald 26

eDialogue 5
Edry, Ronnie 128
Edy, J. A. 51
Egypt: resisting bad government and corruption 125–6; state media 78–9; state satellite channels 98
Eickelman, Dale 223
El Fajr (newspaper) 22
el Gendy, Khaled 225
El Zeitouna television station 22
El-Dakheel, Khaled 214
el-Ouseimi, Majid 5
Elshokary, Ahmed 226
Emotional and Spiritual Quotient 262n28
En Nahdha 22–3

Ennahdha party: contesting conformism 26; described 18–20; electronic militia 23; on Facebook 23–5; media practices by 20–3; monotheism violation 40
Erdogan, Recep 125
European Muslim Network (EMN) 144
European Muslims: contributing to changes in public consciousness 142–3; demographics 140; globalization phenomenon 173; online expressions 143–4; online facilities, use of 154
extremist groups, Internet use of 38

Facebook: anonymity on 39; demographics 203; Group for the fight against tyrants 41; identity expression on 39; Peace Factory 129; peace messaging 129; *see also* social media
Fageeh, Hisham 130
Fallimha 196
Fanon, Frantz 79–80
Farag, Abd al-Salam 70–1
Faris, David 123, 126
fatwas: collaborators 239; consumption of 237–9; creative conformity 240; defined 232; digital 213–14; flow of 212–13; globalization phenomenon 239; hymenoplasty 238; Jewish 234–5; new preachers and 222; online production and consumption of 233–4; production of 234–7; simplification of 213
Federation of Islamic Organizations in Europe (FIOE) 145–6
Fernback, J. 141
F-*fatwas* 213–14
Finn, T. 148
Fiqh, Maliki 34
Fitna film 116
Forum of European Muslim Youth and Student Organisations (FEMYSO) 146
frames/framing: defined 51; in social media 107–8
freedom fighters 97
Freedom Foundation 125
freedom of choice 256–7
freedom of expression, unchecked 42–3
Friday *khutba*: from Abu Dhabi 93; from Algeria 95–6, 97; 'Alim type 92; defined 92–3; described 90; emphasizing Muslim unity 93; *fitna* 94; hybrid approach 95; as identity discourses 91; impaired hearing access to 86; influence of new communication technology 86; to influence public opinion 8; during Israeli-Lebanese war 89; from Libya 96;

Muslims, internal struggles of 93–4; new preachers and 223; as political instrument in religious form 91; from Qatar 95; as religious ritual 90; revolutionary *khutba* 95–8; satellite television and 87–91; from Saudi Arabia 93–4; from Sharjah 93; state channels that broadcast 87–8; from Sudan 97; from Yemen 96

Gaffney, P. D. 90
Gannah, Khadija Ben 272–3
Gatestone Institute 140
Gaza, as ideal Muslim state 97
Geisser, VIncent 18
generational-cultural cleavages in media consumption 178–9
Georgiou, M. 159
Gerges, Fawaz 80
Ghannouchi, Rached 17, 29, 40, 43
global dawah 4
global economy 125
Global Federation of Muslim Scholars 74
global media 40
global network society 107
Goldfarb, Jeffrey 123
Gräf, B. 246
Green, J. 109
Grillo, R. 174
Groshek, J. 108
Ground Zero mosque controversy 111
Group for the fight against tyrants 41
The Guardian newspaper 131
Guha, Ranajit 79

Habermas, J. 142
Haddad, Sanaa 30
Haikal, Muhammad Hassanayn 72
Haleem, Abdel 90
Hamid, Shadi 5
Hannibal TV 21
Happy British Muslims (video) 149–52
Harakat Ennahdha 17
Harb, Z. 178
Hashim, Ahmed Omar 95
Heelas, P. 259–60
Hegghammer, Thomas 77
Helland, C. 3
Here is Silicon Valley 197
heterodoxies 211–14
Hirschkind, Charles 223
Hjarvard, Stig 266
homeland, concept of 179
The Honesty Policy Group 149–51
Hoover, Stewart M. 3, 266
Hosny, Mustafa 225–7

Hough, M. 248
Howard, Phillip N. 133
Hroub, Khaled 269
human sociality 203
Huntington, Samuel 2
Hussain, D. 140–1
Hussain, Muzammil M. 133
hymenoplasty 238
hypermedia 191

identity: anonymous online 38–9; Arab 160–1; concept of 141, 144–5; expression of 39; face-to-face interactions 37; Friday *khutba* and 91; of a journalist 268; Muslim 160–1; online 141–3; online spaces 37; religion shaping 166–8; religious 222; reviving 160; social identity theory 139–41; symbols 30
identity check list 30
identity construction on social media 38–9
identity expression, religious groups 39
Ikhwan revolt 75
Illouz, Eva 259
I'mara, Muhammad 269
inclusiveness 143
information communications technologies (ICTs) 176, 205, 209
Innocence of Muslims (film) 9
Internet: Arab world penetration of 123; as cyber-mufti 232; death, commemoration of 48, 52–4, 57–8; digitizing Islamic content for 205–6; to disseminate religious discourse 11, 205; exchanging religious teachings 44; extremist groups on 38; as form of mass dissemination 36; generational gap in 178; inclusiveness 143; national identity and 37–8; for propaganda purposes 122; radicalization via 142; for remembrance 54; for surveillance 122; *see also* new media; social media
Internet cafes 21
invented homelands 176
invisible community 159–60
Iqraa 87
Islam: controversial issues related to 111–12; and identity 5–7; identity symbols 30; as immigrant religion 140; Internet research and 205–6; and media research 204–5
Islam Online: creation of 246–7; defined 4; editorial team of 235–6; as model of modern *dawah* 4; production of *fatwas* 234–7
Islamic awakening 70–1
Islamic boundaries 253–5

Islamic groups, emergence of 45
Islamic identity 161; *see also* identity
Islamic militant, humanization of 78–9
Islamic movements, influenced by religion 167–9
Islamic revival 108, 274–5
Islamic satellite channels, objective of 89
Islamic State: development of 45; establishing framework of 70–3; horizontal reconstitution of power 72; Islamist responses to 73–4; as revolutionary movement 75; rise of 67
Islamic State in Iraq and Syria (ISIS) 142, 152–3
Islamic State in Iraq and the Levant (ISIL) 67
Islamic tele-preachers 225
Islamic values 253
Islamism, defined 82n6
Islamists: anti-democratic 18; defined 82n6; response to IS 73–4
Islamophobic groups 140
Israeli-Lebanese war 89

Jeffreys, James 125
Jewish *fatwas* 234–5
jihadi Salafism 70–3, 75
jihadi science 153
jihadism: post-colonial police state and 78; socio-political readings of 75–8; Western power systems and 81
Johnson, T. J. 37
Jones, Terry 105, 113, 116
Jordanian *khutba* 97
journalists/journalism: Arab. *See* Arab journalists; centering on compassion 273; cultural analysis of 272–6; goal of justice 269; identity of 268; religious beliefs of 266–7; social responsibility of 268–9
Juhayman's revolt 75–7

Karoui, Nabil 42
Kashgari, Hamza 110
Kepel, Gilles 71, 78–9, 204–5
Kessler, Oren 270–1
Khaled, Amr 221–2, 224, 226
khalifa 77
Khanfar, Wadah 273
Khedher, Habib 25–6, 29
Khiari, Sadri 19, 21
khilafa 74
khutba. *See* Friday *khutba*
King Abdul Aziz City for Science and Technology 188
Kraidy, Marwan 187–8

Krishan, Mohammed 272, 275
Krüger, Oliver 248
Kuwait, bad governance of 126–7
Kwak, Haewoon 210

Laabidi, Meherzia 25–6, 27–8
Labat, Séverine 18, 22
Lacroix, Stephane 77, 187
Lange, P. 109–10
Lanneau, G. 29
Latino migrant minorities 39
Leonardi, P. 39
Libyan *khutba* 96
Life as Politics: How Ordinary People Change the Middle East (Bayat) 123–4
Life Makers project 221–2
linguistic pollution 29
living Islam 257
Löfgren, Orvar 30
Love in a Headscarf (Zahra) 149
Luckmann, T. 44

MAB (Muslim Association of Britain) 147–8
Madar Research 123
Madaville, Peter 1
Mahmood, Aqsa 142
Mahmood, S. 138, 262n28
Mahmoud, Karem 275
mainstream media 10, 107–8, 141, 154, 158–9, 189–90, 211–13, 274
majority-minority categorization 138
Malka, Haim 270
Mandaville, Peter 10, 107
Mando, Abdullah 190, 192
Mansour, Ahmed 271, 273–4
maqasid (intentions) 253
Margalit, Ruth 129
Marks, M. 44
martyrdom: commemoration of 48, 52–4; coping with 58–9; group phenomenon of 55; of Hussein 57; liberating dimension of 58; loyalty towards 54; to rectify past wrongs 57–8; ritualized performance 53; strengthening community bonds through 56; warrior martyr 56
Masoud, Moez 224, 226
Mawlawi, Faysal 235–6, 237
Mazel, Zvi 271
MCB (Muslim Council of Britain) 146–7
Mcinerney, L. 111
media: to construct religious meaning in life 265; and Islam 267–9; Muslim communications 267; religion, relationship between 266–7; religious

beliefs of journalists 266–7; as social agents 266
media censorship 20–3
media consumption: gender differences in 179–80; general modes of 177–8; generational gap in 178–9; new modes of 180–1; segregational modes of 179–80
media globalization 173
media research, Islam and 204–5
Mehdi, H. 276
Meijer, Roel 70
memory boom 49–50
Men Elaa 196
Meraz, S. 108
Merkel, Angela 2
Miladi, N. 178
Millat Ibrahim (al-Maqdisi) 71
minaret ban 111
minority: defined 138; as objective designation 138
Mishra, S. 233
Mitchell, D. 39
Modern *Jihad* 4–5
Mohammed, Prophet, as ideal role model for husbands 258–9
Mohammed cartoon controversy 265
Moll, Yasmin 224
morality 262n28
mosque, function of 90
Mostafa, Zeinab 235–6, 237
Mostefaoui, Belgacem 21
Mourad, Mahmoud 275
Mowlana, Hamid 268
Mubarak, Housni 125–6
multiculturalism 174
Murphy, Caryle 187, 200
Mushaff (book) burning 112; *see also* Quran-burning incidents
Musim code of journalism 267
Muslim Association of Britain (MAB) 147–8
Muslim Brotherhood: Al Jazeera and 271–2; Arab Spring 168–9; defined 69; defining Muslim identity 161; empathy toward 273–4; as moderate force 7; news media and 265; Qatar and 271
Muslim communications 267
Muslim Community Helpline 149
Muslim Council of Britain (MCB) 146–7
Muslim identity, Arab identity v. 160–1; *see also* identity
Muslim media 141–2
Muslim preachers (*da'eyah*) 221–2
Muslim *Ummah*. *See Ummah*
Muslim Village 237–9

Muslim Women Helpline in the UK (MWHL) 149
Muslim youth, Arab youth v. 158
Muslims: British population of 139–40; European demographics 140; European immigrants 2, 173; in France and Germany 2; internal conflicts among 99; as subjects of nation-states 96–7
Mustafa, Shukri 78–9
mutawah, defined 131
Mzoughi, Abdelaziz 28

Nasr, Assem 275–6
National Constituent Assembly (ANC) 17, 27–8
national identity 6, 37–8, 223–4
Neergaard, Helle 89
Neglected Obligation, The (Farag) 70
Neiger, Motti 277
Nessma television 42–3
networked framing 108
new media: clash of cultural values 42–3; to connect to homeland 177; digital memory culture 49–50; to explore Islam 1–2; as form of agency 3; new preachers use of 223; religion and 2–3; reshaping politics 4–5; in Saudi society 191–2; symbiotic relationship between alternative Muslim media and 141; working around the state 124–5; young generations use of 1–2; *see also* Internet; online media; social media
new nationalism, emergence of 176
new preachers. *See dawah*
new Saudi media: closed spaces 191–2; comedy 190–1; defined 188; emergence of 188–91; as modernist nationalism 199–200; news satire 190–1; 'No Woman, No Drive' campaign 197–8; online freedom of expression 195; as political commentary 192–6; public spaces 191; satellite television 192; as social commentary 196–9; taboo subjects 197–9; youth influence on 200
news media: culture of factuality 268; religion and 265; social responsibility 268–9; *see also* Al Jazeera
news satire 190–1
Nisbet, Matthew 107
'No Woman, No Drive' campaign 129–33, 197–8
Nofal, H. 109, 111

Obama, Barack 105
Obeid, H. 148

offline spaces 37
Öktem, K. 140
Omar, Mullah 74
OnIslam.net 234
online communities 37, 52
online flaming 109–10
online graphics 57–8
online media: as alternate source of religion 160; youth's identity and 159; *see also* new media
online religion: v. religion online 3; spiritual activities 3
online religious communities, invisible aspects of 248
online *Ummah* 106–7
online visual components 39–41
On-TV 98
open marriages 253
Orange Revolution 126–7
the other 249–50
Ottoman caliphate 72
Ounissi, Saida 29

Palin, Souad 27
pan-Arab identity 269–70
Pan-Arab media 44, 180
Papacharissi, Z. 108
Peace, T. 147
Peace Factory 129
Pearl, Judea 271
Peek, L. 166
people-to-people peace opportunities 128–9
Persepolis (animated programme) 42–3
personality expression 39–41
Pew Research Center 109, 140
Pew Research Religion and Public Life Project 139
Pintak, L. 176, 267
pious entertainment 224
polemic negation 26
political commentary 192–6
political conceptualization of modernity 76
political Islam 8, 69–70, 169
Politics of Small Things, The (Goldfarb) 123
positioning theory 91
private television stations 21
privately public behaviour on YouTube 110
Problems and Solutions 246–7
Problems and Solutions counselling: correcting erroneous religious interpretations 258–9; creation of 247–8; cultivating an ethical self 256–8; detraditionalizing 259; freedom of choice 256–7; goals of 250; Islamic boundaries 253–5; within an Islamic framework 252–5; objective of 250; philosophy of 248–9; self-awareness 259; self-reflexivity 251; skills emphasis 251; social awareness 259
Project for Excellence 109
protests, in Arab region 8
public spaces 237
publicly private behaviour on YouTube 110
publinets 21

Qana massacre of 1996 95–6
Qana massacre of 2006 96
Qaradawi, Yousef 269
Qatar: financial support for Al Jazeera 270; foreign policy 275; Muslim Brotherhood and 271
Quran-burning incidents 105–6, 113–14, 116–17
Qutb, Sayyid 68, 70, 72, 78

radicalization: as a security issue 80–1; via Internet 142
Ramadan 72–3, 181
Ramadan, Tariq 144
re-Islamization 108
rejectionist Islamism 77
religion: and Arab identity 161–4; British Arab youth 165–6; British Arab youth's identity construction 160; freedom before 165–6; Friday *khutba* 87–90; influencing attitudes 166–8; influencing Islamic movements 167–9; Internet consumption and 167; media and 266–7; and news media 265; news reporting and 268; online religion v. religion online 3; politics v. 170–1; regulatory factors 165; science and 166–7; shaping identities 166; YouTube debates over 109
religions of humanity 259–60
religious activism 9
religious agency 233, 240
religious authority: de-legitimation 231; deterritorialization of 239
religious awakening 250
religious boundaries 253–5
religious edu-tainment 224–5
religious identity: articulating 10; building a diaspora on 6; in Tunisia 34–7; youth and 222
religious leaders: societal role of 214; using Twitter 209–10
Resala 228
retweeting 207
revolutionary *khutba* 95–8
Rida, Rashid 69

righteousness, strengthening community of 55–6
Rinnawi, Khalil 270, 271
Rise and Fall of Al-Qaeda (Gerges) 80
Roy, Oliver 69, 108
Rudnyckyj, D. 262n28

sacramental activities online 3
Said, Khaled 126
Salafism 34–5, 46n3, 68–70
Salvatore, Armando 223
Sanaktekin, O. 167
satellite television 21, 87–90, 98, 192
Saud, Muhammad ibn 69
Saudi Arabia: Internet access 187; political structure 78; social media diffusion 206–7; social media use 187; women's driving campaign 129–33
Saudi *khutba* 93–4
Saudi Twitterverse: demographics 206–7; heterodoxies 211–14; religious orthodoxies and 209–10; trending topics 207–9
Saudi Wahhabism 69
Schielke, Samuli 247
Seddon, M. S. 141
Sedgwick, Mark 175
Seib, Philip 270
self-acceptance 257
self-awareness 259
self-reflexivity 251
self-representation, process of 6
Semaan, G. 233
semiotic theory 51–2
Shahrory, Ahmed 97
Sharjah, Friday *khutba* 93
Shirley, S. 206
Shura Council 132–3
Siddiqi, Muzammil 220, 235, 236–7
Silverstone, R. 159
SingleMuslim.com 149
Sisi, General 126
Small Media, Big Revolution 205
social activists 196
social awareness 250–1, 259
social capital 41
social criticism 196
social identity theory, defined 139
social justice 76–7
social media: active user-generated content producers 43–4; as alternative media channel 107; and Arab Spring 50–2; in Bahraini society 51; citizen-to-citizen 129; to control public sphere 123; controlling 125; decentralized religious authority 44–5; digital memorials 49–50; exposing government corruption 125–8; frames/framing in 107–8; generational gap in 178; identity construction 38–9; to incite public opinion 274; to influence public opinion 9–10; for mobilization 123; 'No Woman, No Drive' campaign 129–33; online visual components 39–41; personality expression 39–41; reshaping politics 4–5; to resist bad government 123; sociological relationship to Islam 203; spreading anti-Islamic sentiments 106; Tunisian revolution and 38; women's use of, for empowerment 131–2; *see also* Internet; new media
social networking: ISIS utilizing 152–3; to resist warmongering states 128–9
social responsibility 256, 268–9
Socialbakers 51
solipsistic introjection effect 110, 116
Soukup, Paul 266
space-transcending technologies 174–5
Spirit 21 (blog) 149
spiritual activities online 3
Spivak, Gayatri Chakravorty 81
Starrett, G. 259
state satellite channels 98
Steele, Janet 269
Stolow, J. 265
Stone, A. R. 141
Stop the War Coalition 147
Strangelove, Michael 109
strong multiculturalism 174
Subaltern Studies project 79
Sudanese *khutba* 97
Suleiman, Y. 140
Suler, J. 110

tabligh, defined 268
Tajfel, H. 139
Tatham, S. 270
Tawfik, Zein al Abeeden 274–5
Taymiyya, Ibn 68–9
televangelists 3
televised preaching programmes 227–9
television: private stations 21; satellite 21
terrorism 40–1, 73, 80, 94, 96, 138, 148, 153, 241
Theobald, S. 110
Thinking Islam 257
Tilley, L. 260n2
transnational media: cultural order and 174–7; social media and 180

Transparency International 125
troika alliance 23–4, 36
Tunisia: Amar 404 21–2; Arab Spring 17; Arabic language as source of Tunisianess 29–30; audio-visual policies of 20–1; binationality v. revolutionary authenticity 27–9; clash of cultural values 42–3; Destourian Socialist Party (PSI) 18–19; Ennahdha party. *See* Ennahdha party; identity check list 30; identity symbols 30; linguistic pollution 29; media censorship 20–3, 34–7; media role in revolution 20; National Constituent Assembly (ANC) 17; national identity 37–8; oral communication in 41; personality of 29–30; religious identity after revolution 34–7; religious revivalism 44; state media 36; troika alliance 23–4; Tunisian Islamist Movement 18–19; veiled women 27; women's autonomy 25–6
Tunisian Islamist Movement 18–19
Tunisian Islamists, anti-democratic 18
Tunisian media 20–3
Twitter: demographics 203, 207; exposing government corruption 125; *fatwas* 212–13; as freedom of thought and expression 213; as primary source of religious content 211; Quran-burning incidents 105; religious leaders using 209–10; as religious tool 203; retweeting 207; in Saudi Arabia. *See* Saudi Twitterverse; as source of information 211–12; as threat to *Ummah* 209; trending topics 207–9; *see also* social media

ulama 76
Ummah: '*Alim* universalizing the 92–4; concept of 106–7; digital 223; on Internet 106–7; *khutba* appeal to 96–7; as reimagined community 10
Ummah films 106
user generated framing 108
Uturn Entertainment 190, 193–5, 197

veiled women 27
Venturelli, Shalini S. 3
virtual public spaces 237
virtual *Ummah* 106–7, 108, 115, 223

Wahhabi movement 34–5, 46n5, 69, 75
Wajda (film) 133
Wamda tv 190–1
Wardi, Alaa 130, 197–8
warrior martyr 56
weak multiculturalism 174
whistle-blowing, to resist corruption 125–8
White, M. 152–3
Woman2Drive movement 130
Woodhead, L. 259–60
Woodthorpe, K. 260n2
Wretched of the Earth (Fanon) 79–80
WsmA13odah series 193–4

Yemen *khutba* 96
Youcef, Ben 18
youth: of ethnic minorities 158; religious identity 222; *see also* British Arab youth
YouTube: age distribution 114; celebrity status from 189–90; demographic distribution 109, 117–18; disinhibition effect 109–10; exposing government corruption 125; gender differences in posters 114; global public sphere 108–11, 115; most discussed topics 109; news satire 190–1; 'No Woman, No Drive' satire 130–1; online flaming 109–10; publicly private behaviour 110; Quran-burning incidents 116–17; to resist harassment 131; Saudi channels on 188–9; Saudi video content on 188; Tunisian 23; virtual *Ummah* 106–7, 108, 115

Zahra, Shelina 149
Zandberg, Eyal 277
Zayani, Mohamed 270
Zelizer, B. 49, 272
Zhao, S. 37, 39–40
Zubaida, Sami 88

9781138639577